T0326253

THE ANTINOMIES OF REALISM

THE ANTINOMIES OF REALISM

FREDRIC JAMESON

VERSO
London • New York

This paperback edition published by Verso 2015
First published by Verso 2013
© Fredric Jameson 2013, 2015
"The Experiment of Time" first appeared in Franco Moretti, ed.,
Il Romanzo, Torino: Einaudi, 2004
"War and Representation" was first published in *PMLA*
124:5, October 2009

All rights reserved

The moral rights of the author have been asserted

1 3 5 7 9 10 8 6 4 2

Verso
UK: 6 Meard Street, London W1F 0EG
US: 388 Atlantic Ave, Brooklyn, NY 11217
www.versobooks.com

Verso is the imprint of New Left Books

ISBN-13: 978-1-78168-817-5 (PB)
ISBN-13: 978-1-78168-133-6 (HB)
eISBN-13: 978-1-78168-191-6 (US)
eISBN-13: 978-1-78168-502-0 (UK)

British Library Cataloguing in Publication Data
A catalogue record for this book is available from the British Library

Library of Congress Cataloging-in-Publication Data
A catalog record for this book is available from the Library of Congress

Typeset in Garamond by MJ & N Gavan, Truro, Cornwall
Printed in the United States

For Kim Stanley Robinson

Contents

Introduction: Realism and Its Antinomies   1

PART ONE: THE ANTINOMIES OF REALISM

I   The Twin Sources of Realism: The Narrative Impulse   15

II   The Twin Sources of Realism: Affect, or, the Body's Present   27

III   Zola, or, the Codification of Affect   45

IV   Tolstoy, or, Distraction   78

V   Pérez Galdós, or, the Waning of Protagonicity   95

VI   George Eliot and *Mauvaise Foi*   114

VII   Realism and the Dissolution of Genre   138

VIII   The Swollen Third Person, or, Realism after Realism   163

IX   Coda: Kluge, or, Realism after Affect   187

PART TWO: THE LOGIC OF THE MATERIAL

I   The Experiments of Time: Providence and Realism   195

II   War and Representation   232

III   The Historical Novel Today, or, Is It Still Possible?   259

Index   315

Introduction: Realism and Its Antinomies

I have observed a curious development which always seems to set in when we attempt to hold the phenomenon of realism firmly in our mind's eye. It is as though the object of our meditation began to wobble, and the attention to it to slip insensibly away from it in two opposite directions, so that at length we find we are thinking, not about realism, but about its emergence; not about the thing itself, but about its dissolution. Much great work, indeed, has been done on these lateral topics: on the former, for example, Ian Watt's canonical *Rise of the Novel* and Michael McKeon's monumental *Origins of the Novel*; and on the latter, any number of those collections entitled "problems of realism" (in which Lukács deplored the degeneration of realistic practice into naturalism, symbolism and modernism), or "towards a new novel" (in which Robbe-Grillet argued the unsuitability of Balzacian techniques for capturing our current realities). I will later explain how these slippages determined the form of the theory about to be presented.

First, however, we must enumerate a number of other possibilities which are not explored here (but which this particular theoretical exercise is by no means intended to exclude). Thus, the most ancient literary category of all—mimesis—still inspires work and thought, enshrined as anthropology and psychology in the Frankfurt School's idiosyncratic notion of the mimetic impulse; and provocatively worked out, following Lenin's reflection theory (*Widerspiegelung*), by scholars like Robert Weimann.[1] (Auerbach's use of the term, not exactly classical, will be mentioned below.) Aristotle did not, of course, know that form we call the novel, a product of Hegel's "world

---

[1] Robert Weimann, "Mimesis in Hamlet," in Geoffrey Hartman and Patricia Parker, eds., *Shakespeare and the Question of Theory*, New York: Routledge, 1985; and see also Dieter Schlenstedt, ed., *Literarische Widerspiegelung*, Berlin: Aufbau, 1981.

of prose"; nor are we taking theatrical practice into account in the present book (so much the worse for it!); and indeed, my suspicion is that later discussions of this term tend to be contaminated by those of the visual arts, and to be influenced either in the direction of representationality or abstraction (in painting) or that of Hollywood or the experimental in film.

This is the moment at which to assert the inevitability, in the realism debate, of what has just been illustrated by the turn to visuality, namely the inescapable operative value, in any discussion of realism, of this or that binary opposition in terms of which it has been defined. It is this, above all, which makes any definitive resolution of the matter impossible: for one thing, binary opposites make unavoidable the taking of sides (unless, as with Arnold Hauser, or in a different way, Worringer, one sees it as some eternal cyclical alternation[2]). Realism, for or against: but as opposed to what? At this point the list becomes at least relatively interminable: realism vs. romance, realism vs. epic, realism vs. melodrama, realism vs. idealism,[3] realism vs. naturalism, (bourgeois or critical) realism vs. socialist realism, realism vs. the oriental tale,[4] and of course, most frequently rehearsed of all, realism vs. modernism. As is inevitably the case with such a play of opposites, each of them becomes inevitably invested with political and even metaphysical significance, as, with film criticism, in the now somewhat antiquated opposition between Hollywood "realism" and formal subversions such as those associated with the *nouvelle vague* and Godard.[5] Most of these binary pairs will therefore arouse a passionate taking of sides, in which realism is either denounced or elevated to the status of an ideal (aesthetic or otherwise).

The definition of realism by way of such oppositions can also take on a historical, or periodizing, character. Indeed, the opposition between realism and modernism already implies a historical narrative which it is fairly difficult to reduce to a structural or stylistic one; but

---

[2] I refer to Arnold Hauser's *Social History of Art* (1954) as well as Wilhelm Worringer's influential and rather cosmological oppositions in *Abstraction and Empathy* (1907).

[3] The provocative concept of an idealist novel was developed by Naomi Schor in her study of George Sand and elaborated by Jane Tomkins in her work on the American western, where it also involved Christian religious and familial traditions (which the traditional western functioned to undermine).

[4] See Srinivas Aravamudan, *Enlightenment Orientalism*, Chicago: University of Chicago Press, 2012.

[5] And with *Screen* magazine in its heyday in the 1960s and '70s.

which it is also difficult to control, since it tends to generate other periods beyond its limits, one of postmodernity, for example, if some putative end of the modern is itself posited; or of some preliminary stage of Enlightenment and secularization invoked to precede the period of realism as such, in a logic of periodization bound to lead on into the positioning of a classical system or a pre-capitalist system of fixed modes and genres, and so forth. Whether such a focus on periodization necessarily leads out of literary history into cultural history in general (and beyond that to the history of modes of production) probably depends on how one situates capitalism itself and its specific cultural system in the sequence in question. The focus, in other words, tends to relativize realism as one mode among many others, unless, by the use of mediatory concepts such as that of modernity, one places capitalism uniquely at the center of human history.

For at this point another combination comes into play, and that is the tendency to identify realism with the novel itself as a uniquely modern form (but not necessarily a "modernist" one). Discussions of either concept tend to become indistinguishable from the other, at least when the history of either is invoked: the history of the novel is inevitably the history of the realist novel, against which or underneath which all the aberrant modes, such as the fantastic novel or the episodic novel, are subsumed without much protest. But by the same token, chronology is itself equally subsumed, and a Bakhtin can argue that "novel-ness" is itself a sign, perhaps the fundamental sign and symptom, of a "modernity" that can be found in the Alexandrian world fully as much as in the Ming dynasty.[6]

Indeed, Bakhtin is himself among the major figures for whom the novel, or realism as such, is both a literary phenomenon and a symptom of the quality of social life. For Bakhtin, the novel is the vehicle of polyphony or the recognition and expression of a multiplicity of social voices: it is therefore modern in its democratic opening onto an ideologically multiple population. Auerbach also invokes democracy in an analogous sense, even though for him the opening is global and consists in the conquest and achievement of a "realist" social life or modernity around the world.[7] But for Auerbach "realism," or mimesis in his sense, is a syntactic conquest, the slow

---

[6]   See, for example, his essay, "Epic and Novel," in Michael Holquist, ed., *The Dialogical Imagination*, Austin: University of Texas Press, 1994.

[7]   Erich Auerbach, *Mimesis: The Representation of Reality in Western Literature*, Princeton: Princeton University Press, 1953, 552, "a common life of mankind on earth."

appropriation of syntactic forms capable of holding together multiple levels of a complex reality and a secular daily life, whose twin climaxes in the West he celebrates in Dante and in Zola.

Lukács is more ambivalent in his reading of the novel's formal and historical record: in the *Theory of the Novel*, the form is essentially distinguished by its capacity of registering problematization and the irreconcilable contradictions of a purely secular modernity. The latter becomes reidentified as capitalism, in the later Lukács, and the novel with realism, whose task is now the reawakening of the dynamics of history.[8]

But in all three apologists for the realist novel as a form (so to speak), it is never very clear whether that form simply registers the advanced state of a given society or plays a part in society's awareness of that advanced state and its potentialities (political and otherwise). This ambiguity (or hesitation) will characterize the evaluative approaches to realism I want to outline in this initial survey, and which grasp the problem in terms of form and content respectively.

Realism as a form (or mode) is historically associated, particularly if you position the *Quijote* as the first (modern, or realist) novel, with the function of demystification. It is a function which can take many forms, in this foundational instance the undermining of romance as a genre, along with the use of its idealizing values to foreground features of the social reality they cannot accommodate. I have mentioned a first period of modernity in which the tasks of enlightenment and in particular secularization were fundamental (in a kind of bourgeois cultural revolution): these are for realism essentially negative, critical or destructive tasks which will later on give way to the construction of bourgeois subjectivity: but as the construction of the subject is always an intervention supported by taboos and inner restrictions of all kinds (one model of which is Weber's "protestant ethic"), the eradication of inherited psychic structures and values will remain a function of realist narrative, whose force always comes from this painful cancellation of tenaciously held illusions. But later on, when the realistic novel begins to discover (or if you prefer, to construct) altogether new kinds of subjective experiences (from Dostoyevsky to Henry James), the negative social function begins to weaken, and demystification

---

[8]   The most succinct summary of Lukács' formal views is to be found in "Narrate or Describe?" in George Lukács, *Writer and Critic*, London: Merlin, 1970. We will see that this opposition is fundamental in explaining his (equally political) rejection of Zola's naturalism.

finds itself transformed into defamiliarization and the renewal of perception, a more modernist impulse, while the emotional tone of such texts tends towards resignation, renunciation or compromise, as both Lukács and Moretti have noted.

But the very ideology of realism also tends to stage it in terms of content, and here clearly the realist mode is closely associated with the bourgeoisie and the coming into being of bourgeois daily life: this, I would like to insist, is also very much a construction, and it is a construction in which realism and narrative participate. Sartre argued that mimesis is always at least tendentially critical: holding up a mirror to nature, in this case bourgeois society, never really shows people what they want to see, and is always to that degree demystifying.[9] Certainly the attacks on realism which have already been mentioned are based on the idea that the literature of realism has the ideological function of adapting its readers to bourgeois society as it currently exists, with its premium on comfort and inwardness, on individualism, on the acceptance of money as an ultimate reality (we might today speak of the acceptance of the market, of competition, of a certain image of human nature, and so forth). I myself argue elsewhere in this collection that the realistic novelist has a vested interest, an ontological stake, in the solidity of social reality, on the resistance of bourgeois society to history and to change.[10] Meanwhile, it could also be argued that in a stylistic and ideological sense, the consumerism of late capitalism is no longer a bourgeois society in that sense, and no longer knows the forms of daily life that emerged in the eighteenth and nineteenth centuries: so that realism inevitably gives way to modernism insofar as its privileged content has become extinct. This argument thus makes a fundamental distinction between a bourgeois class culture and the economic dynamics of late capitalism.

I have outlined these multiple approaches to realism not only to make the point about its contextual variability as an object, but also to admit, finally, that I plan to do none of these things here. Realism, as I argued elsewhere, is a hybrid concept, in which an epistemological claim (for knowledge or truth) masquerades as an aesthetic ideal,

---

[9] Jean-Paul Sartre, "*What Is Literature?" and Other Essays*, Cambridge, MA: Harvard University Press, 1988, 91: "The mirror which he modestly offers to his readers is magical: it enthralls and compromises."

[10] See "The Experiments of Time: Providence and Realism," in Part Two of this volume.

with fatal consequences for both of these incommensurable dimensions.[11] If it is social truth or knowledge we want from realism, we will soon find that what we get is ideology; if it is beauty or aesthetic satisfaction we are looking for, we will quickly find that we have to do with outdated styles or mere decoration (if not distraction). And if it is history we are looking for—either social history or the history of literary forms—then we are at once confronted with questions about the uses of the past and even the access to it which, as unanswerable as they may be, take us well beyond literature and theory and seem to demand an engagement with our own present.[12]

From a dialectical standpoint it is not hard to see why this is so. Both sociology and aesthetics are superannuated forms of thinking and inquiry, inasmuch as neither society nor what is called cultural or aesthetic experience are in this present of time stable substances that can be studied empirically and analyzed philosophically. History, meanwhile, if it is anything at all, is at one with the dialectic, and can only be the problem of which it claims to be the solution.

My experiment here claims to come at realism dialectically, not only by taking as its object of study the very antinomies themselves into which every constitution of this or that realism seems to resolve: but above all by grasping realism as a historical and even evolutionary process in which the negative and the positive are inextricably combined, and whose emergence and development at one and the same time constitute its own inevitable undoing, its own decay and dissolution. The stronger it gets, the weaker it gets; winner loses; its success is its failure. And this is meant, not in the spirit of the life cycle ("ripeness is all"), or of evolution or of entropy or historical rises and falls: it is to be grasped as a paradox and an anomaly, and the thinking of it as a contradiction or an aporia. Yet as Derrida observed, the aporia is not so much "an absence of path, a paralysis before road-blocks" so much as the promise of "the thinking of the path."[13] For me, however, aporetic thinking is precisely the dialectic itself; and the

---

[11] See Jameson, "The Existence of Italy," in *Signatures of the Visible*, New York: Routledge, 1992.

[12] It is not only the content of literature which is itself profoundly historical (and necessarily has its own shaping influence on the form), it is also the sensory medium itself; it is always instructive to recall Marx on the history of the senses (*Early Writings*, London: Penguin, 1975, 351–55).

[13] Jacques Derrida, *Memoires for Paul de Man*, New York: Columbia University Press, 1989, 132.

following exercise will therefore be for better or for worse a dialectical experiment.

But we need to have a better idea of what Deleuze might have called the image of the concept, the shape of some new dialectical solution, before continuing. Hegel's thoughts certainly had some distinctive shapes, but it is not a question of adopting any of those forms here and today; nor does the word "dialectical" give us much help except to revive antiquated formulas, many of which are not even historically accurate.

The unity of opposites, for example, will certainly characterize a situation in which what brings a phenomenon into being also gradually undermines and destroys it. But the content of these fundamental categories is not identifiable: what is negative and what is positive in the trajectory of realism (it being understood that the struggles over its ideological value are not yet even in play here)? Indeed, on any responsible reading of Hegel it will have been clear that what is positive in its own eyes is negative from the standpoint of its opposite number, and vice versa: so nothing much is gained here except the notion of unity—unity not as synthesis but rather as antagonism, the unity of attraction and repulsion, the unity of struggle.

What is also gained—but it may well simply have been some unconscious structuralist premise, smuggled in avant la lettre—is the sense that we still have to do here with a binary opposition. I have argued elsewhere that the play of oppositions we have grown accustomed to since structuralism is not some newfangled linguistic supplement, but already exists fully developed in Hegel's own time and work, who derives them from ancient philosophy.[14] But now what we need to do is not only to give some literary content to this abstract form, but also to demonstrate such an opposition at work within realism itself (and not externally, between realism and some other kind of discourse). Meanwhile, the superficial traits that come at first to mind—the new plain-language écriture versus the language of dialogue, for example—must not only be specific to realism itself but must also entertain some relationship to the seemingly more external question of realism's coming into being and going hence.

Taken all together in bulk, the heterogeneous materials that somehow end up coalescing into what we call the novel—or realism!—include

---

[14] See Michael N. Forster, *Hegel and Skepticism*, Cambridge, MA: Harvard University Press, 1989, 10–13, on "equipollence."

the following: ballads and broadsheets, newspaper sketches, memoirs, diaries and letters, the Renaissance tale, and even popular forms like the play or the folk- or fairy-tale. What is selected from such a mass of different types of writing is its narrative component (even when, as for Balzac or Dickens, that component is first offered as a seemingly static description of characteristic types or activities, of picturesque or costumbrista evocations). To put it this way is to isolate something like a narrative impulse which is also realized in the novel as a form, but perhaps does not exhaust the novel's energy sources.

What could then constitute the opposite of the narrative impulse as such? Taken thus abstractly and speculatively we could surely think of any number of non-narrative sentence types: judgements, for example, such as the moral a storyteller might want to add on at the end, or a bit of the folk wisdom with which George Eliot liked to regale her readers. But the most inveterate alternative to narrative as such reminds us that storytelling is a temporal art, and always seems to single out a painterly moment in which the onward drive of narrative is checked if not suspended altogether. The shield of Achilles!: this is the most famous instance of that suspension of narrative which still remained to be theorized as late as Lessing's *Laocoon* in the late eighteenth century. Will the ancient rhetorical trope of ekphrasis be sufficient to fold this descriptive impulse back into narrative homogeneity?

Everyone knows the patience one must bring to his novels as Balzac slowly sets in place his various components—description of the town, history of the profession, the loving enumeration of the parts of the house, inside and out, the family itself, the physiognomy of the protagonist and his or her favorite clothes, his or her favorite *emploi du temps*—in short, all those different types of discourse which as raw material were to have been fused back together in this new form, but which Balzac unapologetically requires us to plow through on our way to the story itself (which will eventually satisfy any taste for reckless momentum, suspense and action we may have had to hold in check during those opening pages).

But if all it accomplished was to lead us back to Lessing and the status of ekphrasis today, this search for the opposite of the narrative impulse will not have been very productive. Perhaps, indeed, the more satisfactory identification of narrative's opposite number is better sought at the other end of the history of the genre, namely at the moment of realism's dissolution, which we always seem to call modernism, without feeling the need to rummage among the innumerable modernisms, not all of them reducible to a single denominator in the first place.

But this procedure, which assumes that by subtracting the modern from narrative we will be left with the essence of realism, assumes that some general definition of what modernism is (or was) is available, an optimistic assumption which generally results in a few stereotypical formulae (it is subjectivist—the inward turn; reflexive or conscious of its own procedures; formalistic in the sense of a heightened attention to its own raw materials; anti-narrative; and deeply imbued with a mystique of art itself). Roland Barthes took a wiser and more prudent position on the matter: "When it comes to the 'modern,' you can only carry out tactical-style operations: at certain times you feel it's necessary to intervene to signal some shift in the landscape or some new inflection in modernity."[15] But his own experience, to be sure, expressed the preoccupations of the post-war period, in which, in what I have called the "late modern," the effort to theorize and to name what had happened in the first half of the twentieth century became a dominant theoretical ambition.

There are also more paradoxical trajectories to be followed: as for example in film, where Tom Gunning has identified what in our present context might be described as a movement from modernism to realism. D. W. Griffith, who rightly or wrongly is tradition-ally credited with having invented the modern (fiction) film as we know it (relying indeed very heavily on literature and in particular on Dickens), began with atmospheric sketches (of a photographic nature) which it was his mission to develop into plots and narrativity as such.[16]

The example suggests that, whatever thematic clue we choose to follow in our identification of the opposite number to the narrative impulse, its theorization will ultimately involve that most paradoxical of philosophical problems, namely the conceptualization of time and temporality. In the world of art, it is a dilemma compounded by our limited vocabulary: for even the *récit* or tale, whose events are already over and done with before the telling of it can begin, is experienced by

---

[15] Quoted in Alain Robbe-Grillet, *Why I Love Barthes*, trans. Andrew Brown, London: Polity, 2011, 39. My own proposals on modernism can be found in *A Singular Modernity*, London: Verso, 2002.

[16] See Tom Gunning, *D.W. Griffith and the Origins of American Narrative Film*, Chicago: University of Illinois Press, 1991.

listener or reader (and above all, of course, by the viewer) as a present of time, but it is of course our present, the present of reading time, and not that of the events themselves.

So in what follows I will approach the question of realism from the angle of temporality; and I will suggest that the opposite number of that chronological temporality of the récit has somehow to do with a present; but with a different kind of presence than the one marked out by the tripartite temporal system of past-present-future, or even by that of the before and after. For all kinds of reasons, to be developed in the following pages, I will identify this present—or what Alexander Kluge calls the "insurrection of the present against the other temporalities"[17]—as the realm of affect.

As the rather crude misuse of this term will be explained later on, I might as well generalize our other impulse with equally decisive approximation and replace the very general word "narrative" with a far sharper and more limited *Fremdwort*, which is the French "récit," and which transforms narrative into the narrative situation itself and the telling of a tale as such.

This means that we now have in our grasp the two chronological end points of realism: its genealogy in storytelling and the tale, its future dissolution in the literary representation of affect. A new concept of realism is then made available when we grasp both these terminal points firmly at one and the same time.

A number of images come to mind for the shape of this thought: the electrical one of negative and positive currents is perhaps not the most reassuring one. But one can also imagine the strands of DNA winding tightly about each other, or a chemical process in which the introduction of a fresh reagent precipitates a combination which then slowly dissolves again as too much of the element in question is added. But it is the dialectical formulation which, taken as an image of thought rather than a philosophical proposition in its own right, still strikes me as the most suggestive: for in it positive force becomes negative (quantity changing into quality) without the determination of a threshold being required, and emergence and dissolution are thought together in the unity of a single thought, beyond all-too-human judgements that claim to separate the positive from the negative, the good from the bad. Still, what I will want to insist on

---

[17] The title of one of his books: *Der Angriff der Gegenwart gegen die übrige Zeit*, Frankfurt: Europaeische Verlagsanstalt, 1985.

in such images is the irrevocable antagonism between the twin (and entwined) forces in question: they are never reconciled, never fold back into one another in some ultimate reconciliation and identity; and the very force and pungency of the realist writing I here examine is predicated on that tension, which must remain an impossible one, under pain of losing itself altogether and dissipating if it is ever resolved in favor of one of the parties to the struggle.

What we call realism will thus come into being in the symbiosis of this pure form of storytelling with impulses of scenic elaboration, description and above all affective investment, which allow it to develop towards a scenic present which in reality, but secretly, abhors the other temporalities which constitute the force of the tale or récit in the first place.

The new scenic impulse will also detect its enemies in the hierarchy of characters who people the tale, which can scarcely be conceived without a protagonist. In particular, it will wage a ceaseless muffled battle against the structures of melodrama by which it is ceaselessly menaced; in the process also throwing off other genres such as the *Bildungsroman*, which for a while seemed so central to it as to define it. Its final battle will be raged in the microstructures of language and in particular against the dominance of point of view which seems to hold the affective impulses in check and lend them the organizing attribution of a central consciousness. Engaging this final battle will however exhaust and destroy it, and realism thereby leaves an odd assortment of random tools and techniques to its shrivelled posterity, who still carry its name on into an era of mass culture and rival media.

So Part One of the present text is by way of offering a phenomenological and structural model, an experiment which posits a unique historical situation without exploring the content of that situation, as so many indispensable studies of the various realisms have already done. Of the two chronological sequels to the moment of realism—modernism and postmodernism—only the latter outcome will be briefly sketched in conclusion. The essay that comprises Part One is followed by three monographs on the relationships of narrative possibility to its specific raw material. *The Antinomies of Realism* constitutes the third volume of the sequence called *The Poetics of Social Forms*.

April 2013

PART I

THE ANTINOMIES OF REALISM

Chapter 1

The Twin Sources of Realism:
The Narrative Impulse

A happy denouncement has at least as much justification as an unhappy one, and
when it is a matter of considering this difference alone, I must admit that for my
part a happy denouncement is to be preferred.

Hegel, *Aesthetics*

If there is anything distinctive to be discovered about realism, then, we
will not find it without somehow distinguishing between realism and
narrative in general, or without, at least, mapping some vague general
zone of narrative which lies outside it (at the same time including
it as well, since the realisms are presumably narratives themselves).
Single-shot answers always seem possible: the fantastic, for example,
or so-called primitive myth (the very word *mythos* means narrative);
or in some narrower and more literary sense, the epic (insofar as we
distinguish it from the novel), or the oral tale, insofar as we distinguish it from the written one.

This is not the solution I want to begin with here, for I am looking
for a storytelling impulse that precedes the formation of the realist
novel and yet persists within it, albeit transformed by a host of new
connections and relationships. I will call the products of this impulse
simply the tale, with the intent of emphasizing its structural versatil-
ity, its aptness for transformation and exploitation by the other forms
just enumerated. The tale can thereby be pressed into service by epic
performance fully as much as by tribal and mythic storytelling, by the
Renaissance art-novella and its equivalents in the Romantic period,
by the ballad, by sub-forms and subgenres like the ghost story or SF,
indeed by the very forms and strictures of the short story itself, as a
specific strict formal practice in its own right with its own history.

At the level of abstraction at which we are working, then, the tale
becomes the generalized object of which narration is the generalized production process or activity, but this generic specification also becomes a
convenient way of evading psychological or anthropological analysis of
that activity, which would be a distraction in our present context.

Yet we may retain one feature from traditional or modern psychological theories of the faculties and/or functions, in which narrativity might be opposed to cognition for example, or emotion to reason; and that is the requirement that the storytelling function, if we want to call it that, must form part of an opposition, must be defined against something else: otherwise the potentiality we are trying to circumscribe risks extending over the entire field of mental activity, everything becoming narrative, everything becoming a kind of story.[1]

So it is that in an influential pronouncement of the 1920s, Ramon Fernandez developed an opposition between the tale and the novel—or rather, to use the more precise and only imperfectly translatable French terms, between the récit and the *roman*.[2] It was a distinction that proved useful for several generations of French writers from Gide to Sartre; and that will remain helpful for us here, particularly since the same general opposition has taken somewhat different forms in other national traditions.

In effect, Fernandez organized his distinction around two distinct genres, which may be taken as markers for either historical developments or structural variations. Translators have tried to render "récit" in English with its cognate, the recital, which is suggestive only to the degree to which someone might recite an account or even a chronicle of events. But even the word "tale," which I prefer here, bears a weight of generic connotation, and can easily crystallize back into historical forms such as the Renaissance novella or the Romantic art-story.

This is the sense in which the active content of Fernandez' theory lies in the opposition itself and the differentiation it generates. For in itself, the term "novel" is even less structurally operative here than that of the récit: the latter can be more rigorously specified, particularly with the use of those national variants I mentioned. As for the

---

[1] Jack Goody's stern rebuke to pan-narrativists (such as myself) overlooks the distinction between a restricted use of the term for a generic type of discourse (songs, divinations, orations and the like) and a more general, dare I say hermeneutic use of the term in which the object of analysis is temporal movement of a more musical kind (in which, for example, mathematical problems are solved or one follows the adventures of a named concept through a technical philosophical argument): Jack Goody, "From Oral to Written," in Franco Moretti, ed., *The Novel, Volume 1: History, Geography, and Culture*, Princeton: Princeton University Press, 2006.

[2] My impression is, however, that the fortunes of this opposition were in fact based on a misunderstanding: Fernandez, in his essay on Balzac (in *Messages*, 1943) seems to have meant "récit" to mean the background and "backstory" passages which accompanied the various characters, and not a distinct form of discourse in its own right.

novel itself, however (not to speak of the realist novel which interests us here), very little is to be deduced from Fernandez' opposition, and writers have tended to fill in their own blank check according to their aesthetic and their ideology.

So it is that Gide, conceiving of the récit as the tale of a unique personal existence or destiny (mostly, for him, a tale told in the first person), is able to draw the conclusion that the novel ought then to be a "*carrefour*," a crossroads or meeting place of multiple destinies, multiple récits. The only book of his own that he was willing to call a novel, then, *Les faux-monnayeurs* (*The Counterfeiters*), offers just such a convergence of a number of different life stories; and it may be agreed that many writers, particularly those specializing in the short story, have thought of the novel in this general way, as a sort of formal Everest to be confronted.

Sartre, on the other hand, has a much more philosophical and ide-ological conception of this opposition, which he grasps in temporal terms and wields with no little critical and polemic power. Here is his evocation of the Maupassant short story, which he grasps as a kind of bourgeois social institution and translates into a concrete after-dinner situation set in the den of cigar-smoking affluent men:

The procedure is nowhere more manifest than in Maupassant. The structure of his short stories is almost invariable; we are first presented with the audience, a brilliant and worldly society which has assembled in a drawing-room after dinner. It is night-time, which dispels fatigue and passion. The oppressed are asleep, as are the rebellious; the world is enshrouded; the story unfolds. In a bubble of light surrounded by nothing there remains this élite which stays awake, completely occupied with its ceremonies. If there are intrigues or love or hate among its members, we are not told of them, and desire and anger are likewise stilled; these men and women are occupied in *preserving* their culture and manners and in *recognizing* each other by the rites of politeness. They represent order in its most exquisite form; the calm of night, the silence of the passions, everything concurs in symbolizing the stable bourgeoisie of the end of the century which thinks that nothing more will happen and which believes in the eternity of capitalist organization. Thereupon, the narrator is introduced. He is a middle-aged man who has "seen much, read much, and retained much," a professional man of experience, a doctor, a military man, an artist, or a Don Juan. He has reached the time of life when, according to a respectful and comfortable myth, man is freed from the passions and considers with an indulgent clear-sightedness those he has experienced. His heart is calm, like the night. He tells his story with detachment. If it has caused him suffering, he has made honey from this suffering. He looks back upon it and considers it as it really was, that is, *sub specie aeternitatis*. There was difficulty to be sure, but this difficulty ended long ago; the actors are dead or married or comforted. Thus, the adventure was a brief disturbance which is over with. It is told from the viewpoint of experience and wisdom; it is listened to from the viewpoint of order. Order triumphs; order is everywhere; it contemplates an old disorder as if the still waters of a summer day have preserved the memory of the ripples which have run through it.[3]

Gide practiced both "genres"; Sartre has nothing but contempt for the kind of anecdote which forms the structural core of the récit and which he associates with the oppressive cult of "experience" wielded by the older generation over the younger (see *La nausée*). But it is precisely that judgement that allows him to formulate what the novel ought to be—the authentic, existential novel—in temporal terms.

The time of the récit is then a time of the preterite, of events completed, over and done with, events that have entered history once and for all. It will be clear enough what a philosophy of freedom must object to in such an inauthentic and reified temporality: it necessarily blocks out the freshness of the event happening, along with the agony of decision of its protagonists. It omits, in other words, the present of time and turns the future into a "dead future" (what this or that character anticipated in 1651 or in 1943). Clearly enough, then, what Sartre calls upon the novel to reestablish is the open present of freedom, the present of an open, undecided future, where the die has not yet been cast, to use one of his favorite expressions. The aesthetic of the existential novel will then bend its narrative instruments to the recreation of this open present, in which not even the past is set in stone, insofar as our acts in the present rewrite and modify it.

We will not fully appreciate the force of this conception of the novel until we recall the devastating critique of François Mauriac's novels, with their sense of impending doom, their melodramatic rhetorical gestures ("this fatal gesture," "she was not then to know," "this encounter, in retrospect so full of consequences," etc.), their built-in predictable mechanisms of sin and judgement. All this, Sartre tells us, is narrated from above, with a God-like omniscience of past and future alike. "Dieu n'est pas bon romancier," he concludes, "M. Mauriac non plus."[4]

But just as surely, even though more subtly, the Sartrean recipe for

---

3 Jean-Paul Sartre, "*What Is Literature?*" *and Other Essays*, Cambridge, MA: Harvard University Press, 1988, 125–126.

4 Sartre, *Situations I*, Paris: Gallimard, 1947, 67.

the novel is shaped and determined, preselected, by its own historical content: the time of the momentous decision and the impending Event, the effacement of everyday life and the iteratives of peacetime, the pressure of what he called extreme situations. The Sartrean taboo on foreknowledge will be replicated in a somewhat different way by the Jamesian ideology of point of view, and both will be appropriated, as we shall see, for far more inauthentic purposes after the end of realism as such, in what I will call a more commercial realism after realism.

What we can retain of the Sartrean perspective on the récit, however, is its insistence on irrevocability, on which a somewhat different light is shed by the German tradition, relatively poor in novels as it may be, but extraordinarily rich in storytelling of all kinds, particularly in the Romantic era. We have, for example, Goethe's memorable encapsulation of the content of storytelling as an *"unerhörte Begebenheit"*[5]—an unheard-of event or conjuncture, one thereby itself memorable and worthy of retelling over and over again, and of being passed down in the family and even the community: the time of the single lightning bolt that killed three people at once, the time of the great flood, of the invasion of the barbarians, the time Lizzie Borden took an axe, and so forth. It is then this time of the memorable event, of the traditional tale or story, that Walter Benjamin memorialized in his great essay "The Storyteller" (on Leskov).

Indeed, Benjamin makes it clear what so many examples of the *"unerhörte Begebenheit"* have in common: namely death. "Warming your hands on a death that is told" is the way he characterizes the récit[6]; and if we feel that this is too bleak, we may substitute for death simply the mark of the irrevocable. This irrevocability adds a new dimension to Sartre's critique of the inauthenticity of the récit: the temporal past is now redefined in terms of what cannot be changed, what lies beyond the reach of repetition or rectification, which now comes to be seen as the time of everyday life or of routine. The

---

[5]   Johann Peter Eckermann, *Gespräche mit Goethe*, Vol. I, Basel: Birkhäuser, 1945, 210 (January 25, 1827): "denn was ist eine Novelle anders als eine sich ereignete unerhörte Begebenbeit."

[6]   Walter Benjamin, "Der Erzähler," *Gesammelte Schriften*, Vol. 2, Frankfurt: Suhrkamp, 1989, 457: "Das was den Leser zum Roman zieht, ist die Hoffnung, sein fröstelndes Leben an einem Tod, von dem er liest, zu wärmen." It will be remembered that earlier in the same section he compared the construction of a novel to the building of a fire.

irrevocable then comes to stand as a mark of one specific temporality which is separated off from another kind; and Goethe's definition may then be reread to designate, not strangeness or uniqueness, but precisely this shock of a marked time brutally differentiating itself from ordinary existence.

It should be added that for Benjamin, this ordinary existence is itself grasped as collective and historical, as the time of peasants or of the village, in which, as opposed to the great industrial metropolis of a later date, the tale as such flourishes.[7] Indeed, we may further point out that for Benjamin, the opposite number of the tale or récit is not the realistic novel at all: it is the dissolution of the memorable and the narratable in Baudelaire's modernism, or the technological and political recuperation of Baudelaire's fragments in Eisensteinian montage, in the so-called reproducible work of art.[8]

Meanwhile, in a paradoxical turn-about, this new notion of the irrevocable mark as the very basis of the récit is also susceptible of a Sartrean authenticity very different from the bourgeois inauthenticity of the Maupassant smoking den. Indeed, the irrevocable also comes in Sartre to define the heroic, the freely chosen act, one that marks you forever and from which there is no turning back: the act one drags about with one like a ball and chain (again a Sartrean figure). It is then the recoiling in horror before such a choice that is inauthentic; and we may draw on *Peer Gynt* for a comic example. For when Peer is welcomed into the kingdom of the trolls, he is promised everything: the troll king's daughter, riches beyond price, a life of leisure and pleasure, the succession to the throne—and all this, the king assures him, on the most minimal condition, namely, that you let yourself—painlessly, to be sure—undergo hideous defacement as a pledge of solidarity with us and a guarantee that you will never seek to return to the world of ordinary humans. Peer draws the line at that kind of guarantee, that mark of irrevocability, preferring to keep his options open and his "Sartrean freedom" untouched by any such binding commitments.[9]

We may thus grasp the lightning bolt of the récit as the marking

---

[7] The "origin" of storytelling, according to him, lay in the intersection of travelling seamen and merchants with the sedentary life of the villagers.

[8] I believe that Benjamin's three essays, on Leskov, on Baudelaire, and finally on Eisenstein and film, make up a trilogy that stages history as the rise and fall of narrative as it symptomatizes experience itself.

[9] Henrik Ibsen, *Peer Gynt*, Act II.

of a body and the transformation of an individual into a character with a unique destiny, a "life sore," as one American novelist puts it, something given to you uniquely to bear and to suffer[10]: something "*je mein eigenes,*" as Heidegger described individual death. This brings our account of the récit or the tale a little closer to the destinies once offered in spectacle by tragedy as a form. In modern times, however, such destinies at best mark a character as one of Todorov's "*hommes-récits,*" the Thousand-and-One-Nights characters who *are* their own stories,[11] at the high tide of the récit as a form; while at worst, in yet more modern times, they are taken to be little more than bad luck. Still, I will retain the category of "destiny" or "fate" as the deeper philosophical content of this narrative form, which might also be evoked as the narrative preterite, the mark of irrevocable time, of the event that has happened once and for all. What has happened in the course of our discussion—it will be important later on—is that this mark has slowly been turned or rotated in the direction of other people: it is not only my act, for myself, which defines my destiny: the latter also becomes my scar, my sore or limp, my being-for-other-people, which is also to say my existence as a character in a story.

It will not have escaped notice that in this lengthy discussion of the récit, we have completely lost sight of its opposite number, namely the *roman*. Sartre seemed to have made a place for it in that existential present in which the choice was in the process of being made or being refused: a time before destiny, in other words, and perhaps before the récit itself. We need to retain this notion of an existential present as it is opposed to the irrevocable past tense of the récit; but we now need to approach it in a different way, and for this I will turn to yet a third tradition, that of English-language narratology or rather, to be more precise about it, the American tradition.

Here, of course, the fundamental theoretician is Henry James in his *Prefaces*, its ideas codified and popularized in Percy Lubbock's *Craft of Fiction*. And here the distinction between récit and *roman* takes on a much more familiar appearance: it is simply that between "telling" and "showing." You tell, you *recite*, the events; you show them happening in the present of the novelistic scene. To be sure, the novel includes both types of discourse; indeed, the very passage from one

---

[10] See Susan Willis, *Specifying: Black Women Writing the American Experience*, Madison, WI: University of Wisconsin Press, 1987, 70. (The writer referred to is Paule Marshall).

[11] Tzvetan Todorov, *Poetics of Prose*, Ithaca: Cornell, 1977, chapter 5, "Narrative Men."

to the other is itself stylistically and even metaphysically significant—that "choice," as André Malraux put it, "of what is to become scene or to remain récit, the emplacement of those porches where a Balzac or a Dostoyevsky lie in wait for their characters as destiny itself waits on man."[12]

Yet Malraux, along with James himself, is biased in favor of showing rather than telling; and we must factor this prejudice in favor of scene, this commitment to Jamesian "point of view," into their theorization of the opposition.

For James himself, it would seem that mere telling—the récit part of what he describes as a "double pressure" on the novel—means shirking his job.[13] The narrative summaries and foreshortenings are in effect sheer laziness, they are the sign he has not lived up to his calling, the august vocation he invented for himself (and for others). "One's poor word of honor has *had* to pass muster for the show."[14] "The poor author's comparatively cold affirmation or thin guarantee"[15] he calls such passages, on the point of drawing the whole process into an economic transaction (as he does so often), while calling on the literary critics to live up to their vocation and denounce all the "dodges" (his word) the novelist has thereby had recourse to. The more modern language of discourse versus story does not really modify this bias, which I hope my own dual model will redress, giving some of the honor back to the great storytellers and the framers of the great art-novellas.

But James is very clear about the antagonism between the two modes of récit and presence. He characterizes it as

> the odd inveteracy with which picture, at almost any turn, is jealous of drama, and drama (though on the whole with a greater patience, I think) suspicious of picture. Between them, no doubt, they do much for the theme; yet each baffles insidiously the other's ideal and eats round the edges of its position; each is too ready to say, "I can take the thing for 'done' only when done in *my* way."[16]

---

12 André Malraux, *Les voix du silence*, Paris: Gallimard, 1951, 353.

13 Henry James, *The Art of the Novel*, New York: Scribners, 1934, 300. James's foundational distinction between telling and showing now finds confirmation in the light of David Kurnick's remarkable *Empty Houses*, Princeton UP, 2012, which, documenting the theatrical failures at the heart of much of the modernist canon now grasps modernist showing as a formal and structural nostalgia for theatricality.

14 Ibid., 298.

15 Ibid., 301.

16 Ibid., 298. (The quotes are all part of the Preface to *The Wings of the Dove*.)

In defense of telling, however, and by way of redressing the scales so heavily weighted by Sartre against the extraordinary storytelling art of Maupassant, it may be well to insist on the relative insignificance of "showing" in the narratives, not only of the great oral practitioners, but even in that of more sophisticated practitioners such as Boccaccio. Many are no doubt the candidates for the most beautiful story in the world, but I am not far myself from endorsing the view of the distinguished German writer Paul Heyse,[17] who based his so-called *Falkentheorie* on the ninth tale of the fifth day of the *Decameron*, whose "moral" or summary I herewith append:

> 9. In courting a lady who does not return his love, Federigo degli Alberighi spends the whole of his substance, being left with nothing but a falcon, which, since his larder is bare, he offers to his lady to eat when she calls to see him at his house. On discovering the truth of the matter, she has a change of heart, accepts him as her husband, and makes a rich man of him.[18]

Heyse thought that the perfection of this little tale lay in the way in which its convergences were crystallized in a single object, namely the hawk of the title, in such a way as to concentrate the temporality of narrative into something the mind could uniquely appropriate and hold to itself, time made space, in other words, the event material-ized, in a fashion perhaps not so distant after all from Benjamin's conception of a moment which becomes "memorable."[19] This object is not a symbol; it is not its meaningfulness which is essential but rather its unity and density.

Heyse is here clearly enough specifying the properties of the most usable anecdotal starting point (or "subject" as Henry James liked to call it), rather than a structural law of some kind: in contemporary stories objects tend to be far more contingent, resembling Barthes' *punctum*[20] more than they do his *studium*. What gives his theory its plausibility is, however, the part of the story Boccaccio has dropped, either by negligence or by design, from his little summary. For the hawk—in this, paradigmatic of most twist or trick endings, even those which do not turn on a single object—is double-valenced, which is

---

[17] Paul Heyse, "Einleitung," *Deutscher Novellenschatz*, Munich: Oldenbourg, 1971.

[18] Boccaccio, *The Decameron*, London: Penguin, 1995, xiv.

[19] Benjamin, "Der Erzähler," 453–54, section xiii on *Erinnerung*.

[20] Roland Barthes, *La Chambre Claire*, *Œuvres completes, tome III*, Paris: Seuil, 1995, 1126.

to say that it can serve a different function in each of the contexts in which it appears, switching back and forth in a kind of Gestalt effect.

What is curious here is that Boccaccio has omitted both contexts, both storylines which converge here, from his brief outline. For the hawk is not only his master's prize possession (and not merely his only one, as the summary suggests), it is something of a substitute for the desperate and forlorn passion he nourishes for the pointedly indifferent and uninterested Monna Giovanna, so that he will have sacrificed with it everything that still gives any meaning to his sad existence.

But the hawk also stands at the center of the other storyline, the reason for Monna Giovanna's unusual visit to a man she has every reason to avoid, inasmuch as its possession also constitutes the passionate desire of her beloved son, deathly ill and unlikely to recover even if he is able to have this last wish satisfied.

The story shows us that Federigo is willing to do anything she wants, and the banquet with which he regales her is intended to dramatize that willingness. The hawk thereby unites the tragic failure of three passions, and its story thereby triumphantly wins its nomination, not only for the saddest story ever told but also for the most perfect.

But it is a tale that needs no "showing," no scene, no present of narrative at all; and this is the point of its introduction here, as the purest form of the récit. The anecdote not only needs no dialogue and no point of view (it has all these in Boccaccio's brief "telling"), but the whole art of storytelling lies in this possibility of the anecdote, the *fait divers*, to be expanded and contracted at will, and according to the practical necessities of the situation. Even more important from our perspective is the palpable fact that the tale cannot exist in the present, its events must already have happened: this is the "moment of truth" of Sartre's analysis, for whom in this sense the absolute past, what has already happened, the irrevocable, cannot exist, for it can always be rewritten, reevaluated, revised by the power of a new act in the present or the future. The mode of the récit now seals this event off and makes such revision impossible (and the death of the hawk is the figure for this irrevocability of death in general). What confuses the issue is of course the eternal present of the reader, who brings a different temporality to the process.

This is then the moment to distinguish two kinds of time, two systems of temporality, which will be the basis for the argument that follows. The distinction is one between a present of consciousness and a time, if not of succession or of chronology, then at least of the more familiar tripartite system of past-present-future. I want to assert that the present of consciousness is somehow impersonal, that consciousness is itself impersonal; while it is the subject of consciousness or the self that is the locus of personal identity in the ordinary sense. That self, however, is itself only an object for the impersonal consciousness of the present; and in a way all the personal identifications of past-present-future in the other sense are distinct from the impersonal present, mere objects in it, no matter how inseparable they are from it. You can say that theories of this kind reflect the famous "death of the subject" or that they articulate the split subject of poststructuralism or Lacanianism: we won't follow those debates any further here, but will only draw some interesting consequences for the narrative theories in the process of elaboration. In particular, it becomes clear that the regime of the past-present-future and of personal identities and destinies is at its outer limit the realm of the récit; while the impersonal consciousness of an eternal or existential present would at its outer limit govern pure scene, a showing that was altogether divorced and separated from telling and purified of it. Let's see what an event might look like from this second temporal perspective:

> Lunch went on methodically, until each of the seven courses was left in fragments and the fruit was merely a toy, to be peeled and sliced as a child destroys a daisy, petal by petal.

This is a rather different lunch from many we can remember reading about: the one which makes Mr. Bloom belch with satisfaction in *Ulysses*; the immense two-hundred-page lunches in Proust, from which all the gossip and anecdotes fan out like a rhizome; the truly abominable lunch break that sets everything in motion at the beginning of *La bête humaine*; some elegant English luncheon in which, according to the newspapers, someone ingests a virulent particle of radiation; or that infinitely sad lunch to which Boccaccio's impoverished hero invited his beloved. All of those—and I will treat you to yet another lunch later on, a truly wondrous well-nigh salvational one—all of those are inserted into one or another kind of narrative time; the anonymous lunch in which one course is peeled off after another is not.

Many are to be sure the theories of metaphor from time immemorial, from Ricoeur's identification (based on Aristotle) of metaphor as the very source of Being itself[21] to any number of tropological systems, let alone systems of resemblance and recognition. In our context, however, what is inescapable is the function of metaphor to detemporalize existence, to dechronologize and denarrativize the present, indeed, to construct or reconstruct a new temporal present which we are so oddly tempted to call eternal. The word is evidently an attempt to escape the temporal overtones of the normal vocabulary for experiences of time, and is consistent with the "eternity" of individual consciousness itself as long as it lasts (inasmuch as in that sense, consciousness has no opposite and we are in it, even in sleep, in some absolute and inescapable fashion).

What we can at least conclude from this discussion is that we have here finally located the definitive formulation for the discursive opposition we have been trying to name. Now it can be articulated not as *récit* versus *roman*, nor even telling versus showing; but rather destiny versus the eternal present. And what is crucial is not to load one of these dies and take sides for the one or the other as all our theorists seemed to do, but rather to grasp the proposition that realism lies at their intersection. Realism is a consequence of the tension between these two terms; to resolve the opposition either way would destroy it; James's guilt feelings are not only justified, they are necessary. And this is also why it is justified to find oneself always talking about the emergence or the breakdown of realism and never about the thing itself, since we will always find ourselves describing a potential emergence or a potential breakdown.

---

[21] Paul Ricoeur, *The Rule of Metaphor*, Toronto: University Press, 1977, 307.

Chapter II

The Twin Sources of Realism: Affect, or, the Body's Present

We have, to be sure, ourselves omitted something significant from our account of "The Hawk," and it is the happy ending: the boy recovers from his illness (despite the absence of his beloved falcon), Monna Giovanna relents, and, although she fails to develop any genuine passion for Federigo, consents to the marriage, in which "they all live happily ever after" and so forth. But this involves a lowering of tone, and as it were a decompression, a return to the flatlands of everyday life, a slow disengagement from the intensities of the Event (the narrative or récit itself) and a consent to the less exhilarating yet ultimately more humanly bearable comfort of the everyday (using this last word in Auerbach's heightened sense, with its connotation of a realism to come).

The shift, then, from tale to daily life simply confirms the point being made about the two temporalities at stake here. Yet also to be noted, if not unduly stressed, is the mild desolation that accompanies this narrative, whether in its major mode as a récit or in the coda. I have used the word "sad" (to which we will return in a more official context): is this feeling only to be attributed to the reader or is it possible that it suggests a dimension of narrative we have not yet taken into consideration?

This observation will then serve to introduce the second agency in my story, and the other impulse—affect—I want to associate with the emergence of realism as such. I will first stage this second impulse as the opposite of the narrative one: that is to say, I will approach it from the standpoint of temporality, for which the récit has seemed to embody a temporality of the past and of the preterite, a temporality of the chronological, in which, everything having happened already, events succeed each other in what is today loosely called "linear time" (a rather faddish expression I believe we owe to Marshall McLuhan).

Is it possible to imagine a temporality so different from this conventional one that the word "time" ceases to seem altogether appropriate for it (something we already mused about in connection with the term "eternal")?

In the hindsight of the theory (and historical experience) of the postmodern, and of what I have called "the end of temporality," perhaps we can add greater specificity to the kind of temporality (or lack of it) at stake here. "The End of Temporality" theorized a shrinking of contemporary (bourgeois) experience such that we begin to live a perpetual present with a diminishing sense of temporal or indeed phenomenological continuities[1]: this perpetual present was, I believe, what Deleuze and Guattari described as a schizophrenic present (in the *Anti-Oedipus*)[2], but theirs was an altogether Utopian account which takes its place in a tradition of literary celebrations of temporal immediacy from Wordsworth's imbeciles and Flaubert's "simple heart"[3] on down to modern times. I believe that the contemporary or postmodern "perpetual present" is better characterized as a "reduction to the body," inasmuch as the body is all that remains in any tendential reduction of experience to the present as such. But I would not necessarily want to argue that in such temporal isolation the body's senses gain a heightened existence, something that is more likely to happen when, for whatever reason, one sense is given priority over the others (as in the evolving specializations of nineteenth-century painting and music). Rather, the isolated body begins to know more global waves of generalized sensations, and it is these which, for want of a better word, I will here call affect.

It is a technical term which has been strongly associated with a number of recent theories which alternately appeal to Freud or to Deleuze and which, like the theory of postmodernity, also take this phenomenon as evidence for a new turn in human relations and forms of subjectivity (including politics).[4] I do not here mean to

---

[1] See Jameson, "The End of Temporality," in *Ideologies of Theory*, London: Verso, 2009.

[2] See the first chapter of Deleuze and Guattari's *L'Anti-Œdipe* (Paris: Minuit, 1972), as celebrated, for example, in the following account: "Il y a une expérience schizophrénique des quantités intensives à l'état pur, à un point presque insupportable—une misère et une gloire célibataires éprouvées au plus haut point, comme une clameur suspendue entre la vie et la mort, un sentiment de passage intense, états d'intensité pure et crue dépouillés de leur figure et de leur forme" (25).

[3] To Felicité's blessed simplicity should be added the very different longing expressed in Saint Antoine's final cry: "Être la matière!"

[4] Various conceptual streams meet in this concept: Deleuze's commentaries on

appropriate it for a different theory of all these things, nor do I mean to endorse or to correct the philosophies of which it currently constitutes a kind of signal or badge of group identity. Indeed, I want to specify a very local and restricted, practical use of the term "affect" here by incorporating it into a binary opposition which historicizes it and limits its import to questions of representation and indeed of literary history.

I will therefore begin by distinguishing affect (in my sense of the word) from emotions as such. The opposition between feelings and emotions is a long-standing one, based mostly on tradition rather than any successfully articulated structural difference. The replacement of the vague word "feeling" by the more technical if not clinical term "affect" does seem to promise a little more rigor in the debate, if not indeed to promise some renewal of it in the reconsideration of an old problem, which has become the unexamined sedimentation of common sense thought.

I will clarify it by modifying the terminology of the opposite number as well: for I wish to redefine emotion as "named emotion," and thereby not only to mark a structural difference between emotion and affect but also to underscore yet a further dimension of this problem, which involves the intervention of language as such. The new implication is that affect (or its plural) somehow eludes language and its naming of things (and feelings), whereas emotion is preeminently a phenomenon sorted out into an array of names. Traditionally those names—love, hatred, anger, fear, disgust, pleasure, and so forth—have been grasped as a system of phenomena (like the system of the colors, for example); and like colors, the system is a historical one which varies from culture to culture and from period to period. Many are the handbooks which seek to map out the then current systems of emotions, from Aristotle's *Nichomachean Ethics* to Descartes' *Treatise on the Passions.*[5] But what needs further clarification in our context—

Spinoza, Eve Sedgwick's meditations on Sylvan Tompkins, trauma theory, queer theory and a whole new generation of work, which is usefully summarized by references to Jonathan Flatley, *Affective Mapping*, Cambridge, MA: Harvard, 2008—but see his bibliographic note on 198–99—or to Sianne Ngai, *Ugly Feelings*, Cambridge, MA: Harvard University Press, 2005.

[5]   I have not found a suitable structural history; but see Amélie O. Rorty, ed., *Exploring Emotions*, Berkeley: University of California Press, 1980; Daniel M. Gross, *The Secret History of Emotion*, Chicago: University of Chicago Press, 2006; and, in order not to omit the humors from this picture, Noga Arikha, *Passions and the Tempers*, New York: Harper Collins, 2007.

for such systems eventually seem to dissolve in the era of affect, and yet to survive residually like so many traditions—is not so much the system as such as rather the reifying effects of the name itself.

It is indeed a delicate philosophical problem, if not a false one altogether, to distinguish between a phenomenological state of being—say, the experience of anger—and the word by which it is named: "Sing, Muse, the wrath of Achilles"—*thumos*. The philological dialectic deflects our interest in the thing itself—how the ancients felt anger—to the history of the word: but is the existence of the word altogether foreign to the experience of the emotion? If it does not bring it into being in the first place, as some absolute constructivism might claim, then at least the articulation language brings to the as yet unexpressed feeling will surely open all kinds of new channels into which it can spread and thrive.

By habit and tradition, the notion of reification now strikes us as a negative or critical one; and the implication that the name necessarily reifies the emotion at once suggests the possibility of some more authentic experience that preceded the baleful spell of nomination (and that could in a pinch perhaps be recovered). But this is to forget Hegel's judiciously ambivalent deployment of the original concept: humans objectify their projects and their desires, thereby enriching them: life is itself then a series of reifications which are themselves reabsorbed and enlarged by way of the new project. Naming is a fundamental component of such objectification, and alienation is only one possible fate for what is a universal process.

"If the word love comes up between them I am lost!" Count Mosca's famous apprehension (on seeing Gina and Fabrice together) is perhaps only the most dramatic expression of the way in which the name can suddenly bring a whole new world into being (for good or ill!).[6] Meanwhile, many are the examples of words which have historically articulated undiscovered states of being which, while perhaps not newly emergent, were at least dormant if not unconscious in everyday human existence, and which then begin to play their own role as agents in a reorganization of life. Such was, for example, the appropriation of the old word "*ennui*" for the new state of nineteenth-century boredom, which brought all kinds of new questions about activity and even existence into being around it. Such was also, in my opinion, the word "anxiety," which rescued a daily and unnerving experience

---

[6] Stendhal, *La Chartreuse de Parme*, Paris: Cluny, 1948, 165 (chapter 8).

from the melodramatic and quasi-religious grandeur of words like "anguish." Such finally is also the designation of an ancient scholastic term for that register of feeling we now call "affect" itself, not to speak of medicalization.[7] Yet the onto-philological dilemma remains (or is it the Sapir-Whorff hypothesis?): were there affects before this name raised them into the light of consciousness, or did the word somehow slowly begin to modify the field of existential reality itself in such a way as to endow us with a bodily dimension absent from the bodily experience of, say, the ancient Greeks?

As I suggested, I believe that the problem is unsolvable in that form, but also that, if we specify a restriction on what the historical language can and cannot express at any given point, the ontological question will not disrupt the historical one. (Meanwhile, the question of whether affects cannot themselves be reified in the naming process must also remain open: Did the medieval term "acedia" not modify the experience of medieval clerks? Does the word "melancholia," itself long present in Western discourse, not do something significant to our own internal subjectivities? And does not the very word "affect," itself henceforth powerfully reorganize the latter's force field?)[8]

At any rate, it will have become clear that by positing the named emotion (rather than emotion tout court) as the binary opposite of affect per se (or at least as the term whose difference allows us best to articulate the latter's identity), I am also insisting on the resistance of affect to language, and thereby on the new representational tasks it poses poets and novelists in the effort somehow to seize its fleeting essence and to force its recognition. For in its insatiable colonization of the as yet unexplored and inexpressed (it is an impulse in which realism can be said to share the telos that modernism only more stridently affirms and sloganizes), the system of the old named emotions becomes not only too general but also too familiar: to approach the emotions more closely is microscopically to see within them a Brownian movement which, although properly unnamable in its own right, calls out imperiously for all the stimulation of linguistic innovation. It is towards mid-century, let us say in the 1840s of the bourgeois era, that such linguistic demands begin to become audible and inescapable, at least for the most alert arts that scan the era for the new.

---

7   See Ivan Illich, *Limits to Medicine*, London: Marion Boyers, 1995.

8   We will see that the very word "body," unifying and totalizing as it is, can itself scarcely escape the reproach of reification either.

But now we must introduce another feature of affect: I provisionally follow Rei Terada's idea (derived ultimately from Kant) that affects are bodily feelings, whereas emotions (or passions, to use their other name) are conscious states.[9] The latter have objects, the former are bodily sensations: it is the difference between the *coup de foudre* and a state of generalized depression. But this is then to endow the concept of affect with a positive content: if the positive characteristic of the emotion is to be named, the positive content of an affect is to activate the body. Language is here opposed to the body, or at least the lived body (which may itself be a "modern" phenomenon). And therefore, alongside a crisis of language, in which the old systems of emotions come to be felt as a traditional rhetoric, and an outmoded one at that, there is also a new history of the body to be written, the "bourgeois body" as we may now call it, as it emerges from the outmoded classifications of the feudal era. (Foucault's historical periodization of the emergence of "life" or of the new biosciences offers one possible context for what I here mean to be an existential and class-social phenomenon, related to the emergence of new forms of daily life.[10])

One has only to compare the descriptions in Balzac's novels, concocted by someone who came of age in the Restoration, to the organization of narrative discourse in Flaubert only a generation later, to grasp the truly historical changes in what is asked of language by each novelist, and what is represented in the way of the representation of subjectivity, and of its perceptions.

In that case, it will be appropriate to associate rise of affect with the emergence of the phenomenological body in language and representation; and to historicize a competition between the system of named emotions and the emergence of nameless bodily states which can be documented in literature around the middle of the nineteenth century (literary representation furnishing the most comprehensive evidence as to a momentous yet impossibly hypothetical historical transformation of this kind). Flaubert and Baudelaire can stand as the markers for such a transformation of the sensorium, which can perhaps best be demonstrated by way of Balzac's dealings with the senses in the previous generation. Balzacian descriptions are well-known: here is the most famous, of the salon of the Maison Vauquer:

---

[9] Rei Terada, *Feeling in Theory: Emotion After the "Death of the Subject,"* Cambridge, MA: Harvard, 2001, 82.

[10] See also Donald Lowe's pathbreaking *History of Bourgeois Perception*, Chicago: University of Chicago Press, 1983.

Cette première pièce exhale une odeur sans nom dans la langue, et qu'il faudrait appeler *l'odeur de pension*. Elle sent le renfermé, le moisi, le rancé; elle donne froid, elle est humide au nez, elle pénètre les vêtements; elle a le goût d'une salle où l'on dine; elle pue le service, l'office, l'hospice. Peut-être pourrait-elle se décrire si l'on inventait un procédé pour évaluer les quantités élémentaires et nauséabondes qu'y jettent les atmosphères catarrhales et *sui generis* de chaque pensionnaire, jeune ou vieux.

This room gives off a smell for which our language has no special word; it can only be described as a *boarding house smell*. It smells stuffy, mouldy, rancid; it is chilly, clammy to breathe, permeates one's clothing; it leaves the stale taste of a room where people have been eating; it stinks of backstairs, scullery, workhouse. It could only be described if some process were invented for measuring the quantity of disgusting elementary particles contributed by each resident, young or old, from his own catarrhal and *sui generis* exhalations.[11]

Everything would seem to confirm the first impression, that it is an affect that is at question here: it is nameless and unclassifiable, the senses are mobilized, Balzac is keenly aware of his linguistic and representational problem and fusses with his recording apparatus. But this description is not the evocation of an affect, for one good reason: namely that it *means* something.

The passage makes clear why the elaborate descriptions in Balzec do not invalidate the historical proposition I want to advance about the body in literature. For in Balzac everything that looks like a physical sensation—a musty smell, a rancid taste, a greasy fabric—always means something, it is a sign or allegory of the moral or social status of a given character: decent poverty, squalor, the pretensions of the parvenu, the true nobility of the old aristocracy, and so on. In short, it is not really a sensation, it is already a meaning, an allegory. By the time of Flaubert, these signs remain, but they have become stereotypical; and the new descriptions register a density beyond such stereotypical meanings.

Roland Barthes, a keen amateur of the new vibrations modernity brought with it, has spoken authoritatively of the irreconcilable divorce between lived experience and the intelligible which characterizes modernity, between the existential and the meaningful.[12]

---

[11] Honoré de Balzac, *Le père Goriot*, in *Oeuvres III*, Paris: La Pléiade, 1976, 53. Note the wistful longing for a quantitative turn in this description. English translation by A. J. Krailsheimer, Oxford, 1991, 4–6.

[12] Roland Barthes, "L'Effet de réel," in *Oeuvres*, Vol. II, Paris: Seuil, 1994, 483. And see my own commentary in "The Realist Floor Plan," in *Ideologies of Theory*, London: Verso, 2009.

Experience—and sensory experience in particular—is in modern times contingent: if such experience seems to have a meaning, we are at once suspicious of its authenticity. Balzac, however, will not give up on meaning: he continues energetically to deploy the twin weapons of metaphor ("Old Goriot was a lion!") and of metonymy, as in this passage and indeed everywhere in his work, where the nameless smell is composed of the decent or desperate miseries of pensioners who have deposited their traces in this haven.

To this we might well oppose the contingencies enumerated by Flaubert in his descriptions (Barthes terms them "l'effet de réel" or the "reality-effect"). Baudelaire is just as useful:

> dans une maison déserte quelque armoire
> Pleine de l'âcre odeur des temps, poudreuse et noire.
>
> "Le flacon"

where the musty smell of time drifts in indeterminable synesthesia across the grimy tactility of the armoire. These unnamable sensations have become autonomous, as Balzac's odor might have been had it been converted into some distasteful melancholia. At any rate they no longer mean anything: states of the world, they simply exist.

Yet this is a historical proposition which raises serious philosophical problems. Are we to suppose that before the construction of the secular or bourgeois body in the course of the nineteenth century, affects simply did not exist, and an older pre-modern humanity had to make do with the various systems of emotions referenced above? But it is not exactly this kind of sweeping and peremptory affirmation which I am advancing here, but rather a hypothesis that, with the change in nuance, differentiates it absolutely from this or that statement about human nature. For what I suggest is that before this mid-century, such affects had not been named, had not found their way into language, let alone become the object of this or that linguistic codification. To be sure, this is also a historical proposition, but one about language itself and the way in which the nomination of an experience makes it visible at the very moment that it transforms and reifies it. And what is presupposed is that affects or feelings which have not thus been named are not available to consciousness, or are absorbed into subjectivity in different ways that render them inconspicuous and indistinguishable from the named emotions they may serve to fill out and to which they lend body and substance. This is to say that any proposition about affect is also a proposition about the body; and a historical one at that.

We have so far (in our examples) characterized affect in terms of physical sensation or sensory perception. Odor, the most repressed and stigmatized of the senses as Adorno pointed out,[13] seems everywhere, from Baudelaire to Proust, to be a privileged vehicle for isolating affect and identifying it for a variety of dynamics (we should not forget Teresa Brennan's startling proposal that the contagion of affect—its interpersonal transmission—is historically the result of smell, of which sexual pheromones are only a particularly dramatic example[14]). But these sensory vehicles of affect present a representational problem inasmuch they are easily confused and identified with the bodily senses as such, and thereby reduced to merely physical perceptions or sensations. It is clear, for example, that the usefulness of smell as a vehicle for different types of affect derives at least in part from its marginalized status, its underdevelopment, so to speak, as a symbolic element.

We need then, before continuing, to enumerate some of the features affect seems to present (or to require): the variety of such features then begins to suggest the multiplicity of ways this new element can pervade nineteenth-century realism and open up its narratives, not only to scene and consciousness as such, but above all to some new realism of affect, some heightened representational presence.

We have already insisted on the namelessness of this new reality. It can certainly be constructed, and not only in literature but also in the other arts; but that very operation is dialectical and expresses both faces of a tenacious representational nominalism, for the name, whatever its vocabulary field—the celebration of the *body* or the positing of something like *melancholy* as the fundamental ground-tone of human existence—necessarily turns the affect into a new thing in its own right. The *symboliste* doctrine of suggestion here betrays a deeper truth, that of a radical distinction between naming and representational construction, which, distantly evoking our more fundamental distinction between telling and showing, explains why affect cannot be present in the regime of the *récit*.

Yet the temptation to name is encouraged by another feature of affect, namely its autonomization. It seems to have no context, but to float above experience without causes and without the structural relationship to its cognate entities which the named emotions have

[13] T. W. Adorno and Max Horkheimer, *Dialectic of Enlightenment*, Stanford, CA: Stanford University Press, 2007. See the chapter "Elements of Anti-Semitism."

[14] Teresa Brennan, *The Transmission of Affect*, Ithaca: Cornell, 2004.

with one another.[15] This is not to say that in reality affect has no causes whatsoever, no relationship to its situation of emergence: for any number of chemical, psychoanalytic, or interpersonal factors may well plausibly be proposed or experimentally tested. But its essence is to remain free-floating and independent of these factors (which only exist for other people), and this is obviously a function of its temporality as an eternal present, as an element which is somehow self-sufficient, feeding on itself, and perpetuating its own existence ("all joy wants eternity!"). This is then the point at which we must evoke another feature (explored in recent times by Deleuze and Lyotard)[16], namely intensity: that is, the capacity of affect to be registered according to a range of sonority, from minute to deafening, without losing its quality and its determination. Indeed, Lyotard's usage makes it clear that we could just as well substitute the term "intensity" for that of "affect" itself, provided we use it in the plural—yet here too it is no longer a matter of form and content, but rather of that other contemporary verbal-fetish, which is singularity. Affects are singularities and intensities, existences rather than essences, which usefully unsettle the more established psychological and physiological categories.

This was indeed what Roland Barthes meant by his notion of the "reality effect," a formulation designed to replace any substantive idea of realism (and in particular those based on its content) by a semiotic one, in which "realism" is only one of the possible signs and signals given off by the text in question. That texts designed to be called "realism" and recognized as such give off signals or connotations of the type Barthes described in *Writing Degree Zero* (and which he called "*écriture*" as such) is unquestionable, even though the type of realism they may have wanted to convey necessarily had a historical and ideological status. Yet I believe there is a more satisfactory way of dealing with realism than its reduction to signs alone (this book attempts to justify that belief).

For with his uncanny sense of intellectual consequences, Barthes then at once historicizes his position: "In the ideology of our time, the obsessive reference to the 'concrete' ... is always trained like a

---

15   But who says autonomization also necessarily implies differentiation and institutionalization: just as music became an autonomous art with it own rules and properties, so also the musical institutions and material instruments developed around it, from music schools to orchestras, from new instruments to new kinds of municipal funding, etc.

16   See, for example, Jean-François Lyotard, *Economie libidinale*, Paris: Minuit, 1974.

weapon against meaning as such, as though, de jure, what lives could not signify—and vice versa."[17] This irreconcilable divorce between intelligibility and experience, between meaning and existence, then can be grasped as a fundamental feature of modernity, particularly in literature, whose verbal existence necessarily inclines it to idealism. If it means something, it can't be real; if it is real, it can't be absorbed by purely mental or conceptual categories (the ideal of the "concrete" then attempting an impossible synthesis of these two dimensions: clearly enough phenomenology conceived the most strenuous modern vocation to achieve it.) Yet what Barthes in fact describes here already has another name, it is "contingency"; for the intellectuals of his generation, the novel that gave its discovery the most indelible expression was Sartre's *Nausea*, a unique and unrepeatable solution to an endemic form-problem. Barthes has himself here reincorporated it by transforming Flaubert's non-meaningful non-symbolic objects into so many rhetorical signs (signs of realism). But we can also keep faith with the aims of phenomenology by suggesting that the affect released in Flaubert by the disappearance of Balzac's symbolic and allegorical possibilities shares with Barthes' contingency the "property" of being unassimilable to meaning, to verbal and intellectual abstract (names) and to rational conceptualization as such. So in reality, it is not existence and meaning which are incompatible here (although they may well be in the context of some other philosophical inquiry), it is allegory and the body which repel one another and fail to mix.

And as we shall show elsewhere,[18] allegory in this traditional sense means personification, it means naming and nomination; and it is therefore words themselves (the medieval universals) which are incompatible with the body and its affects. Such is then the first lesson we will want to draw from this foray into the affective realm, namely, that we need a different kind of language to identify affect without, by naming it, presuming to define its content. Metaphor and the metaphorical are not themselves a reliable guide; that the lunch-flower of Virginia Woolf[19] that has been quoted above has an affective dimension is little more than a presumption, the reader must somehow introduce it from the outside; yet we can nonetheless retain at least one feature from its temporality, in which, with each petal

---

17   Barthes, "L'Effet de réel," 483.

18   The second volume of the *Poetics of Social Forms* will be devoted to allegory.

19   Virginia Woolf, *The Long Voyage Out*, New York: Random House, 2000, 143.

plucked the lunch disintegrates into a pitiable collection of ruined and inedible objects.

For affect to achieve a genuine autonomization, either in its experience or in its representation, however, it must somehow achieve independence from the conventional body itself (which as Sartre taught us is the body of other people). This is why I have for some time found suggestive Heidegger's inaugural invocation of affect—the starting point, not only of Sartrean phenomenology but also of Merleau-Ponty's attempts to formulate embodiment—and that turns on the German word "*Stimmung,*"[20] of which the English "mood" is but a pale and one-dimensional equivalent. Heidegger wanted to show that *Stimmung* was neither subjective nor objective, neither irrational nor cognitive, but rather a constitutive dimension of our being-in-the-world; and his term goes well beyond the characterization of a cloudy sky as "ominous" or a particular kind of lighting as "sinister," as in Gaston Bachelard's psychoanalysis of the elements (joyously rippling streams, stagnant pools)[21]—although the primacy of light is significant here, as we shall see later on.

In fact, Heideggerian or Sartrean *Stimmung* adds something like an object-pole to the subject-pole suggested by the word "affect" (thus demonstrating in the process how difficult it is for us to escape this fatal prejudice by which we are obliged to decide whether something is subjective or objective from the outset). For us, in the present context, however, the alternative opens up a welcome enlargement of the field, in which it is either the world or the individual subject who is thereby the source of what we have until now simply called affect.

The German term has the additional advantage of introducing an auditory dimension, not so much in its relationship to *Stimme* or voice, as rather to what the term suggests of musical tuning, of the according of a musical instrument (as well as the jangling of the unharmonized)—not for nothing does German use the expression "*das stimmt!*" for "it's true!" or "it's correct!" (and their opposites).

More extensive musical reference suggests not only the moods of major and minor (and of the variety of the old Greek modes as well[22]), it also moves us on to the matter of affect's chromaticism, its

---

20 Martin Heidegger, *Sein und Zeit*, Tübingen: Niemeyer, 1967, 134, Par. 29.

21 The first in his series of explorations was *La psychanalyse du feu* (1938).

22 On the other hand, the Greek system of the seven modes (which are even referenced in Plato and Aristotle's political theories) might well be considered an equivalent of

waxing and waning not only in intensity but across the very scale and gamut of such nuances. Not for nothing is Wagner's *Tristan* (1865) counted (along with Flaubert and Baudelaire, and with Manet) as a fundamental date in modernism's liberation from tradition and convention, in this case, I am tempted to say, from the musical récit and that completion into which Beethoven led sonata form and instrumental music. Chromaticism here means a waxing and waning of the scale, a slippage up and down the tones which dismisses all respect for their individual implications (their inner logic of tonic and subdominant), and which also develops each tone into its own specific coloration (articulated by the material development of the instruments themselves).

The evolution of music is thus a vivid way to describe the logic of affect, and indeed the very notion of a sliding scale seems already to suggest quarter-tones and their eventual disaggregation of the Western tonal system (at one, according to Max Weber, with the emergence of Western modernity and "rationality").[23]

But in this mid-century period, it is best to limit ourselves to the disaggregation of the "rationality" of the sonata form (or its completion and exhaustion by Beethoven), in order to appreciate the Wagnerian innovations—the reorganization of sonata-form temporality into the repetitions of the *Leitmotiven*, the transformation of heightened dissonance (the diminished seventh and ninth) into vehicles for affect rather than simple preparations for resolution; chromaticism itself and the very conversion of the key system into precisely that sliding scale of which I have spoken. In all this, there is perhaps a strange regression into the modal systems of pre-Western music; while the Wagnerian "endless melody" itself projects a temporality notably distinct from the past-present-future of the sonata, indeed it brings into being very precisely that "eternal present" we have already evoked in another context. Wagner's own remark about "an art of transitions"[24]

---

the traditional systems of named emotions to which we have alluded (and also to have their analogues in other cultures as with the Indian ragas). Yet the reappearance of unfamiliar modes in a modern music from which all traces of that systematicity have long since disappeared might well offer suitable occasions for the registration of uncodified affect.

23 Max Weber, *The Rational and Social Foundations of Music*, trans. Don Martindale, Johannes Riedel and Gertrude Neuwirth, Carbondale: Southern Illinois University Press, 1958.

24 Richard Wagner, *Selected Letters*, trans. S. Spencer and B. Millington, New York: Norton, 1988, 475: "The characteristic fabric of music ... owes its construction to

not only uncannily anticipates what modern critics have had to say about Flaubert's style, but itself constructs a pure present in which little by little transition itself replaces the more substantive states (or musical "named emotions") that precede and follow it.

None of this, to be sure, takes into account that immense material development and expansion of musical coloration (and material instruments) which Wagner pioneered along with Berlioz and which would seem the most essential, but also the most obvious, way of characterizing everything that is proteiform, metamorphic, shimmering and changeable-ephemeral about affect itself, not excluding its immense (but unmotivated) crescendoes and diminuendi. Meanwhile, Wagnerian affect determines a crisis and a revolution in external form (and the very conception of the music drama) which, although without any immediate analogy with the realistic novel, nonetheless portends significant formal changes to come.

But Wagnerian chromaticism offers a useful staging of the concept (and the new bodily reality?) of affect in yet another way than in its tension with sonata form, for its continuities (the so-called "endless melody") can also be seen as the systematic exclusion of closed entities and episodes essential to the more traditional Italian opera Wagner wished to displace: namely, the aria. It is enough to recall the occasional "songs" that punctuate Wagner's musical continuities—either the official songs of *Meistersinger* or *Tannhäuser*, or the "Du bist der Lenz" of *Walküre*—indeed, it might also be argued that Wagner's long retrospective storytelling passages are something of a replacement for the old aria as such—to understand that the aria was designed to express what we have called the named emotion as such (love! vengeance! grief!); and indeed, to express that expression: ideologically to stage the existence of the emotion and to draw attention to itself as that emotion's embodiment. Whence the flourishes that offer the voice its properly rhetorical vehicle, combining material sound with emotional content. Wagner's repudiation of the aria is thus a profound critique and repudiation of the "named emotion" as such,

---

the extreme sensitivity which gudes me in the direction of mediating and providing an intimate bond between all the different moments of transition that separate the extremes of mood. I should now like to call my most delicate and profound art the art of transition." (October 29, 1859, to Mathilde Wesendonk). One might well juxtapose this remark with Jean Rousset's study of "l'art des modulations" of Flaubert, in *Forme et signification*, Paris: Corti, 1963; and, on the strength of Charles Rosen's *Romantic Generation*, Cambridge: Harvard, 1998, add Chopin into the picture.

both in reality and in its concept; and what he replaces it with is very precisely affect as such.

The very notion of orchestral coloration, to be sure, reminds us of the tendency of such accounts of one art to borrow the terminology and logic of another, and return us to the parallel developments in painting, where Manet's attention to material color (Gertrude Stein would say, material oil paint) surreptitiously drains his storytelling content of its primacy. Indeed, the word "chromaticism" itself is derived from the Greek *chroma*, which first means "skin" or "skin color," thereby reaffirming the constitutive relationship with the body itself, and not merely one of its reified senses.

Time is thus famously eternalized by Monet's impressionism, as the latter painted his haystacks or cathedrals at every moment of the day from dawn to dusk, seizing each shade of light as a distinct event which the surfaces in question are but a pretext for capturing. It is the intimate relationship between this new conjuncture of light and temporality with Wagner's chromaticism that we now need to grasp, as it constructs a virtually imperceptible passage of perception from one level to the next. Here then, in impressionism as well, an absolute heterogeneity of the elements is translated into some new kind of homogeneity in which a new kind of phenomenological continuum is asserted.

The vogue of the pseudo-scientific experiments with perception (and of such mythical concepts as the meaningless "sense-data" from whose combinations our sense-perceptions are allegedly derived) also suggests this double movement whereby the body is analytically broken down into its smallest components and then scientifically reconstructed as an abstraction, all the while releasing a flow of affect hitherto stored and bound by its traditional unities and their named feelings. Yet it would be wrong to see this development as the exclusion of narrative, as does the conventional account, grasping narrative only in the representational or storytelling content of the painting. This new "pure present" of the visual data of paint and painting in reality harbors new kinds of narrative movement and awakens new trajectories in the movement of the eye and new conceptions of the visual event and its new temporalities.

At any rate, in all these contemporary symptoms, a certain sensory heterogeneity is disguised as that absolute homogeneity we call style, and a new phenomenological continuum begins to emerge, which is that of the play and variations, the expansion and contraction, the intensification and diminution, of that nameless new life of the body which is affect. Affect becomes the very chromaticism of the body itself.

Such changeability endows the dimension of affect with a capacity for transformation and metamorphosis which can register the nuances of mood fully as much as it can mutate into its opposite, from the depressive to the manic, from gloominess to ecstasy. And the Greek derivation then ultimately returns us to the body itself, along with its temperatures, from the feverish to the deathly chill, from blushing to the pallor of fear or shock.

Affect thus ranges chromatically up and down the bodily scale from melancholy to euphoria, from the bad trip to the high—from Nietzsche's most manic outbursts to the unquenchable depression and guilt of a Strindberg. And this is, as I have stressed, to be radically distinguished from the play of the named emotions as such, even though as modernism develops, their representations will not fail to be tinged and colored, as it were tuned and orchestrated, by the new affective phenomena and the new registering apparatuses designed to capture them.

This puts us on the track of a temporality specific to affect, which I will call the sliding scale of the incremental, in which each infinitesimal moment differentiates itself from the last by a modification of tone and an increase or diminution of intensity. The reference to the other, more material arts is unescapable in this context, not only because it is here a question of the body and its sensations, far more tangibly deployed in music and the visual arts; but also because such an account must necessarily remain external to the thing itself, a language from the outside, which must necessarily be called upon to characterize the structure of language effects, let alone the lived experiences of the body as such.

Impressionism and post-impressionism in painting, the Wagnerian revolution in music—these are only the most obvious analogies to the new affective styles invented by Flaubert and Baudelaire: all are indeed contemporaneous with that historic emergence of the bourgeois body which I want outrageously to affirm here as a historical fact and date. (And if we follow the now conventional story of the emergence of existentialism as a revolt against Hegelianism, then both Kierkegaard's discovery of anxiety and Marx's dramatization, by way of his theory of alienation, of "naked life" can also be summoned to document this radical transformation of the experience of the body in the European 1840s.) At its outer limit, then, affect becomes the organ of perception of the world itself, the vehicle of my being-in-the-world that Nietzsche and after him phenomenological philosophy begin to discover at much the same time.

I now want to explore some of the forms such affect can take, it being understood that our primary interest here lies in what this affective dimension of the new existential present does to the novelistic and in particular the scenic possibilities it opens up and begins to undermine at one and the same time.

But the content of affect is of course itself variable, and even if melancholia remains a kind of constant, in Flaubert, in *Tristan*, in Munch, in Gogol, its opposite is very different in all these cases, as also in Zola, where an expected excess of orgiastic excitement is far less authentic than the domestic shelter and metaphysical comfort of what the French call "*bonheur*," something again quite different from the trivial and truly petty-bourgeois state which English names "happiness." Here, for example, is the truly wondrous moment, in all the heat and dust of the campaign, the fatigue of endless forced marches and the confusion of rumor and fear, in which the protagonist of Zola's *Debacle* is able to know "*un dejeuner rêvé*" in a little garden as yet spared from the sound of artillery and the whistling of flying bullets:

> Dans la joie de la nappe très blanche, ravi du vin blanc qui étincelait dans son verre, Maurice mangea deux oeufs à la coque, avec une gourmandise qu'il ne se connaissait pas.

> In his delight at the snowy tablecloth and the white wine sparkling in his glass, Maurice ate two soft-boiled eggs with such an appetite that he surprised himself.[25]

It is an interlude in white utterly distinct in tone from the sad debris of Virginia Woolf's luncheon, and confirmed later on by the luxuriation of his fellow soldier, Jean, when, for one single solitary night of rest and quiet, he is able to sleep in a real bed:

> Ah! ces draps blancs, ces draps si ardemment convoites, Jean ne voyait plus qu'eux … C'était une gourmandise, une impatience d'enfant, une irrésistible passion, à se glisser dans cette blancheur, dans cette fraicheur, et à s'y perdre.

---

[25] Émile Zola, *Les Rougon-Macquart*, Volume V, *La Débacle*, Paris: Pleiade, 1967, 446. English translation by Elinor Dordray, Oxford: Oxford University Press, 2000, 54.

Oh! All Jean could see were those white sheets, the sheets he'd longed for so fervently! ... He was greedy and impatient as a child, feeling an irresistible passion urging him to slip into the whiteness, the freshness, and lose himself inside it.[26]

Many more will however be the metamorphoses of white in this work before we have done with it. Indeed, it is with the development of Zola's extraordinary bodily and linguistic sensibility that the realistic novel is able to deploy the possibilities of what James was to call "the scene as such."

We may conclude this introductory discussion of affect with a table in which the variety of its forms is systematically contrasted with those of the older named emotions:

EMOTION	AFFECT
system	chromaticism
nomenclature	bodily sensation
marks of destiny	perpetual present/eternity
generalized objects	intensities
traditional temporality	singularities
human nature	diagnosis, medicalization
motives	experiences, existentialisms
arias	endless melody
representation	sense-data
closed sonata form	the problem of endings
narration	description

---

[26] Ibid., 555; Dordray, 161–2.

Chapter III

Zola, or, the Codification of Affect

The novelist who offers some of the richest and most tangible deployments of affect in nineteenth-century realism is Émile Zola, inheritor of the Flaubertian narrative apparatus, contemporary of Wagner, an art critic who was one of the most fervent and perceptive defenders of Manet, and a profound political and social observer, whose own codification of the naturalist novel as a form then serves as a standard for the practice of mass culture and the bestseller up to our own time and all over the world. His unrequited claim to stand among Lukács' "great realists" should not be shaken by his political opinions nor by his enthusiastic practice of melodrama and a dramatic rhetoric often bordering on vulgarity; nor is the naturalism debate—as it is perpetuated by generations of critics intent on somehow separating Zola from the mainstream of nineteenth-century realism—relevant for our own purposes here, except insofar as it plays its part in a contemporary literary tug-of-war. As Susan Harrow has astutely observed, this categorical, conservative view situates Zola as a confirmed Realist-Naturalist whilst Flaubert's modernity allows the author of *Madame Bovary* and *Bouvard et Pécuchet* to be read forwards (by Sarraute or Robbe-Grillet).[1] We may prefer to follow Deleuze's extraordinary analysis (he is speaking of film and of the relationship of Stroheim, whose *Greed* is an adaptation of one of the greatest of American naturalist novels, to Buñuel)[2]: where the opening of the social and the uncharted exploration of its "lower depths" (*"flectere si nequeo superos"*) leaves the psyche exposed to seismic tremors and eruptions from the unconscious. It is precisely of such openings and possibilities that we have to speak here.

---

[1] Susan Harrow, *Zola: The Body Modern: Pressures and Prospects of Representation*, London: Legenda, 2012, 3.

[2] Gilles Deleuze, *Cinéma I*, Paris: Minuit, 1983. See chapter 8, "De l'affet à l'action."

Famously, and one may even say notoriously, Zola organized his multivolume project around the pseudo-scientific notion of "tainted heredity," going so far as to establish elaborate genealogical charts of his characters and their relationships from book to book. Here we find most tangibly the survival of that "mark of destiny" which defined the récit, a biographical framework (shared by the other novelists of the period) which has however here been melodramatically intensified into an extravagant sense of impending doom (doing double-duty for the usual naturalist pessimism). We will here, however, see this less as a regression into some older Hugolian if not Gothic excess, than a unique form taken by the temporality of destiny when it is drawn into the force field of affect and distorted out of recognition by the latter. It will indeed even be possible to show that the pseudo-scientific doctrine of heredity Zola articulates in his final volume (the discovery of Dr. Pascal) is itself an affective schema. Meanwhile, the melodramatic endings and climaxes that regularly terminate these novels foretell, *a contrario* and as a kind of anticipatory compensation, the dissolution of the compact between chronology and the present that makes realism possible in the first place, and thereby signals the crisis of plot which has regularly been taken to spell the end of realism as such: in that, Zola's endings play out what will later become the dialectic of mass culture, as in contemporary action film and its specific "end of temporality."

Yet it is important to remember that our interest in affect lies primarily in the combinations it forms with the longer-range temporalities of storytelling, of récit and of destiny. Indeed, everything that is admirable and productive in Zola to this effect can also be judged as a shameless exploitation and manipulation of poetic perception that has been harnessed to a commercial project and that scarcely merits the "distinction" of the literary in the first place (whence Zola's endemic exclusion from the canon).

It is precisely this skill in the utilization of his raw materials that the word "codification" is meant more neutrally to designate. Still, even that exploitation, and the very properties of his remarkable new raw material, has had to be learned; and the earlier novels of the Rougon-Macquart series testify to the stages of this process.

It is perhaps in the second and third novels in the series, *La Curée* (1871) and *Le ventre de Paris* (1873), that the registration of affect as such begins its work. The first novel of the series (1840), which sets the political stage as such with Louis Napoleon's coup d'état and its provincial equivalents, was still written under the Empire and thus still bears the traces of a satiric exposé and denunciation. *La Curée* itself is begun in the same spirit; but with the Franco-Prussian war and the abrupt collapse of the Empire as such, Zola is able to change his focus: few writers, indeed, have had this kind of luck, where History obligingly redistributes your material for you in a more workable form.

Zola's investigation now has closure, and a different kind of experimental spirit takes the place of the older, politically committed one. Now the viruses of the Empire may be allowed to develop autonomously, in their own local petri dishes and according to their own specificities; the laboratory itself is now sealed, we have to do with a historical settlement and not a partisan struggle. It is in this new space of "observation" (to speak for a moment the language of Zola's scientistic rhetoric) that the resonances of affect will be registered.

Yet this registration begins modestly enough with simpler exercises in perception, about which this is the moment to observe that it is itself no more affect than named emotion was. Perception is still a concept located within the subject/object split, it is a rationalization of the sensory and its expression a codified form of rhetoric under the rubric of description.

Affect is perhaps here present as a kind of invisible figuration, which doubles the literal invisibly; a convex that shows through, as though reality itself blushed imperceptibly, and some strange new optical illusion separated the trees from one another stereoscopically, allowing their three dimensions to be visible three-dimensionally. Such are, for example, the great opening lines of *La Terre* (1887), in which Jean plows the field, seeing his village ahead of him in one direction, and then, turning on the next furrow, the whole vast plain of the Beauce spread out before him in the other:

> Jean, qui remontait la pièce du midi au nord, avait justement devant lui, à deux kilomètres, les bâtiments de la ferme. Arrivé au bout du sillon, il leva les yeux, regarda sans voir, en soufflant une minute … Mais Jean se retourna, et il repartit, du nord au midi, avec son balancement, la main gauche tenant le semoir, la droite fouettant l'air d'un vol continu de semence. Maintenant, il avait devant lui, tout proche, coupant la plaine ainsi qu'un fossé, l'étroit vallon de l'Aigre, après lequel recommençait la Beauce, immense, jusqu'à Orléans.

> The farm buildings themselves lay only about a mile and a half in front of Jean as he moved up the field from the south to the north. Pausing at the end of the

furrow, he lifted his head and stared blankly as he took a breather … Jean now turned back and set off once again, this time from north to south, his left hand still holding open the bag while his right swept through the air and dispersed its cloud of seed. Directly ahead of him now lay the narrow little valley of the Aigre, cutting through the plain, while beyond it the flat lands of the Beauce began once again, their vast expanses stretching as far as Orleans.[3]

The furrows coming and going, the boustrophedon of the camera eye, giving us now the landscape, now the town, Jean as a mere servant of the apparatus. This movement has become itself so productive and creative that old-fashioned description can itself be diminished and streamlined: to describe this as cinematographic (as well as opportunistic, in the way in which it allows Zola to lay his double background in place) is already to refocus the visual in the form of the camera's figuration.

In much the same way, these early descriptions, like Gestalt images, can be taken either as rhetorical flourishes that still function allegorically as in Balzac: thus the vegetation of *La Curée*—

Pour gazon, une large bande de Sélaginelle entourait le bassin. Cette fougère naine formait un épais tapis de mousse, d'un vert tendre. Et, au-delà de la grande allée circulaire, quatre énormes massifs allaient d'un élan vigoureux jusqu'au cintre: les Palmiers, légèrement penchés dans leur grâce, épanouissaient leurs éventails, étalaient leurs têtes arrondies, laissaient pendre leurs palmes, comme des avirons lassés par leur éternel voyage dans le bleu de l'air; les grands Bambous de l'Inde montaient droits, frêles et durs, faisant tomber de haut leur pluie légère de feuilles; un Ravenala, l'arbre du voyageur, dressait son bouquet d'immenses écrans chinois; et, dans un coin, un Bananier, chargé de ses fruits, allongeait de toutes parts ses longues feuilles horizontales, où deux amants pourraient se coucher à l'aise en se serrant l'un contre l'autre. Aux angles, il y avait des Euphorbes d'Abyssinie, ces cierges épineux, contrefaits, pleins de bosses honteuses, suant le poison. Et, sous les arbres, pour couvrir le sol, des fougères basses, les Adiantums, les Ptérides, mettaient leurs dentelles délicates, leurs fines découpures. Les Alsophilas, d'espèce plus haute, étageaient leurs rangs de rameaux symétriques, sexangulaires, si réguliers, qu'on aurait dit de grandes pièces de faïence destinées à contenir les fruits de quelque dessert gigantesque. Puis, une bordure de Bégonias et de Caladiums entourait les massifs; les Bégonias, à feuilles torses, tachées superbement de vert et de rouge; les Caladiums, dont les feuilles en fer de lance, blanches et à nervures vertes, ressemblent à de larges ailes de papillon; plantes bizarres dont le feuillage vit étrangement, avec un éclat sombre ou pâlissant de fleurs malsaines. (II, 354–5)

---

3   French notes are referenced in the text to the five volume Gallimard/La Pléiade edition of Zola (1960–1967), as here: IV, 367–8. English translation mine.

By way of turf, a broad edging of selaginella encircled the tank. This dwarf fern formed a thick mossy carpet of light green. Beyond the great circular path, four enormous clusters of plants shot up to the roof: palms, drooping gently in their elegance, spreading their fans, displayed their rounded crowns, hung down their leaves like oars wearied by their perpetual voyage through the blue; tall Indian bamboos rose upwards, hard, slender, dropping from on high their light shower of leaves; a ravenala, the traveller's tree, erected its foliage like enormous Chinese screens; and in a corner a banana tree, loaded with fruit, stretched out on all sides its long horizontal leaves, on which two lovers might easily recline in each other's arms. In the corners were Abyssinian euphorbias, deformed prickly cactuses covered with hideous excrescences, oozing with poison. Beneath the trees the ground was carpeted with creeping ferns, adianta and pterides, their fronds outlined daintily like fine lace. Alsophilas of a taller species tapered upwards with their rows of symmetrical branches, hexagonal, so regular that they looked like large pieces of porcelain made specially for the fruit of some gigantic dessert. The shrubs were surrounded by a border of begonias and caladiums: begonias with twisted leaves, gorgeously streaked with red and green; caladiums whose spearheaded leaves, white with green veins, looked like large butterfly wings; bizarre plants whose foliage lives strangely, with the somber or wan splendor of poisonous flowers. [4]

—flora and fauna which can be taken as signs of the sickness of the Second Empire, the morbidity or indeed decadence of its social relations, whose properly abnormal growths (happily paralleling the efflorescence of the tainted heredity of Zola's two conjoined families) stand as a culture critique of this political and economic system; or else it begins to foreground new kinds of perceptions, whose microscopic convexities now serve as vehicles for affect itself.

This is perhaps then the place to say a word about the famous "pathetic fallacy" denounced by New Criticism, which rightly deplored the facile use of an external nature—even though the key text is the storm on the heath in *King Lear*—to express the emotions raging within the protagonist.[5] But they were talking about the expression of named emotions, that is to say, the aesthetic of expression as such;

---

[4]   *The Kill*, trans. Brian Nelson, Oxford: Oxford University Press, 2004, 37.

[5]   Ruskin's original concept (*Modern Painters*, Volume III, chapter 12) seems to have had more to do with the mendacity of artificial tropes, more spontaneous outbursts being tolerated. He deplores the subject-object split, but on the other hand wishes to preserve objectivity and accurate observation. Perhaps it would be better in this context to suggest that the manifestations of affect, whatever they are, are not tropological. (*Lear* is a New Critical importation, but see W. K. Wimsatt and Monroe Beardsley, "The Affective Fallacy," in *The Norton Anthology of Theory and Criticism*, Vincent Leitsch, ed., New York: Norton, 2001, 1246–61.)

and in our context here we might reverse their judgement and suggest that what is poetically inauthentic in traditional "pathetic fallacy" is not so much its illicit use of nature as its presupposition of named emotions as such, which reacts back on the former to endow it with those "meanings" we found in Balzacian description, that is to say, a signifying system and no longer really a physical perception at all.

But Zola discovers his own narrative space with the third novel of the Rougon-Macquart, *Le ventre de Paris*. The opening novel laid the political situation in place with Louis Bonaparte's coup d'etat; the second, *La Curée*, was a relatively didactic exposé of the corruption of the Second Empire—corruption in sexuality (incest), corruption in money (gentrification), even corruption in botany (exotic, dangerous tropical plants) and corruption in architecture (Saccard's "palace"), etc. The problem is that all of these richly explored dimensions, when juxtaposed, simply give off the univocal meaning of the hieroglyph (or ideogram) for "corruption." In other words, as in Balzac, they still mean something, no matter how rich their sensory overload.

With *Le ventre de Paris*, that excess of the sensory becomes autonomous, that is to say, it begins to have enough weight of its own to counterbalance the plot, it begins to fill its function as affect calculated to stand in a successful tension with the belief in "destiny" to which Zola is also committed. (Yet we will see later on how the theory of heredity itself subtly and not so subtly inflects the pole of destiny and makes of it a sensory and bodily form as well, susceptible to all kinds of affective investment, as though it were precisely affect that had a destiny of its own…).

Obviously, the very project of a novel on Les Halles (begun in 1854) originated spatially (*La Curée* centered on a villa, with the new Haussman quarter not yet fully built; while *La Fortune de Rougon* turned on a whole national region), and thus of itself proposed description, landscape painting, and with the multiplicity of vegetables and edible objects, a variety of strokes, colors, textures and smells. To these meanwhile Zola has added time itself, the time of day, the nighttime in which its produce is brought to Les Halles, slowly lightening into the dawn when the market opens. He has in other words had to "set it in motion" à la Monet, thereby also adding the jolts of the cart through the darkness as the farmers laboriously bring their produce to market. All of this would make for a transformation of description into action—indeed, it may be said that if it is a question of technique, in the reified cut-and-dried meaning of that term, then it is precisely this transformation which is Zola's method and his discovery.[6] Balzac made everything stop until he was finished, first his laborious descriptions, and second, his account of the past history of his characters. Zola has not developed a means for innovating with the latter—he will still interpolate lengthy flashbacks or récits—but the former he has completely revolutionized, bringing all his narrative intelligence to bear on the problem of "exposition," as the great dramatists from Molière to Ibsen faced that technical difficulty.[7] Still, there the second problem remained, that of the past of the characters and their situations. Now it is ekphrasis, which demands planning something like a camera movement through the object world, so that *attention to each item* is motivated, as in early film.

Yet with *Le ventre de Paris*, we are not quite at that point, and Zola still seems to need a point of view; indeed, it is, at least in part, of the very notion of point of view that we will be speaking here and throughout this theory of realism, speaking of it not only as a technique but also as a concept, indeed as something like a technique-concept (the film-theory version of camera agency will have autonomized and reified some of this ambiguity), and finally as an ideology; but in any case not as some empirical common-sense datum on the order of the eyes of bodily daily life. That obvious phenomenological reality will have first had to be made strange, to be differentiated (autonomization means that as well), somehow separated out from the existence we take for granted, only in order then to be added back in as a specific and ideologized technique.

What Zola does here, however, is something a little more complex and extraordinary than simple Jamesian point of view. James might have argued that Zola was still insufficiently aware of point of view as a technical problem and necessity, and allowed himself the slovenliness of all the other omniscient narrators, without realizing that Zola's shrewdness with respect to point of view had just taken on another, more psychoanalytic form.

Thus, to the degree to which description sheds its allegorical

---

6   This might be the argument to make in the face of Lukács' opposition of the active and temporal, profoundly historical virtue of narration as opposed to what is static and contemplative in description (an argument by virtue of which the great Hungarian philosopher is able to condemn naturalism and symbolism alike, and to devalue Zola in the face of Balzac). See note 8, "Introduction."

7   Goethe thought the opening of Molière's *Tartuffe* was the most dramatic and successful exposition in the history of dramatic literature.

meanings and approaches the state of a more purely physical and bodily registering of external contingency, to that extent it lies open to affective investment. Such is now the case with the opening chapters of *Le ventre de Paris*, a novel set in the old Les Halles now newly constructed, and into which the protagonist arrives by night, as if parachuted ex nihilo by the great carts which provision the enormous market before the dawn.

Here Florent will confront a chaotic multiplicity of goods organized according to their species with much the same engineering sensibility Zola himself brought to his subjects (to each novel, a specialty or a specialization—the railroad, disease, painting, the stock market, etc.). Immense quantities of objects are collected and enumerated for us (under the pretext of Florent's new position as inspector):

> Quand il déboucha dans la grande rue du milieu, il songea à quelque ville étrange, avec ses quartiers distincts, ses faubourgs, ses villages, ses promenades et ses routes, ses places et ses carrefours, mise tout entière sous un hangar, un jour de pluie, par quelque caprice gigantesque. (I, 621)

> As he turned into the broad central avenue, he imagined himself in some foreign town, with its various districts, suburbs, villages, walks and streets, squares and intersections, all suddenly placed under a huge roof one rainy day by the whim of some gigantic power.[8]

As with animation or miniaturization, this unification redeems the bewildering and contingent chaos of the immense commercial center by suggesting that it has been constructed by a single intelligence (like a miniature train set).

And it is always worth emphasizing the degree to which such apparently static catalogues and enumerations are symbolic forms of praxis and of construction, invisibly harboring the work of the hand itself in some more fundamentally physical sense than the autoreferential imagination of its writer.

Yet a bewildering multiplicity returns within this rational organization: masses of vegetables first (627), then the heaps of edible flesh and blood, Quenu's storehouse of dairy products, sausages and sausage-making, and finally, in a kind of delirious climax, the world of seafood (697) in which the category of fish differentiates into pages of monsters and weird otherworldly beings:

---

[8] *The Belly of Paris*, trans. Brian Nelson, Oxford: Oxford University Press, 2007, 20.

Pêle-mêle, au hasard du coup de filet, les algues profondes, où dort la vie mysté-
rieuse des grandes eaux, avaient tout livré: les cabillauds, les aigrefins, les carrelets,
les plies, les limandes, bêtes communes, d'un gris sale, aux taches blanchâtres;
les congres, ces grosses couleuvres d'un bleu de vase, aux minces yeux noirs, si
gluantes qu'elles semblent ramper, vivantes encore; les raies élargies, à ventre pâle
bordé de rouge tendre, dont les dos superbes, allongeant les noeuds saillants de
l'échine, se marbrent, jusqu'aux baleines tendues des nageoires, de plaques de
cinabre coupées par des zébrures de bronze florentin, d'une bigarrure assom-
brie de crapaud et de fleur malsaine; les chiens de mer, horribles, avec leurs têtes
rondes, leurs bouches largement fendues d'idoles chinoises, leurs courtes ailes de
chauves-souris charnues, monstres qui doivent garder de leurs abois les trésors des
grottes marines. Puis, venaient les beaux poissons, isolés, un sur chaque plateau
d'osier: les saumons, d'argent guilloché, dont chaque écaille semble un coup de
burin dans le poli du métal; les mulets, d'écailles plus fortes, de ciselures plus
grossières; les grands turbots, les grandes barbues, d'un grain serré et blanc comme
du lait caillé; les thons, lisses et vernis, pareils à des sacs de cuir noirâtre; les bars
arrondis, ouvrant une bouche énorme, faisant songer à quelque âme trop grosse,
rendue à pleine gorge, dans la stupéfaction de l'agonie. Et, de toutes parts, les
soles, par paires, grises ou blondes, pullulaient; les équilles minces, raidies, ressem-
blaient à des rognures d'étain; les harengs, légèrement tordus, montraient tous,
sur leurs robes lamées, la meurtrissure de leurs ouïes saignantes; les dorades grasses
se teintaient d'une pointe de carmin, tandis que les maquereaux, dorés, le dos
strié de brunissures verdâtres, faisaient luire la nacre changeante de leurs flancs, et
que les grondins roses, à ventres blancs, les têtes rangées au centre des mannes, les
queues rayonnantes, épanouissaient d'étranges floraisons, panachées de blanc de
perle et de vermillon vif. Il y avait encore des rougets de roche, à la chair exquise,
du rouge enluminé des cyprins, des caisses de merlans aux reflets d'opale, des
paniers d'éperlans, de petits paniers propres, jolis comme des paniers de fraises,
qui laissaient échapper une odeur puissante de violette. Cependant, les crevettes
roses, les crevettes grises, dans des bourriches, mettaient, au milieu de la douceur
effacée de leurs tas, les imperceptibles boutons de jais de leurs milliers d'yeux; les
langoustes épineuses, les homards tigrés de noir, vivants encore, se traînant sur
leurs pattes cassées, craquaient. (I, 697–8).

The seaweed that lies on the ocean bed where the mysteries of the deep lie sleep-
ing had jumbled everything into the sweep of the net: cod, haddock, flounder,
plaice, dabs, and other sorts of common fish in dirty grey spotted with white;
conger eels, huge snake-like creatures, with small, black eyes and muddy, bluish
skins, so slimy that they seemed to be still alive and gliding along; broad flat
skate, their pale underbellies edged with a soft red, their superb backs, bumpy
with vertebrae, marbled to the very tips of the bones in their fins, in sulphur-red
patches cut across by stripes of Florentine bronze, a sombre assortment of colours
from filthy toad to poisonous flower; dogfish, with hideous round heads, gaping
mouths like Chinese idols, and short fins like bats' wings, monsters who doubtless
kept guard over the treasures of the ocean grottoes. Then there were the finer fish,

displayed individually on wicker trays: salmon, gleaming like chased silver, whose every scale seemed to have been exquisitely chiselled on highly polished metal; mullet, with larger scales and coarser markings; huge turbot and brill, their scales pure white and closely knit like curdled milk; tuna fish, smooth and glossy, like bags of black leather; and rounded bass, with gaping mouths, as if some outsize spirit, at the moment of death, had forced its way out of the surprised creatures' bodies. Everywhere there were soles, grey or pale yellow, heaped in pairs; sand eels, thin and stiff, like shavings of pewter; herrings, slightly twisted, with bleeding gills showing on their silver-worked skins; fat bream, tinged with crimson; golden mackerel, their backs stained with greenish brown markings, their sides shimmering like mother-of-pearl; and pink gurnet with white bellies, placed with their heads together in the middle of the baskets and their tails fanned out, so that they seemed like strange flowers in a bloom of pearly white and brilliant scarlet. There were red rock mullet, too, with their exquisite flesh; boxes of whiting, like opal reflections in a mirror; and baskets of smelt—neat little baskets as pretty as punnets of strawberries and giving off a strong smell of violets. The tiny jet-black eyes of the prawns, in covered baskets, were like thousands of beads scattered across the piles of soft-toned pink and grey; the spiky lobsters and crayfish, striped with black and still alive, were dragging themselves about on their broken legs.[9]

What seems crucial here is the relationship between the perceptual and language or naming. It would appear at first glance, and in the light of Zola's remarkable organizational procedures, that what is at stake here is a resolution of multiplicity back into unity, of difference back into identity. The enormous lists and catalogues would seem to be subsumed under generic categories and everyday common-sense universals: from life to the edible, from the edible to plants and animals, from the latter to meats and fish, and so on. In fact, I believe that this impression is at the least ambiguous; and that simultaneously with this first centrifugal movement of mastery and subsumption, of the ordering of raw nameless things into their proper genetic classifications, there exists a second movement which undermines this one and secretly discredits it—a tremendous fermenting and bubbling pullulation in which the simplicity of words and names is unsettled to the point of an ecstatic dizziness by the visual multiplicity of the things themselves and the sensations that they press on the unforewarned observer. The unexpected result is that far from enriching representational language with all kinds of new meanings, the gap between words and things is heightened; perceptions turn into sensations; words no longer take on a body at prey to its nameless

---

[9] Ibid., 91.

experience. Finally the realm of the visual begins to separate from that of the verbal and conceptual and to float away in a new kind of autonomy. Precisely this autonomy will create the space for affect: just as the gradual enfeeblement of named emotions and the words for them opened up a new space in which the unrepresentable and unnameable affects can colonize and make their own.

But this autonomy is itself subject to imminent dissolution from both sides at once. For language (and conceptualization) rises to the challenge, and matches this new proliferation of beings by a differentiation that generates ever newer generic categories, themselves quickly filled and subsequently overwhelmed by the sensory. Thus the world of marine life is multiplied (not to speak of the opposition between fresh water and salt water fish as such), and expands through the crustaceans to the eels and so on and so forth. At the same time, as though by the very force of its intensifying multiplicities, it generates a new and autonomous realm of the sensory alongside itself, namely that of Odor, so that Florent begins to have in his very body the lived experience of Baudelairean synesthesia, whose specificity lies in the ambiguity of separation and identification. Does it combine the senses or rather affirm the coming into being of a new and heightened sense in which they are combined? And even this new experience of the nausea of a dizzying continuity of smells whose apprenticeship he makes in his new domain as the inspector of the fish market will reach a rather different climax in the subterranean world of the cheeses.

But in order to appreciate the new autonomization of the sensory as it here first emerges in Zola, we must first note a significant displacement in what will later on be called point of view (as well as in the protagonicity it marks and certifies). Florent is of course the nominal hero of the novel: a demonstrator against the regime of Louis Philippe, he has been arrested and shipped off to the penal colony in Cayenne (Devil's Island)—a *séjour* whose memories mark the intrusion of a flora and fauna even more exotic than Renée's plants, but less amenable to Utopian reorganization than the levant of Saccard's daydreams in *L'Argent*. He escapes, after eight years, and returning to Paris, offers a double defamiliarization for reader and writer alike: first, because he recognizes nothing any more, and second, because there is nothing he can recognize owing to the prodigious transformation of Paris begun by Haussman (and memorialized by Baudelaire), in which the construction of Les Halles is a functional centerpiece.

So far so good, and this is a trope readily available even to the most inexperienced would-be novelist (the Persian visit, as it were).

But to this mediatory outsider's point of view, Zola adds a Virgil: it is the painter Claude Lantier, himself an authentic member of the eponymous Macquart clan (he is the son of the ill-fated Gervaise of *L'Assommoir* [1878], the later novel whose success will precipitate Zola into the front ranks of the literary world, and later on the protagonist of a novel of his own [*L'Oeuvre* (1886)] based on Zola's childhood friendship with Cézanne.)

To be sure, Zola did not have the benefit of later Jamesian statutes on the proper use of point of view, and there is a deplorable, or opportunistic, and at least wholly unregulated displacement of the narrative center from one participant to another in all of Zola's novels. But this particular doubling of perception, in which the aesthetic perspective of the painter does not replace that of the explorer-protagonist, but rather imperceptibly slips in beside it, in a kind of stereoscopic view which is no doubt initially multi-dimensional, but which, we will argue, ultimately tends to release its sensory material from any specific viewer or individual human subject, from any specific character to whom the function of observation has been assigned.

Florent is the ideal of the Russian Formalist reader: for him everything is estranged, partly because he has never seen this unique quartier of Paris before (for the obvious reason that it did not then exist, something which would seem to render the evocation of the *ostranenie*, or making strange of habitual objects, less relevant); but also partly because he has not been among people for a long time, and particularly not in cities, nor, above all, in the kind of milling, asphyxiating crowd he here encounters, with its welter of noises and smells (of which more later). His is thus the privileged point of perception for the onslaught of raw sensation, for sheer intensity.

Claude meanwhile brings the painterly eye to this confusion; it is the era of Zola's defense of Manet and of nascent impressionism, and we may assume that Claude's eye tends to master its material in analogous fashion. It would then be tempting to assume that Florent brings the raw material which Claude then organizes in ways propitious for Zola's descriptive practice (which is prodigious and voracious).

And this seems to me a significant, experimental moment in Zola's approach to affect, and a preparation for the later and more programmatic exercises in the sensory sublime, as when that blissful white of the tableclothes and sheets which we have evoked in the previous chapter is in *Au Bonheur des Dames* (1883) whipped into a frenzy by the inventor of the new department store (himself obviously a surrogate for the novelist and inventor of the new literary series) into masses of white intensities which stagger the patrons and rivalize with one another like repeated orchestral tutti, each one distinct, each one the same:

Ce qui arrêtait ces dames, c'était le spectacle prodigieux de la grande exposition de blanc. Autour d'elles, d'abord, il y avait le vestibule, un hall aux glaces claires, pavé de mosaïques, où les étalages à bas prix retenaient la foule vorace. Ensuite, les galeries s'enfonçaient, dans une blancheur éclatante, une échappée boréale, toute une contrée de neige, déroulant l'infini des steppes tendues d'hermine, l'entassement des glaciers allumés sous le soleil. On retrouvait le blanc des vitrines du dehors, mais avivé, colossal, brûlant d'un bout à l'autre de l'énorme vaisseau, avec la flambée blanche d'un incendie en plein feu. Rien que du blanc, tous les articles blancs de chaque rayon, une débauche de blanc, un astre blanc dont le rayonnement fixe aveuglait d'abord, sans qu'on pût distinguer les détails, au milieu de cette blancheur unique. Bientôt les yeux s'accoutumaient: à gauche, la galerie Monsigny allongeait les promontoires blancs des toiles et des calicots, les roches blanches des draps de lit, des serviettes, des mouchoirs; tandis que la galerie Michodière, à droite, occupée par la mercerie, la bonneterie et les lainages, exposait des constructions blanches en boutons de nacre, un grand décor bâti avec des chaussettes blanches, toute une salle recouverte de molleton blanc, éclairée au loin d'un coup de lumière. Mais le foyer de clarté rayonnait surtout de la galerie centrale, aux rubans et aux fichus, à la ganterie et à la soie. Les comptoirs disparaissaient sous le blanc des soies et des rubans, des gants et des fichus. Autour des colonnettes de fer, s'élevaient des bouillonnés de mousseline blanche, noués de place en place par des foulards blancs. Les escaliers étaient garnis de draperies blanches, des draperies de piqué et de basin alternées, qui filaient le long des rampes, entouraient les halls, jusqu'au second étage; et cette montée du blanc prenait des ailes, se pressait et se perdait, comme une envolée de cygnes. Puis, le blanc retombait des voûtes, une tombée de duvet, une nappe neigeuse en larges flocons: des couvertures blanches, des couvre-pieds blancs, battaient l'air, accrochés, pareils à des bannières d'église; de longs jets de guipure traversaient, semblaient suspendre des essaims de papillons blancs, au bourdonnement immobile; des dentelles frissonnaient de toutes parts, flottaient comme des fils de la Vierge par un ciel d'été, emplissaient l'air de leur haleine blanche. Et la merveille, l'autel de cette religion du blanc, était, au-dessus du comptoir des soieries, dans le grand hall, une tente faite de rideaux blancs, qui descendaient du vitrage. Les mousselines, les gazes, les guipures d'art, coulaient à flots légers, pendant que des tulles brodés, très riches, et des pièces de soie orientale, lamées d'argent, servaient de fond à cette décoration géante, qui tenait du tabernacle et de l'alcôve. On aurait dit un grand lit blanc, dont l'énormité virginale attendait, comme dans les légendes, la princesse blanche, celle qui devait venir un jour, toute-puissante, avec le voile blanc des épousées. (I, 768–9)

It was the stupendous sight of the great exhibition of household linen which had caused the ladies to stop. First of all, surrounding them, there was the entrance hall, with bright mirrors, and paved with mosaics, in which displays of inexpensive goods were drawing the voracious crowd. Then there were the galleries, dazzling in their whiteness like a polar vista, a snowy expanse unfolding with the endlessness of steppes draped with ermine, a mass of glaciers lit up beneath the sun. It was the same whiteness as that displayed in the outside windows, but heightened and on a colossal scale, burning from one end of the enormous nave to the other with the white blaze of a conflagration at its height. There was nothing but white, all the white goods from every department, an orgy of white, a white star whose radiance was blinding at first, and made it impossible to distinguish any details in the midst of this total whiteness. Soon the eye grew accustomed to it: to the left in the Monsigny Gallery there stretched out white promontories of linens and calicoes, white rocks of sheets, table-napkins, and handkerchiefs; while in the Michodière Gallery on the right, occupied by the haberdashery, hosiery, and woollens, white edifices were displayed made of pearl buttons, together with a huge construction of white socks, and a whole hall covered with white swansdown and illuminated by a distant shaft of light. But the light was especially bright in the central gallery, where the ribbons and fichus, gloves and silks were situated. The counters disappeared beneath the white of silks and ribbons, of gloves and fichus. Around the iron pillars were twined flounces of white muslin, knotted here and there with white scarves. The staircases were decked with white draperies, draperies of piqué alternating with dimity, running the whole length of the banisters and encircling the halls right up to the second floor; and the ascending whiteness appeared to take wing, merging together and disappearing like a flight of swans. The whiteness then fell back again from the domes in a rain of eiderdown, a sheet of huge snowflakes: white blankets and white coverlets were waving in the air, hung up like banners in a church; long streams of pillow-lace seemed suspended like swarms of white butterflies, humming there motionless; other types of lace were fluttering everywhere, floating like a gossamer against a summer sky, filling the air with their white breath. And over the silk counter in the main hall there was the miracle, the altar of this cult of white—a tent made of white curtains hanging down from the glass roof. Muslin, gauzes, and guipures flowed in light ripples, while richly embroidered tulles and lengths of oriental silk and silver lamé served as a background to this gigantic decoration, which was evocative both of the tabernacle and of the bedroom. It looked like a great white bed, its virginal whiteness waiting, as in legends, for the white princess, for she who would one day come, all powerful, in her white bridal veil.[10]

---

[10] *The Ladies' Paradise*, trans. Brian Nelson, Oxford: Oxford University Press, 1995, 397–8.

But here, for the moment, in *Le ventre de Paris*, we are merely being trained in this new sensorium, forming new habits of perception in accordance with the new realms and dimensions of bodily reality thereby opened up to us.

We now need no intermediaries in this novel ontological exploration, and characters become the most perfunctory pretexts for what is virtually an autonomous unfolding of sense data, as in the virtuoso chapter on the cheeses, in which the two hostile observers, Mme. Lecoeur and the conniving Mlle. Saget exchange their gossip about Florent and his criminal past in the underground storeroom of the former's dairy shop:

> – Vous savez, ce Florent ?… Eh bien, je peux vous dire d'où il vient, maintenant. Et elle les laissa un instant encore suspendues à ses lèvres.
> – Il vient du bagne, dit-elle enfin, en assourdissant terriblement sa voix.
> Autour d'elles, les fromages puaient. Sur les deux étagères de la boutique, au fond, s'alignaient des mottes de beurre énormes; les beurres de Bretagne, dans des paniers, débordaient; les beurres de Normandie, enveloppés de toile, ressemblaient à des ébauches de ventres, sur lesquelles un sculpteur aurait jeté des linges mouillés; d'autres mottes, entamées, taillées par les larges couteaux en rochers à pic, pleines de vallons et de cassures, étaient comme des cimes éboulées, dorées par la pâleur d'un soir d'automne. Sous la table d'étalage, de marbre rouge veiné de gris, des paniers d'oeufs mettaient une blancheur de craie; et, dans des caisses, sur des clayons de paille, des bondons posés bout à bout, des gournays rangés à plat comme des médailles, faisaient des nappes plus sombres, tachées de tons verdâtres. Mais c'était surtout sur la table que les fromages s'empilaient. Là, à côté des pains de beurre à la livre, dans des feuilles de poirée, s'élargissait un cantal géant, comme fendu à coups de hache; puis venaient un chester, couleur d'or, un gruyère, pareil à une roue tombée de quelque char barbare, des hollandes, ronds comme des têtes coupées, barbouillées de sang séché, avec cette dureté de crâne vide qui les fait nommer têtes-de-mort. Un parmesan, au milieu de cette lourdeur de pâte cuite, ajoutait sa pointe d'odeur aromatique. Trois bries, sur des planches rondes, avaient des mélancolies de lunes éteintes; deux, très secs, étaient dans leur plein; le troisième, dans son deuxième quartier, coulait, se vidait d'une crème blanche, étalée en lac, ravageant les minces planchettes, à l'aide desquelles on avait vainement essayé de le contenir. Des port-salut, semblables à des disques antiques, montraient en exergue le nom imprimé des fabricants. Un romantour, vêtu de son papier d'argent, donnait le rêve d'une barre de nougat, d'un fromage sucré, égaré parmi ces fermentations âcres. Les roqueforts, eux aussi, sous des cloches de cristal, prenaient des mines princières, des faces marbrées et grasses, veinées de bleu et de jaune, comme attaqués d'une maladie honteuse de gens riches qui ont trop mangé de truffes; tandis que, dans un plat, à côté, des fromages de chèvre, gros comme un poing d'enfant, durs et grisâtres, rappelaient

les cailloux que les boucs, menant leur troupeau, font rouler aux coudes des sentiers pierreux. Alors, commençaient les puanteurs: les mont-d'or, jaune clair, puant une odeur douceâtre; les troyes, très épais, meurtris sur les bords, d'âpreté déjà plus forte, ajoutant une fétidité de cave humide; les camemberts, d'un fumet de gibier trop faisandé; les neufchâtels, les limbourgs, les marolles, les pont-l'évêque, carrés, mettant chacun leur note aiguë et particulière dans cette phrase rude jusqu'à la nausée; les livarots, teintés de rouge, terribles à la gorge comme une vapeur de soufre; puis enfin, par-dessus tous les autres, les olivets, enveloppés de feuilles de noyer, ainsi que ces charognes que les paysans couvrent de branches, au bord d'un champ, fumantes au soleil. La chaude après-midi avait amolli les fromages; les moisissures des croûtes fondaient, se vernissaient avec des tons riches de cuivre rouge et de vert-de-gris, semblables à des blessures mal fermées; sous les feuilles de chêne, un souffle soulevait la peau des olivets, qui battait comme une poitrine, d'une haleine lente et grosse d'homme endormi; un flot de vie avait troué un livarot, accouchant par cette entaille d'un peuple de vers. Et, derrière les balances, dans sa boîte mince, un géromé anisé répandait une infection telle que des mouches étaient tombées autour de la boîte, sur le marbre rouge veiné de gris. (I, 826–8)

All around them the cheeses were stinking. On the two shelves at the back of the stall were huge blocks of butter: Brittany butter overflowing its baskets; Normandy butter wrapped in cloth, looking like models of bellies on to which a sculptor had thrown some wet rags; other blocks, already cut into and looking like high rocks full of valleys and crevices. Under the display counter of red marble veined with grey, baskets of eggs shone like white chalk; while on layers of straw in boxes were *bondons* placed end to end, and *gournays* arranged like medals, forming darker patches tinted with green. But for the most part the cheeses stood in piles on the table. There, next to the one-pound packs of butter, a gigantic *cantal* was spread on leaves of white beet, as though split by blows from an axe; then came a golden Cheshire cheese, a *gruyère* like a wheel fallen from some barbarian chariot, some Dutch cheeses suggesting decapitated heads smeared in dried blood and as hard as skulls—which has earned them the name of "death's heads." A *parmesan* added its aromatic tang to the thick, dull smell of the others. Three *bries*, on round boards, looked like melancholy moons. Two of them, very dry, were at the full; the third, in its second quarter, was melting away in a white cream, which had spread into a pool and flowed over the thin boards that had been put there in an attempt to hold it in check. Some *port-salut*, shaped like ancient discuses, bore the printed names of their makers. A *romantour* in silver paper suggested a bar of nougat or some sweet cheese which had strayed into this realm of bitter fermentations. The *roqueforts*, too, under their glass covers, had a princely air, their fat faces veined in blue and yellow, like the victims of some shameful disease common to rich people who have eaten too many truffles; while on a dish next to them stood the *fromages de chèvre*, about the size of a child's fist, hard and grey like the pebbles which the rams send rolling down stony paths as they lead their flock. Then came the strong-smelling cheeses: the *mont-d'ors*, pale yellow, with a mild sugary smell; the *troyes*, very thick and bruised at the edges, much stronger, smelling like a damp cellar; the *camemberts*, suggesting high game; the *neufchâtels*, the *limbourgs*, the *marolles*, the *pont-l'évèques*, each adding its own shrill note in a phrase that was harsh to the point of nausea; the *livarots*, tinted red, as irritating to the throat as sulphur fumes; and finally, stronger than all the others, the *olivets*, wrapped in walnut leaves, like the carcasses of animals which peasants cover with branches as they lie rotting in the hedgerow under the blazing sun. The warm afternoon had softened the cheeses; the mould on the rinds was melting and glazing over with the rich colours of red copper verdigris, like wounds that have badly healed; under the oak leaves, a breeze lifted the skin of the *olivets*, which seemed to move up and down with the slow deep breathing of a man asleep. A *livarot* was swarming with life; and behind the scales a *géromé* flavoured with aniseed gave off such a pestilential smell that all around it flies had dropped dead on the marble slab.[11]

The multiplicity comes before us not as things or visible objects but rather as names, it is the alien guts and insides of the words themselves that are overwhelmingly juxtaposed and arrayed against us in such catalogues, which are very far from expressing their original Whitmanian gusto. Here perhaps the Sartrean opposition between centrifugal and centripetal poetics has its relevance, the Whitman lists and catalogues being at one and the same time the explosion of the self, inhaling its impossibly large breath and appropriating the outside world itself, and yet at one and the same time making that world object by object a little like Fichte's big bang of the first Subject producing a universe of objectivity outside of itself. Here, however, the world multiplies and pullulates over against the observing subject, delirious from the cascading names as they begin to translate themselves into infinite space itself. Certainly the Flaubertian delectation with the weirdest stones and ritual jewelry from antiquity—leaving its traces in Huysmans and Wilde and a truly decadent fin de siècle— has somehow released this orgiastic compilation, but without any of Flaubert's morbidity or the antiquarian and perverse spirit in which he revels in the past and its grotesque documents. That peculiar taste has suddenly left Zola free in the present to collect the names of our own richly commercial and exploratory world in a present open to the senses.

Yet names are not enough, and now the piles and well-nigh infinite variety of commodities find their way into the other senses at the same time that they borrow their distinct temporalities, and along with smell, a sonorous dimension appears which reorganizes

---

[11]   *The Belly of Paris*, 210–11.

the trajectory of the eye into the temporality of something which is neither noise nor music, neither the deafening sound-pollution of the crowd all around us, nor the fragile path of an instrument pursuing its unfamiliar course towards an unknown note which can never be the last word.

We must then here distinguish two distinct allegorical levels: the sensory one, in reality itself multiple, which is necessary in order to endow the inert multiplicity of these material things—fish or cheeses—with their appropriate intensities; and then the parallel with the gossiping women, for whom the multiplicity all around them is in fact the multiplicity of Rumor itself, as it sends its horde of messages and distortions into an outside world as vast as outer space. The object world cannot immediately parallel the drama of human exchange, in which Florent's past and state crimes, his politics and his unavowable exile, will come to light, like a bad smell whose origins become apparent. Rather, as the theorists of film theory have suggested, from Eisler to Marie-Claire Ropars, there must be an essential disjunction of the image and the sound track, no longer to be considered as background music or voice-over, but rather in its semi-autonomy to be counterpointed with the visible events, syncopated with them as Gertrude Stein says about drama, either a little too early or a little too late.

So it is that this delirious multiplicity, itself already animated by figures and metaphors of all kinds, will now, from its status as a kind of background music, sonorous, from silent partner in the "vile" drama of gossip and incitement, become agents and actors in its own right. The sun's rays heat the cheeses, whose wafting odor passes from sight and mere visual inspection to temporality itself:

> Le soleil oblique entrait sous le pavillon, les fromages puaient plus fort. À ce moment, c'était surtout le marolles qui dominait; il jetait des bouffées puissantes, une senteur de vieille litière, dans la fadeur des mottes de beurre. Puis, le vent parut tourner; brusquement, des râles de limbourg arrivèrent entre les trois femmes, aigres et amers, comme soufflés par des gorges de mourants. (I, 829)

> The sun was slanting into the market, the cheeses stank even more. The smell of the *marolles* seemed strongest; it released powerful whiffs into the air, like the stink of stable litter. Then the wind changed, and suddenly the deathly presence of the *limbourg* struck the three women, pungent and bitter, like the last gasps of a dying man.[12]

---

[12] Ibid., 212.

Now the cheeses assert their individuality, and begin to struggle among each other, in a kind of odorous polyphony and dissonance:

> Le camembert, de son fumet de venaison, avait vaincu les odeurs plus sourdes du marolles et du limbourg; il élargissait ses exhalaisons, étouffait les autres senteurs sous une abondance surprenante d'haleines gâtées. Cependant, au milieu de cette phrase vigoureuse, le parmesan jetait par moments un filet mince de flûte champêtre; tandis que les bries y mettaient des douceurs fades de tambourins humides. Il y eut une reprise suffocante du livarot. Et cette symphonie se tint un moment sur une note aiguë du géromé anisé, prolongée en point d'orgue. (I, 830)

> As they were all rather short of breath by this time, it was the *camembert* they could smell. This cheese, with its gamy odour, had overpowered the milder smells of the *marolles* and the *limbourg*; its power was remarkable. Every now and then, however, a slight whiff, a flute-like note, came from the *parmesan,* while the *bries* came into play with their soft, musty smell, the gentle sound, so to speak, of a damp tambourine. The *livarot* launched into an overwhelming reprise, and the *géromé* kept up the symphony with a sustained high note.[13]

This semi-autonomous "symphony" will now begin to intervene in the toxic gossip of the old women and as it were orchestrate their machinations at the same time that it exasperates them, in a new and heightened cacophonous counterpoint:

> Elles restaient debout, se saluant, dans le bouquet final des fromages. Tous, à cette heure, donnaient à la fois. C'était une cacophonie de souffles infects, depuis les lourdeurs molles des pâtes cuites, du gruyère et du hollande, jusqu'aux pointes alcalines de l'olivet. Il y avait des ronflements sourds du cantal, du chester, des fromages de chèvre, pareils à un chant large de basse, sur lesquels se détachaient, en notes piquées, les petites fumées brusques des neufchâtels, des troyes et des mont-d'or. Puis les odeurs s'effaraient, roulaient les unes sur les autres, s'épaississaient des bouffées du Port-Salut, du limbourg, du géromé, du marolles, du livarot, du pont-l'évêque, peu à peu confondues, épanouies en une seule explosion de puanteurs. Cela s'épandait, se soutenait, au milieu du vibrement général, n'ayant plus de parfums distincts, d'un vertige continu de nausée et d'une force terrible d'asphyxie. (I, 833)

> As they stood there taking their leave of each other, the cheeses seemed to stink even more. They all seemed to stink together, in a foul cacophony: from the oppressiveness of the heavy Dutch cheeses and the *gruyères* to the sharp alkaline note of the *olivet*. From the *cantal*, Cheshire, and goat's milk came the sound of a bassoon, punctuated by the sudden, sharp notes of the *neufchâtels*, the *troyes*, and

---

13 Ibid., 213.

the *mont-d'ors*. Then the smells went wild and became completely jumbled, the *port-salut*, *limbourg*, *gé*romé, *marolles*, *livarot*, and *pont-l'évèque* combining into a great explosion of smells. The stench rose and spread, no longer a collection of individual smells, but a huge, sickening mixture.[14]

At which point Zola adds, quite unnecessarily: "Il semblait que c'étaient les paroles mauvaises de Mme. Lecœur and de Mlle. Saget qui puaient si fort." ("It seemed for a moment that it was the vile words of Madame Lecoeur and Mademoiselle Saget that had produced this dreadful odour.")

But what is also crucial here is not so much the allegorical function of the cheeses as their veritable liberation from meaning in all their excess, so that they come to know their own temporality, in which even the silences of the body play their role. For such an onslaught of sensation seems to require something like a zero degree, what Deleuze calls a surface of inscription, in order to sound its specific note and make its effect. In Zola that role will often be played by cleanliness:

Mais, au déjeuner, il fut repris par la douceur fondante de Lisa. Elle lui reparla de la place d'inspecteur à la marée, sans trop insister, comme d'une chose qui méritait réflexion. Il l'écoutait, l'assiette pleine, gagné malgré lui par la propreté dévote de la salle à manger; la natte mettait une mollesse sous ses pieds; les luisants de la suspension de cuivre, le jaune tendre du papier peint et du chêne clair des meubles, le pénétraient d'un sentiment d'honnêteté dans le bien-être, qui troublait ses idées du faux et du vrai. (I, 681–2)

When he returned for lunch, however, he was quite won over by Lisa's soft, gentle manner. She again spoke to him about the fish inspector's job, without undue insistence but as something that deserved consideration. As he listened to her, his plate piled high, he was affected, in spite of himself, by the prim comfort of his surroundings. The matting beneath his feet seemed very soft; the glitter of the brass hanging lamp, the yellow tint of the wallpaper, and the bright oak of the furniture filled him with a sense of appreciation for a life of well-being, which confused his notions of right and wrong.[15]

Yet this last, unexpected development warns us that in sensation as well, there can be no ultimate "zero degree" in perception, that all such seemingly pure data are still haunted by a meaning of some kind, which is to say an ideological connotation (to use Barthes' early word)—here the way in which cleanliness and neatness is somehow

---

[14] Ibid., 215–6.
[15] Ibid., 77.

infiltrated by *bien-être*, which is to say by bourgeois comfort, itself then libidinally personified in Lisa. At this point cleanliness, the surface against which all the content-laden sense-data of smells and visual stimuli, sounds and fabrics, are perceived, itself is secretly subverted by the surface of inscription of a bourgeois value or ideal. We will see the process again later on, it constitutes the mastering of affect by ideology, of the body open to sensations by the bourgeois ideology of the body and its training, manners, stances and practice.

Yet the very multiplication of these sensory onslaughts raises the question of their succession in time, where the gradual autonomization of the various affects slowly begins to release them from their relationship to plot as such and suggest whole new forms of temporal organization. I have implied that in Octave's climactic new fashion exhibit, the oases of white which the visitors happen upon can no longer really compete with each other: even though the clients' movements are organized according to a trajectory through the now enlarged and immense department store, reaching some climactic altar to whiteness itself, yet at the same time confronting them as so many musical variations on a single theme. Yet these climaxes must not be allowed to become symbolic either, and the residual meanings of white (innocence, virginity and so forth) are precisely what are to be drowned out by the new sensibility (Zola's prophetic vision of addictive consumerism, with strong sexual overtones and undertones).

Thus, in order to maintain a focus on this strange and disembodied element which is affect, we must vigilantly separate it from its material supports or bearers, whether in the body (where it becomes simply one more sensory impression or perception) or the psyche (where it is reduced to the merely subjective). What happens, indeed, is that the registration of affect must become allegorical of itself, and designate its own detached and floating structure within itself. Here, for example, is Jean Macquart looking out across the Paris of the Commune, set on fire by extremists (the infamous *pétroleuses* of anti-Commune propaganda[16]):

> Jean, plein d'angoisse, se retourna vers Paris. À cette fin si claire d'un beau dimanche, le soleil oblique, au ras de l'horizon, éclairait la ville immense d'une ardente lueur rouge. On aurait dit un soleil de sang, sur une mer sans borne. Les vitres des milliers de fenêtres braisillaient, comme attisées sous des soufflets

---

[16] See for example Paul Lidsky, *Les écrivains contre la Commune*, Paris: La Decouverte, 2011.

invisibles; les toitures s'embrasaient, telles que des lits de charbons; les pans de murailles jaunes, les hauts monuments, couleur de rouille, flambaient avec les pétillements de brusques feux de fagots, dans l'air du soir. Et n'était-ce pas la gerbe finale, le gigantesque bouquet de pourpre, Paris entier brûlant ainsi qu'une fascine géante, une antique forêt sèche, s'envolant au ciel d'un coup, en un vol de flammèches et d'étincelles? Les incendies continuaient, de grosses fumées rousses montaient toujours, on entendait une rumeur énorme, peut-être les derniers râles des fusillés, à la caserne Lobau, peut-être la joie des femmes et le rire des enfants, dînant dehors après l'heureuse promenade, assis aux portes des marchands de vin. Des maisons et des édifices saccagés, des rues éventrées, de tant de ruines et de tant de souffrances, la vie grondait encore, au milieu du flamboiement de ce royal coucher d'astre, dans lequel Paris achevait de se consumer en braise. (V, 911)

Filled with dread, Jean turned back towards Paris. At the end of a beautiful Sunday, on such a fine, clear evening, the slanting rays of the sun, skimming the horizon, lit up the immense city with a burning, red light. It looked like a bloody sun over a boundless sea. The panes of the thousands of windows glowed as if fanned by invisible bellows; the rooftops blazed like beds of hot coals; yellow walls and the tall, rust-coloured monuments were licked by flames like flickering fires in the evening air. Wasn't this the final burst of sparks, the enormous, purple bouquet, the whole of Paris burning like some giant sacrificial fire, a dry, ancient forest suddenly flaming sky-high, in a sparkling, crackling whirl? The fires burned on, there were still great clouds of russet-coloured smoke rising up into the air, and a huge noise could be heard, perhaps the last cries of those being shot in the Lobau barracks, or perhaps the joy of the women and the laughter of children, as they dined in the open air after their happy stroll, sitting outside the cafés. From the devastated houses and buildings, from the gutted streets, from all the ruins and all the suffering, life was stirring once more, amidst the flames cast by this regal sunset, by whose light the fire of Paris was finally burning itself out.[17]

We must carefully distinguish the levels of a passage of this kind, beginning with the awkward reminiscences of Balzac (*"on aurait dit"*), who ever invited us, with his rhetorical questions, to compare his scenes with this or that great painting of the past, as much theatrically to stage a tableau as to elicit our admiration. Such echoes are part and parcel of a whole rhetoric in Zola, which one might term a rhetoric of things (like the famous *"leçon de choses"*) systematically arranged to produce that theatrical effect against which Michael Fried has famously warned us. In particular here, on the last page of this immense war novel *La débâcle* (1892) (which Henry James admired

---

[17] *The Debacle*, trans. Elinor Dorday, Oxford: Oxford University Press, 2000, 513–4.

despite himself[18]), the descriptive amplification is allegorical of the ending of the novel as well, the final climactic recapitulation of a whole thematics of fire which informs the narrative as a whole (and the Rougon-Macquart more generally). This practice of the Wagnerian leitmotiv (to which Thomas Mann compares it), as well as of the variational system of the impressionists (Manet's haystacks and cathedrals at all hours of the day in every weather), then makes for a somewhat different temporality, one of repetition and of memory, than the stock melodramatic one. Meanwhile, the symbolic value of the passage, as a vision of the end of the world itself, can be corroborated by a wild outburst of the then Bakuninite Wagner himself (in the revolution of 1848), who claimed that nothing can be changed in music or in anything else until Paris is burnt to the ground![19] Semantically, however, this apocalypse announces a more local and historical one, namely the end of the Second Empire; and on this level the various appearances of fire are in hindsight revealed to be so many grim prolepses of this real holocaust, as in the festivities of the *Exposition Universelle* of 1867:

> Ce fut le 1er avril que l'Exposition Universelle de 1867 ouvrit, au milieu de fêtes, avec un éclat triomphal. La grande saison de l'empire commençait, cette saison de gala suprême, qui allait faire de Paris l'auberge du monde, une auberge pavoisée, pleine de musiques et de chants, où l'on mangeait, où l'on forniquait dans toutes les chambres. Jamais règne, à son apogée, n'avait convoqué les nations à une si colossale ripaille. Vers les Tuileries flamboyantes, dans une apothéose de féerie, le

---

[18] Henry James, *Literary Criticism, Volume II: European Writers; Prefaces to the New York Edition*, New York: Library of America, 1984, 898: "I recall the effect [*La débâcle*] then produced on me as a really luxurious act of submission. It was early in the summer; I was in an old Italian town; the heat was oppressive, and one could but recline, in the lightest garments, in a great dim room and give one's self up. I like to think of the conditions and the emotion, which melt for me together into the memory I fear to imperil. I remember that in the glow of my admiration there was not a reserve I had ever made that I was not ready to take back. As an application of the author's system and his supreme faculty, as a triumph of what these things could do for him, how could such a performance be surpassed? The long, complex, horrific, pathetic battle, embraced, mastered, with every crash of its squadrons, every pulse of its thunder and blood resolved for us, by reflection, by communication from two of the humblest and obscurest of the military units, into immediate vision and contact, into deep human thrills of terror and pity—this bristling centre of the book was a piece of 'doing' (to come back to our word) as could only shut our mouths."

[19] Ernest Newman, *The Life of Richard Wagner, Vol. IV*, Cambridge: Cambridge University Press, 1947, 272, notes.

long défilé des empereurs, des rois et des princes, se mettait en marche, des quatre coins de la terre. (V, 228)

It was on April 1, in the midst of *fêtes*, that the Universal Exhibition of 1867 was opened with triumphal splendor. The Empire's great "season" was beginning, that supreme gala season which was to turn Paris into the hostelry of the entire world—a hostelry gay with bunting, song, and music, where there was feasting and love-making in every room. Never had a *régime* at the zenith of its power convoked the nations to such a colossal spree. From the four corners of the earth a long procession of emperors, kings, and princes started on the march towards the Tuileries, which were all ablaze like some palace in the crowning scene of an extravaganza.[20]

But all these levels need to be distinguished from the invisible materiality of light itself, as a medium that is allegorical of the affect for which it is the recording device, a transparency capable at certain moments of thickening into an object in its own right, with its own kind of visibility, as with certain hours of the day in Los Angeles or Jerusalem, where light can be perceived in and for itself, and where the surfaces of the buildings are best observed as sheets whose pores and rugosities capture the new element and hold it for a moment, or those receding planes where pebbles and their determinate shadows serve as sundials, as in a Dali painting.

What we have not yet pointed out in this passage is the way in which the materiality of light is here secured by its redoubling: within the clear light of the afternoon sun there is enveloped the light of the city burning day and night, a different kind of light about which one cannot tell which one reflects the other, deepening it or revealing its secret essence. This is a very different contrast than that of light and dark ("in the gloom the gold gathers the light against it"), in which difference is represented by means of identity itself. It is the abstract form we need to glimpse here, as in a candle still burning in the dawn light:

Le jour naissait, une aube d'une pureté délicieuse, au fond du grand ciel clair, lavé par l'orage. Aucun nuage n'en tachait plus le pâle azur, teinté de rose. Tout le gai réveil de la campagne mouillée entrait par la fenêtre, tandis que les bougies, qui achevaient de se consumer, pâlissaient dans la clarté croissante. (V, 1024)

Day was breaking, a dawn of a delicious purity at the heart of the great clear sky washed clean by the storm. Not a cloud stained its pale rosy azure. A gay

---

[20] *Money*, trans. Ernest A. Vizetelly, New York: Mondial, 2007, 185.

awakening of the dampened countryside everywhere came through the window, while the candles, melting and dwindling away, grew pale in the ever stronger light.[21]

The light within the light—each one derealizing the other, dawn turning the candle flame yellow and garish, the flame itself making of dawn light something watery and unhealthy—betray one of the deepest secrets of affect. Its inner mirroring and division, an internal *pli*, prepares it as a vehicle for the investment of affect insofar as it mimics scale and differentiation, save that, as in this case and unlike music, it is a lateral dissociation, an opposition of the thing to itself which produces it as a thing at the same time that it effaces itself. A strange evanescent dissonance within unison as such, rather than the slippage of chromaticism: Baudelaire was onto this property, which, however, "Correspondences" theorizes in terms of harmony, as I noted. And yet he practices it: "*doux comme les hautbois*," where all the sweetness is in the sour oboe itself; "a green so delicious it hurts," in which the pleasure is in the pain itself.

Yet there is another reason why the representation of intensities (which is also their expression) should require the reduplication or redoubling we have been describing here: and this has to do with the separation of the affect from its physical bearer. For if it becomes indistinguishable from physiological experiences or reactions, it vanishes as an autonomous entity and folds back into explanatory habits and stereotypes in which subjectivity or the physiology of the body suffice as some ultimate ground or cause. Here however the mind is obliged to move back and forth between alternate mirror-images, neither of which is satisfactory in itself—candle or sun, sun or fire?— in such a way that the effect transcends either. The relevant example here might be the magic potions in Wagner—the love potion in Act I of *Tristan*, and the potion of oblivion in *Götterdämmerung*: there has indeed been much idle debate about the dramatic necessity of these contrivances—are they necessary, are we really to believe in their efficacy, or are they not rather distracting tricks the dramatist might better have avoided?

In short, do they really cause anything? If Tristan and Isolde fall in love because of the potion, then the whole love-death ethos of the work as a whole is nothing but an illusion; while Siegfried's forgetfulness of Brünnhilde comes before us as a mere plot mechanism

---

[21] *Doctor Pascal* (1893), trans. mine.

like the deus ex machina or the *reitender Bote*. If the famous pair are in love already, then the love potion is superfluous; as for Siegfried, Carl Dahlhaus has ingeniously observed that he lives in any case in the present and is unlikely to remember anything anyway, even so significant a moment in his own past.[22] The physical potion, or cause, is then equally unnecessary, particularly since we are no longer in the fairy-tale world of the preceding opera, *Siegfried*. Yet I think these discussions can be seen to be misplaced if they are taken to be examples of the affective redoubling we have been trying to theorize here: the physical brew makes it impossible for the spectator to take these developments as purely subjective ones, that happen to this or that individual or are subject to the psychological vagaries of this or that contingent identity. On the other hand, the very autonomous force of the passion in *Tristan* (and the radical innocence that makes of Siegfried again a blank slate and a perpetual present) differentiate both these effects from the material causes, all the while endowing them with a kind of materiality that grounds their autonomy in the first place.

But as idealists from Berkeley to Bergson have persuasively demonstrated, the idea of matter is itself an idealistic fiction (not a good concept, as Deleuze might say!); so that our various experiences of affect (above) are in a paradoxical way more materialistic than the concept of matter itself, along with that of the body. It may therefore be useful, in pursuing this chiasmus, to turn to a different category on which affect inscribes itself, one equally as invisible as light but which Kant took to be a formal precondition of perception (like time) and in no way a feature of the latter's content. This is the category of space, whose possible intensities we may explore in the following passage, a characteristic moment in *L'argent*, in which the novelist describes the pitiful enclosed back garden of an impecunious mother and daughter, last remnants of an aristocratic lineage, who wash their own clothes in secret and eat scraps behind closed doors, in order to avoid public disgrace:

> Tous les jours, lorsqu'il ne pleuvait pas, elles apparaissaient ainsi, l'une derrière l'autre, elles descendaient le perron, faisaient le tour de l'étroite pelouse centrale, sans échanger une parole. Il n'y avait que des bordures de lierre, les fleurs n'auraient pas poussé, ou peut-être auraient-elles coûté trop cher. Et cette promenade

---

[22] Carl Dahlhaus, *Richard Wagner's Music Dramas*, Cambridge: Cambridge University Press, 1979, 98.

lente, sans doute une simple promenade de santé, par ces deux femmes si pâles, sous ces arbres centenaires qui avaient vu tant de fêtes et que les bourgeoises maisons du voisinage étouffaient, prenait une mélancolique douleur, comme si elles eussent promené le deuil des vieilles choses mortes. (IV, 68–9)

Every day, when it did not rain, they thus appeared, one behind the other, and, descending the steps, made the circuit of the little central grass-plot, without exchanging a word. The path was merely edged with ivy; flowers would not have grown in such a spot, or perhaps they would have cost too dear. And the slow promenade—undoubtedly a simple constitutional—made by those two pale women, under the centenarian trees which long ago had witnessed so many festivities, and which the neighbouring *bourgeois* houses were now stifling, was suggestive of a melancholy grief, as though they had been performing some mourning ceremony for old, dead things.[23]

Phenomenology has taught us to read such descriptions, not as projections, but rather as accounts of our being-in-the-world; and older ideologies, such as vitalism, would have been as keenly sensitive to all the symptoms of this palpable stunting and disfiguration of the life force as Zola himself. Nor is the suggestion that nature has become a prison some mere rhetorical and metaphorical flourish, it is realized in the object world itself, as at the bottom of a well, a metaphor which has exchanged its vehicle for its tenor, becoming tangibly accessible to the starved senses. It is instructive once again to compare this garden with the miserable salon of Balzac, where the social meaning has become the meaning we read on the room's qualities. Here, the garden does not testify to the indigent situation of its inhabitants, nor to their pre-history or their pitiful stratagems (about which Zola tells us): rather, it offers a phenomenologically meaningful state of the world in and of itself, which can only be juxtaposed with and compared to the other vivid spaces explored in this novel with which it coexists—filthy hovels, seedy houses of assignation, the Bourse itself from dawn to dusk, indeed Paris itself lit up in that festival of the Universal Exposition we have already witnessed.

This variety of phenomenological spaces, however, suggests another interpretation of affect which demands comment in passing, and that is the unique status of melancholia among the various kinds of affects presumed or implied by the definition. Is it really so that melancholia is the very prototype of affect, as so much contemporary theory seems to believe; or better still that affect is simply another word for

---

[23] *Money*, op. cit., 51, translation modified.

melancholia as such? I tend to want to include the properties of a given national language in the account of these general representational or registrational possibilities. Indeed, the unique sociability of French lends its expressions for feelings a collective resonance that many other languages, such as English, lack. This is true of gestures and commonplaces as well, but I here limit myself to affect alone, where it can be affirmed that the word "*triste*" has graver musical and phenomenological connotations which only Milton and T. S. Eliot have been able to convey with the English word "sad." The French word opens up that whole landscape of desolation which is the very allegory of melancholy itself, and which tolls throughout Flaubert and Baudelaire. It is enough to recall Flaubert's remark about the writing of that great historical construction which is *Salammbô*:

> Peu de gens devineront combien il a fallu être triste pour ressusciter Carthage.

> Few will guess how melancholy one had to be to want to bring Carthage back to life.[24]

Yet before we thus absolutize melancholia, we must remember and take into account not only the doctrine of intensities (which actually, as we shall see, turns out to find some expression and grounding in Zola's pseudoscientific theories), but also the notion of a chromatic scale, according to which affect would be no more exempt than anything else from the semiotic play of oppositions in general. Affect is somehow felt in isolation from all relationship, and yet at the same time it remains defined by its opposites, the nobler melancholy standing nonetheless in an imperceptible relationship with its more vulgar opposite number, euphoria.

But the content of these scales is of course itself variable, and even if melancholia remains a kind of constant, in Flaubert, in *Tristan*, in Munch, in Gogol, its opposite is very different in all these cases, as also in Zola, where an expected excess of orgiastic excitement is far less authentic than the peacefulness of "*bonheur*."

---

[24] Famously quoted by Walter Benjamin in his description of the experience of historical defeat, in a passage worth quoting more extensively: "The nature of this sadness stands out more clearly if one asks with whom the adherents of historicism actually empathize. The answer is inevitable: with the victor ... There is no document of civilization which is not at the same time a document of barbarism." "Theses on the Philosophy of History," in *Illuminations*, trans. Harry Zohn, New York: Schocken, 1969, 256.

Indeed, the very generalization of affect beyond specific named feelings, such as melancholy or joy, affords an unexpected answer to that reproach of the pathetic fallacy formulated by the New Critics. We have suggested above that this diagnosis in reality takes as its object emotion rather than affect, and in a technical sense, one may even claim that the literary representation of affect develops precisely as a response to this objection, and has as its function to replace the opposition between mind and body which such older representations presupposed. For the latter very much posit a Cartesian dualism, of the type which Heideggerian phenomenology took as its fundamental philosophical target; it is thus not only the various modernisms that sought to overcome it. Is this to attribute to Zola a secret or nascent modernism? That would certainly incapacitate the theory of realism we are trying to outline here; but only at the price of disregarding the other temporal axis of Zola's novels, namely the system of the récit and of chronological temporality and narrative in which a nascent phenomenological consciousness is embedded and with which the latter stands in productive tension.

A revealing indication of this tension is to be found in the ambiguity of the narrative structure, which, famously in Zola, posits the dead weight of the past and of heredity on his immensely varied cast of characters: their various hereditary taints, vices, obsessions and the like are so many scars and marks that testify to the tenacious survival of the past-present-future system of the récit and would seem to corroborate Sartre's warnings about its "*passéiste*" determinism with a vengeance.

Yet Zola's pseudo-science vindicates the theory of affect in another, unexpected way. To be sure, we have already observed that Zola's great plan for a series of novels socially and politically critical of the regime in which he lived was suddenly ratified by the collapse of the system at the moment in which he began to write. Now suddenly a dictatorial government, set in place by the coup d'état which was to have been the subject of the first novel of that series, is dramatically ended in such a way that the series itself knows closure and can now have something like a happy ending. The year in which Zola publishes the beginning of the Rougon-Macquart series will thus turn out to open the setting for the last novel of that series, written some twenty-five years later (at the same time that it furnishes the Empire's most dramatic moment in the military defeat which would be the subject of its penultimate work). History, then, is a more than suspiciously complicit collaborator in the project, whose closure (known to the novelist in advance) allows all its episodes to be "historical" in the literary sense, and the object of a diagnostic already confirmed in advance.

The series, to be sure, abounds in vitalistic rhetoric and the invocation of life, nowhere quite so strident as in Jean's premonition of a rebirth of France at the end of *La débacle*, and the birth of the nameless child at the end of the final work, *Le docteur Pascal* (1893). But these appeals to the future are decorative against the background of the narrative preterite and the social and personal diseases of the period in question, now forever ended. The power of this temporal frame may well explain the weaknesses of Zola's novelistic projects after the end of the Rougon-Macquart, where little is left of a once oppressive and fateful History save the pious hope and the energetic optimism.

But it is important to rate that the great series has two distinct endings and not merely the political one, the disaster of a rotten power structure. For there is still heredity and tainted blood, corruption and obsession rooted in bodily unsoundness. Society and heredity are still the long shadows cast by the mind-body problem; nor does Zola dispose of a pineal gland whereby to hypothesize their causal interactions. Indeed, if anything, the political protagonists of this unhappy family are far more energetic than their kinsmen in a more grotesque private sphere.

The series will therefore require a second happy ending on that level as well, and it comes in the form of Dr. Pascal's medical solution to the problem of bad blood in the eponymous final volume. Nothing seems to grow old-fashioned more swiftly than the cures and diseases of yesteryear, which turn into superstition in the blink of the eye. This is indeed also the fate of Zola's medical speculation (if it ever had scientific verisimilitude for its contemporary readers in the first place). And it seems, in fact, to have been based on a far more ancient and tenacious superstition, namely the magical idea that like cures like. Thus, if you suffer from heart or kidney weakness, the ingestion of those organs will be helpful, and Yeats' monkey glands are only the most notorious recent avatar of this remedial conviction, which may well extend back into the earliest cannibalisms. The modern hypodermic needle, however, confers a certain technical cast to the practice, along with the concept of the scientific experiment, with its records and charts (Dr. Pascal's laboriously assembled files play a significant role in this novel, where they constitute a kind of shadow rivalry to Zola's novel series itself, Pascal constituting no doubt a more fundamental creative alter ego of the novelist than the fraternal Cezanne-figure of the painter in the earlier works).

But we have not yet come to Pascal's great discovery. Suffering himself from all kinds of physical ills (to which Zola, a confirmed hypochondriac, will no doubt add the obsessive pursuit of a cure, not unlike his own monumental perseverance in a novelistic task worthy of the most impossible ambitions of the modernists themselves), he has begun to inject himself, at which point an accident reveals the truth. It is the injection as such, and not its contents, which give the patient relief: "a simple mechanical effect," remarks Pascal modestly (V, 1084): "j'ai été frappé dernièrement par ce singulier résultat que les piqûres faites avec de l'eau pure étaient presque aussi efficaces... Le liquide injecté n'importe donc pas, il n'y a donc là qu'une action simplement mécanique." (V, 1177).[25] Pascal concludes that the effect of the injection does not lie in its action on the individual organ, but rather its restoration of the equilibrium of all the organs together and the restoration of the totality of relationships within the organism itself.

It is worth reiterating this finding in the words of the medical authority from whom Zola/Pascal derived it (a certain Dr. Chéron): "all hypodermic injections produce the same effects, whatever the liquid introduced beneath the skin... The difference bears only on the greater or lesser intensity of the reaction produced."[26]

It is revealing and suggestive to come upon the word "intensity" in this context, for it confirms our intuition that Pascal's discovery is in fact an allegory of the very theory of affective narrative we have been outlining here, and that Zola's series thus culminates in a kind of autoreferential consciousness of its own representational procedures. Think of it this way: Chéron/Pascal's discovery is that of the super-session of content by form as such. Hitherto, each blighted destiny was analogous to a diseased organ, and in the case of the organs, they are treated by an injection of their own substance, distinct from the substances of all the other organs of the body. The temptation is to imagine a multiplicity of diseases and corresponding organs, just as

---

[25] "I was recently struck by an unusual result, namely that injections of pure water were just as efficacious ... The nature of the injected liquid is thus unimportant, the action is a purely mechanical one."

[26] See Henri Mitterand's note, V, 1654.

Zola imagined himself to be documenting the multiplicity of destinies played out on his immense social stage, each destiny with a specific and unique content of its own. But this is substantialist thinking rather than a concept of relationality. For just as all these human destinies are linked together by heredity into a single family, so also their multiplicity is mere appearance: they are in fact all the same, whether they look like obsession, neurosis, psychosis, morbid ambition, erotomania, the lust for power and so forth.

They differ, not in substance, but in intensity: they thereby correspond, not to the specific types of the named emotions, but to the purely formal play of affect. What look like the unique individual destinies of so many récits are in fact now transformed into the abstract fever-chart of affects and intensities rising and falling; and Zola's narratives are what happen to individuals and their destinies when their récits fall into the force-field of affect and submit to its dynamic, in a situation in which the two forces, the two temporalities, are still for one last moment more or less equal in their power and influence.

Here, then, we witness the autoreferentiality of the representation of affect, as a form becomes its own content and Zola's requirement of a scientific "motivation of the device" becomes in effect a formal account of his representation. The doctrine of intensity thereby becomes an aesthetic ideology for this novelistic practice, which in retrospect looks less like an account of the destiny of anthropomorphic characters than it does an immense collection of distinct phenomenological spaces. Meanwhile, his people begin to exist as bodies first and foremost, despite their identification as characters in the older sense. Zola's novels are immense accumulations of bodies in movement and intersection across such spaces, from rooms to streets, from the fetid darkness of *L'assommoir* and the underground nightmare of *Germinal* to the rococo excesses of the most vulgar Second Empire salons: bodies in full effervescence, paralysis or decay, landscapes increasingly thronged with new buildings and the wreckage of older ones, the phenomenology of History and histories caught in a dynamic of toxic expansion. Here, then, affect has become a symptomatology reinforcing the great realist project at the very moment it imperils it.

Yet this is only one way in which affect appropriates a whole narrative apparatus and colonizes it; there are as many varieties of realism as there are features and potentialities in the phenomenon of affect itself, and in the tensions between the two temporalities with which we began. We will take several more in review in the following chapters, beginning with an affective temporality quite different from Zola's stubborn single-mindedness, which some may feel more illustrative of *Stimmung* than of affect, I mean the changeable narrative temporality of Leo Tolstoy.

Chapter IV

Tolstoy, or, Distraction

Tolstoy presents a unique practice of affect which shapes his work and which is in fact responsible for many of the features stereotypically associated with it (the multitude of characters, the seemingly "natural" rhythm of the narrative, etc.). To discuss this under the heading of psychology, however, and to abound in wonderment about Tolstoy's feeling for the psychological states and reactions of his characters, no longer seems to me particularly helpful, especially since the contemporary exploration of affect has undermined many of the standard categories and concepts which organized the system of this "discipline" (as traditional as Aristotle). The theoretical interest in affect, indeed, was prepared by the structuralist/poststructuralist "death of the subject," which is to say the problematization of notions of personal identity and of centralized consciousness. In what follows, I will proceed on the basis of a radical dissociation of these two phenomena—identity and consciousness—and indeed the theory of realism I am presenting here is itself organized around that dissociation; identity as a social mark of a relatively objective kind, which specifies individual history and indeed temporal chronology; consciousness as an impersonal field which can probably no longer even be described in terms of subjectivity. But more of that as it informs a reading of Tolstoy later on.

The literary historians invoke *War and Peace* in terms of an opposition between "domesticity" and the political, an opposition which itself has its own deeper relationship to the debates between slavophiles and Westernizers in this period but which is misleading to the degree to which the positions of the slavophiles are themselves political, as well as presupposing too simple a transfer of ideological positions onto aesthetic ones and their translation into issues of representation. On the other hand, perhaps this distinction between the ideological and the aesthetic can also clarify the matter: for what Tolstoy's opposition to the political consists in is very precisely a loathing for what we might today call left intellectuals, that is to say, "liberals" with their pamphlets and pronouncements, their polemics and above all their practice of literature as a vehicle for political opinion. Chernyshevsky's name is the obvious tag here, as the aesthetic embodiment of all the political things Tolstoy (and after him, Nabokov) finds viscerally intolerable.

It is a position that we can identify in many of our own anti-political contemporaries, whom we should therefore describe less as reactionaries than as aesthetes. But this is the point I want to come to, namely that his hostility to political literature and a political aesthetic does not necessarily mark Tolstoy out as a slavophile in that parallel opposition which is the ideological one. (Indeed, later on in life he will discover himself to be as passionately anti-aesthetic as he is anti-political.) We must therefore be cautious in dealing with Tolstoy's anti-liberalism; another century has taught us that anti-liberalism can be as radical as it is conservative: and also that liberal modernizers, in the light of the construction of capitalism, need not automatically be judged progressive, although their enemies are often reactionary. Eikhenbaum in any case proposes that we shift the terms of the debate, and call Tolstoy's position an anti-historical one,[1] and this seems a good deal more promising as an approach to what is supposed to be the greatest historical novel ever written. Meanwhile, it is appropriate to recall Dostoyevsky's characterization of Tolstoy's work as "landowner's literature"; and Lenin's of Tolstoy's identification with the peasantry; descriptions which shift the discussion helpfully from nationalism to class.[2]

But now we need to step back from these general questions and take a closer look at affect in Tolstoy and at the kind of narrative texture it develops. It will be useful, in this regard, to examine chapter

---

[1] Boris Eikhenbaum, *Tolstoi in the Sixties*, trans. Duffield White, Ann Arbor: Ardis, 1982, 135: "The historical novel had been chosen precisely with the intention of being anti-historical." The companion volumes, *The Young Tolstoi* (Ardis, 1972), and *Tolstoi in the Seventies* (Ardis, 1982), are equally valuable and among the most insightful literary as well as biographical studies of Tolstoy ever written. I discuss the position of *War and Peace* in the tradition of the historical novel in "The Historical Novel Today" below.

[2] V. I. Lenin, "Leo Tolstoy as the Mirror of the Russian Revolution," in *Collected Works*, Vol. XV, Moscow: Progress, 1973. See also Pierre Macherey's discussion of this essay in his *Pour une théorie de la production littéraire*, Paris: Maspéro, 1966.

6 of Book II of *War and Peace*, an episode in the 1807 war in which Prince Andrew brings the news of Kutuzov's victory over Mortier (to be sure, a relatively minor encounter with a division that had become separated from the main body of Napoleon's army) to the Austrian court.[3] Still, coming after the Austrian disaster at Ulm, this minor Russian victory is most welcome indeed and seemingly auspicious.

Prince Andrew, in the coach carrying him to Brno, is elated ("excited but not weary"), not least at the prospect of a promotion his choice as messenger implies: yet he understands this primarily through a fantasy about the reception of other people ("picturing pleasantly to himself the impression his news of a victory would create"). These two features—the reward and the attention to "society" and its reactions—are in Tolstoy always ominous signs.

We do not yet reach the level of affect when we identify, in Tolstoy, a kind of moralizing system of the psychological which is itself a kind of ideology and which serves to evaluate his characters' feelings and to explain their dynamics. In this ideology, to be sure, we touch Tolstoy's Rousseauian convictions about the evils, not so much of society as of "civilized" society: "*le monde*," drawing rooms, gossip, manners, deceitful politeness and etiquette, reputation, in short, of everything Rousseau himself associated with Paris and with "progress." And over against this, what exactly? The natural, the deeper self, true feeling— and as opposed to society, the family, which is to say the extended family or clan, in other words what has already been ideologically identified as "domesticity," an ideology very much in keeping with the literature of landlords and landowners (and finally rather different from that of Rousseau's agonizing solitude).

But we must hold firmly to the premise that this Tolstoyan system of psychology, this *Weltanschauung* or view of human nature, is itself an ideology, an ideological construction and by no means the mere expression of that human nature nor of Tolstoy's own psychological makeup either. Clearly overdetermined by class (and by generational and historical realities, by social change as much as intellectual fashion and debate), this level of the text—Tolstoy's explanations of Prince Andrew's feelings—is far from being the ultimate one and itself demands explanation.

---

[3] I here use the Norton Critical Edition of *War and Peace*, in the translation of Louise and Aylmer Maude, ed. G. Gibian (New York: Norton, 1966), page number references given in the text. Book II, chapter 6 is to be found on 158–62.

But it certainly explains why Tolstoy would qualify Prince Andrew's elation in the following charged terms: "enjoying the feelings of a man who has at length begun to attain a long-desired happiness." The text pointedly avoids saying that Prince Andrew is "happy": and this is the moment to pause on this term as well, and to specify the unique meaning it has for Tolstoy and its symptomatic value as a sign wherever it appears in the novel.

It is here worth citing Boris Eikhenbaum in some detail:

Tolstoy's key word, his catchword, is "happiness." He writes in his diary on March 3, 1863: "Whoever is happy is right!" This is a quote from the final draft of *The Cossacks*, from Olenin's letter to his friend: "My goal—I am happy; this is my goal. Whoever is happy is right! ... I am good and I am right because happiness is absolutely obvious. A person who is happy knows it more certainly than 2 x 2 = 4."

These aphorisms do not simply express abstraction: Tolstoy directed them at his times, as a demonstration against its slogans. When spoken by Tolstoy, the very word "happiness" assumes a special meaning, as the opposition of "natural" human right to all other "civil" rights and obligations, as the juxtaposition of feeling to mind and of nature to civilization. In an 1863 diary entry we read: "Everything that people do they do according to the demands of their natures. And the mind only fabricates for each action its imaginary causes, which for one person may be called convictions or faith and for the people (acting collectively in history) is called *idea*. This is one of the oldest and most harmful fallacies." This is a formulation of Tolstoy's long-standing animosity toward "convictions" and ideas, or, in other words, toward the new Russian intelligentsia, toward the whole movement of the sixties.[4]

Happiness is in Tolstoy a moment and in that sense necessarily an event; but we may also say that it is somehow outside of time, although not "eternal" in the way in which non-temporal states (such as mathematical truths) are thought to be by those temporal beings which we are. What it is outside of can better be identified as the temporal continuum, the structure of past-present-future: and therefore the kind of temporal present it occupies (always referring here to the Tolstoyan system) would demand a different word than the one in current use, which is inextricable from its chronological structure. But there is no such word; and its absence opens up a space for representational innovation at the same time that it condemns theoretical presentation to the inescapable attempt to distinguish two homonyms which have nothing to do with each other. (To say that

---

4 Eikhenbaum, *Tolstoi in the Sixties*, 105.

these two types of "present" make for existential problems as well is an understatement.[5])

"Happiness" as a peculiar kind of Tolstoyan present designates a reconciliation with life and the world, with being, by definition an ephemeral one, or as Heidegger says, one that withdraws in the same moment that it appears. It has preconditions but cannot be caused; and clearly, it cannot be the aim or end of any action or project, save in the sense in which Prince Andrew imagines "the feelings of a man who has at length begun to attain a long-desired happiness," that is to say, who imagines it from the outside or in the future, and also substitutes for it some other kind of satisfaction.

Its centrality and its uniqueness for Tolstoy can be judged comparatively by juxtaposing the words available for this state in the other languages ("*bonheur*" is in French a far more specific physiological condition, the English word is diluted with some general bourgeois sense of comfort, etc.); but also by comparison with its relative functional value in comparable texts. In Stendhal, for example, a writer so close to Tolstoy in this and other ways, what prevents happiness in Tolstoy—ambition, vanity, society and the opinions of other people—also blasts and denatures a comparable spontaneity ("la pensée du privilège avait desséché cette plante toujours si la délicate qu'on nomme le bonheur"[6]); but one cannot say that the deeper authentic self in Stendhal is Tolstoyan, absorbed as it is in love and longing. (And we might also add that the very framework of a single protagonist, like Julien or Fabrice, limits the perspective on such psychic processes to a single type of content and thereby a single interpretation. "Freeing himself from the initial constraint of a central personality," as Eikenbaum puts it of Tolstoy,[7] attaining what the same critic calls "mass parallelism" or what we might term "cross-cutting," thus allows for a greater variety of such processes and indeed tends to depersonalize the process itself. It should also be added that the tyranny of "point of view" is thus something Tolstoy was thereby able to do away with, rather than, as Henry James thought, a goal he was too primitive to attain.[8])

---

5 See above, Chapter I.

6 *La Chartreuse de Parme*, Paris: Cluny, 1950, 165.

7 Eikenbaum, *The Young Tolstoi*, 84.

8 This is probably a central reason for James's famous characterization of the great Russian novels (and others) as "large, loose, baggy monsters": "Art of the Novel," in Henry James, *Literary Criticism, Volume II: European Writers; Prefaces to the*

In Proust, also, the will is a powerful force for alienation and sterility, but what it alienates (creativity) is specified in still different ways from the two writers we have mentioned. Probably the Kantian aesthetic which posits a suspension of interest or practical intent has its kinship as well (indeed, as Lukács has shown, the most influential models of social and political disalienation are already anticipated in this aesthetic[9]); but to see Tolstoy from this perspective (however correct and interesting it might be) would classify his ethico-psychological referent as an essentially contemplative and aesthetic one and thereby return it to those worldly judgements and systems from which he represented it as an escape.

It therefore seems best to me to think of such crucial moments of Tolstoyan happiness as an affect, one which he constructs as the fundamental one, and which is ideologically privileged in his thought, but which for us must be grasped as a compositional element, to return to the perspective of the Russian Formalists. Indeed, Eikhenbaum lays great stress (as did the contemporary Russian critics) on the episodic structure of *War and Peace*, that is to say, on the way in which an attention to affect denarrativizes and dechronologizes the action ostensibly being narrated. This is of course preeminently the structure we have sought to disengage here: a tension between plot and scene, between the chronological continuum and the eternal affective present which, realized in quite distinct ratios in the various great realists, nonetheless marks out the space in which realism emerges and subsists, until one of the two antithetical forces finally outweighs the other and assures its disintegration.

But let us now return to Prince Andrew; he is generous with some wounded soldiers on the way to the town; arriving at dark "he felt even more vigorous and alert," recalling the details of the battle and imagining the questions that might be put to him (161). But now, approaching the door of the minister's room, his "joyous feeling was considerably weakened" by the formality of the adjutant. "He felt offended" at being asked to wait; "his fertile mind instantly suggested to him a point of view which gave him a right to despise the adjutant." The minister receives him with the artificiality "of a man who is continually receiving many petitions one after another," shaken

---

New York Edition, New York: Library of America, 1984, 84 (Preface to *The Tragic Muse*).

[9] See his essay on Schiller, "Zur Asthetik Schillers," in *Probleme der Asthetik*, Berlin: Lucterhand, 1969.

only by news of the death of the Austrian general Schmidt. And the chapter concludes thus: "When Prince Andrew left the palace he felt that all the interest and happiness the victory had afforded him had now been left in the indifferent hands of the Minister of War and the polite adjutant." It is a well-nigh Lacanian conclusion: now that this affect has been entrusted to the other, it will no longer be necessary for me to feel it.

Clearly enough, except for moving Prince Andrew to the army headquarters in Brünn, this chapter, which confirms the Russian's suspicion that the Austrians are less interested in a Russian victory than they are by the Austrian defeat at Ulm, has very little plot significance. Nothing much happens to Prince Andrew; we have already encountered the prickliness of his character in earlier chapters, so nothing further is supplied on that score; all that transpires here is a gamut of affects, of which the chapter is a kind of fever chart or musical partition. Nor is this series of moods of any great importance to the portrayal of Prince Andrew as a character, although we may well be surprised at the degree to which his fantasies are driven by ambition, startled indeed at the degree to which his reverie is taken up with fantasies and day-dreams in the first place (from the outside he seemed altogether a graver and more dignified personage). In the long run, however, all Tolstoy's characters are thus contaminated by the other in one way or another, and this particular inner life will not uniquely distinguish any one individual figure, will not in other words serve as a psychological distinguishing trait or individualizing characteristic. It is the character's name and place in the action or the chronological continuum which will hold each gamut of affects together (or, if you prefer, serve as their pretext and container).

Finally, we will not appreciate the operation of form here if we reduce Andrew's reactions to some common-sense psychological stereotype, such as disappointment at his bureaucratic reception, or exhaustion of his eagerness and excitement in advance by the exercise of fantasy. Not the content of these moods but rather their rapid succession is the mark of Tolstoy's peculiar sensibility.

What is thus crucial here is the changeability of the affects, which in turn provides the registering apparatus, the legibility of the various states. For they can only be read distinctly against a constant variation: a single affective tonality, like a single note or pedal-point held without variation, becomes in the long run indistinct or imperceptible against its background, or else slowly takes on a pathological dimension which demands motivation in its own right. But what the chapter in question demonstrates is the ceaseless variability from elation to hostility, from sympathy to generosity and then to suspicion, and finally to disappointment and indifference: there are in principle in Tolstoy no moments of the narrative which lack their dimension of affect, to the point at which one is tempted to say that these movements and variations are themselves the narrative. The chapter is the story of the affects themselves, and not of external events or plot developments; and vivid as the characters are, the very density of the affects themselves secures an impersonal existence for them, above and beyond those individual subjects which were once the protagonists of realism.

It is this changeability and variability, this capacity for sensitivity (in the sense of irritation) and for sudden bouts of ennui, for passing enthusiasms, obsessions, drops in enthusiasm and niveau—it is all this which seems to have been characterized by Tolstoy himself as a "stream of consciousness" (a term better reserved for this play of affect than for the verbal monologues which of course Tolstoy also pioneered before the official modernists). It is not a return of the old-fashioned biographical criticism to say so; for the journals and testimony that confirm the diagnosis are yet another set of texts to be added to the literary ones. But the evidence is abundant, not least owing to his incessant self-examinations, which seem to have been provoked by his own bewilderment at this temperament, which he understood to be something a little more significant than a mere character trait.

At this point it will perhaps be worthwhile to compare a stronger, "modernist" form of such changeability in the music of Gustav Mahler, in which at first we seem to confront a simple opposition between agitation and its soothing, its calming down. But the calming down will itself depend on the variety of forms the agitation can take—noble-heroic, neurotic, anticipatory, anxiety-laden, foreboding, euphoric, rhetorically operatic, declamatory, sublime or pathologically sublime, morbid, manic, jolly, frivolous-ceremonial, etc. Each of these must be momentarily subdued according to its dynamic, while the mode of calm—always ephemeral—will itself be dissolved into a new kind of agitation. Temporality is agitation in its very nature, it cannot remain in a state of tranquility for long, the latter always evolves back into a new form of agitation. This is why the whole does not simply resolve itself into a series of variations, why the sonata form does not explain this dynamic, whose fundamental formal question is how this restless alternation from high to low, from somber to ethereal, can possibly be concluded, and on what key. (And as for Mahler, it will be remembered that Freud's diagnosis of him was based on the composer's childhood memory of turmoil at the parents' violent quarrels, when, shutting himself in the bathroom, at one and the same time he heard the inescapable sound of the hurdy-gurdy in the streets.)

We may then juxtapose two evaluations of this libidinal restlessness at its two extremes: one a Utopian anticipation and the other a clinical diagnosis. At the one pole lies Fourier's inclusion of the "butterfly passion" as one of the three fundamental drives in human nature, whose harmonious combination is bound to ground the institutions of a Utopian society. The butterfly passion is the incessant movement from one interest to another, from one activity to another. Let Roland Barthes be the spokesperson for the Utopian dimensions and uses of this existential distraction:

> La Variante (ou Alternante, ou Papillonne) est un besoin de variété périodique (changer d'occupation, de plaisir, toutes les deux heures); c'est, si l'on veut, la disposition du sujet qui n'investit pas d'une façon stable dans le «bon objet»: passion dont la figure mythique serait don Juan: individus qui changent sans cesse de métiers, de manies, d'amours, de désirs, dragueurs impénitents, infidèles, renégats, sujets à «humeurs», etc.: passion méprisée en Civilisation, mais que Fourier place très haut: c'est elle qui permet de parcourir rapidement beaucoup de passions à la fois, et telle une main agile sur un clavier multiple, de faire vibrer *harmonieusement* (c'est le cas de le dire) la grande âme intégrale; agent de transition universelle, elle anime ce genre de bonheur attribué aux sybarites parisiens, *l'art de vivre si bien et si vite, la variété et l'enchaînement des plaisirs*, la rapidité du mouvement (on se rappelle que pour Fourier le mode de vie de la classe possédante est le modèle même du bonheur).

> The Variating (or Alternating or Butterfly) is a need for periodic variety (changing occupation or pleasure every two hours); we might say that it is the disposition of the subject who does not devote himself to the "good object" in a stable manner: a passion whose mythical prototype is Don Juan: individuals who constantly change occupation, manias, affections, desires, "cruisers" who are incorrigible, unfaithful, renegade, subject to "moods," etc.: a passion disdained in Civilization, but one Fourier places very high: the one that permits ranging through many passions at once, and like an agile hand on a multiple keyboard, creating an *harmonious* (appropriately put) vibration throughout the integral soul; an agent of universal transition, it animates that type of happiness that is attributed to Parisian sybarites, *the art of living well and fast, the variety and interconnection of*

pleasures, rapidity of movement (we recall that for Fourier the mode of life of the possessing class is the very model of happiness).[10]

The clinical version of all this is that syndrome named Attention Deficit Disorder, whose symptoms are well-known[11]: it is by now well-known that naming a cluster of features of this kind is also a construction of the disease itself, which is to say, the bringing into being of a new disease that did not really exist as such before the name. In an age of self-diagnosis, the name then functions to alert the subject to further introspection and as a consequence to the "discovery" of new and richer evidence for its existence. The semiotics of the process, and the critique of the medical clinic they imply, are of relevance only insofar as they complete a dialectical union of opposites with the productivity of a subject unaware of the reifying medical designation, and particularly of the negative symptomatology of frequent bouts of boredom and loss of interest with which such a subject's "stream of consciousness" is bound to have been plagued.

In the case of Tolstoy, it is not merely the self-doubt and the evanescence of whole projects and commitments (the abandonment of the early works in mid-course, the very turn away from literature itself) which are noteworthy, but also features that might at first glance seem to be positive: in particular the multiplicity of characters in *War and Peace* and also the brevity of its multiple chapters and episodes (we may well wish to recall here Nietzsche's extraordinary characterization of Wagner as a miniaturist[12]). Are these not also marks of Tolstoy's

---

[10]   Roland Barthes, *Sade, Fourier, Loyola,* Paris: Seuil, 1980, 106–7. The English translation is by R. Miller, Berkeley: University of California Press, 1989, 101.

[11]   As seems customary in the DSM, fourteen characteristics form the criteria for an official clinical diagnosis, any of which suffice. I quote three that seem characteristic: "stimuli extraneous to the task at hand are easily distracting; holding attention to a single task or play activity is difficult; frequently will hop from one activity to another, without completing the first." Thom Hartmann, *Attention Deficit Disorder: A Different Perception,* Grass Valley, CA: Underwood Books, 1997, 11. The reader may not find it so difficult to square this description with a "characteristic" portrait of Prince Andrew: "As he said this Prince Andrew was less than ever like that Bolkónski who had lolled in Anna Pávlovna's easy chairs and with half-closed eyes had uttered French phrases between his teeth. Every muscle of his thin face was now quivering with nervous excitement; his eyes, in which the fire of life had seemed extinguished, now flashed with brilliant light. It was evident that the more lifeless he seemed at ordinary times, the more impassioned he became in these moments of almost morbid irritation." (28)

[12]   Friedrich Nietzsche, *The Case of Wagner,* chapter 7, *Basic Writings,* New York:

mercurial temperament, of his need for constant distraction and variation, of his impatience with this or that individual character and his subsequent interest in passing to another one, for the moment more absorbing? The multiplicity of characters, then, the variety of the fictive personages (and their situations), which attract Tolstoy's attention in turn—this as it were external variety is the exact correlative of his subjective mood swings, or what I have called the continuum of affect we have been able to observe within the individual scenes and attributed to each of the individual characters. It is also, of course, the opposite pole of that structural tension we are here in the process of attributing to realism itself and to its construction. The expansion and deployment of affect in a range of moods is what makes for the presence of the scene, the timeless or existential consciousness at one with its showing (and its reading); while the multiplicity of the characters—each one with a name and a potential story or destiny, and all somehow defined and marked by that truly external destiny which is war and History itself—these make up the telling as such, the time continuum, the past-present-future of the *fabula* (as opposed to the *syujet*) of the realist novel.

But now we need to invent some closer approach to Tolstoy's production of his characters. (That he is on his way to a thoroughgoing effacement of protagonists in favor of secondary characters as such is also a premise of this account, as we shall see in the next chapter. But it is the *how* of this transformation which now requires its own theorization.) We may first observe the physical externality of his characterization, even in the ostensible protagonists, Pierre and Natasha, (or perhaps I should say especially in them). We should first recall Eikhenbaum's analysis of the Tolstoyan portrait as a virtually fixed form (inherited from the eighteenth century, another source of kinship with Stendhal): it requires the treatment of three topics—psychology, speech and appearance[13]—in a rather mechanical procedure which would seem to have little in common with the introspective registration of affect on which we have commented in the discussion of Prince Andrew. All these attributes of a character would seem to objectify such a figure and indeed to reify it to the point where we would expect it to remain fixed in externality and radically distinct from any first or third "point of view." To be sure, Lacan's

---

Modern Library, 2000, 627.
[13] Eikhenbaum, *The Young Tolstoi*, 37.

"*trait unaire*" (Dolokhov's blue eyes, Natasha's childish gleefulness, the "little princess'" upper lip, Pierre's spectacles—Nikolai and Boris are in this respect far less distinct) can furnish one bridge between the physiognomic description and the inner state. But for the most part these descriptions seem merely to underscore the arbitrariness of the corporeal; or better still, its contingency. The trick to description is, of course, not to lock the character so firmly into any single physiognomy that the reader might be unable or unwilling to accept. The acceptance will generally stand or fall on the way in which the external description harmonizes with the "inner" character of the personage in what is essentially a symbolic or metaphoric process.

(Meanwhile, it seems possible that what stunned Tolstoy about the writing of his young peasant pupils was the unerring precision with which the children isolated a single "trait"—physiological or linguistic, a habit or a sudden interjection—to characterize their imaginary figures.)[14]

Yet Jakobson famously observed that Tolstoy had moved from a metaphoric to a metonymic mode of character portrayal; while Eikhenbaum insists on the essential fragmentation of Tolstoy's portraits: commenting on a remark of the novelist ("it seems to me that to actually describe a man is impossible"), Eikhenbaum suggests that for Tolstoy "a portrait should be composed of separate, concrete features, and not of general attributes ... the bearers of separate human qualities and features which are for the most part combined paradoxically."[15] This is why Tolstoy gradually develops a method whereby he shows his character thinking or saying one thing, while physically absorbed in doing something else, something unrelated (brushing his uniform, lighting a match, watching a dog in the yard). We must consequently posit the Tolstoyan character not as some organic unity, but as a heterogeneity, a mosaic of fragments and differences held together by a body and a name (that is to say, a past, a unique destiny, a specific story).[16]

---

[14] "Should we teach the peasant children to write, or should they teach us?" Leo Tolstoy, in Alan Pinch and Michael Armstrong, eds., *Tolstoy on Education*, London: Athlone Press, 1982, 222–70.

[15] Eikhenbaum, *The Young Tolstoi*, 34.

[16] It is regrettable that so knowledgeable and subtly intuitive a critic of Tolstoy as Boris Eikhenbaum, on whom any student of Tolstoy must rely as massively as I have here, should have found the character of Natasha improbable and unconvincing as she passes from adolescence to the matronliness of the epilogue. (In addition, he calls "the domestic, family part of Tolstoy's novel ... principled, tendentious," *Tolstoi in the*

The strong form of such a presentation (which is also a whole novelistic conception of the phenomenology of individual identity) appears
when these unrelated traits enter into opposition with each other: this
seems to be what Eikhenbaum means by his expression "combined
paradoxically," but which I will be so bold as to call a contradiction. Here is Prince Vassili calling his two sons fools ("a quiet one"
and "an active one"): "He said this smiling in a way more unnatural
and animated than usual, so that the wrinkles round his mouth very
clearly revealed something unexpectedly coarse and unpleasant."[17]
And here is one of the sons in question: "Le charmant Hippolyte
was surprising by his extraordinary resemblance to his beautiful sister,
but yet more by the fact that in spite of this resemblance he was
exceedingly ugly."[18]

But this does not yet get us to the heart of Tolstoy's relationship to
his characters and in particular to their multiplicity, which almost,
but not quite, effaces the very category of protagonicity as such, to
the distress of many of its early readers; others simply thought many
of the characters were trivial and uninteresting—unworthy of the
novelist's attention. It is to that attention that we must now turn,
remembering that from another perspective it was precisely Tolstoy's
moody loss of attention to this or that character which made for the
rapid crosscutting from one to the other (what Eikhenbaum calls
"parallelism") in the first place.

I will describe this novelistic attention as a kind of "narcissism of
the other," which momentarily fulfills the commandment to "treat
thy neighbor as thyself." The healthy self (but we need not enter on
the long tradition for which it is the health and vitality of Tolstoy
which is extolled all above all[19]) necessarily includes a "healthy" dose

---

Sixties, 149). Here the biographical method leads him astray, since he finds different models concealed under each of these stages, whose unexpected transformations
Proust will later foreground as one of his fundamental themes and effects. Yet these
characterological changes over time reveal the same phenomenon of dissonance to be
found in individual scenes, and betray the deeper impersonality Tolstoy has discovered
beneath the surface variability of character, temperament and indeed mood and affect.

17 *War and Peace*, 6.

18 Ibid., 12.

19 See especially Thomas Mann, "Dostoevsky—in Moderation," in *The Short Novels of
Dostoevsky*, New York: Dial, 1945, vii: "the divine and the fortunate, the children
of nature in their exalted simplicity and their exuberant healthfulness" (referring
to Goethe and Tolstoy, whom he had contrasted with the debility and sickness of
Nietzsche and Dostoyevsky in a earlier essay).

of narcissism which dictates the conferral of special privileges on itself (to the point of *mauvaise foi*), and which motivates a permanent fascination with all kinds of features of ourselves not necessarily fascinating or even attractive to other people. This is the conatus of the biological individual, what keeps it interested in life, in survival, in the satisfaction of its desires and even of its whims: Agamben's "bare life" appears at the moment in which this narcissism is extinguished and the organism survives itself.

I believe that Tolstoy's attention to his characters, his interest in them, can best be described as a kind of momentary transfer of narcissism to these external beings, whose vitality fascinates him for the briefest of periods, so that whether it is the youthful delight of Natasha or the cold vindictiveness of Dolokhov (this last unexpectedly entering into contradiction with his love for his mother and his family)—on each of these manifestations, as on so many others, Tolstoy's own narcissism warms itself for a moment. The description is not complete unless we specify repulsion as another form of this well-nigh carnal fascination: for antipathy or repugnance (very much also including indifference) are also modes in which the rapt mesmerization with the other can be expressed.

This is the sense in which there are no villains in Tolstoy (another feature of the great realists to be discussed later on): for categories of good and evil are, as we shall see, survivals of those melodramatic forms and stereotypes that realism must necessarily overcome. Even Napoleon, the supreme object of Tolstoy's censure in *War and Peace*, and perhaps the character who less than any other profits from Tolstoy's secret indulgences, is the object of a visceral loathing and not any disinterested Kantian moral judgement. Yet we must here add in a qualification: part of the negative judgement on Napoleon is a judgement on society and on its glamorization of him, a judgement on a collective hero-worship akin to vanity and social ambition on the individual level. And it is certain that the fascination with characters like Prince Vassili (whose social status and influence is as subject to judgement and disapproval as his more materialist schemes and ambitions) must necessarily be transmuted by that ideological and Rousseauian ideology of nature and of the condemnation of society and its artificiality which was one of Tolstoy's "philosophical" messages and motivations in writing *War and Peace*. Repulsion is thus a form of fascination like any other; and Tolstoy distinguishes himself from Stendhal by a novelistic practice in which, in the latter, characters deadened by their identification with society and the social—characters distinguished by "*la sécheresse du coeur*"—are handled differently from protagonists who still retain a possibility of spontaneity and authenticity.

Perhaps a somewhat different model can be adduced for this peculiar dynamism: in *The Transmission of Affect*, Teresa Brennan finds telling evidence for her theme in an anecdote related by Montaigne in which an old man draws vitality from the mere presence of the young Montaigne, "feasting his senses on my flourishing state of health."[20] His conclusion—that the younger man would thereby "find his energy depleted"—is less relevant than the phenomenon itself, which suggests a kind of affective contagion, a glowing enlargement of affect well beyond the natural limits and boundaries of the individual subject, a kind of "transmission," to use Brennan's term, susceptible of modifying our current conceptions of intersubjectivity and indeed of subjectivity itself as some purely inward, private and psychological matter. This is, at any rate, the kind of reenergizing force I attribute to that relationship which is Tolstoy's fascination with his own characters.

That he himself is aware of it can then be documented by its return in the very content of the narrative as an affective phenomenon in its own right. Thus, for example, the first appearance of the "little princess" (Prince Andrew's wife Lise), whose radiating power is not merely to be attributed to sensual beauty (indeed the passage in question is preceded by the evocation of the "defect" of the *trait unaire* we have mentioned above):

> Everyone brightened at the sight of this pretty young woman, so soon to become a mother, so full of life and health, and carrying her burden so lightly. Old men and dull dispirited young ones who looked at her, after being in her company and talking to her a little while, felt as if they too were becoming, like her, full of life and health. All who talked to her, and at each word saw her bright smile and the constant gleam of her white teeth, thought that they were in a specially amiable mood that day.[21]

---

[20] Teresa Brennan, *The Transmission of Affect*, Ithaca: Cornell, 2004, 16; in the same way, perhaps, the ageing Goethe found renewal in the mere existence of the youthful, rebellious Byron, the path not taken.

[21] *War and Peace*, 8.

Thus we have come full circle, and from the homology between the affective continuum and the multiplicity of characters we return to the ways in which that multiplicity itself feeds the power of affect in both content and form, and in which both these developments enrich the scene of narrative consciousness and the destinies and continuities of past/present/future to the point of straining realism to its limits, to a threat of its ultimate dissolution, just as they strain the very limits of the individual subject itself and "personal identity."

Perhaps, indeed, in the light of what has been argued here, it might be time to invent a different way of reading Tolstoy, something more intimate to substitute (at least for a time) for the orchestral interludes of the epic with which he is stereotypically associated. But as a recorder of war, Tolstoy was perhaps more original in his late novella *Hadji Murad*, which deals with the guerrilla warfare he himself experienced in what is today Chechnya. As a modern war novel, *La débâcle* is surely a greater accomplishment than *War and Peace*, the military parts of which in any case spring from Stendhal's Waterloo episode, something Tolstoy himself would readily admit.

It is when we come to affect, whether registered in solitude or in interpersonal relationships, that Tolstoy is surely unequaled. And perhaps, if it is true that La Rochefoucauld's maxims are in reality miniature novels, we might want to invert this "genre," not for purposes of literary classification, but for new models of singularity. At any rate, such notations[22] cannot but have their effects on older

---

[22] I cannot resist quoting a miniaturist evocation of affect in Natasha's attraction to Karagin (or better still, her feeling of his attraction to her): *War and Peace*, 624–25:

"And do you know, Countess," he said, suddenly addressing her as an old, familiar acquaintance, "we are getting up a costume tournament, you ought to take part in it! It will be great fun! We shall all meet at the Karagins'! Please come! No! Really, eh?" said he.

While saying this, he never removed his smiling eyes from her face, her neck, and her bare arms. Natasha knew for certain that he was enraptured by her. This pleased her, yet his presence made her feel constrained and oppressed. When she was not looking at him, she felt that he was looking at her shoulders, and she involuntarily caught his eye so that he should look into hers rather than this. But looking into his eyes she was frightened, realizing that there was not that barrier of modesty she had always felt between herself and other men. She did not know how it was that within five minutes she had come to feel herself terribly near to this man. When she turned away she feared he might seize her from behind by her bare arm and kiss her on the neck. They spoke of most ordinary things, yet she felt that they were closer to one another than she had ever been to any man. Natasha kept turning to Helene and to her father, as if asking what it all meant, but Helene was engaged in conversation with a general and did not answer her look, and her father's eyes said nothing but what they always said: "Having a good time? Well, I'm glad of it!"

categories of character and of narrated interaction; and it is now to one such body of work, as saturated with named characters as Tolstoy, yet characters as distinctive in their development and as full of consequences for the evolution of realism as such, that we now turn.

Chapter V

Pérez Galdós, or, the Waning of Protagonicity

If Zola is the Wagner of nineteenth-century realism (and George Eliot perhaps its Brahms), then Benito Pérez Galdós is its Shakespeare, or at least the Shakespeare of the late comedies and romances. The absence of Galdós from the conventional nineteenth-century list of the "great realists"—even one limited to Europe—is more than a crime, it is an error which seriously limits and deforms our picture of this discourse and its possibilities. Coming at the end of the tradition, he enjoyed the great good fortune of the historical conjuncture, not only arriving at the moment when everything remained to be said about the belatedly nascent bourgeois world of nineteenth-century Spain and of Madrid as the last great European metropolis; he also inherited fully developed all those novelistic innovations and instruments of representation which, since Balzac, a century of novelists had worked to perfection. In addition, an immense series of historical novels—the *Episodios nacionales*—is superadded to the prodigious *Novelas contemporaneos* which from the maturity of 1880 on rivalize with *La Comédie humaine* or the Rougon-Macquart.

Galdós's Madrid is as full of mystery as Balzac's Paris, and the former's receptivity is as open to all the levels of social life as it is to all the intellectual currents of the last decades of the century. Full of curiosity about servants and of sympathy with women of all classes (he was a life-long bachelor, one of those characteristic practioners of what Jean Borie once called *"la littérature des célibataires"*[1]), as exploratory of the lower depths as Dickens, as sympathetic to his ambitious young men but with more indulgence for the slackers than Balzac himself, as alert to the vibrations of civil war and political tension as Stendhal, as ironic as Thomas Mann, as gossipy as Proust, as familiar

---

[1] Jean Borie, *Le Célibataire français*, Paris: Le Saegittaire, 1976.

with the urban terrain and the streets of the city as Joyce, as prolific as Trollope, he felt the energizing influences of French naturalism and Russian spirituality as enlargements of his outsider's view (he came to Madrid from the Canary Islands) of the prosperity of bourgeois Spain, whose 1867 revolution avoided the convulsions of Italian or German reunification as well as the militant nationalisms of Eastern Europe, well before 1898 casts a grim shadow over Spanish destiny. Like Dostoyevsky, his vocation was awakened by a reading of *Eugénie Grandet*; he was the Spanish translator of *Pickwick Papers*, and later on, in his final blindness, became a senator for the nascent Socialist Party; nor is his worldly-wise moralizing without its distant family likeness to George Eliot's sententiousness.

My argument will turn on a rather different form of the tension between the two temporalities—between plot and consciousness, or telling and showing—than what we were able to perceive in the emergence of affect. Now it will be a matter of the character system as such, organized around the prodigious Balzacian "method" of the "*retour des personnages*," at the point at which Galdós (like Faulkner later on) realized that he had a whole novelistic world to administer, and not just one or two local episodes to record. Yet what I will show is that the effects of this serial organization in Galdós are quite different from the consequences in *La Comédie humaine*, where in principle even the most minor characters have the right to become protagonists of their own separate novels. Here in Galdós, on the contrary, we will witness what I will call a deterioration of protagonicity, a movement of the putative heroes and heroines to the background, whose foreground is increasingly occupied by minor or secondary characters whose stories (and "destinies") might once have been digressions but now colonize and appropriate the novel for themselves. Clearly any discussion of secondary characters will want to rely on one of the most important contributions to the study of the novel in recent years, namely Alex Woloch's *The One vs. the Many*;[2] in effect, I want to historicize his findings in what follows, and assert a historical trend in the relationship of these groups to each other, or in other words a structural modification of the character system which is necessarily an integral part of narrative as such (and which can also know individual reconfigurations at the hands of stylistically original novelists as well, as distinguished from the momentous structural trend I have in mind here).

---

[2] Alex Woloch, *The One vs. the Many*, Princeton: Princeton University Press, 2003.

But let's begin with a collection of the many: they are lodged in an enormous building near the very center of Madrid, a palace with 2800 rooms (Versailles only has 700), which houses the Queen, to be sure—Isabela II—but also offers private apartments and rooms for hangers-on of the court, ranging from the middle bourgeoisie to aristocratic and royal relatives of various conditions. This fascinating social space, although immensely larger and more various, might well have demanded comparison with Zola's apartment building in *Pot-Bouille*, save that here Galdós's line of sight will be trained on a single habitation alone: it is the suite of a rather scatter-brained woman who thinks she is distinguished and has a mania for consumption, especially clothes and expensive finery. She is married to an uptight bureaucrat with a hobby, who is extremely miserly, intent on avoiding not merely unnecessary expense but also, if possible, even the necessary kind: and yet the hobby is a curious, artisanal one, the weaving of pictures out of human hair (evidently a recognized artistic activity in the nineteenth century, about which one would be curious to learn more[3]—Galdós does not often insert such handicraft figures, allegorical or not, into his cast of characters). At any rate, this is an eccentricity of the type associated with the Great Detectives of the period; and it is characteristic of the distinguishing traits that mark secondary characters off from protagonists, reminding us of Woloch's extraordinary observation: "two existential states lie behind the two pervasive extremes of minorness within the nineteenth-century novel: the *worker* and the *eccentric*, the flat character who is reduced to a single functional use within the narrative, and the fragmentary character who plays a disruptive, oppositional role within the plot."[4] Bringas's thrift is functional, and required in order to bring the catastrophe of debt to a climax; his eccentricity however marks him as an individuality in his own right, but a constitutively minor individuality of no particular interest to us.

The Bringas wife, however (the novel is entitled *La de Bringas* [1884]), is for all intents and purposes the protagonist of this novel: through her point of view and her drama we are allowed to meet a steady stream of minor figures, from a complacent princess, through various friends and would-be yet curiously half-hearted suitors, along with the usual maids and clerks, arriving finally at the infamous usurer,

---

3   See on this curious art form, which is the "hair picture" the translator's introduction to *That Bringas Woman*, trans. Catherine Jagoe, London: J. M. Dent, 1996, xxi–xxii.

4   Woloch, *The One vs. The Many*, 25.

Torquemada, into whose hands she ultimately falls, and to whom, as we shall see, Galdós devoted no less than four novels in his own right. Throughout this increasingly desperate quest, we are subjected mercilessly to the inner monologue of this stupid woman, whom Galdós ventriloquizes with a wit that makes this intolerable stream of language delicious for the reader. It must be observed that, like all the great realists, Galdós is a great mimic, not only coining the unique accents of authentic dialogue, but also inventing the tonality in which the thoughts of his characters are to be noted, as in a musical score.

One of the features, indeed, that distinguishes Galdós (and many of the other late-nineteenth century novelists) from the novelizing pioneers of the early century is the sharpness, the spirit and wit, of their characters' dialogue. In part, clearly this results from the imperceptible shift in the reader's attention from the plot line to the immediacy of the characters' encounters with each other; but also from the attention to the sound and timbre of the spoken voice, reflected in the attempts to capture accent and dialect (as in early George Eliot), and that heightened value attached to the personal intonation as such, to the unique sound which is henceforth, in the realm of affect, the sound of the individual body. The transmission of information about plot development is no longer the principal function of the voice here, but rather its qualities in the present of time.

Plays are not prose, Gore Vidal once observed: the implication is that dialogue, to be sure not poetic in any bad or regressive sense, now has a substance and density of its own, distinct from the surrounding fabric of the prose context. Joyce meanwhile proudly and wistfully described the characters of *Ulysses* as "the last of the great talkers." Something of that is also involved in this promotion of speech and its registration: and in the case of Galdós it is clear—his characters are talkers par excellence, they love to talk, and not only to gossip, but to express themselves volubly on the occasion not merely of every feeling, but of every *acontecimiento*, which is to say that it is their speech that transforms every moment into an event. Nothing is too minor to pass without the exercise of fulsome opinion; and the delight of Galdós's novels is this inexhaustibility of the spoken word (even in inner monologue) called forth by the new primacy of affect in the realm of voices and their bodies.[5]

---

[5] It should be noted that in his old age Galdós wrote a number of "novels" (which cannot strictly be called plays) exclusively in dialogue.

But I hazard the guess that such mimicry essentially holds—in all the like-minded novelists with whom we have here to do—for minor characters rather than protagonists: the language of protagonists is the language of poetic drama or of tragedy, expressiveness which demands a stage and a public, as in Corneille or in opera: otherwise the reader's empathy and identification (whatever those are) is enough to motivate us to lose ourselves in the protagonist (if that is what we do). Their inner life must not be marked or personalized; they must not be allowed to become other to us or to be visible from the outside. It is our old friend the impersonal consciousness, the eternal present of an anonymous and purely formal awareness without content, that is required for them.

But in the world of secondary characters irony is back in place: the movement out of point of view to the observer of otherness and back, the paradoxical combination of outer and inner distance which brings the external judgement of the récit to bear on the internal experience of the temporal present. To be sure, the novel is generally a combination of both perspectives, and as such irony is always structurally possible (as most often in the *Bildungsroman*, where it plays on the naïveté of the inexperienced protagonist); but it is wrong to erect irony into the fundamental building block of the form as such, as Henry James tried to do. Yet the perspective seems to demand some further engagement on the part of the novelist, as Wayne Booth famously demonstrated—some ultimate judgement, which can range from savage to indulgent but which in Galdós takes the form of a permissiveness which can intensify into a glacial indifference, as the character who is its object inevitably destroys herself.

The point I have wanted to make here, but have only presupposed, is that in fact "the Bringas woman" is not a protagonist at all: she is preeminently a minor character who has unaccountably been allowed to become the center of a novel in her own right.[6] That novel is not a récit, but one might well imagine it as one, in the form of the gossip retailed by other characters in other novels of the series. Can we somehow allegorize the subject of such a narrative, and parlay debt, mindless consumerism and prodigality into obsession and punishment, as Balzac often did? In other words, can we endow a story like this with the kind of significance hitherto reserved for real protagonists, thereby also redeeming author and form as well, and restoring

---

[6]   She also figures in the earlier novel *Tormento* (1884).

their dignity and status?[7] I suppose that such narrative exercises are receivable in the context of an enormous literary production, in which each stands as yet another virtuoso performance by its now famous maker. Yet under normal circumstances, this kind of reaction would make sense only when a lighter or more occasional product of this kind stands side by side with the truly central or major productions with which we compare it: the narrative masterpieces for which this episode can in a pinch be seen as a preparation and warming up. The problem is that there are no major novels in Galdós's immense corpus.

I'm aware that this is a scandalous thing to say, about one of the country's great classics (but there is always Cervantes, after all, whose ethos is of course as omnipresent in Galdós as in so much else of the Spanish tradition). Meanwhile, one risks the appearance of true ignorance, given the existence of *Fortunata y Jacinta*, Galdós's longest novel and for many his masterpiece; but as Stephen Gilman has observed (and he is everywhere acknowledged as one of the fundamental authorities on the subject), *Fortunata y Jacinta* is in fact not one novel but four[8]; which brings each down to the standard length of what one does not want to call a novella in Galdós's production. Still, as the very title suggests, this one certainly seems to have protagonists, and it will be in order for us to test our hypothesis against so monumental a text.

It is the story of a happy marriage, a "marriage made in heaven," as they say, which only faces two seemingly minor problems to overcome before it can fade into that non-narrative state Tolstoy's famous dictum seems to foretell. On the one hand, the perfect wife, Jacinta, cannot bear children; on the other, the perhaps less than perfect husband, Juanito, without being at all dissatisfied with his wife, also knows a second love—or perhaps it is better to call it *amour*—with a lower-class girl (Fortunata) who does in fact bear him a son. The novel will then, after many peripeties, be resolved with the predictable return to equilibrium achieved by a swap: Jacinta will receive Fortunata's child as her own, and Fortunata will become a kind of saint and go to heaven.

But is there any point in telling this immemorial story again, or rehearsing its now structuralist restoration of order? The fatal

---

[7] Does transforming it into a sociological example do so? On Rosalia's temperament as a cultural trait, see Maurice Vallis, *The Culture of Cursileria*, Durham: Duke University Press, 2003; I am indebted to Stephanie Sieburth for this reference.

[8] Stephen Gilman, *Galdós and the Art of the European Novel, 1867–1887*, Princeton: Princeton University Press, 1981.

encounter of the upper-class male with the lower-class female is to be sure always full of sociological promise: but Galdós's sympathy with women is omnipresent and dispenses him from the suspicion of patriarchal bias. What is more significant from the standpoint of plot construction is its gradual withdrawal from the conventional drama of the love triangle (or the novel of adultery). The only way, indeed, for the young Santa Cruz family to know any kind of story or récit is by way of the accident of barrenness; their marriage is quickly dispatched in the opening pages, and both recede, leaving the foreground to Jacinta and her milieu.

Meanwhile, these pages are crowded with minor characters of all kinds; numerous family acquaintances and schoolchums of Juanito, for example, the latter giving rise to any number of Galdósian novels in their own right, the former providing at least one stellar figure, the notable philanthropist and founder of a monumental hospice for fallen women, Guillermina; and later on, Jacinta's husband, the unfortunate Max, along with his aunt the usurer (and friend of Torquemada) and his brother the priest; Max's employer (he is a pharmacist); Fortunata's erstwhile partner in crime, the frightening Mauricia la dura, and her more respectable counselor, Feijoo; and many more, not excluding the narrator himself, who turns out to be yet another distant acquaintance of Juanito. The prestidigitation whereby the formerly "omniscient narrator" is transformed, by a touch of the magic wand, into yet another minor character (not unlike the one who appears for the first and last time on the first page of *Madame Bovary*)—nothing is more appropriately emblematic for our purposes here: Henry James—himself just such a minor character in real life, a listener and observer, a voyeur and a gossip, the eager recipient of hearsay and tall tales of all kinds (preferably usable ones!)—would have been indignant at being assigned so humiliating a position.

The reader will have suspected that we are moving towards a momentous assertion, namely that Fortunata is herself a minor character! In spite of the disproportionate attention she receives in this novel (about which on the contrary it might equally be asserted that she herself becomes the protagonist, consigning both Jacinta and Juanito to minor roles in the wings), there cling to her the marks and scars of the protagonist of the récit: we are interested in the development of her consciousness (as so many moralizing interpreters have been), but from the outside, as one of Guillermina's cases, and not as the true center of consciousness. The "other woman" is always a secondary character: in the novel of adultery it is the wife (guilty or offended) who seizes protagonicity from the husband, the male lead. She is able to combine the récit-like destiny of the victim with the central consciousness of the primary figure, thereby (for a time) winning that possibility of authenticity on which we have already commented. But the object of the husband's infidelity (or of her own) is a mere pretext, and the extraordinary attention she receives here has no ready-made paradigm to house it, so that indeed Fortunata's story passes through any number of generic discontinuities on her way to beatitude (yet another narrative paradigm!).

Can we speak, in so illustrious a case as this, of narrative digression? What is clear is that Galdós is easily distracted by his minor characters, in that very much like Tolstoy; and we are tempted to apply to him the same characterization we offered of the Russian novelist —that of a "narcissism of the other"—save that Galdós is already so selfless as to problematize the idea of narcissism itself. Perhaps it might be better to wonder whether he does not seize a chance to live himself in each of his characters, major or minor, and thereby, like "*el amigo Manso*," to populate a somehow posthumous life.

At any rate, as far as the formal developments are concerned, some obvious sociological contexts can be mentioned. We can for example float the hypothesis that Galdós's content, the social raw material at his disposal, strikes an uneasy compromise between the atomized individualism of more fully bourgeois societies with their nuclear families, and the more archaic traces of the older feudal clans and castes.

The population of Galdós's novels is indeed organized into households, an ambiguous category which does not preserve the blood jealousies of the older clans but yet is not technically purely familial either, in the sense of some later extended family. Rather, these households very much include servants,[9] often the first approach of bourgeois novelists to the lower classes; they include the other families who circulate in their orbit, sometimes somewhat subordinate in their gravity to the central family, in the case of *Fortunata y Jacinta*, the Santa Cruz family (and this distribution of social weight includes the partnership of the two families of husband and wife); they touch on the less often seen "connections," of a political and a social type;

---

9 See Bruce Robbins, *The Servant's Hand*, Durham: Duke University Press, 1993.

and finally on those characters I will categorize under the rubric of the "friend of the family," someone who is not related, yet sups at the table, performs all manner of favors and services, and often operates, with his handyman's know-how, as the fixer on a social rather than an odd-jobs level. So it is that at the very outset of this immense journey which is *Fortunata y Jacinta*, immediately after a summary account of the hero and his generational friends, the students, and then a sketch of the family itself, suddenly a single figure absorbs our attention in a brilliant and detailed portrait: it is Estupiñá, the "friend of the family." Introduced obliquely, we quickly receive his whole life-story and then, at the opening of a new chapter, are treated to this from the novelist: "When I personally met this illustrious child of Madrid he was on the brink of his seventieth birthday, but he carried his years very well."[10]

El llamado Estupiñá debía de ser indispensable en todas las tertulias de tiendas, porque cuando no iba a la de Arnáiz todo se volvía preguntas: «Y Plácido, ¿qué es de él?» Cuando entraba le recibían con exclamaciones de alegría, pues con su sola presencia animaba la conversación. En 1871 conocí a este hombre, que fundaba su vanidad en *haber visto toda la historia de España* en el presente siglo. Había venido al mundo en 1803, y se llamaba hermano de fecha de Mesonero Romanos, por haber nacido, como éste, el 19 de julio del citado año. Una sola frase suya probará su inmenso saber en esta historia viva que se aprende con los ojos: «Vi a José I como le estoy viendo a usted ahora.» Y parecía que se relamía de gusto cuando le preguntaban; «¿Vio usted al duque de Angulema, a lord Wellington?…» «Pues ya lo creo.» Su contestación era siempre la misma: «Como le estoy viendo a usted.» Hasta llegaba a incomodarse cuando se le interrogaba en tono dubitativo. «¡Que si vi entrar a María Cristina!… Hombre, si eso es de ayer…» Para completar su erudición ocular, hablaba del *aspecto que presentaba Madrid* el 1 de septiembre de 1840 como si fuera cosa de la semana pasada. Había visto morir a Canterac; ajusticiar a Merino, «nada menos que sobre el propio patíbulo», por ser él hermano de la Paz y Caridad; había visto matar a Chico…; precisamente ver no, pero oyó los tiritos, hallándose en la calle de las Velas; había visto a Fernando VII el 7 de julio cuando salió al balcón a decir a los milicianos que *sacudieran* a los de la Guardia; había visto a Rodil y al sargento García arengando desde otro balcón, el año 36; había visto a O'Donnell y Espartero abrazándose; a Espartero solo, saludando al pueblo; a O'Donnell solo; todo eso en un balcón; y por fin, en un balcón había visto también en fecha cercana a otro personaje diciendo a gritos que se habían acabado los Reyes. La historia que Estupiñá sabía estaba escrita en los balcones.

---

10 Benito Pérez Galdós, *Fortunata y Jacinta*, trans. Agnes Marcy Gullon, London: Penguin, 1986, 40.

La biografía mercantil de este hombre es tan curiosa como sencilla. Era muy joven cuando entró de hortera en case de Arnáiz; allí sirvió muchos años, siempre bien visto del principal por su honradez acrisolada y el grandísimo interés con que miraba todo lo concerniente al establecimiento. Y a pesar de tales prendas, Estupiñá no era un buen dependiente. Al despachar, entretenía demasiado a los parroquianos, y si le mandaban con un recado o comisión a la Aduana, tardaba tanto en volver, que muchas veces creyó D. Bonifacio que le halbían llevado preso. La singularidad de que teniendo Plácido estas mañas no pudieran los dueños de la tienda prescindir de él, se explica por la ciega confianza que inspiraba, pues estando él al cuidado de la tienda y de la caja, ya podían Arnáiz y su familia echarse a dormir. Era su fidelidad tan grande como su humildad, pues ya le podían reñir y decirle cuantas perrerías quisieran sin que se incomodase. Por esto sintió macho Arnáiz que Estupiñá dejara la casa en 1837, cuando se le antojó establecerse con los dineros de una pequeña herencia. Su principal, que le conocía bien, hacía lúgubres profecías del porvenir comercial de Plácido trabajando por su cuenta.

The man called Estupiñá must have been indispensable to the *tertulias* in all the shops, because when he didn't go to Arnáiz's somebody always asked, "What have you heard from Plácido?" When he appeared, they would receive him with happy exclamations; his mere presence enlivened the conversation. In 1871 I met this man whose vanity rested on his "having seen all of Spain's history" in the nineteenth century. He was born to the world in 1803, and dubbed himself Mesonero Romanos' "birth twin" because they were both born on July 19 of that year. A single sentence of his is enough to prove his immense knowledge of the kind of history one can learn simply by looking around: "I saw José I the same as I'm seeing you right now." And he seemed to lick his chops whenever he replied to a question like "Did you get to see the duke of Angulema and Lord Wellington?" "You bet I did." His answer never varied: "The same as I'm seeing you right now."

He was annoyed if someone interrogated him skeptically. "Did I actually *see* María Cristina when she arrived to marry the king? Why, that was just the other day!"

To substantiate his ocular erudition, he used to talk about "the way Madrid looked" on September 1, 1840, as if it had been a week ago. He had seen Canterac die and Merino being executed—"on his own scaffold, no less"—for being one of those Samaritans who comfort prisoners condemned to death. He had seen Chico (the chief of police) being killed; … well, not exactly seen him, but he'd heard the shots from where he was, on Velas Street. He had seen Fernando VII on July 7 when he appeared on the balcony to tell the militiamen to "shake up" the Royal Guard. He had seen Rodil and Sergeant Garcia haranguing from another balcony, back in '36. He had seen O'Donnell and Espartero when they embraced. And Espartero once, greeting the people. And O'Donnell doing the same; all on balconies. And finally, he had seen another historical character on a balcony not long ago, proclaiming in a high-pitched voice that it was all over for the kings. The history Estupiñá knew was written on the balconies of Madrid.

This man's business biography is as curious as it is simple. He was very young when he started out as a clerk at Atnáiz's. He served there many years, always highly regarded by the owner for his unfailing honesty and great interest in everything concerning the firm. Yet despite such virtues Estupiñá was not a good clerk. When he made a sale, he kept the customers too long, and when he was sent on an errand or a commission to the Customs House, it took him so long that in many instances Don Bonifacio thought he'd been put in jail. The reason why Plácido, even with all his shenanigans, was indispensable to the shop's owners was that he inspired blind trust. With him in charge of the shop and the cash register, Arnáiz and his family could forget about the business. Plácido's loyalty was as great as his modesty; they could scold him or insult him all they wanted—it didn't bother him a bit. That's why Arnáiz was very sorry when Estupiñá left in 1837; he'd inherited some money and gotten the idea of striking out on his own. His boss, who knew him well, made dire predictions about the commercial future awaiting Plácido once he was his own boss.[11]

Galdós goes on to launch into an account of Estupiñá's multiple daily activities and his busy trajectories about the city. There is no condescension towards this secondary or minor character: Spain is a far more socially egalitarian society than its "advanced" neighbors (except in the upper spheres of its emergent bourgeoisie)—and yet Estupiñá is there for reasons of plot, for it is through him that the young man we will continue for another moment to call the hero—Juanito Santa Cruz—will meet the second love of his love and the first-named eponymous heroine, Fortunata. I think that Galdós needed the accident and the pretext for this chance meeting, but that the richness of his imagination was such that he couldn't let it alone, that he compulsively elaborated the necessary link into this extraordinary family dependent (on whom the family truly itself depends) and in whom the deeper genius of Galdós's character elaboration is somehow allegorized, but on the strength of a quasi-familial household relationship. Estupiñá is a member of the family, and he merits all the sympathy and good will we are to bring to this family, from whom, however, we are also distant as from a zoological or biological exhibit arranged for us by Galdós's unique combination of tolerant affection and cold-blooded scientific observation. For Galdós, the most inveterate and archetypal of bachelors, is also a family man and the head of a household, however exasperating it may be: and his construction of his character systems reflect this profound structural dualism and

---

[11] Benito Pérez Galdós, *Fortunata y Jacinta*, Madrid: Casa Editorial Hernandez, 1968. Translation by Agnes Nancy Gullon, ibid., 34–35.

ambivalence. (In that, Estupiñá can be considered a kind of double of the author himself: but as we shall see, there are many kinds of these in Galdós.)

The evolution of the usurer Torquemada will now offer a virtual allegory of this process: the protagonist of four novels and a minor character in others, he is clearly a fundamental element in this realism in which money is a central fact of life, from inheritances to the condition of beggars, from the anxiety of debt to the frivolity of the spendthrift and the credulous admiration of the multitude for the wealthy.

But the paradox of this thematic centrality is this: that Torquemada remains a protagonist as long as he is technically a minor character; it is when he becomes a protagonist in his own novels that he loses this "protagonicity," if I may put it that way, and truly becomes a minor or flat character in fact, if not in name or appearance. Indeed, Galdós seems himself to have become aware of this strange evolution, for he interrupts the central panel of his Torquemada tetralogy to make the following lengthy digression:

> Zárate ... Pero ¿quién es este Zárate?
>
> Reconozcamos que en nuestra época de uniformidades ya de nivelación física y moral se han desgastado los tipos genéricos y que van desaparaciendo, en el lento ocaso del mundo antiguo, aquellos caracteres que representaban porciones grandísimas de la familia humana, clases, grupos, categorías morales. Los que han nacido antes de los últimos veinte años recuerdan perfectamente que antes existían, por ejemplo, el genuine tipo military, y todo campeón curtido en las guerras civiles se acusaba por su marcial facha, aunque de paisano se vistiese. Otros muchos tipos habia, *calvados*, como vulgarmente se dice, consagrados por especialísimas conformaciones del rostro humano y de los modales y del vestir. El avaro, pongo por caso, ofrecia rasgos y fisonomía como de casta, y no se le confundía con ninguna otra especie de hombres, y lo mismo puede decirse del *Don Juan*, ya fuse de los que pican alto, ya de los que se dedican a doncellas de server y amas decría. Y el beato tenía su cara y andares y ropa a las de ningún otro parecidas, y caracterización igual se observaba en los encargados de chupar sangre humana, prestamistas, vampiros, etcetera. Todo eso pasó, y apenas quedan ya tipos de clase, como no sean los toreros. En el scenario del mundo se va acabando el amaneramiento, lo que no deja de ser un bien para el arte, y ahora nadie sabe quién es nadie, como no lo estudie bien, familia por familia y persona por persona.
>
> Esta tendencia a la uniformidad, que se relaciona en cierto modo con lo mucho que la Humanidad se va despabilando, con los progresos de la industria y hasta con la baja de los aranceles, que ha generalizado y abaratado la buena ropa, nos ha traído una gran confusion en material de tipos.

Zárate? But who is this Zárate?

Let us recognize that in our time, a time of uniformity and a physical and moral leveling process, generic types have become outworn and that, in the slow twilight of the old world, those traits represented by large portions of the human family—classes, groups, moral categories—are gradually disappearing. Persons born more than twenty years ago, for instance, can remember perfectly that a real military type used to exist, and that every warrior who had been seasoned in the civil wars proclaimed his status by his martial appearance, even though he wore civilian clothes. There were many other types, "ringers for each other" as is popularly said, established by very particular conformations of the human countenance and by ways of behaving and dressing. The miser, for example, had the traits and facial characteristics of his caste and could not be confused with any other kind of man, and the same can be said of the "Don Juan" type, either those who aim high or those who expend their efforts on servant girls and nursemaids. And the exaggeratedly pious person had a face, and a way of walking, and clothing, that were like no others, and the same sort of characterization could be observed in those who sucked human blood, moneylenders, vampires, etc. All this is gone now, and scarcely any types are left who betray the class to which they belong, unless it be bullfighters. Mannerism is disappearing from the world scene, which is probably a good thing for art, and nowadays no one knows who anyone is except by studying the question carefully, family by family and person by person.

This tendency toward uniformity—connected to some degree by the great progress humanity is in process of achieving, with the progress of industry and even with the lowering of tariffs, which has made good clothing more common and cheaper—has caused great confusion in the matter of types. [12]

To be sure, Galdós will go on to propose new kinds of character types, emerging from the levelling democratization of the new bourgeois society and the symbolic integration of the older aristocracy. But it is rather with Torquemada that we can grasp this process more concretely (indeed, the character to whose presentation all this is a kind of introduction—Zárate—is himself something of the instrument of Torquemada's transformation). First, we must think back to the literary antecedents: without going as far back as Molière, we need only confront the larger-than-life usurer who is Balzac's Gobseck, with his terrifying yellow tiger's eyes (characteristically, Balzac transforms him into a source of wisdom).

The story of Galdós's Torquemada, however, comes closer to Molière's "*bourgeois gentilhomme,*" for among other things, the eponymous

---

[12] *Torquemada en el Purgatoria.* (1894) Benito Pérez Galdós, *Obras Completas*, tomo V Madrid: Aguilar, 1967, 1040. *Torquemada*, trans. F. M. López-Morillas, New York: Columbia University Press, 1986, 265–6.

novels show him learning cultivated language, dressing appropriately for his fortune and status in society, and inhabiting a mansion with his now noble family; indeed, the climax of the series is a ridiculously ornate speech which he delivers to the high society of Madrid. All of this Galdós characterizes as "the metamorphosis that has changed the very nature of metaphysical usury, rendering it positivistic."[13] And Casalduero quite rightly describes this change as the evolution from mercantilism (and value calculated in terms of gold) to finance capitalism in its fully developed senses, "from the figure of the usurer to that of the great modern financier."[14] But from our present perspective, this evolution is also an allegory of the evolution of the novel from the Balzacian system to the Galdósian, and from a network of novels in which, according to the famous *retour des personnages*, potentially any minor character can become a protagonist of a novel or tale in his own right, to the new Galdósian system in which even the protagonists are in reality minor characters, and their return as such reveals the new formal truth of their apparent "protagonicity."

(And what of Galdós's other villains if it comes to that? There remains the dissolute priest of *Tormento*, a source of universal harm, for example, and of trouble if there ever was one, under the guise of a voluble and seductive, self-pitying and unquenchably demanding suitor: he reminds me of Fyodor Karamazov in his sudden, unwanted and unexpected reappearances, but above all of the incomparable Jules Berry, in his ultimate role as the newspaper editor in Jean Renoir's epic of the Popular Front, *Le crime de M. Lange* [1936]. Here evil has been transformed into the appearance of evil, its sensory and theatrical attributes, its infinite gestuality: everything it might have meant and done in an older world like that of Balzac, it now shows in the present—"Essence must appear!" as someone once said; but only minor characters have essences!)

These formal developments in Galdós, coming at the end of the nineteenth century and at the climax of the development of its most characteristic form (along with opera), reflect two distinct and opposing trends or tendencies which miraculously complement each other.

---

[13] *Fortunata y Jacinta*, trans. Agnes Marcy Gullon, 8.

[14] Joaquín Casalduero, *Vida y Obra de Galdós*, Madrid: Gredos, 1970, 115; and see also Carlos Blanco Aguinaga, "De Vencedores y vencidos en la restauracion," in *De Restauracion a Restauracion*, Seville: Benacimiento, 2007, as well as the relevant pages of his *Historia social de la literatura espanola*, with Julio Rodríguez Puértolas and Iris M. Zavala, Madrid: Castalia, 1978.

On the one hand, with the nascent public sphere, there is an increasing fatigue with plot and with the standard narrative paradigms—that is to say, not merely with the chronicles of world-historical figures, but also with the destinies of protagonists generally in whatever form. The repertory of récits (freshened by music in the opera—all those adaptations of Sir Walter Scott's novels!) is no longer so attractive in the longer and longer narrative forms, where the experience of the everyday has begun to assert its claims on our interest and our attentions. The nineteenth century, indeed, may be characterized as the era of the triumph of everyday life, and of the hegemony of its categories everywhere, over the rarer and more exceptional moments of heroic deeds and "extreme situations." The end of Wagner's *Ring* is a virtual parable of the process: the protagonists—gods and heroes alike—all disappear, whether immolated in their conflagration or killed off by one another according to the logic of the curse they have brought upon themselves, leaving behind them nothing but the human world of all the others, the secondary characters and hitherto minor figures, who will now have to find some other form in which to tell their stories: "From the ruins of the fallen hall," Wagner tells us, "the men and women watch, moved to the very depths of their being, as the glow from the fire grows in the sky."[15]

At the same time, another tendency is at work in bourgeois society, and that is social equality. It would be remarkable if this trend, whose other face is what we call individualism, did not leave its traces on the form of the novel as well. And thus we find George Eliot interrupting herself as she patiently follows the events and reactions that define her protagonist Dorothea, and famously crying out:

> But why always Dorothea? Was her point of view the only possible one with regard to this marriage? I protest against all our interest, all our effort, at understanding being given to the young skins that look blooming in spite of trouble; for these too will get faded, and will know the other and more eating griefs which we are helping to neglect. In spite of the blinking eyes and white moles objectionable to Celia, and the want of muscular curve which was morally painful to Sir James, Mr. Casaubon had an intense consciousness within him, and was spiritually a-hungered like the rest of us.[16]

---

[15] Stewart Spencer and Barry Millington, *Wagner's Ring: A Companion*, London: Thames and Hudson, 1993, 351. Chéreau's centennial production at Bayreuth restores the sense of this ending, when, after the conflagration, the assembled townspeople turn and face the audience.

[16] George Eliot, *Middlemarch*, London: Penguin, 1994, 278 (chapter 29).

It will be objected that George Eliot is here merely seeking to reestablish the protagonicity of a figure hitherto minor and caricatured from the outside. But this attempt at justice and at equal rights for all her characters will not only be pursued further by Galdós, but will also take new and revealing forms in her own work, where they have to do with vocation and with success or failure. She, for whom novel writing was not a profession in the continental sense and for whom the sublime and unclassifiable role of the Poet had been replaced by that—not yet fully codified—of the literary intellectual, had a keen sense of vocation (the secularized version of the Protestant *Beruf* or "calling") which was quite different from the professionalism of a Zola, even though it addressed the same problem of the differentiation of society into new kinds of métiers. For she took the matter at its onset, in the very moment of the discovery of the vocation, which she daringly assimilated to passion and to the *coup de foudre*: "we are not afraid of telling over and over again how a man comes to fall in love with a woman."[17] This novelist's implicit boast is therefore that she will now expand the very conception of passion to include the lightning bolt of the vocation itself. In Balzac, such discoveries were the feverish dawn of the great obsessions and manias; in Zola, when successful, they are more akin to the first stirrings of the artist's creativity (as witness not only Octave's invention of the department store, comparable to Zola's own invention of the Rougon-Macquart project itself, but not excluding Saccard's speculative drives, both sinister and Utopian). Eliot's notion then cuts across the traditional epic alternative—love and war—but it also cuts across that of private and public, and in our own time, between science and the "humanities." Her subtle account, in chapter 15, of the complex preconditions for this concrete vocation (state of medicine, relationship to practice, provincial life, etc.) shows that the narrative category of the vocation can accommodate and organize all kinds of local and empirical narrative data as well.

Meanwhile, it also modifies what can be counted as the outcome of such a vocational destiny, already complicated in advance (as everywhere else) by the emergence of money as the unassimilable element. In Balzac, the alternative remained the simple one of success or failure: the former included fame and fortune ("*à nous deux, Paris!*"), the latter catastrophe, as in the case of poor Lucien (Rastignac, it will be

---

[17] Ibid., 144.

remembered, becomes prime minister). Zola perpetuates this tradition, where failure is accompanied by even greater and more explosive physical catastrophe (even though, in one of the most delicate of his political touches, we glimpse the shadow of the defeated and physically debilitated Napoleon III behind his bedroom curtain, on his way to exile);[18] while success—Octave again!—leads directly on into the wish fulfillments of the bestsellers.

(We may here open a parenthesis on the effacement of protagonicity implicit in Georg Lukács' discussion of "world-historical figures" in *The Historical Novel*: the discussion is in reality a contribution to historiographic debates of the period, in which Lukács was not himself involved and of which he may have had no particular knowledge, namely the crusade of the *Annales* school against the dynastic tradition of history writing and historical narrative, which was essentially a story of the kings and queens and the achievements of the great, that is to say individuals, who are grasped in our own spirit of the word as the protagonists of historical actions and narratives. As is well known, he believes that such figures must always be seen from the outside and in the distance, save for historical dramas in which, virtually by the definition of theatrical form and performance, they are necessarily seen without interiority, even where they are at the center of the action. For in the theater there can be no question of empathy or point of view, and Lukács' requirement is thus here preserved as well, that world-historical figures must remain minor characters. This withdrawal of protagonicity thus confirms our sense of the formal tendency in which realism is moving in this respect, but it adds something useful to it: namely the historiographic context in which a whole new theory of history is emerging in which such individualism is no longer meaningful. Lukács' diagnosis is astute enough to register the compensation for this withdrawal in the rise of romantic or hero-worshipping biography as a mass-cultural attempt to reinstate protagonicity, as it were in another place and another genre.)

As for the others, Tolstoy's heroes withdraw back into the landowner's country estates, outside society and history, to pass their days in dealing with recalcitrant peasants and projects of agricultural reform;[19] while Galdós's people simply sink back into the modest world of Madrid society, where they are received with comfortable

---

[18] *La débacle*, Paris: Gallimard, 1892 (La Pleiade, Vol. V).
[19] See his obviously autobiographical story, *Metel* (1856).

and amiable irony. The story of these figures is then that of abdication: they renounce their right to be protagonists of the novel and now cheerfully or with resignation accept their democratic future in the new world of secondary characters as such.

This is of course Lydgate's "destiny" as well (to lose his right to a destiny); and we must also remember that Dorothea has a vocation as well, even though—that of the Saint Theresa evoked in the opening and closing pages of *Middlemarch* alike—it can have no modern name or professional status. But for Eliot this development (a personal dénouement which is also the resolution of a novelistic form-problem) is only apparently to be considered a failure and a loss of fame: or rather it is on those very categories themselves that the work of the novel is to be expended, transforming them into something else, that is to say, their newly theorized position in the "web" of the social totality, of the social interrelationships. Here, it is no longer significant that such former protagonists (including Lydgate as well as Dorothea) "lived faithfully a hidden life," in the memorable last words of the novel, "and rest in unvisited tombs." *Middlemarch* was written, not so much to celebrate or to elegize those forgotten agents as it was to describe the process whereby their protagonicity was slowly dissolved in the name of a very different conception of the social totality, thereby also allowing this last to be represented in one final form, before it becomes so vast as to demand a different kind of evocation—as the presence of an enormous and omnipresent absence, rather than an empirical entity we can still barely glimpse.

(But we must not leave this topic without some final word on Lydgate and the scientific vocation, which can only be compared to the destiny of Zola's Dr. Pascal: both also still, like Balzac's madman Balthasar Claes, in search of the philosopher's stone, the ultimate alchemical element. Lydgate searches for "the primitive tissue" which holds the complex heterogeneity of the individual organs together in an organic totality: he fails in this, and we know that the narrative unity of the web is not to be found in its individual substances or anything they share with one another, but rather with that far less tangible thing, which is sheer relationship. But as we have already seen in an earlier chapter, Dr. Pascal succeeds, for he has been able to isolate, not the totality itself, but the very force of affect which makes the realistic novel possible as a totality in the first place.)

In that case, Dr. Pascal becomes yet another form of the secondary character, namely the author himself: for like Estupiñá at the other end of the characterological ladder, this eponymous figure comes, by virtue of his all-encompassing knowledge of society—like Zola himself he has researched all the family members of the preceding novels of the series—the afterimage of another new bourgeois vocation, namely that of the professional writer. Indeed, modernism may be said to emerge when the writers of literature begin to resist their assimilation with this professional figure—the poets, who are the direct ancestors of the "great modernists," were never fully assimilated into it in the first place—and claim the supplementary status of a return to "calling" and to genius as such. But even in realism, autoreferentiality emerges in these more elusive signatures of the novelist within his own cast of characters.

Galdós, for example, slyly inserts himself twice over into his novels: first in the nameless first person who went to school with Juanito or met someone else at the club; and then in the delirious novelist and man of letters Ido del Sagrario, who everywhere erupts, turning the prosaic events of the novel in question into the most shamelessly fantastic and commercial fantasies, very much in literary emulation of the paradigmatic Quijote himself. The characters then, including the author(s), now all become minor or secondary, reorganizing themselves into Hegel's "*geistiges Tierreich*"—the zoology of the human differentiation by trades and métiers: a collection in which, however, the professional novelist must take his place alongside everyone else as a minor character.

Still, even with the waning of protagonicity and the more democratic mass assimilation of novelistic characters to the levelling of the minor or the secondary, there remains one actantial exception, and it is a narrative anomaly to which George Eliot's work will most usefully draw attention.

Chapter VI

George Eliot and *Mauvaise Foi*

So even with this structural and as it were evolutionary change in the status of the characters (or perhaps it would be better to say, in our distance from them), there remains one actantial feature that, surviving from out of a distant narrative past, continues to seem indispensable for plot as such: this is something like the other face of the protagonist, namely the villain, the agent of conflict and opposition, the hero's obstacle and the enemy of desire. We recall that the villain remains fundamental to Propp's analysis of the structure of the fairy tale. This function is assuredly distinct from the possibilities of local or minor resistance which this or that secondary character may be capable of offering; yet it is not to be grasped as symmetrical with that of the hero or protagonist either (as when Satan is affirmed as the "true hero" of *Paradise Lost*), even though it does seem possible in most cases to imagine a revisionist work in which the former villain becomes the protagonist of some new revisionary narrative.[1] In some ways, indeed, the villain's function (I continue to use Propp's technical language) would seem to rest on simpler foundations and presuppositions—to operate on the basis of a simpler category—than the innumerable protagonists of literary history, insofar as the sympathy or identification the latter generate (two philosophically vexed and socially extremely problematic processes in their own right) are socially and historically varied and can range from admiration for physical prowess (the *Iliad*) to a fellow-feeling for lovers, a satisfaction in the efforts of the underdog, a respect for genuine innocence, an energizing collective vision of the traits of a given culture hero, and so on.

---

[1] Thus the hero of the *Niebelungenlied*, the warrior Hagen, has become the villain of Wagner's *Ring*.

But perhaps in fact this situation is less contingent and less complex than what such historical contexts might suggest; perhaps indeed it is simply dependent on the point of view constructed by the narrative voice and lens, so that whoever is given as the initial subject—observer or participant—will project an "identification" and a protagonicity which only a good deal of irony—internal as well as external—can undo. In that case, protagonicity is simply a function of narrative structure, and that of the opponent or villain will follow suit and equally be identified positionally.

But this is where the dissymmetry of the two figures comes in; and I must feel that the narrative position of the villain rests on a very different categorial basis than this positional one of the hero, which I am willing provisionally to accept (at least until the onset of the dissolution we have described in the previous chapter). For the actantial role of the villain necessarily presupposes and depends on a preexisting binary opposition between good and evil (which does not come into play for the hero or heroine: Dorothea is after all not Saint Teresa).

The binary opposition between good and evil is a most peculiar opposition indeed, about which one might well claim that it is the fundamental binary opposition as such, the one that generates all those other innumerable oppositions at work in life and thought, from masculine/feminine to black and white, from intellect versus emotion to the one and the many, from nature and culture to master and slave (by the same token any number of ideologies claiming in their turn to interpret and to derive it from one of these secondary oppositions taken as its deeper underlying cause, as we shall indeed do here).

The ethical binary is nonetheless unusual and powerful insofar as it is a social opposition which can be and generally is expressed in individual terms, absorbing the eudaimonic and the body (pleasure and pain) as its code of expression and organizing the opposition of self and other as its principal terrain of struggle. It can be appropriated by the most complex theologies and philosophies and at the same time serve the mechanism of folk culture and popular entertainment. It is, finally, in my judgement, the object of an immense tendential deconstruction in modern times which can be seen as the last stage in the secular struggle against religion and superstition as well as the most fundamental political drive towards democratization.

But the ethical binary is also, as philosophers from Nietzsche to Sartre and Foucault have insisted, an immense swindle. Nietzsche's genealogy of morals, arguing from philology, finds the origin of this opposition in social class, in the disdain of the feudal or military elite for the commoners (in middle French the "villains"). By way of the latter's slave religion, Christianity, the commoners then reappropriate this class system and reverse it, undermining and punishing the class enemy by pronouncing strength and violence evil and weakness and humility good. This is a plausible account, but required supplementation by contemporary philosophy, which diagnoses the very concept of evil as a "thought of the other": for Sartre (and for Foucault in a somewhat different way) the good is the center and evil is the marginalized other. It is in the very nature of this phenomenology, then, that the self cannot originally and virtually by definition feel itself to be evil:[2] that is a judgement on me that must necessarily come from the outside and be interiorized as a judgement of other people I perpetuate within myself. The widespread existence, not only of shame but above all of guilt, is enough to testify that such an interiorization is structurally possible; yet the very diagnosis of the social function of the ethical binary necessarily goes hand in hand with the will to eradicate it from a democratic society in which there are to be no "others" in this sense, and in which the category of evil, as it lives on in psycho-social ideologies such as racism and sexism, no longer functions.

The form problem for the novel lies in the very source of the villain's evil as a concept of otherness. The stage villain is all exterior, and can declare his essential villainy as largely as he likes, in spoken language and in gesture. Even the villains of epic must declare themselves in soliloquy: "Which way I fly is Hell; myself am Hell"; "Evil, be thou my Good!"[3] But that is, indeed, the philosophical conundrum par excellence, namely how my "good" could ever be evil. For philosophy, indeed, all evil must be "radical evil," in Kant's sense, evil done for evil's sake;[4] we do it because we like it; a boot in the face for a thousand years! Diagnoses such as those of sadism—clinical attempts to explain radical evil—are all symptoms of the historical dissatisfaction with the ethical binary and the fruitless attempts to replace it with

---

[2]   Sartre's monumental *Saint Genet* is in fact dedicated to demonstrating this paradox.

[3]   John Milton, *Paradise Lost*, book iv, lines 75 and 110.

[4]   Kant's reasoning on the subject is to be found in *Religion within the Limits of Reason Alone* (1793), trans. T. M. Greene and H. H. Hudson, New York: Harper, 1960; an interesting contemporary discussion of this text is to be found in *Radical Evil*, ed. Joan Copjec, London: Verso, 1996. One may still wonder what difference there can be between radical evil and evil *tout court*.

something else, with motivations drawn from some other system. Perhaps, indeed, only Spinoza's notion of the "sad passions" (along with Nietzsche's of *ressentiment*) count as truly philosophically inventive attempts to square this circle and to produce a concept of evil which is self-motivating and does not depend on a motor force from outside itself, which is to say an explanation still mired in the otherness it was meant to account for in the first place.

For the novel and its progressively enlarging explorations of the inwardness of its characters, then, the representational problem arises in the contradiction between such thought of the other and the self to which it is to be attributed. Contemporary writers have evolved a technical solution to this problem which will be discussed it our penultimate chapter; but in classical narrative the success of representations of villainy as it were "from the inside" has been exceedingly limited. Indeed, one thinks of only a single supreme example; and even here one hesitates to characterize the most remarkable serial killer in all literature, Musil's Moosbrugger, as a "villain," inasmuch as the author has narrated his crimes in the mode of a drop in niveau, a psychic lowering and confusion which cancels them out as crimes in the first place and corresponds to what the lawyers call diminished responsibility.[5]

There thus remains for the serious novelist only the excuse of sheer obsession. How else to explain the characteristic power of Thackeray's Mr. Osbourne, who on the strength of his son's mismatch refuses to acknowledge his daughter-in-law and grandson and pursues the marriage with a hatred as it were beyond the grave:

> It seemed a humiliation to old Osborne to think that his son, an English gentleman, a captain in the famous British army, should not be found worthy to lie in ground where mere foreigners were buried. Which of us is there can tell how much vanity lurks in our warmest regard for others, and how selfish our love is? Old Osborne did not speculate much on the mingled nature of his feelings, and how his instinct and selfishness were combating together. He firmly believed that everything he did was right, that he ought on all occasions to have his own way—and like the sting of a wasp or serpent his hatred rushed out armed and poisonous against anything like opposition. He was proud of his hatred as of everything else. Always to be right, always to trample forward, and never to doubt, are not these the great qualities with which dulness takes the lead in the world?[6]

---

[5]   Robert Musil, *Der Mann ohne Eigenschaften*, Hamburg: Rowohlt, 1952. See especially Book I, chapter 18.

[6]   Thackeray, *Vanity Fair*, London: Penguin, 1985, 421.

But Mr. Osbourne is scarcely to be classified as a villain either, even though he functions like one in the narrative; and indeed the whole technique derives from an earlier aesthetic, which I will call allegorical, and in which the psychology of the passions is staged as a gradual possession of the entire personality, a concentration in which the human subject is gradually invested to the point of becoming the very personification of the passion itself: thus Spenser's poor Malbecco, whose wife has gone to live among "the jolly Satyres." He becomes a "hollow shell," a veritable insect, withdrawing into a cave, eaten away by his passion:

> Yet can he never dye, but dying lives,
> And doth himselfe with sorrow new sustaine,
> That death and life attonce unto him gives.
> And painefull pleasure turnes to pleasing pain.
> There dwels he ever, miserable swain,
> Hatefull both to him selfe, and every wight;
> Where he through privy griefe, and horrour vain,
> Is woxen so deform'd, that he has quight
> Forgot he was a man, and *Gealosie* is hight.[7]

Here passion or emotion lose their defining characteristics and become pure reification as such, as it were underscoring the very dynamic of the traditional system, for which the word "psychological" is anachronistic, inasmuch as this system opens up a development in which at least tendentially all passions, all obsessions, are the same.

These obsessives are therefore no longer true villains; Spinoza's theory of the sad passions explains them away and leaves only pity in the place that fear should have occupied. Such representations then reinsert "evil" as a unique category of otherness back into a system of named emotions of which, henceforth reified, each one stands as an allegory and thereby challenges the novel, and realism itself, to dissolve it into relationality. In this sense, then, the novel's most fundamental impulse resists psychology as a system (this was the spirit of our earlier analysis of the affect that comes to replace the named emotions), and the word "psychological" must be used with great care in the characterization of even the most seemingly introspective kinds of narrative discourse.

Nietzsche, to be sure, delighted in his self-ascribed mission as a "psychologist": but he meant thereby the genealogical act that unmasked

---

7   Spenser, *The Faerie Queene*, Book Three, Canto X, Stanza 60.

and discredited conventional systems of the classification of passions and the various ethical and moral methods devised to deal with them. His aim was not to construct some new and more satisfactory system of psychology (a construction going on all around him in his academic contemporaries whose research founded a whole new discipline), but rather to altogether preempt and destroy all such emergent forms of introspective reification. It is a program we can best grasp by way of the hostile analysis (by one of Nietzsche's modern followers) of a characteristic passage on the "psychology" of love in a text by the most illustrious of modern novelists (and "psychologists"):

> As soon as the desire to take her away from everyone else was no longer added to his love by jealousy, that love became again a taste for the sensations which Odette's person gave him ... And this pleasure different from all others had ended by creating in him a need of her.[8]

It is true that Proust astutely describes this process as a kind of chemistry ("after having created jealousy out of his love, he began to manufacture tenderness, pity for Odette"), so that the whole passage might well be taken as an elaborate figure. What it reveals, however, is that all such psychological description is in fact figural, positing a "symbolic chemistry" (Sartre) whose reified "elements," separated from each other on the chart or system of the former passions, can only somehow "interact" as "the cloud of cream 'added' to the coffee," (to borrow Sartre's famous analysis). It is, he concludes, "a mechanistic interpretation of the psychic," without adding that virtually all modern psychological descriptions rehearse the same kind of chemical analogy.[9]

For Sartre, then, Proustian "psychology" is to be grasped as a reifying operation in which meaningful acts (it will be remembered that Sartre's own phenomenological theory of the emotions grasps them as intentional forms of behavior)[10] are rewritten as things or substances. In the present book we have emphasized the reification of emotions implicit in the very process of naming as such, as well as the way in which invariably such named emotions then come to form systems, albeit systems which vary according to their historical and cultural

---

[8] Marcel Proust, "Swann in Love," quoted in Jean-Paul Sartre, *Being and Nothingness*, trans. Hazel Barnes, New York: Washington Square Press, 1956 [1943], 235.

[9] Ibid., 235–6.

[10] *Esquisse d'une théorie des émotions*, Paris: Hermann, 1939.

moments (so that Aristotle's is distinguishable from Descartes', and the latter's from the system of named emotions presupposed by contemporary academic psychology or neuroscience).

Nietzsche's own pathbreaking (historical, genealogical) analyses took as their fundamental target a rather different ideological operation, namely (as his famous title suggests) morality and moralizing as such, something which will swiftly be identified as the ethical binary of good and evil. It is not irrelevant in our present context to remember that one of his choicest objects of critique was the novelist George Eliot (and behind her, the English tradition in general). This was, indeed, by way of returning the favor, since of all nineteenth-century English thinkers Eliot was the one to whom German philosophy meant the most and on whom it had the greatest impact (her literary career began, in effect, with her translation of David Strauss's *Life of Jesus*, which in effect conjoined the German philosophical tradition with the Victorian ethical commitment to religion).

And it is certain that no reader of George Eliot can escape the feeling that her pages are obsessively devoted to an intricate moralizing of the most minute psychological reactions and perturbations. It will therefore seem perverse to argue, as I will, that the moralizing style with which she renders and represents inner movements and reactions can in fact be identified as a strategy for weakening the hold of ethical systems and values as such, and ultimately as a move consistent with modern denunciations of the ethical binary very much in the spirit of Nietzsche or Sartre.

The argument would begin with the archaizing habit of her style, in which what look like psychological explanations are conveyed in the form of folk wisdom and pseudo-proverbial sagacity: the deeper ideological intent here is, I believe, to affirm historical continuity (as against the radical breaks of modernity) as well as to integrate a deeper affirmation of the "people" and the abiding spirit of the yeoman farmer (in a rather different strategy from that of Leavis or a Raymond Williams). This is an essentially political choice which can be seen either as explaining or as resulting from her ideological distaste for overt political practice[11] (as most openly in *Felix Holt*). But this political or anti-political instinct can only be fully assessed in relationship to her conception of community as such.

---

[11] See my discussion of the political ontology of realism in "The Experiments of Time," below, in the present volume.

This conception is in fact a figural one, insofar as the very content of the novels explicitly details the historical disintegration of the traditional communities, and the political thinking of the period is not yet in a position to conceptualize that "*peuple à venir*" evoked by Deleuze. Yet her famous image of "the web" is a little more complex than mere picture-thinking and in fact constitutes the space in which we can identify a logic of dereification very much in Sartre's spirit. For it emphasizes relationality over substance: the "individual lots," the individual human lives or destinies, are meaningful only in terms of their interrelations, which make up a totality, however local:

> I at least have so much to do in unravelling certain human lots, and seeing how they were woven and interwoven, that all the light I can command must be concentrated on this particular web, and not dispersed over that tempting range of relevancies called the universe.[12]

The philosophical subtlety of the image lies not only in its displacement of attention from the individual (reified) item to its relationship with all the others, but also and above all, as David Ferris has so powerfully demonstrated, in its inevitably deconstructive (or indeed dialectical) function.[13] For one is a part of the web whether included or excluded; disjunction is relationship fully as much as positive interaction. Everything is a part, even when it affirms its individuality against an oppressive whole. This omnipresent collectivity persisting beneath the appearance of fragmentation and disintegration in concrete social life no doubt constitutes a deeper ideological excuse for the abstention from overt and intentional projects of change on the political level; but it also reinforces the decentering and gradual equalization of life on the social one, which we have emphasized in the preceding chapter as a kind of narrative democratization, a waning of protagonicity and a foregrounding of secondary characters as such. For weaving knows no hierarchy, whatever momentary centers the web may seem to throw up; and the tendency of Eliot's novels (particularly the later ones) to have multiple centers, corresponding to multiple "protagonists," is only the outward symptom of this process.

Still, this is the moment at which the question of evil and the form-problem of villains must fatally return. For it is no longer with the

---

[12] Quoted in David Ferris, *Theory and the Evasion of History*, Baltimore: Johns Hopkins University Press, 1994, 222–3.

[13] Ibid., 184–90.

centrality of heroes and heroines that we need be concerned here, but rather with Eliot's other moralizing project (in fact identical with Nietzsche's anti-moralizing one), namely her intent to persuade us that there are no villains and that evil does not exist.

This startling proposition is perhaps better grasped in the light of its solution; and no one has expressed it more concisely than her great admirer Proust, who understands her to demonstrate "que le mal que nous faisons est le mal (nous faisons du mal à nous et aux autres), et qu'au contraire le mal qui nous arrive est souvent la condition d'un plus grand bien que Dieu voulait nous faire."[14] The insight is dependent on the ambiguity of the French word "*le mal*," which means evil and harm at one and the same time: "Evil is the evil we do—harm to ourselves and to other people—while the evil (harm, misfortune) that happens to us is often the condition for some greater good God has had in mind for us." It is a formulation which has the added advantage of including that providential turn of Eliot's imagination discussed elsewhere in this book,[15] while at the same time conveying that "*rayonnement*" or benign or malignant emanation, the infection of good and evil, that so many realists attempted to convey in the great webs of collective interrelationship their narratives work to construct.

To grasp the originality of Eliot's solution to the form-problem of the villain or of what we may call "represented evil," we may briefly turn to her first novel, *Adam Bede*, in which one of the great paradigms of eighteenth-century class conflict is again rehearsed. This is the seduction of a peasant or even a bourgeois girl by an aristocratic figure, which results most often in the disaster of pregnancy. Gretchen is indeed executed for this "crime" in Goethe's *Faust*, while the most villainous of such seducers, Richardson's Lovelace, is responsible for Clarissa's death (an abstracted and concentrated version of this "evil" is then dramatized in *Les Liaisons dangereuses*, which Gide thought the greatest novel in the language, for reasons that might be convincingly argued from our present context). Biology can most often be appealed to for the ethical palliation of such "evils"; but guilt must still be dealt with, and Arthur's reflections here may serve as a starting point for what is in Eliot a remarkable new way of dealing with evil as such:

---

14 Marcel Proust, "Sur George Eliot," in *Contre Sainte-Beuve*, Paris: Gallimard, 1971, 657.

15 See "The Experiments of Time" below.

Gone a little too far perhaps in flirtation, but another man in his place would have acted much worse; and no harm would come—no harm *should* come, for the next time he was alone with Hetty, he would explain to her that she must not think seriously of him or of what had passed. It was necessary to Arthur, you perceive, to be satisfied with himself; uncomfortable thoughts must be got rid of by good intentions for the future, which can be formed so rapidly that he had time to be uncomfortable and to become easy again before Mr. Peyser's slow speech was finished, and when it was time for him to speak he was quite lighthearted.[16]

For the problem lies not so much with the act itself, as with the way in which the subject can be understood to have chosen to be evil, when by definition "evil" is a judgement and a characterization that can only be assigned to the other. Arthur's thoughts may so far be taken as a fairly conventional sort of self-justification, something which it will be important to grasp in the context of an interiorized argument in which one replies to the indictments of other people and of external judges: such replies are then most often made in what we call bad faith.

How this conventional representation unexpectedly develops in George Eliot's work we may then observe in what is often thought to be her transitional novel, her one historical novel *Romola* (1862), which separates the first more rural and nostalgic novels from *Middlemarch* and *Daniel Deronda*. It would be misleading to call *Romola* her only historical novel, as all the others are set in a more recent, yet carefully dated past; yet it is certainly her only costume drama along the lines designed by Sir Walter Scott and conforming to at least two of his principles: 1) the background of a world-historical, generally revolutionary event (in this case the short-lived revolution of Savonarola in Florence); and 2) the inclusion of historical figures familiar from the manuals whose recognition in the novel in question provokes a satisfaction of its own (in flesh and blood: so this is what she looked like, what he sounded like, etc.), a reaction comparable to the present-day passing glimpse of a celebrity in the street. In this case, in the era of the Grand Tour and the first Baedekers, there is also the satisfaction of seeing your favorite Florentine historical streets and monuments as it were set in historical motion and recreated complete with their bustling original casts (George Eliot has done her research very thoroughly indeed, and not only on the scholarly level).

---

[16] George Eliot, *Adam Bede*, London: Penguin, 1985, 265.

This book is not a favorite with the public today, whose interest in the Italian Renaissance has diminished, and whose appetite for philosophical and aesthetic debate and for intellectual history in general, insofar as it exists at all, has found other channels. Yet Henry James thought *Romola* was "on the whole the finest thing she wrote,"[17] and the astute selection of the historical situation, in Pocock's "Machiavellian moment," shows a keen sense of political significance, even if she fails to shed any new light on the paradoxical emergence of a religious and even millenarian interlude within the most productive constitutional experiment in the West.

Romola is also, as Scott's new genre required, the most melodramatic of all George Eliot's novels and thereby worthy of especial attention in our present context. Yet the complex plot is less interesting than the destiny of one of the protagonists, who is not, paradoxically, the eponymous heroine. Of the three ultimate fates of the nineteenth-century woman (assuming the failure of her marriage), namely renunciation (*Eugénie Grandet*), death (*Madame Bovary*), or sainthood (*Fortunata y Jacinta*), Romola is awarded the last (which might of course uncharitably be seen as the synthesis of the first two). She is for the most part a witness rather than an actor, and one is almost tempted to reprise Leavis's judgement on *Daniel Deronda* and suggest that the novel can in its layers be prised apart into two distinct and uneven narratives: in this case, however, it is the man's story which is far and away the most original one. James himself indeed found this character, Romola's young Greek husband Tito Melema, the most tantalizing figure in the novel, and had this to say about his unique dilemmas:

> In Tito we have a picture of that depression of the moral tone by falsity and self-indulgence, which gradually evokes on every side of the subject some implacable claim, to be avoided or propitiated. At last all his unpaid debts join issue before him, and he finds the path of life a hideous blind alley.[18]

It is a true Jamesian subject, perhaps more stark and violent than anything the author himself ever undertook.

The implication that Tito and his drama constitute the central plot line of the novel finds confirmation in Romola's concluding summing up:

---

[17]   Henry James, *Literary Criticism, Volume II: European Writers; Prefaces to the New York Edition*, New York: Library of America, 1984, 1006.

[18]   Ibid., 931.

There was a man to whom I was very near, so that I could see a great deal of his life, who made almost every one fond of him, for he was young, and clever, and beautiful, and his manners to all were gentle and kind. I believe when I first knew him, he never thought of anything cruel or base. But because he tried to slip away from everything that was unpleasant, and cared for nothing else so much as his own safety, he came at last to commit some of the basest deeds—such as make men infamous. He denied his father, and left him to misery; he betrayed every trust that was reposed in him, that he might keep himself safe and get rich and prosperous. Yet calamity overtook him.[19]

We will come back to this judgement later on, which seems to exonerate Tito from much that is villainous in the role he plays in the plot, selling her father's monumental library (we are here in full Humanism), betraying the Savonarolan experiment and conspiring with the Medicean counterrevolution, and finally bringing destruction on his own father (and on himself in the process).

But Romola's excuses are not at all what was meant by the weakening of melodramatic trappings here; and if that were all that was wanted we might have proposed a kind of Freudian splitting in the way in which the attractive son has been separated from the ferocious father, a former humanist whom Tito has abandoned to Turkish captivity and who returns in the form of a veritable allegory of old-style Elizabethan vengeance (only a chance military venture has freed him to search out and punish his guilty son). But Tito does feel guilt (without remorse) and he is also anxious to conceal this episode (and other equally shameful ones later on) from his virtuous spouse. A good deal of psychological complexity is thus to be found here, and it is in the dynamics of that complexity, rather than in her assignment of what are relatively conventional motivations, that the originality of George Eliot's novelistic solution is to be found.

We must begin its examination by declining the terms of Romola's own explanation, which we have just read and which she shares with the author, who tells us that Tito "had simply chosen to make life easy to himself—to carry his human lot, if possible, in such a way that it should pinch him nowhere" (219). "And the choice had," adds the novelist in George Eliot, "at various times, landed him in unexpected positions."

These positions, indeed, will make up the novel's plots, but the reproach of a lack of strenuousness and self-discipline will lead on

---

[19]   George Eliot, *Romola*, London: J. M. Dent, 1907, p. 566. Hereafter all page numbers in the text refer to this edition.

into something worse: "What, looked at closely," thinks Tito, "was the end of all life, but to extract the utmost sum of pleasure?" (113). This lazy hedonism is then quite enough, for minds possessed of the Protestant ethic, to account for whatever corruptions destiny has in store for Tito: but it is not enough to make the character interesting, and indeed, if it does not seem enough to qualify him for the role of the villain in melodrama, there remain enough other stock parts available for an innocent misled into this or that reprehensible deed. But Tito's character is a little too complicated for that stock role as well.

Still, we may begin with this "innocence," this blank slate on which George Eliot will begin to write something new. It is first of all an innocence for other people, as Sartre might put it: "gentle and kind," as we are told in Eliot's summary; or, following the impression of another minor character, "it was not less true that Tito had movements of kindliness towards her apart from any contemplated gain to himself" (293). Indeed, from the very first page (where we begin the novel with Tito's arrival in Florence) his joyousness and charm, his sympathies and good impulses, are underscored at some length.[20]

What happens to these qualities is then unexpected: first, he becomes a type, but a new type, not altogether unknown in nineteenth-century realism (see, for example, the ubiquitous Dobbin of *Vanity Fair*), but one relatively untheorized and certainly unnamed in the way Eliot does it: "His face wore that bland liveliness, as far removed from excitability as from heaviness or gloom, which marks the companion popular alike amongst men and women—the companion who is never obtrusive or noisy from uneasy vanity or excessive animal spirits, and whose brow is never contracted by resentment or indignation" (83–4). In short, the minor character par excellence, except for the fact that this minor character is the protagonist.

What becomes of this curious modulation of Tito's initial innocence is then even more curious: the handsome blandness of his features slowly becomes negative; the lack of vanity, resentment, indignation now becomes a more suspect expressionlessness:

On the day of San Giovanni it was already three weeks ago that Tito had handed his florins to Cennini, and we have seen that as he set out towards the Via

---

[20] He is also given an attractive physique: "Tito's bright face showed its rich-tinted beauty without any rivalry of color above his black sajo or tunic reaching to the knees. It seemed like a wreath of spring, dropped suddenly in Romola's young but wintry life" (57).

de' Bardi he showed all the outward signs of a mind at ease. How should it be otherwise? He never jarred with what was immediately around him, and his nature was too joyous, too unapprehensive, for the hidden and the distant to grasp him in the shape of a dread. As he turned out of the hot sunshine into the shelter of a narrow street, took off the black cloth berretta, or simple cap with upturned lappet, which just crowned his brown curls, pushing his hair and tossing his head backward to court the colder air, there was no brand of duplicity on his brow; neither was there any stamp of candour: it was simply a finely formed, square, smooth young brow. And the slow absent glance he cast around at the upper windows of the houses had neither more dissimulation in it, nor more ingenuousness, than belongs to a youthful well-opened eyelid with its unwearied breadth of gaze; to perfectly pellucid lenses; to the undimmed dark of a rich brown iris; and to pure cerulean-tinted angle of whiteness streaked with the delicate shadows of long eyelashes. Was it that Tito's face attracted or repelled according to the mental attitude of the observer? Was it a cypher with more than one key? The strong, unmistakable expression in his whole air and person was a negative one, and it was perfectly veracious; it declared the absence of any uneasy claim, any restless vanity, and it made the admiration that followed him as he passed among the troop of holiday-makers a thoroughly willing tribute. (100)

And now, by some peculiar dialectical transformation within the novel's raw material itself, this indifference of Tito's features, their expressionlessness, which the description certifies to be "veracious," turns out to be the very expression of secretiveness and concealment itself:

Tito had an innate love of reticence—let us say a talent for it—which acted, as other motives do, without any conscious motive, and, like all people to whom concealment is easy, he would now and then conceal something which had as little the nature of a secret as the fact that he had seen a flight of crows. (92)

Thus, by a mysterious alchemy known only to Eliot herself, the joyous openness of the innocent youth has been transformed by a touch of the wand into a suspect secretiveness and a propensity for concealment (and thereby for intrigue and conspiracy) which will not long wait for the appropriate context. Indeed, it is never altogether clear which comes first, the secret or the secretiveness, or perhaps this is in the very nature of this particular vice (and its concrete existence as a habit, or as what habit itself perpetuates and nourishes). But with this we are already within the multiplicity of Tito's motives alluded to earlier: he does not feel like saving his father (this is itself already a feeling that has been overdetermined); while now he does not want Romola to know about this betrayal (and for purposes of the plot, it will be her long-lost brother, become a monk, who brings him positive news of his father's captivity which will then infallibly be transmitted to her once the brother realizes his identity, etc.). But this particular secret has been multiplied in other areas (such is indeed the inevitable consequence of the "channel" deepened by so many "little rills of selfishness"); Tito has rescued a peasant girl and found her a lodging—all quite innocently, but inexplicably undivulged to his spouse; he has also sold her father's library, something she is bound to find out about; and his numerous friendships have led him into relationships which in the current revolutionary situation cannot but take on a political, and thereby conspiratorial, function, thereby securing for him the guilt of the overthrow and execution of Savonarola.

This multiplicity of sins and secrets is in the very nature of George Eliot's conception of the nature of what was formerly called evil:

> Under every guilty secret there is hidden a brood of guilty wishes, whose unwholesome infecting life is cherished by the darkness. The contaminating effects of deeds often lies less in the commission than in the consequent adjustment of our desires—the enlistment of our self-interest on the side of falsity; as, on the other hand, the purifying influence of public confession springs from the fact, that by it the hope in lies is for ever swept away, and the soul recovers the noble attitude of simplicity. (99)

The notion of infection is no doubt also part and parcel of a late Victorian episteme (Marc Angenot's discussion of the period's medical obsessions is illuminating):[21] in this instance, however, it is also the other face of what is perhaps the most luminous vision in her late work of the providential web, the way in which the good is also infectious, and radiates outward across the network of social relations (at least those of the traditional community).[22]

But in the present instance, the immediate result of this multiplicity is quite different. On the one hand, all these multiple motivations not only perpetuate each other, but reciprocally ensure each other's existence. It is preferable, indeed, to state this peculiar consequence in a negative way, by insisting on the way in which each one prevents the other from being removed or neutralized. But she says it much better: "He had made it impossible that he should not from henceforth

---

[21] On the ideological rhetoric of disease and infection, see Marc Angenot, *1889*, Longueuil, Quebec: Le Préambule, 1989; see also my discussion of this remarkable book in the *Ideologies of Theory*.

[22] See "The Experiments of Time" below.

desire it to be the truth that his father was dead; impossible that he should not be tempted to baseness rather than that the precise facts of his conduct should not remain for ever concealed" (99).

A remarkable construction of negatives, achieved by Tito's own inner efforts—by his own free choice, Sartre would say, albeit a choice that remains unknown to him. Yet how can one's free choice remain unknown to one's self?

The answer lies in Eliot's narrative anticipation of what is only much later theorized as a philosophical concept, namely Sartre's notion of *mauvaise foi* or bad faith. The technical expression is borrowed from daily life and in particular from those disputes in which one of the interlocutors (or even both, as the case may be) produces one after the other reasons and demonstrations palpably in contradiction with one another for the sole purpose of winning the argument (and not even of persuading himself, since he henceforth no longer believes in any of those reasons and demonstrations). In Sartrean bad faith, this argument is interiorized, and consists in a struggle against my "being-for-another," namely the trauma of my image in other people's eyes which I am powerless to modify.

It is this mechanism which, in the absence of anything like a Freudian notion of the unconscious, must be grasped against the background of the phenomenological theory of consciousness as an essentially impersonal state which for that very reason cannot *be* anything, whether good or evil. These attributes are then somehow related to the construction of the self, an object for that impersonal consciousness. For Sartre, therefore, it becomes a paradox and a fundamental philosophical problem how and why any consciousness would judge itself to be evil, would even go so far (in cases of "radical evil") to affirm itself as such ("Evil, be thou my good!"). For, as we have already suggested, evil is a judgement rendered from the outside, a sentence passed on the Other: in order to feel myself as evil, I must have interiorized that judgement in a way that remains to be explained.

Sartre's critique of this concept therefore faces technical difficulties more complex than those confronted by his great predecessors (or competitors) in this problematic—Spinoza with his notion of the "sad passions" and Nietzsche with his idea of *"ressentiment."* Sartre's is an ontology and must for that reason somehow show how an entity which has no being (or has the being of not-being)—namely human reality or *Dasein*—can convince itself of its possession of that attribute of being which is badness or evil; and we speak here not of hypocrisy or the feigning of appearances, as when a villain pretends to be good and righteous, but rather of the deep and agonizing inner conviction of being wrong, sinful, born to do harm, cursed by sheer otherness and outcast from the society of the righteous. (Presumably a similar drama would lie in wait for those who are persuaded of their own goodness; yet here hypocrisy does seem to propose itself more insistently, even though, as in the contemporary instance of "celebrity," positive judgements by other people can no doubt be no less traumatic. Sartre's own "self-sequestration" in later life would seem to have been his own solution to just such a trauma.)

In any case, this interiorization of an external judgement is explicitly registered here in *Romola*.

"This first distinct colloquy with himself" (99): so George Eliot names and dates Tito's initial pangs of conscience, as they are traditionally termed; and we will suggest that this moment is also the one in which George Eliot invents the concept of mauvaise foi avant la lettre. We here illustrate the discovery with Tito in order to mark the emergence of the new… shall we call it "technique"? (For I will later on want to discuss it on the level with "*style indirect libre*" and point of view as an alternative means of representation.) Yet it comes into its own only in the great moments in *Middlemarch*, in the agonies of Casaubon and Bulstrode; and recedes again somewhat in *Daniel Deronda*, where for reasons yet to be suggested, Grandcourt marks something of a return to the old-fashioned romantic—and I may even say eighteenth-century—villain. Casaubon and Bulstrode are, so to speak, former villains: and what they do and do not do for the plot in that status forms the supreme proof and example of that dissolution of melodrama I am here arguing for, with all its results for the classic form of novelistic realism which it fulfills and undermines at one and the same time.

"Colloquy with himself": Eliot here betrays traces of her Hegelianism with this positing of an initial moment of self-consciousness ("I = I," as Hegel terms it), in which the self becomes divided and confronts itself in some novel and fresh, historically new mode of awareness, one which seems to mimic and to reproduce the encounter of two separate individuals with each other. (Hegel indeed describes it that way, in the famous encounter of what will become the Master and the Slave; an encounter which comes first and phenomenologically precedes the inner split as which the subsequent "self-consciousness," whatever that may be, is described).

At any rate, it is clear that for Sartre (the source of the well-known Lacanian "split subject") the word "self" will be technically quite inappropriate and misleading for such a description (and in the preceding paragraph), inasmuch as self-consciousness does not proceed from some doubling within the self but can rather better be characterized as the very production of the self as such. Self-consciousness is my way of dealing with that "object for consciousness" which is the self, and which I can live, Sartre says, in shame or in pride, but which is not really me, in the sense in which the "me" in question is an utterly impersonal consciousness which cannot *be* anything in the strong sense, nor can it have any properties or characteristics which might occasion shame or its opposite.[23] Such impersonal consciousness could never feel itself to be evil (or good) inasmuch as it cannot feel itself to *be* the way things (or other people) are, to have attributes to which we might attach such adjectives in the first place. What impersonal consciousness can feel is the unjustifiability of its existence.

So mauvaise foi in this respect will involve a peculiar kind of inner prestidigitation, in which I manage to talk myself into *being* something: the process seems to involve speed—I must work very fast indeed in order to prevent the whole construction from falling apart (Sartre's description in *Saint Genet*, a veritable case study of this kind of construction), in order to confuse myself into momentarily believing the things I want to affirm or deny about myself. Self-justification? Yes, in a sense; and yet it is about my very self that I have to affirm the matter, and although the self may well be imaginary (in the Lacanian sense) or a mere object of consciousness (in Sartre's), it is nonetheless real and something I can scarcely my whole life long do away with. Sartre has had the terminological good fortune to find a technical term in the language of everyday situations, so that (like Hegel's notion of self-consciousness) it has an interpersonal relationship sedimented within what looks like a philosophical nomenclature.

This ambiguity entitles us to insist on the representational, rather than the philosophical, nature of Sartre's concept. It is organized around a dualism we can express in any number of ways: facticity versus freedom, matter and spirit, what can't be changed and what can, thing and process, or finally, the body and consciousness. But we must

---

[23] Already outlined in Sartre's first philosophical work, *La Transcendance de L'Ego*, Paris: Vrin, 1936.

also understand that representationally, the Sartrean demonstration is staged as a confrontation between a judge and a defendant (whether these are embodied in separate individuals or within a single mind); and also that, as befitting an ontology, the accusation is couched in terms of being. The casuistry of the defendant, then, his mauvaise foi or bad faith, consists in shifting the terms of the accusation back and forth across this basic dualism which is human reality. To the accusation of betrayal, then, the subject replies that he has indeed done this or that, but that he is not a traitor in the way in which things (facticity) *are*; and that he is always free to change and to become something different (to become loyal or trustworthy). To which the judge replies that he knows that the defendant is not ontologically untrustworthy in the manner of the being of things, and that we have here to do with freely chosen acts rather than essences and static properties or qualities; and yet the judge remains convinced that the defendant will nonetheless never change and become anything other than a traitor.[24] And so an endless, impossible argument continues, which is in mauvaise foi reproduced within the mind of the character seeking self-justification and claiming that it is always within his power to change and to become someone different. Sartre also insists on the tempo of this inner argument, which must rotate from one term to the other with such dizzying rapidity that the subject is himself never able to grasp the deceitfulness of this ontological double standard: and the speed of this flight is tantamount for Sartre to the unconscious as such. "In bad faith there is neither cynical lie nor knowing preparation for deceitful concepts ... the first act of bad faith is to flee what it cannot flee, to flee what it is."[25]

Sartre's characters, then, taking mauvaise foi here as a representation of consciousness rather than a philosophical concept, tend to couch their arguments with themselves at a high philosophical and ontological level, one not particularly appropriate to the more traditional religious vocabulary of sin, shame and guilt which would have been available to any of George Eliot's characters. In the latter's "colloquys with self," that nimble leaping back and forth between two incompatible alternatives which is mauvaise foi tends to take the form of a substitution of incompatible motives, which is why I have insisted above on the structural significance of a multiplicity of such

---

[24] *Being and Nothingness*, trans. Hazel Barnes, Part One, Chapter Two.
[25] Ibid., 115–6.

motives in Eliot's novels. Guilt can indeed be evaded by playing these motives off against each other rapidly enough for each one to excuse the other. Thus betrayal can be justified by the need for secrecy, secretiveness and lying by the shamefulness of the betrayal, and so forth. It is a demanding process, something one must keep in constant circulation all the time, not without its affinities with Brecht's unhappy demon: "the swollen veins of his forehead testifying to the effort it takes to be evil."

And this is why the procedure, whether in real life or in its representation, is no longer adequate for the construction of those genuine villains on which the structure of melodrama depends. In Sartrean terms, we might have said that there can be no villains because no one can *be* evil as a thing is (brown, solid, heavy, large or whatever); even though anyone can freely commit evil acts (something with obvious consequences for any Sartrean politics, which must replace moralizing judgements with the act of commitment [*engagement*]).

Eliot is perhaps more Spinozan in her insistence on the toll of psychic misery to be exacted by the "sad passions." Yet, this is precisely what allows her to resolve her fundamental form-problem: how to prevent the denial of the category of evil from leaving her with a sanitized world, an idyllic fantasy à la Rousseau or Bernardin de Saint-Pierre, in which all her characters have no other recourse than to be "good" in the most uninteresting fashion. To neutralize the effects of her own pedagogical and moralizing temperament, to steer a course between the two formal alternatives of melodrama and the most saccharine Utopian fantasies—this is Eliot's fundamental technical dilemma, and one to whose triumphant solution, after the crucial experiment of Tito in *Romola*, the characters of Casaubon and Bulstrode in *Middlemarch* offer remarkable testimony.

We cannot deal with them in the detail they deserve: suffice it to say that they incarnate the two types of oppression to which George Eliot was the most sensitive—the first, that of women, and the second, that of money: and the context of their respective dramas having the added advantage of allowing her, in the first case, to raise the issue of intellectuals, and in the second, of religion. Meanwhile, their contrast also allows of another ironic contrast, namely the common fate reserved for failure and success alike, when both are lived in bad faith.

Mr. Casaubon's misery, no doubt, finds its occasion in the failure of the great work, indeed its impossibility (and the bad totalization projected by the Key to All Mythologies is perhaps the caricature and distorted mirror image of Eliot's own achieved totalization in *Middlemarch* itself). But in reality it finds its deeper source in the intersection of two other feelings (if we may hastily call them that), which the traditional psychology of the named or reified emotions ordinarily terms vanity and jealousy.

Both are complicated; and the first is no doubt related to the great project and to the "morbid consciousness" related to it "that others did not give him the place which he had not demonstrably merited"[26] (417). But this wounded vanity crystallizes around the sense that Dorothea does not herself give him that place, and indeed that he has underrated her intelligence, which now houses itself within his mind as a place of implacable, inescapable judgement on him.

The other feeling is a more conventional and not unjustified jealousy for Will Ladislaw and the interest he has palpably awakened in Dorothea. "Suspicion and jealousy of Will Ladislaw's intentions, suspicion and jealousy of Dorothea's impressions, were constantly at their weaving work" (419). The point is that either of these preoccupations might well, if only briefly and intermittently, lead to moments of self-lucidity for Casaubon, moments in which mauvaise foi might have given way to self-knowledge. But the ruse of mauvaise foi lies in the way in which each obsession then excuses itself on the grounds of the other, turning round in that inexhaustible perpetual motion we have already identified.

As for Mr. Bulstrode, his case has more to do with deeds than with suspicions: indeed, it bears an uncanny resemblance to Tito's situation, in the existence of a long-lost relative thought to be dead and the moral laziness with which Bulstrode justifies his failure to follow up the traces of this claimant on his fortune as well as the secrecy with which he keeps his wife ignorant of the matter, and of his own culpability. The whole situation is then overdetermined by the shameful origin of the fortune (usury) as well as by the consolations of self-righteousness provided by his religion, neither of which particularly obtain in Tito's case. Still, Eliot goes out of her way to distinguish this complex and agonizing state of mind from simple hypocrisy:

> The spiritual kind of rescue was a genuine need with him. There may be coarse hypocrites, who consciously affect beliefs and emotions for the sake of gulling the world, but Bulstrode was not one of them. He was simply a man whose desires had been stronger than his theoretic beliefs, and who had gradually explained the

---

26 George Eliot, *Middlemarch*, London: Penguin, 1994, 417.

gratification of his desires into satisfactory agreement with those beliefs. If this be hypocrisy, it is a process which shows itself occasionally in us all, to whatever confession we belong, and whether we believe in the future perfection of our race or in the nearest date fixed for the end of the world; whether we regard the earth as a putrefying nidus for a saved remnant, including ourselves, or have a passionate belief in the solidarity of mankind.

The service he could do to the cause of religion had been through life the ground he alleged to himself for his choice of action: it had been the motive which he had poured out in his prayers. Who would use money and position better than he meant to use them? Who could surpass him in self-abhorrence and exaltation of God's cause? And to Mr. Bulstrode God's cause was something distinct from his own rectitude of conduct: it enforced a discrimination of God's enemies, who were to be used merely as instruments, and whom it would be well if possible to keep out of money and consequent influence. Also, profitable investments in trades where the power of the prince of this world showed its most active devices, became sanctified by a right application of the profits in the hands of God's servant. (419)

This is the point, before moving on to consider the survival of melodramatic elements in George Eliot, to open a terminological digression which will also be relevant for topics discussed in Chapter VIII, most notably *style indirect libre* and point of view.

We can stage the problem dramatically by asking our question in this form: is mauvaise foi, which we have found to be a specific narrative mode (however occasionally or rarely put to use), to be called a narrative technique? In a technological age like our own it is clear that words like "technique" or "method" arouse their own kind of suspicion and vigilance; they seem at once to reify their content, the procedure they seek to describe or name, and by the same token they tend to transform their content, the narrative material which they organize and distribute, into a kind of industrial raw material, which can be processed by certain technical methods alone (or which at least convey a kind of progress in the invention of ever newer and more efficient technical methods). In this respect, it cannot be said that what we have called mauvaise foi was a very successful innovation; examples of its later use are infrequent; meanwhile the systems of reified or named emotions it was supposed to neutralize certainly returned with a vengeance and are very much with us.

Meanwhile, the very notion of a technique standardizes all these literary procedures, and accounts for the surprise we may feel when a formation like mauvaise foi is ranged in the same category of that of *style indirect libre* (and indeed, when the latter is considered on the same level as point of view, as we will be doing in Chapter VIII). The empirical classification systems implicit in such technological thinking at once exclude the kinds of dialectical comparisons opened up by focusing on the philosophical, or better still, the phenomenological meanings of such "techniques," on the way they organize experience, and the rivalry they pose with other comparable forms of the organization of experience. The very fact that mauvaise foi as such takes its origin in the production of a philosophical concept testifies that both meaning and the nature of the raw material (experience) have been omitted from notions of technique or method.

On the other hand, the exclusion of the latter permits the text in question to slip back into pure conceptuality and the promotion of ideological or didactic theses, the history of ideas, or the specific storehouse of idiosyncratic opinions and values of the writer in question. Both faces of the textual object, then—its production as a specific moment of narrative production (of the solution of a narrative problem) and its phenomenological and ideological content—need to figure in any adequate theorization of the object in question.

Indeed, such language then raises yet a third dimension that needs to be present in our account, and that is its coherence and density as a particular kind of discursive object, which can be identified as such (and thus itself named and theorized). Such is the implication of terms like *style indirect libre* or point of view: their very presence can be detected at certain moments of the narrative discourse, allowing them to be studied as structural phenomena, and not only as symptomal production or historical ideology.

This is indeed one of the sources of effectivity of recent French theory, to have sought to name such objectal states, whether as *appareils*, *agencements*, *dispositifs*, and the like—words which have the advantage of professing a certain materialism in the approach (the objects so named are not mere ideas, nor are they mere technical skills), at the same time that their connotations suggest combination, and the conjuncture of various features of complex machinery. (Of the few German equivalents, we may compare Heidegger's notion of the *Gestell* or standing reserve, meant to convey a conception of how the forces of nature are appropriated and stored.) These seemingly technical terms borrowed from the age of industrial machinery are unrelated to the earlier conceptuality of technique and method, if only because the latter imply a far greater activity on the part of the human agent or manager. What we may call the machinic notions, many of them derived from or in cinema theory, presuppose a well-nigh physical apparatus such as the camera or the projector, which are interposed between the narrative and the human agent; I believe that it is proper to separate the latter's know-how decisively from the objectal status of the object in question (which may be linguistic or narrative as the case may be).

Cinema theory has obviously been attractive in what it seems to furnish of a scientific or at least technological objectivity; only a few "literary techniques" have seemed to lend themselves to this kind of approach, even though the critic and analyst may so often yearn for equipment of this empirical and objective type. At any rate, I believe we have said enough to posit at least three dimensions which need to be present and satisfied or fulfilled in any "technical" discussion of this kind; in other words, which need somehow to be theorized in their mutual interrelationship. Those three dimensions are then 1) the object as a technique; 2) the object as a phenomenological meaning; and finally 3) the object as a kind of apparatus.

But we have still not named that "object" with the kind of specificity it demands; I propose, without much hope of any general consensus on the matter, to call it a "narrative formation." Mauvaise foi is thus a narrative formation among others, and yet to put it this way is also to glimpse a shadowy fourth dimension beyond the ones we have already discussed, namely its function in a given historical situation. What is this particular narrative formation for? Why has it been evolved? What is its function or purpose?

But at least in this instance we know the answer to these questions: mauvaise foi exists in order to undermine the ethical binary and to discredit the metaphysical and moral ideologies of evil at the same time that the latter's uses in plot formation and construction are replaced with at least some rough equivalent.

Chapter VII

Realism and the Dissolution of Genre

I.

We have not yet done, however, with evil. For the problem of the villain is not only a philosophical one, nor even one of subjectivity and representation, but also one of plot itself and of those codified narrative structures we call genres. To be sure, there has been a long-standing and desultory debate about whether the novel itself should be classified as a genre in its own right: its differentiation from the lyric, the dramatic and the epic would seem to be decisive, and yet also peculiarly dialectical, insofar as (not only for Lukács and Bakhtin) the novel has seemed to be a very different kind of animal from those, and something peculiarly associated with a modernity from which most of the earlier triad have waned. Meanwhile, however, we often speak of sub-genres of the novel, such as the letter novel or the mystery story, a usage which would seem to return us to some generic genus of which those are the species. This is indeed the feature that will interest us here and motivate us to dismiss the entire terminological debate by simply calling these last the "genres" of the novel as such, genres which not only disappear under modernism, but whose disappearance indeed is at one with their construction and emergence in realism itself, as I will show in the present chapter.

So there is a perspective in which the problem of the villain can now be rethought in terms of just such genres or kinds of the novel itself; at which point it is transformed into a different kind of discussion, namely that of melodrama, and predictably brings with it a new set of terminological confusions which seem uncannily to mirror the old ones of generic classification. Early on, we counted melodrama among the numerous foils (such as romance or modernism) against which realism was often defined. Now, however, we must admit that all these oppositions are somehow also internal: and that (to take the inaugural moment itself) realism is opposed to romance only because it carries it within itself and must somehow dissolve it in order to become its antithesis: the *Quijote* is a laborious work on the romance it still contains, and the later Spanish tradition[1] might cause us to wonder whether the dissolution of romance leaves us with something radically different or merely with an *Aufhebung* of the impulse onto a higher and perhaps unrecognizable level.

Here at any rate we are confronted with innumerable projects and research programs, insofar as each consequent realization will demand analysis in its own right as well as an experimental laboratory of its own in which to inspect the processes at work in the slow purgation of that reified generic structure with which it is threatened. The analysis is then immeasurably complicated by the supplementary requirement that it also register the way in which the novel in question must first construct the structure whose dismantling is the primary work of its narration in the first place.

Melodrama might offer some first key insofar as its villain is quintessentially a prototype of those marked characters and destinies we earlier associated with the récit as such. In this sense, melodrama—and perhaps the other novelistic genres or sub-genres with which we are about to associate it—can be identified with that narrative impulse in whose quintessential struggle and inseparability with its affective opposite number we saw the very emergence of realism (or of the novel as such). The mission of affect in that case would lie in the very weakening of the melodramatic structure, the gradual effacement of the villain (as we have just observed it in George Eliot), and the systematic dismantling of its rhetoric, its specific address to the audience and the demands it makes on their reactions—terror, pity, fear and sympathy, breathless anticipation, and the like. In this sense, melodrama might also be theorized as the literary equivalent of that "theatricality" in painting which Michael Fried opposed to the

---

[1]   One notes in Spain, particularly after 1898, the emergence of all kinds of "philosophies of the Quijote" (Ortega, Unamuno) and evocations of the "Cervantine," in which even the shape of the master's sentences project a whole *Lebensphilosophie*: I know of nothing comparable in any other nation's literature. Meanwhile, it would be ill-advised to underestimate Cervantes's literary impact down through the ages: all of Galdós, for example, is suffused with the fundamental themes of the *Quijote*.

turning away from the audience of its figures and the abandonment of its rhetorical appeals to their emotions.[2]

Is Fried's "absorption" then to be identified with what we have been calling affect, or does it result in the end of realism altogether and the emergence of modernism and of non-figuration? Such questions would also lead us into the multiple meanings and uses of the term "melodrama" itself, which we have associated almost exclusively with the villain and the narrative of evil. But Fried's terminology reminds us that melodrama can also be associated with the theatrical as such, both in its origins in drama and it its afterlife in silent movie acting (along with a parallel existence in music, as its etymology suggests; and particularly in opera and its arias, and thereby in a whole aesthetics of expression closely linked to the system of named emotions).[3] Meanwhile, contemporary film theory[4] and production has thrown up what seems to be yet another influential usage in the genre of sentimental film organized around women's films—Douglas Sirk—and that return of the lachrymose so closely identified with its eighteenth-century form.

Yet the very notion of a dissolution of melodrama can clearly enough take as many forms as melodrama itself does; and the current chapter can scarcely claim even to theorize those, let alone explore them. Thus, if melodrama is taken to be a mode whose essence is theatricality, paths and approaches are thrown open which lead to the problem of rhetoric on the one hand and to the evolution of painting on the other. The denunciation of rhetoric in emergent modernism is already present in the repudiation by Wordsworth and Coleridge of allegory and decoration in the language of the ancien régime; and perhaps the florid acting of opera and the silent film deriving from theatrical texts may also be ranged under this category, which seeks first and foremost to make an effect on its public. Unexpectedly,

---

2   Michael Fried, *Absorption and Theatricality*, Chicago: University of Chicago Press, 1988. We should also note the implications of this position for modernism (Fried, *Art and Objecthood: Essays and Reviews*, Chicago: University of Chicago Press, 1998) as well as its return in unexpected contemporary practices such as that of photography (Fried, *Why Photography Matters as Art as Never Before*, New Haven: Yale University Press, 2008).

3   The classic work on the meaning of melodrama is that of Peter Brooks, *The Melodramatic Imagination*, New Haven: Yale University Press, 1995.

4   Here, the inaugural text is that of Thomas Elsaesser, "Tales of Sound and Fury," in *Movies and Methods*, Volume II, ed. Bill Nichols, Berkeley: University of California Press, 1985.

then, Michael Fried will diagnose these same motives at work in eighteenth-century painting and in modernity as "conceptual art," and will identify what he calls absorption as the process of rejecting this equally rhetorical "theatricality." There is yet one final possible meaning of the word I wish to reserve for plot construction as such and to which I will return later in this chapter.

But let me now come at this question of genre from a very different perspective, namely from Auerbach's work on realism (quite different from this one). I have in mind the way in which Auerbach's notion of *sermo* and the three levels or modes of style can supplement and reinforce our argument about genre.[5] In fact, Auerbach's scheme is a simplified one, in which the high style of Roman rhetoric and the *sermo-humilis* that characterizes early Christian texts and that is based on the models of the New Testament open an intermediary space for a so-called mixed style. In his discussion of modern realism, then, of which the prototype is the analysis of *Madame Bovary*[6] which probably initiated the project of *Mimesis* (without, paradoxically, being included in it, save for a passing comment), the deployment of this mixed style is essentially defined by what it is meant to exclude or prevent in advance. We may translate Auerbach's enumeration of these stylistic exclusions in any number of other sets of terms—as modes or voice, as social points of view and distances taken, as tone, as preexisting rhetorical categories, and so forth: in fact we will here take them as the starting point for various genres and the opening up beyond them of a narrative discourse which is not a genre, namely what will become the realistic novel itself.

The excluded tones are conveniently summarized by Auerbach as follows: "the tone can be tragic, sentimental, idyllic, comical or burlesque."[7] The example of this new subject-matter, which eludes all of the above possibilities, is a scene in which Emma and Charles have a perfectly ordinary evening meal, through which Emma's nameless dissatisfactions are conveyed, ("*elle n'en pouvait plus*," "*toute l'amertume de l'existence*," etc.). Auerbach's list of possible alternative tones projects all the alternative genres in which the drama of such a scene might be staged: the high tragic dissatisfaction of Clytemnestra

5   Erich Auerbach, *Literary Language and its Public in Late Latin Antiquity*, New York: Pantheon, 1965.

6   Erich Auerbach, "On the Serious Imitation of the Everyday," in Flaubert, *Madame Bovary*, Norton Critical Editions, ed. Margaret Cohen, New York: Norton, 2005.

7   Ibid., 427.

(on stage rather than in narrative prose) might there rub elbows with a peasant girl's idyllic yearning for an ideal lover very different from this one (something which in its turn is easily imaginable in terms of comedy—the eighteenth century—or even burlesque, from Shakespeare back to medieval fabliaux, etc.) All such genres, we might say, insist on the meaningfulness of the scene, whether tragic or comic: it is not only that it becomes easily classified literarily (and thereby socially) in genres which then reflect a conventional class differentiation of the situations in life and the status of the characters involved (higher than us, lower than us, as Frye might have put it).[8]

The more crucial point in Auerbach's differentiation of this "everyday" reality from all the other traditionally named and categorized situations lies precisely in the fact that there is no name for what this one represents, for it does not seem to convey any of the lofty metaphysical themes nor is it suitable for vaudeville humor, nor for idyllic distraction and restful contemplation either. The dinner scene (it contrasts both with the interrupted supper in *Manon*—a different chapter of *Mimesis*—and with the various lunches enumerated in Chapter I) is the occasion for a feeling of Emma's which escapes all easy categorization. It is not boredom in any strict sense, nor frustration, she does not as yet have any precise object of desire, she has not even worked out in her own mind the disillusionment Flaubert conveys by way of objective details.

But we have to be sure that we do not ourselves too readily identify this dissatisfaction after the fact, and add in diagnoses which, old or new, tend in advance to reify something it was the very intent and burden of Flaubert's art to leave unidentified—better still, to identify as being unidentifiable and unavailable in the first place. Thus, a new disease called "*bovarysme*" was named and described by Jules de Gaultier in 1892, long after the publication of Flaubert's novel; the case is interesting in as much as it would seem to ratify the disease itself as nameless in the very act naming it. More recently, Flaubert has rightly been celebrated as having discovered the way in which desire is itself shaped by its own representation in novels and other media, which displace some simple idea of (inner and outer) reality by a preexisting stereotype: Mme. Bovary is unsatisfied because she has read novels in which true satisfaction is supposed to exist (Girardian

---

8 Northrop Frye, *The Anatomy of Criticism*, Princeton: Princeton University Press, 1957, 33–4.

mediation, other media theories all the way to poststructuralism).[9] But when this theme threatens to become a causal theory in its own right, it threatens the fragile equilibrium of the novel, which precisely takes affect, and the unnamable, as its fundamental subject.

It is therefore this flight from classification that Auerbach so brilliantly describes in his essay, then himself naming it with the words "everyday" and "existential." Insofar as one has nonetheless to talk about it, these words are as harmless as possible, since they designate the two faces of that unnamable thing which we have ourselves named as affect—the everyday as the outside, or *Stimmung*; the existential as the lived or inside, namely affect as such. The point is that both depend absolutely on the avoidance of genres which would tend to reify and thereby to explain this lived material by associating it with this or that prototype of a destiny which is enshrined in the plot-type of a specific genre.

It is precisely against just such a reification of destinies that the realist narrative apparatus is aimed, which reaffirms the singularity of the episodes to the point at which they can no longer fit into the narrative convention. That this is also a clash of aesthetic ideologies is made clear by the way in which older conceptions of destiny or fate are challenged by newer appeals to that equally ideological yet historically quite distinct notion of this or that "reality," in which social and historical material rise to the surface in the form of the singular or the contingent.

Such is then the way in which all the great realists have thought of their narrative operations as an intervention in the "superstitious" or religious, universalizing conceptions of life, and as the striking of a blow for truth ("reader, this is not a fiction") which is still part and parcel of the whole Enlightenment secularization of the world. But in each historical situation, the claim for truth will be a somewhat different one; the overall strategy or argument for realism in general and as such (the word only really enjoys a brief literary currency around the mid-point of the nineteenth century)[10] is nowhere near as durable and as powerful as its modernist equivalent, in which notions of formal innovation are able to be transferred from one generation

---

[9] René Girard's "mimetic desire" (*Desire, Deceit and the Novel*, Baltimore: Johns Hopkins University Press, 1976) is only the most striking exemplification of this kind of theory, of which simulacrum theory and spectacle-society theory develop other aspects.

[10] With Duranty and the supporters of painters like Courbet.

to another over what turns out to have been a period of about a century.

But now it is time to observe that, despite this attack on the very system of the genres as the realists find it still in place when, in the early eighteenth century, they begin their work in various national situations, realism as a formal strategy gradually begins to form new genres in its own right: hardening over, as it were, in a few tale-types, genres which the novel sometimes inherits but most often invents or reinvents, in a process in which they serve as a scaffolding which must in turn be dismantled. It is a curious and dialectical process which may be identified as the increasing tension between universalism and particularity (or even singularity) in modern times, where the genre eventually comes to be identified as the universal and thereby the target of critical isolation and eventual demolition, particularly insofar as such genres work virtually by definition with social and ideological stereotypes. Any consequent realism will therefore aim formally at dispensing with such stereotypes, at penetrating to the unique situations, cityscapes and individuals which make up the reality of a given moment of language, nationality and history. Yet this is a drive that will eventually reveal itself as one of the sources of modernism, insofar as it seeks to arrive at this or that unique phenomenon which bears no recognizable name and thereby becomes utterly unrecognizable: names and the familiar are of course themselves humble forms of the universal, and stereotypes its disreputable family members. It is, if you prefer, a matter of repetition, and later on mass culture will inaugurate a whole aesthetic of repetition, based on that same generic recognition, which in Lukács' high theorization bore the characterization of the typical.[11]

But, returning to the temporal categories with which we began this whole analysis, we may also describe the process in terms of reification, where some new attention to scene and to the present proves incompatible with the reifications of the older tale or story types in which general images of the various shapes of a reified destiny were vehiculated. Thus the story or tale will select this or that reified turn of events—a comic quid pro quo, a tragic accident, an ironic outcome, the woman scorned, the braggart given his comeuppance,

---

[11] See Georg Lukács, *Writer and Critic*, London: Merlin, 1970; and *Studies in European Realism*, London: Merlin, 1972. It is important to add that for Lukács, the "typical" was what ultimately registered the subterranean movements of History itself and not the merely stereotypical.

and the like—as the reified narrative form along which to string a set of contingent exemplifications, in such a way that the actual story becomes predictable and even formulaic, motivating later realists (not to speak of the modernists themselves) to subvert and destroy those in their turns. Unfortunately, however, as the history of nominalism testifies, new universals always begin to form around the wreckage of the old ones, and what had deservedly been revealed to be unnamable inevitably gets named and generalized in its turn. Such are then the new plot-types that begin to emerge within realism itself and to be codified and marked in their turn for narrative deconstruction.

2.

Besides melodrama as such (considered as a genre), I will briefly touch on four more of the new genres or sub-genres characteristic of realism. These are the *Bildungsroman*, the historical novel, the novel of adultery, and naturalism—taking this last now as a new type of narrative, rather than as a perfectly natural and evolutionary expansion of realism itself.

The ideological hesitations and compromises of the *Bildungsroman* have been too extensively documented by Franco Moretti for me to have to dwell on here,[12] save to say that his analysis raises for me another question about realism which turns on its ontological commitment to the status quo as such. This is not so much an overt political commitment (although the personal conservatism of most of the great realist novelists can be demonstrated biographically) as it is an artistic one: realism requires a conviction as to the massive weight and persistence of the present as such, and an aesthetic need to avoid recognition of deep structural social change as such and of the deeper currents and contradictory tendencies within the social order. To posit the imminence of some thoroughgoing revolution in the social order itself is at once to disqualify those materials of the present which are the building blocks of narrative realism, for from the revolutionary perspective they become mere appearances or epiphenomena, transitory moments of history, a sham calm before the storm, habits which are merely those of an ephemeral social class and which are about to be swept away forever. Realism can accommodate

---

12 Franco Moretti, *The Way of the World*, London: Verso, 2000.

images of social decadence and disintegration, as already in Balzac; but not this quite different sense of the ontology of the present as a swiftly running stream. I have argued elsewhere at some length[13] that this structural bias is visible in the satiric portraits all the great realists offer of intellectuals as such, a discrediting of all such radical commitments to history, to change and to social reform.

But the *Bildungsroman* also suggests a different reason for this unexpected reemergence of genre within a narrative mode seemingly dedicated to replacing such reified forms by a different kind of representation. For the young man of the *Bildungsroman* is as it were an instrument for the exploration of the new possibilities of bourgeois society, a kind of registering device, the establishment of a laboratory situation in which those possibilities can be acted out before our eyes. The protagonist is then not exactly a new social type, but rather a recurrent space in the new society which offers the way in for the new realist narrative.

The other three generic possibilities are to be regarded in the same way. The historical novel isolates the new sense of history emerging at the time of the French revolution, a historicity which determines the very emergence of modern historiography from the older chronicles and corresponds to the new dynamisms of capitalism after the industrial revolution. One can surely argue that all great realist novels are in some sense already historical ones: and Balzac's are already always situated in dated historical time as well as in a specific region or named space, while the others, even if they are not officially about past time, eventually become historical documents on the very strength of their ... dare I say it? ... realism.

Thus one can argue, as Lukács does,[14] that the realist novel is already itself profoundly historical, its new sense of everyday life now transforming the latter from the static sketches of custom or folkloric urban scenes into a sense of change—destruction, rebuilding, ruins, scaffolds, new and unrecognizable quarters, a feeling which will famously become ever more pronounced when one gets to Baudelaire and Haussmann (and Zola!). It is a feeling of change, already present, imminent, threatening, sometimes warmly anticipated, which will be underscored in any number of ways—debts accumulating and the interest fatally coming due, as everywhere from Balzac to Galdós; the

---

[13] See "The Experiments of Time" in this volume.

[14] See note 11 above, as well as Lukács, *The Historical Novel,* Lincoln: University of Nebraska Press, 1983.

crises of inflation; ageing and the generations (*La Cousine Bette*);[15] changes of regime; the notations of fashion (it being understood that change is inherent in the very concept of fashion): the external forces buffeting the stability of the married household and the domestic foyer. This is then the historicity already present and active within the new everyday, and offering the secondary stimuli of the narrative construction, impelling the central plot forward like an uneasy restless element through which it must move.

The historical novel as such and as a specific subgenre then constitutes something like a hypostasis of this inner historical reality: isolating the virus of historical change as though in a test tube and attaching this "history in a pure state" to something like the *images d'Epinal* which bourgeois households hang on their walls. The intersection between daily life and the great historical Event—most often political rather than economic—is one of the marks of the new historicity of the realist novel as already in Scott's *Waverley* (1811). It is as though the historical novel reverses this intersection and follows the historical Event through to the various intersections with private life rather than the other way round. This specialized form obviously has other determinants, which we cannot deal with here.[16]

As for the novel of adultery, Marcuse has observed[17] that it is the very space of negativity in nineteenth-century bourgeois life. Women, not yet fully absorbed into capitalism and the vehicles of unpaid labor, are more likely narrative occasions for revolt and resistance than men. The latter, unless they are young and dissatisfied (thereby becoming the narrative occasions for the *Bildungsroman*), are more likely to be absorbed into the dynamics of business, and by way of success to open up the paradigms of the mass-cultural bestseller, as in Zola's Octave (in *Au bonheur des dames*) or Maupassant's *Bel ami*. (Masculine failure is rather the province of naturalism, as we shall see in a moment.) But women cannot be successful in this sense (unless domestic contentment and satisfaction is considered to be something

---

15 I hope the lamentable absence of any discussion of Balzac in the present work will be remedied by a reminder of the two chapters of my *The Political Unconscious* (Ithaca: Cornell University Press, 1981) on *La Cousine Bette* and *La Rabouilleuse* (*The Black Sheep*), respectively.

16 But see "The Historical Novel Today," below, as well as Perry Anderson's provocative and stimulating survey of the history of this genre in "From Progress to Catastrophe," *London Review of Books* 33:15, July 2011.

17 Herbert Marcuse, *Eros and Civilization*, New York: Routledge, 1987.

positive, at which point the woman character falls to the second rank of minor character and of Dickensian "angel of the hearth" or Mediterranean matriarch). The novel of adultery (taken in the largest sense) is thus a unique space in which the negation of the social order can be narrativized in the person of this other half of "mankind": it is paradoxical and even a contradiction that women figures, like the great dancers of nineteenth-century ballet, become the great stars of the nineteenth-century novel—only compare Madame Bovary to the ineffectual Frédéric, or Anna Karenina to the vacillating Pierre!—a situation in which the role of the adulteress becomes the negative or privative one of showing that there is no place for them in that bourgeois society whose representation was to have been the object of the novel in the first place!

As for naturalism, it will then be the literary slot assigned to the fourth great new player in nineteenth-century society—alongside the young man, the political "world-historical individual," and the woman, naturalism opens a space for the worker and along with him the more heterogeneous population of the "lower depths," of lumpen-proletarians and outcasts generally. The perspectival distortion of this new naturalist sub-genre can be measured by comparing naturalism with the sentimental accounts of the poor in Dickens or Victor Hugo, in which the threat of collective *déclassement* is not present (despite Dickens's own childhood trauma). Philanthropy and its pity and sympathy turn out to be quite distinct from this late-nineteenth-century panic as it confronts a sinister and radically different space. Yet is it appropriate to characterize naturalism as a sub-genre of realism? Certainly its relations with realism have been much debated, and as a form the category of the naturalist novel does not quite seem "on all fours" with that of realism: where the stereotype of the latter involves social observation and the detailed rendering of urban settings, the naturalist text, with its *nostalgie de la boue*, seems rather to breathe a kind of *Stimmung* or affect associated with pessimism or melancholy, to the point where Deleuze's association of naturalism (Norris's *McTeague*) with the surrealism of Buñuel, with its shuddering symptoms of the unconscious and of deep impersonal volcanic forces, offers a welcome twist on these old theoretical debates.[18]

But is the naturalist movement and the unique expressivity its texts seems to breathe to be associated with a specific plot-line in such a

---

[18] Gilles Deleuze, *Cinéma I*, Paris: Minuit, 1983, chapter 8.

way that it can be classified as a sub-genre? My proposition is that naturalism's various and quite distinct exemplifications all share in a more general narrative paradigm, which could be described as the trajectory of decline and failure, of something like an entropy on the level of the individual destiny. And this is a phenomenon to be sharply distinguished from whatever representations of death or finitude are to be found in the mainstream realist novels. For this falling curve of the naturalist narrative shares in that more general late-nineteenth-century ideology which Marc Angenot has described[19] as a simultaneous belief in progress and a conviction of decadence and of a well-nigh biological deterioration, which expresses itself socially in the panics about degeneracy and widespread decadence. Here a fundamental contradiction is articulated in which the dynamic of capitalism is registered as progress (in urbanism, technology, business, civilization) at the same time that the deepest social anxieties take the form of an omnipresent perception of entropy on all social levels.

It is important for the understanding of naturalism, however, to identify this curiously contradictory ideology as a class perspective, reflecting the bourgeoisie's doubts of its own hegemony and its fears of a rising working class, of immigration and the populations of the colonies, of the overwhelming competition from the other imperial nation-states, and finally of its own inner loss of nerve. What stands at the center of the naturalist narrative paradigm is the perspective of the bourgeoisie and its vision of the other (lower) classes. Nor is this a purely epistemological matter: for included in this collective "point of view" is a desperate fear, that of déclassement, of slipping down the painfully climbed slope of class position and business or monetary success, of falling back into the petty bourgeoisie and thence on into working class misery itself. Indeed, the very perspective of misery with which the observing bourgeoisie envelops its image of lower-class life (in naturalism almost indistinguishable from marginality) expresses that anxiety of immanent decadence and decline, the condition into which Gervaise sinks back and from which Hurstwood saves himself by suicide. This middle class and the way in which it realizes its fantasies in the form of a clear-cut narrative paradigm is a better and more striking example of the relationship between class and literature than any of the vaguer and more triumphalistic expressions of the trajectory of the "rising" class in the Balzacian success stories

---

Marc Angenot, *1889*, Longueuil, Quebec: Le Préambule, 1989.

(themselves intermittent—Rastignac wins offstage, as it were—and carrying conviction only by the multiplicity of tales of failure that accompany them). For this reason, naturalism is far more class marked and localized than realism in general, and strikes the reader as far more specialized than the latter to the degree that the public no longer shares those particular fin-de-siécle terrors.

What the special case of naturalism also suggests is that, in an era of the differentiation of the various reading publics and of the increasing fragmentation of a general bourgeois reading public into a multiplicity of more specialized readerships (for whom the "niche" production of more differentiated sub-genres is designed), the other three basic realist narrative paradigms will themselves be reified and become more distinct sub-genres, with a tendency to find themselves degraded into mass-cultural forms and versions. At the same time, they become targets for the defamiliarizations of the various emergent modernisms, which stigmatize their conventions in the form of satire or absorb and sublimate their narratives into generalized allusions, transforming what were still narratives in the heyday of realism into so many synchronic literary connotations.

It is thus instructive to reread *Ulysses* as a compendium of these residual realist narrative lines and as an extraordinary new combinatory play with such residues. The presence of the *Bildungsroman* is the most obvious of these well-nigh extinct remanent forms, inasmuch as Joyce had explicitly walked Stephen through that form on his way to the brief teaching stint in Dalkey. We do not have to decide whether a later Stephen will fail in his pretentious *symboliste* literary ambitions or will on the contrary become Joyce himself, for the perspective of the single day radically interferes with the temporality of the older form which it effectively cancels, while leaving its negation behind as a trace.

It cannot be said that *Ulysses* is a parody of the *Bildungsroman* even if one takes the revisionist view that Stephen is a caricature and not to be estimated by his own manner of gravity and self-consciousness. Yet it is a diversion of that older form into a new combination, in which the novel of adultery is also inserted. Indeed, if supplied with the final point of view of Molly (and strengthened by the evidence of Brenda Maddox's *Nora*, which makes it clear that this book is not mere male writing but rather a collaboration in which Nora's own voice very much has its share), *Ulysses* can be seen as modernist after-image of *Madame Bovary* itself. That Molly stands as a cruder (yet more artistically gifted) version of the latter's protagonist, and Mr. Bloom a more comical yet more sympathetic version of Charles, may be obvious. But if one takes Blazes Boylan to be a version of Rodolphe and Stephen of Léon (always admitting that the latter's ultimate courtship is only realized in Molly's [and Bloom's] fantasies), then the entire complex of Flaubert's novel is as it were copied onto *Ulysses* and amalgamated into it in much the same way an old pair of blue jeans is pasted onto a Rauschenberg canvas; or better still, the way one photographic perspective is distorted by its anamorphic reproduction. Here the narrative of *Madame Bovary* has been projected onto another kind of plane surface, and the resultant segments then added into the new construction in various ways. It is as though Flaubert's realism survived in the form of a ruin, which a new (modernist) building then incorporated, as allusion, as memory, as museum piece, as derisory potsherd.

As for the historical novel, to be sure *Ulysses* is doubly a historical novel, in Joyce's own setting (eighteen years before publication) and for us, as a memorial to the pre-war colonial metropolis in general. But two dates mark it internally and externally: from the outside it is less the unexpected event of World War I which is unsuspected by the characters (but not by us), a war in which Irish regiments fought for the crown; but more especially that other utterly unanticipated event (in part itself a reaction against the War) which was the Easter Rising of 1916. Internally, deep history is embedded, not so much in Stephen's prehistory (which exists outside the book in other books, so that it can be taken by us as external historical fact), but also by the fitful glimpses of the Central European and Palestinian past of the Jews in Mr. Bloom's reveries.[20]

But what is centrally marked in the text as a different dimension of time is the anarchist violence of the Invincibles, the assassination in Phoenix Park twenty years earlier, which survives in the public sphere of gossip and rumor, and of folk memory, and is resurrected in the form of one of the ancient survivors of the guerrilla band, who makes an appearance in the cabman's shelter late at night and late in the book. Here history intersects, not with the present, but with the past—although it can be said that the governor general's procession (relayed by Woolf in the form of the king's limousine in *Mrs.*

---

[20] The non-Irish reader perhaps needs to be reminded of the precedent of Hungary, as described by Arthur Griffith in 1898 in *The Resurrection of Hungary: A Parallel for Ireland* (1904).

Dalloway) marks the imperial presence around which the administration of the colonial city, if not its real society, is organized. The newer postcolonial readings of *Ulysses* have served to translate it back into this sub-genre of the historical novel far more effectively than did the earlier standard mythical ones.

Naturalism, as we have said, is not exactly a sub-genre of realism, but Joyce's debt to the naturalists has often been evoked,[21] in the lower class status of most of his characters as well as in the uncensored urban detail and the journey through a nightmarish underworld or "*bas fonds*." I would myself prefer to evoke a naturalist perspective in the suggestions of a temporal prolongation and in Bloom's presentiment of his own future and decline, his own proletarianization (which I have discussed elsewhere).[22]

Such is then the afterlife of the sub-genres that emerge from realism and become visible in its breakdown. To be sure, Joyce was obliged to unify these remnants of the older synthesis by imposing a new and pseudo-mythic narrative structure (the *Odyssey* parallel) upon this heterogeneity in order to hold its multiplicities together.

Here genre is itself hypostasized and projected outside the novel by the *Odyssey* parallels: the synchronic structure of the single-day novel does not really allow us to read Stephen's brief contact with Bloom in any really familial or psychoanalytic way, whatever the latter's fantasies. That "theme" is, however, projected out of the novel into an unwritten narrative version, which is seized and absorbed by the Odysseus/Telemachus plot and as it were projected, reified, out into legend, much as humans were frozen and lifted into the stars' constellations in ancient times. The *Odyssey* parallel preserves the diachrony of these interpersonal situations, as it were *pour mémoire*, while we are reading and observing them in a quite different dimension: it is as though generic structure, no longer current or available, were acknowledged only as a memory from the distant epic past. And this is then a reified generic essence in which both later sub-genres of realism—the *Bildungsroman* and the novel of adultery—find their place, historicity itself floating above the text in the form of the ancient catastrophe of the Trojan War.

It is as though the idea of genre had taken the place of its practice in this ultimate moment; and that a series of powerful affective moments

---

[21] Harry Levin's pathbreaking *James Joyce* of 1942 described Ulysses as a synthesis of symbolism and naturalism.

[22] See my essay "Joyce or Proust?" in *The Modernist Papers*, London: Verso, 2007.

of an all-immersing present could only be unified—whether at the level of the chapter or the work itself—by way of an idea of unification symbolically concentrated in an ancient, classical, pre-novelistic form.

Yet perhaps another tendency—less a breakdown than a glimpse of some deeper textuality beneath the narrative forms—can be deduced both from Joyce's simultaneous narrativization and denarrativization of *Madame Bovary* and from Auerbach's initial reading of it: this is the persistence of some non-narrative everyday behind the structures of the narrative genres. This non-narrative "reality," which Auerbach also calls "existential," is at one with that impulse towards scene and the present which we initially associated with affect as such. But we may also identify it with another tendency at work within the triumphant realist paradigm, and that is its increasingly episodic character, which will eventually mark the supercession of plot by scene, of imagination by fancy, and of narrative by a kind of non-narrative perceptuality. A reversion to beginnings no doubt, in one sense: for the novel is an omnibus form cobbled together out of heterogeneous materials, chief among which is the sketch (as Dickens called it) or Balzac's *physiognomie*, the newspaper columns on the various and colorful sights of the big city, the journalistic observation and notation which adds to the very density of the narrative text itself. But with serialization, this centrifugal tendency is then once again intensified; and the installment, with its recurrent internal dynamic and its relative autonomy, encourages a tendency once again to break up the continuity of the narrative or story-telling process, albeit in a new way.

We may call this new tendency one towards autonomization; here what Luhmann called "differentiation" is at one with reification itself as process. But where in poetry reification results in the increasing transformation of words into objects, as in Baudelaire's strict forms, in the novel it can better be detected, not only in the emergence of descriptive set pieces, but even more in the tendency of the secondary characters to move forward and to eclipse the relationships of the main characters around whom narrative itself is chiefly organized and Imagination invested and rehearsed. Galdós offers the supreme illustration of this process whereby the novel becomes a kind of tour around the secondary characters of the city and its narrative space, at least insofar as the city is most fully realized and externalized form of the narrative space towards which the realist novel tends. Here again *Ulysses* casts a privileged light backwards on the older form, whose multiple plots and intersections prove to be something like narrative cities in their own right.

3.

A final return to melodrama may be instructive here; but not to the generic substantive; to the melodramatic as such, which we have also consistently identified with the theatrical and with the rhetorical. What is most commonly associated with these epithets, particularly when they are used in a critical or negative spirit, is not so much their effect as the sense that they constitute something like narrative supplements, structures which are superimposed or added on, the survival of an outdated aesthetic of expression which is called upon to compensate for a different kind of chemical deficiency.

For Fried's own discussion (and that of many of the theatrical discussions of melodrama as well) makes it clear that the association of melodrama with theatricality raises the more general issue of rhetoric in modern times and its repudiation (as in Verlaine's famous poem), not only in modernism as such but also in the course of the development of the realist novel. Rhetoric here means not only the theatricality of an essentially expressive language (based as we have already shown on the primacy of the named emotion), but also, from Scott and Hugo on down, the shorthand explosive devices whereby a plot can be begun, turned in a new direction, or brought to a timely end (in an untimely fashion). This is essentially the function of a kind of narrative rhetoric in Zola, as we have seen: the need to finish it all off with a catastrophe, or the insertion of grotesque figures à la Hugo, such as Saccard's demon child in *L'argent*, in order to give a forward momentum to events easily seduced into lethargy by the suffusion of affect (and eschewing any great interest in introspection or psychology as such).

Yet Zola's melodramatic moments not only remind us that he is the inheritor of Hugo fully as much as of Balzac; they also mark a significant disjunction in his raw material. We are inclined to deplore these narrative excesses at the same time that we admire them (if only in the thrill of the execution): which is to say that already in the very reading of the text they project themselves as supplements, the raw material acts out its own inner rifts and discontinuities. It seems to want to demonstrate, on its own, the gap between the lavish, indeed libidinous and garish *jouissance* in daily life and in routine, in the great lists and catalogues of objects, the body's swoons and its *bonheur*, its exhilarations and ecstatic glimpses; and on the other hand the gratuitous explosions, the fires, the bankruptcies, the monstrosities and gratuitous (yet "fatal") catastrophes, which are the price we have to pay for the novel's closure. The excess lies thus in the very subject-matter itself rather than in its creator's bad taste. It foreshadows as it were some future distance between the two temporalities of iteration and Event, of boredom and historical cataclysm; but it also announces the imminent breakdown of narrative as the form in which such "reality" can be registered and conveyed.

As far as George Eliot is concerned, the assertion of some resistance to melodrama cannot but seem paradoxical in the light of the innumerable melodramatic elements in her novels, from the seduction of Hetty in *Adam Bede* to the trials of Gwendolyn in *Daniel Deronda*, from the mysteries of the birth of that novel's hero to Romola's drama of vengeance, from the fortunes and bankruptcies of any number of these stories to their accompaniment by secrecy and blackmail so persuasively documented by Alexander Welsh.[23]

Yet the significance of such elements needs to be grasped in the light of the heterogeneous construction of these works, where a variety of narrative paradigms (and not only those of melodrama) have been superimposed in omnibus constructions which do not betray carelessness or inexperienced workmanship so much as they suggest a will to the inclusion of multiple impulses, a variety of social and psychological types, and an ambitious multiplicity of themes.

The *costumbrismo* of *Adam Bede* is thus combined with a class tragedy à la *Faust I*, the disastrous fraternization of the girl of the people with a young aristocrat (who assuredly occupies the place of a certain kind of traditional villain). *The Mill on the Floss* is an even greater hodgepodge of "subjects" (as Henry James liked to call them) and of plot lines, not all fully explored or brought to conclusion. *Romola*'s status as a historical novel demands a heterogeneity as distinct from the relative single-mindedness of purpose of *Silas Marner* or, in its different way, of *Felix Holt*. Only *Middlemarch* triumphantly succeeds in fusing its plot strands into a coherent landscape, while the unusual upper-class milieu of *Daniel Deronda* equally unexpectedly

---

[23] Alexander Welsh, *George Eliot and Blackmail*, Cambridge: Harvard University Press, 1985.

opens a large fissure in this work and encouraged Leavis outrageously to propose that its political half (the tale of Deronda's ethnic identity) simply be excised.[24]

Yet it is more instructive to see this variety of Eliot's forms as so many exercises in technical experimentation. Indeed, of the other great nineteenth-century novelists, only Flaubert is comparable in the strategic deliberation of his projects and in their limited number. Neither Eliot nor Flaubert were professional novelists of the type of Dickens or Zola, of Balzac or even of Henry James; and each of their works can be seen as a laboratory experiment which poses a distinct form-problem in its own right, however satisfactory the solution.

It is therefore not surprising that the problem of melodrama should find a self-conscious working through in Eliot: in this work a narrative dilemma has come to historical fruition and at the same time has encountered a philosophical motivation to sustain it. We do not need to speculate on the timeliness of the dilemmas of ethics for a Victorian and evolution-minded public (Nietzsche is there to document its wider cultural resonance).

David Ferris has indeed pointed out, with great acuity, that *Middlemarch* itself contains a significant autoreferential digression on melodrama as a form, in the interlude (chapter 15) which recalls Lydgate's early affair in Paris with a young French actress.[25] The moment involves a melodrama in which an unfaithful wife kills her jealous husband on stage: yet in the moment in question the heroine really does kill her counterpart (who is or was in fact her husband "in real life"). Here the separation between melodrama as a genre and the realism that must always resist it, cancel it, unveil something more real behind its formulaic stereotype, is absolute. What "realism" then adds in the process is the revelation that the next layer of representation —her foot slipped, it was an accident—is also false and that the young woman in fact meant to kill her spouse in the first place. This minor discovery is in fact rather momentous for George Eliot's work in general, and we will come back to it.

A more serious objection to the theory of the effacement of melodrama confronts us in the very existence of George Eliot's last great work, *Daniel Deronda*, in which melodrama is inexplicably reinstated

---

[24] "As for the bad part of *Daniel Deronda*, there is nothing to do but cut it away," *The Great Tradition*, London: Chatto and Windus, 1948, 122.

[25] David Ferris, *Theory and the Evasion of History*, Baltimore: Johns Hopkins Univsersity Press, 1993.

in all its glory, with an implacably victimized yet admirably energetic heroine and a villain whose cold passion equals anything the eighteenth century might have bequeathed us. In the case of Grandcourt, indeed, Eliot has availed herself of none of those representational techniques of bad faith which might have made this character more attractive to the reader, or at least more comprehensible: the few brief flashes of his inner life (and the memory of his love for Mrs. Glasher and her children) are scarcely enough to mar this powerful image of the libertine-villain, whose coldness, from Laclos and Sade, from Lovelace, to Byron and Balzac, is the traditional sign of the energies of vice. Nor does the secondary foil of Lush (the corrupt domestic familiar from the Don Juan legend onwards) account for everything that is inexplicable about the existence of this archetype of a certain evil: the inexplicability of radical evil as that is indeed reflected in Grandcourt's manner, which is the unforseeability and capriciousness of the refusal, the unexpected affirmation of the unjustifiable demand, the serene conviction as to the necessity of dominating the other.

When seen in this light and replaced in this particular cultural tradition, the figure of Grandcourt, surely one of Eliot's most fully realized characters, belongs unmistakably in the cast of characters of archetypal melodrama. Yet what can account for this remarkable formal regression on George Eliot's part, in a work which otherwise in formal and stylistic energy and intelligence is in no way inferior to *Middlemarch*? Surprisingly enough, I believe that the reasons are political, and that they also account for that seemingly unrelated development of the Deronda plot, which we have seen a reader so eminent as Leavis suggest its surgical removal from the Gwendolyn half, which he greatly admired.

James's pronouncement on Eliot's conservatism—"Both as an artist and a thinker ... our author is an optimist; and although a conservative is not necessarily an optimist, I think an optimist is pretty likely to be a conservative" [26]—needs some revision, particularly when coming from so apolitical a writer as James himself, whose characterization suggests nothing particularly progressive on his part, but merely that in her "conservatism" he still detected something political, a survival of political impulses and values in what should have been nothing but art. I think it might have been better to characterize these remnants

---

[26] Henry James, *Literary Criticism, Volume II: European Writers; Prefaces to the New York Edition*, New York: Library of America, 1984, 933

of the political in Eliot as anti-political, or better still, as anti-activist. Certainly she had a keen sense of oppression, and just as obviously she deplored both working-class agitation (*Felix Holt*) or militant feminism as such, without for all that ceasing to deplore the wrongs they (mistakenly) set out to correct by outright political action. The providential[27] lent a Utopian glow to such contradictory situations without diminishing the damaging critical vision she exercised in the portrayal of intolerable confinements such as the marriages of Dorothea or Gwendolyn.

Might it not be suggested that the outright political conflicts and social struggles she wished to avoid in contemporary social life, with their taking of sides and the antagonistic structure they necessarily generated, were for her not without their relationship to those melodramatic structures she sought to minimize in her novelistic constructions?

Meanwhile, idyllic visions of an older rural and village life become less and less "realistic" with the development of industrial capitalism, and neither reform bill seems to justify the reconciliation of "progress" with that rural and nostalgic restoration which an optimist like George Eliot might have been expected to hope for. Instead, everywhere in Europe, nationalist movements unexpectedly begin to take the place of the kinds of internal social conflicts that had left their traces in her earlier work. To encompass this new and larger world, a new kind of political thinking is required, which we find Gwendolyn confronting with dismay and good will alike. *Daniel Deronda* as a novel does the same; and it seems plausible enough that, whatever discomfort George Eliot may have felt with the relatively separatist movements of workers or women, her keen sense of the "web" of community and of collective relations would have found the nationalist movements in principle more congenial.[28] Yet they are not to be activist, whence the choice of the Jewish revival as the most appropriate vehicle for this new and evolving political consciousness. In evaluating it we must utterly put aside anachronistic connotations of a later political Zionism (let alone the *Realpolitik* of the state of Israel) and grasp it as a purely cultural nationalism (leaving aside the later connotations of this phrase as well), or in other words a collective

---

[27] Once again, see "The Experiments of Time" elsewhere in this volume.

[28] Her idiosyncratic interest in Zionism is to be sure not the only form of political rethinking to be observed in this latter half of the nineteenth century, after the triumph of representational politics and the onset of imperialism.

national movement wholly organized around the cultural tradition and without the activist political program Eliot so systematically eschewed.

This Eliot, whose interest in the continental nationalisms is, like her philosophical commitments, so far in advance of the more parochial British concerns, may then be seen as revising her view of local social life as well; and here we return to the question of melodrama, but now in order to underscore its political content as a symbolic act. For the tradition in which we have ranged Grandcourt is inescapably, along with the Gothic in general, an expression of the Enlightenment critique of the aristocracy and the ancien régime. The villainy of the libertine protagonists is a class oppression; politics and sexuality are both conjoined in the fundamental eighteenth-century signifier of "virtue"; and Grandcourt like all the others is the quintessential aristocrat battening on commoners. *Adam Bede*, for the Germanophile who was George Eliot, is as we have said a replay of *Faust I*, with its tragedy of the seduced peasant girl; *Daniel Deronda*, is more akin to the Gothic, and to the tyranny of the nobility over its imprisoned female victims. At any rate, I suggest that the deeper plot structure of this last of Eliot's novels consists in a conjuncture between the melodramatic denunciation of the persistence of an English ancien régime and the Utopian vision of another kind of organic community now set, not in the English past, but in some unfamiliar future landscape in which, with Deronda himself, our lives and selves may be utterly transformed.

Yet in all this we have overlooked as it were the other melodrama, the other villain. For surely one of the theatrical (and operatic) staples of melodrama was always the family romance, which is to say the rediscovered paternity of the orphaned child, the dramatical revelation or the birth of hero or heroine, the anagnorisis whose cries of joy and amazement allow the work to be completed and the plot to be finished off (we will return to this matter of narrative closure in a moment). Meanwhile, we also seem to have forgotten that the villain can very often take the form of the other sex, persisting from time immemorial (as in the Chinese tradition of "white-boned demons" and evil princesses) all the way down to the femmes fatales of Hollywood film noir.

It is a reminder that must at once draw our attention away from Grandville (in Eliot's first plot) to the Princess Halm Eberstein, the true melodramatic center of the second plot line: the bad mother, who abandons her son Daniel to become a world-famous diva, and who radiates the coldness conventionally associated with the actantial villain. But we cannot properly evaluate this figure and her climactic position in both plots without returning to its "*mise en abyme*" in that little anecdote of the earlier novel, the tale of Lydgate's first love and disillusionment. For there, in passing, we find enunciated what is really explosive and political in George Eliot's work, in the offhand explanation of his actress lover after the admission of guilt: "'You are a good young man,' she said, 'But I do not like husbands and will never have another.'"[29] In this sentence, and not in any of her moral sententiousness, nor even in sympathetic figures like Dorothea, we find the beating heart of George Eliot's work and the place in which the conventional sub-generic narratives both of melodrama and of the drama of adultery are revealed to be the merest of disguises and fronts for an unequalled drama of liberation. Just as the male villain, the seducer, constituted the civilized avatar of the age-old cannibal ogre (Freud's master of the primal horde), and the coldly villainous woman that of the witch and evil sorceress who kills her own offspring (Medea), so the work of realism lies in dissolving these archetypes (and not, as the old myth criticism tried to assure us, of staging their survival) and in appropriating their archetypal plots for new acts of freedom.

Still, we must also not forget that, emptied of its content and traditional meaning, melodrama, as well as the other tale-types we have mentioned here, is also an empty form, which survives to supply the structure of narrative and in particular that by which it can be set in motion and that with which it can find closure: the ending itself, the catastrophe—explosion, conflagration, flood, financial cataclysm, or indeed, in some cases (*Fidelio*) the providential rescue, the "*reitender Bote*" of Brecht, the Queen's pardon, hope against hope. In all these cases, negative or positive, what is then reinforced is the fundamental category of Ending as melodramatic closure and ultimate satisfaction —if not the destruction of the villains then at the very least the end of the world.

But we have repeatedly argued that realism does not mean the utter effacement of that manifestation of destiny and its récits which is the melodramatic mode: but only its weakening and tendential attenuation in the face of its opposite number, the scene, affect, the eternal present, consciousness or whatever form indeed that

---

[29] George Eliot, *Middlemarch*, London: Penguin, 1994, 154

incomapible impulse might take. Zola's cataclysms, Balzac's frantic denouements, all testify to the persistence of this temporal structure and its indispensability to a form which, particularly in the mode of nineteenth-century serialization, would be sorely challenged without some such device, some such signal of closure and completion.

Is it necessary to add that in this respect George Eliot is herself a master of the melodramatic ending? The great flood that sweeps away the protagonists of *The Mill on the Floss* is surely as Zolaesque as anything in Dickens; and it is no accident, surely, that both *Romola* and *Daniel Deronda* conclude with drownings that are highly melodramatic indeed. Fear death by water. It is that fear, and the formal innovations she devised to conjure as well as to satisfy it, that make George Eliot so interesting an overnight stop on the path from realism's emergence to its dissolution.[30]

Yet there exists one final form of genre which it is virtually impossible for realism to dissolve without completely undoing itself in the process: and that is the novel itself. One of Barthes' central literary observations was the idea that the novel as a form was less to be defined by plot and structure than by the "*romanesque*" itself, by a novel-ness that extended down into the very pores of the language and the individual sentences, transforming even ostensible fact and alleged nonfiction into the inescapable connotation of the supplementary declaration, "I am a novel." I have elsewhere used the following sentence from a nonfictional journalistic work as an example, and it remains a dramatic one:

> The morning air was frigid in Greenwich, Connecticut. At 5:00 a.m. on March 17, 2008, it was still dark, save for the headlights of the black Mercedes idling in the driveway, the beams illuminating patches of slush that were scattered across the lawns of the twelve-acre estate. The driver heard the stones of the walkway crackle as Richard S. Fuld Jr. shuffled out the front door and into the backseat of the car.[31]

Now this is an opening sentence, and thereby all the more significant insofar as it programs the reader and proposes a certain narrative and

---

[30] The two classic studies of endings and beginnings are of course Barbara Herrnstein Smith, *Poetic Closure*, Chicago: University of Chicago Press, 1974; and Edward Said, *Beginnings*, New York: Columbia University Press, 1985.

[31] Andrew Ross Sorkin, *Too Big to Fail*, New York: Penguin, 2009. It is important to note that even if all the details of these sentences are factually true and not merely *vraisemblable* (the snow, the headlights, etc.), the sentences remain no less "fictional."

ultimately novelistic stance on what follows. But if this is so, and if "the novel" is at one and the same time Barthes' "novelistic" and the last genre to be dissolved in realism's struggle against reification and reified form, then it becomes paradoxically clear that realism's ultimate adversary will be the realistic novel itself.

Chapter VIII

The Swollen Third Person, or,
Realism after Realism

What determined the speech that startled him in the course of their encounter scarcely matters, being probably but some words spoken by himself quite without intention—spoken as they lingered and slowly moved together after their renewal of acquaintance.

Until now, we have been telling this story in terms of the largest and most manageable categories: plot, character systems, genres and the like; only the traditional conception of description or ekphrasis has seemed to introduce any attention to style, or rather, to be more precise about the nature of this analysis, to rhetoric. The division, however, already suggests some split between macro and micro, fable and *syuzhet*, story and treatment, which suspiciously echoes the opposition between object and subject, if not even between telling and showing; and which demands scrutiny, that is to say, historicization. The preceding chapters have indeed consisted in an effort to historicize the larger categories mentioned above, and to replace generic plots and systems of characters within a process of change in which their functions undergo fundamental restructuration. It should be obvious enough that the very narrative language in which these materials are staged and conveyed is no less subject to historical modification or evolution; and more than that, necessarily also furnishes clues, when properly scrutinized, as to the transformations underway.

Once again, however, we are confronted with a properly dialectical ambivalence in which the very syntactical machinery that was fundamental to the construction of realism at one and the same time turns out to participate in its deterioration (and then, perhaps, to its rebirth as something else, as yet to be named). Auerbach's great lesson in this area was, to be sure, the correlation between the conquest of ever more complex syntactical forms and the "representation of reality" as such; he was less interested in the appropriation of such syntactic constructions for what we might call anti-realistic tendencies, and it is on this dialectic of ambivalence that we will be concentrating here.

We will find, for example, that Irony (normally listed as a trope and perhaps unduly enlisted and overworked in their practice by tropological thinkers such as Paul de Man and Hayden White) cannot be divided quite so neatly and dialectically into stable irony (good!) and unstable irony (bad!) as it is by Wayne Booth.[1] Above all, however, we will have to come to terms with perhaps the most notorious, or at least the most exhaustively studied forms of linguistic and stylistic innovation in the nineteenth century—"*style indirect libre*," free indirect discourse or *Erlebte Rede*. Such "unspeakable sentences" (Ann Banfield) are preeminently associated with Flaubert, even though scholars have traced their ancestry as far back as Jane Austen (if not Ariosto); and their emergence clearly marks a fundamental event in the history of language. This event has in my opinion most often been misinterpreted; but it would be wrong to underestimate its importance or to relegate it to a marginal state, as Pasolini reminds us ("its presence for a diagnostician is the proof of an ideology that cannot appear in only a few extreme cases but which completely characterizes the entire work").[2]

For the moment it suffices to associate it with the gradual primacy of another category, which it is as difficult to characterize as a linguistic phenomenon as it is as a narrative technique. This is the "law" or norm of "point of view," now taught in creative writing courses, and erected as a hegemonic ideology under the authority of Henry James and by innumerable literary censors, who scan texts for its infringement, which they might as well have discovered on every other page of Tolstoy or Zola. The emergence of this ideology then also demands historical explanation.

But I begin here with a linguistic phenomenon far less often remarked, no doubt on account of its apparent triviality, which (like a virus) primarily affects the pronoun: "The speech that startled him…" It would be tempting to speculate on the practice of the pronoun in traditional (oral) storytelling, in social situations in which its opposite number—the proper name—is itself the locus of no little

---

[1] Wayne Booth, *The Rhetoric of Fiction*, Chicago: University of Chicago Press, 1983; and especially *A Rhetoric of Irony*, Chicago: University of Chicago Press, 1975.

[2] Pier Paolo Pasolini, *Heretical Empiricism*, Washington: New Academia Publishing, 1988, 82.

significance (where it comes from, is it a new name given by circumstances, or a secret name, does it designate kinship, and so on and so forth). But in the modern languages it has become, we are told, a "rigid designator,"[3] and the pronouns which take its place from time to time must therefore be equally rigid. The classical word for such substitution is "*anaphora*," namely the reference of the term—generally a pronoun—back to the named object for which it stands. But in our reference text—the opening sentence of a novella—no named object is given.

This very structure participates in the dialectical ambivalence we have already anticipated: for nothing is more ancient and more traditional than the "*in medias res*" recommended by Horace and surely practiced well before Homer, a narrative procedure equally effective on the microlevel of the sentence itself and its syntax. Modern linguists or rhetoricians have reasonably enough baptized this construction "cataphora":[4] yet its very absence from the ancient manuals is suggestive. For just as the ancient mariners feared the approach to an edge of the world from which they fantasized a drop into nothingness, so this peculiar beginning seems to betoken a nothingness, a void, before the opening of the text itself. The cataphora articulates some inauguratory mystery, some absolute darkness before the voice begins, which no doubt carries intimations of all the primal fears of beginnings, creations, the waking up without a memory or an identity, birth itself. But in fact, the cataphora, far from being a rarity, has been elevated, in much contemporary literature, to the status of an incipit:

> He was there, waiting. He was the first one, standing, lounging, trying to look occupied or at least innocent.

The cataphora, however, rarely succeeds in looking innocent; nor does it really mean to. For this kind of sentence most often announces a thriller of some kind, and the unidentified pronoun stands in fact for the unidentified serial killer of the novel in question. Nothing further, indeed, from the classic opening sentence, in all its nominatory solemnity:

---

[3] The expression is Saul Kripke's, in *Naming and Necessity*, Cambridge: Wiley-Blackwell, 1991.

[4] Most notably in the work of A. J. Greimas.

Those two girls, Constance and Sophia Baines, paid no heed to the manifold interest of their situation, of which, indeed, they had never been conscious.

Alexey Fyodorovich Karamazov was the third son of a landowner in our district, Fyodor Pavlovich Karamazov, so noted in his time (and even now still recollected among us) for his tragic and fishy death, which occurred just thirteen years ago and which I shall report in its proper context.

Detective Inspector Napoleon Bonaparte, of the Queensland police, was walking along a bush track on his way to Windee Station.[5]

To which we should add that sometimes this named character with whom the novel announces itself is in fact a named landscape (through which, for example, a distant horseman is riding).

The reader will anticipate the relationship to be established between these two kinds of actantial openings (with or without the proper name) and the "namelessness" we have been attributing to affect in earlier chapters. For the moment it is important to insist that what is at stake here does not concern the matter of narrative beginnings only, but as Pasolini put it, betrays the working of a deeper and more general ideology at work throughout the narrative text as a whole, most visibly detectable in the system of pronouns and their stable or unstable relationship to names and nouns as such.

But we cannot evaluate changes in pronominal use without forming such a larger view of the status of narrative sentences as such, a view I wish to adapt from Käthe Hamburger's well-known but perhaps today little read study *The Logic of Literature*.[6] On the face of it, Hamburger's 1957 treatise (much like that of her adversary Roman Ingarden, whose *Literary Work of Art* of 1931 reached English at much the same time in the early 1970s)[7] constituted a phenomenologically oriented aesthetics, with particular attention to the status of language in literature, which she called "fictional." This is,

---

[5] The four openings can be identified as follows: William Faulkner, *Intruder in the Dust*, Random House, 1948; Arnold Bennett, *The Old Wives' Tale*, London: Penguin, 2007 [1908]; Fyodor Dostoyevsky, *The Brothers Karamazov*, trans. Richard Pevear and Larissa Volokhonsky, New York: Farrar, Straus and Giroux, 2002; Arthur Upfield, *The Sands of Windee*, London: Hutchinson, 1931.

[6] Käthe Hamburger, *The Logic of Literature*, trans. Marilynn J. Rose, Bloomington: Indiana University Press, 1973.

[7] Roman Ingarden, *The Literary Work of Art*, Evanston: Northwestern University Press, 1979.

however, not a work of linguistics, and is only distantly related to the great German school of romance philology (with its distinctive "style studies" such as are to be found in Spitzer or Auerbach), but is rather more distantly inspired by the exchange between Goethe and Schiller on "epic" language (it being understood that the German *episch* most often simply means narrative, as also in Brecht's "epic" theater).[8] The crisis in philosophy in recent years, and not least the evident plunge in the prestige of aesthetics as a subfield (in the context of an immense enlargement of culture in general in postmodernity, with the recent exception of a doubtful ideological revival of the essentially aesthetic question of "beauty"), has reduced scholarly interest in problems of aesthetic ontology, such as the nature of fictive language, and along with it in treatises like those of Hamburger (or Ingarden) respectively. Although I generally share the distaste for the word "fiction," I will not argue the merits of this neglect further here.

Yet we thereby lose the benefit of everything paradoxical or scandalous in Hamburger's positions in this seemingly conventional work: and it is precisely those heretical judgements that will be most useful for us here. Her articulation of the nature of the narrative sentence for example—what she calls the "*Aussage*" or "statement"—can easily be confused with more traditional formulations of the nature of "fictive" language: that of dematerialization (Hegel), intuition and expression (Croce), quasi-judgements or pseudo-statements (Ingarden) or neutralization (Husserl and Sartre). But the conclusions she draws from her view of the narrative statement are startling, and quite different from those of her predecessors. To be sure, she will dwell insistently on Schiller's idea of literature's *Vergegenwärtigung* or presentification; but she radically detemporalizes the idea:

> Here and now, i.e., presentified, the action in narrative literature unfolds, but this Now, this presentification, must not necessarily have the sense of the temporal present, although it can assume this sense—rather easily, too—as a fictive present. But if literary art, as Schiller, in disagreement with Goethe, believed (and many shared this notion), necessitates that even the epic poet "presentify," this concept nevertheless becomes erroneous once one means, as did Schiller, that "something which has happened," something past, must be made present. The preterite in narrative literature no longer functions to designate past-ness solely because literature does not presentify in a temporal sense. The concept of presentification is in its ambiguity not only inexact, but, as a designation for the structure of fictional,

---

8   See the exchange of letters between Goethe and Schiller in April and May of 1797.

mimetic literature, it is also incorrect and misleading. What it means here is fictionalization. And it does not stand in contradiction to this when we nevertheless say that the action of a novel unfolds "here and now." For "here and now"—and with this we close the circle of our proof of the preterite's loss of temporal function—means epistemologically, and therefore also in terms of theory of language, primarily the zero-point of the system of reality, which is determined through the coordinates of time and space. It means the I-Origo, in reference to which the Now has no precedence over the Here and vice versa. Rather, all three terms designate the originary point of experience. Even if a "present time" (which in the temporal sense is not a series of points, but rather a duration which is arbitrary, extended according to subjective experience) is not indicated at all, such as by the word "today" or a specific date, etc., we experience the action of the novel as being "here and now," as the experience of fictive persons, or, as Aristotle said, of men in action. In turn, this means nothing other than that we experience these fictive persons in their I-originarity, to which all representational particulars, including all possible temporal ones, are referred.[9]

We will return to the interesting question of the use of words like "here" or "now" later on. What is far more unsettling is the consequence, implacably drawn by Hamburger—that the narrative (or fictional) *Aussage* is distinguished by its suspension of the subject-object relationship: it is a statement without a subject (unlike ordinary reality-statements). The power of the distinction can be measured by her ingenious reversal of the traditional terms of the problem: fictionality does not depend on the existence or not of the object, but rather on that of the subject position.

At any rate, it is evident that Hamburger's seemingly perverse yet absolute position here at one stroke frees us from the interminable literary-theoretical theorization of Implied Authors, Implied Readers, and the like, which only add unnecessary entities to such discussions; while at the same time preserving a kind of literary or narrative objectivity from those realms of fantasy and fantasizing, of the imaginary or of the imagination, in which at length this activity seems indistinguishable from that idle daydreaming with which the first readers of novels were so often taxed. Narrative thereby, without ceasing to be fictional, ceases to be unreal: and it is perhaps a consequence of the society of the spectacle, and the simulacrum, a society invested at all points with images and the Imaginary, with daydreams, wish fulfillments and other quasi-fetishistic intensities, that such a position will today seem less paradoxical than it once was.

---

[9] Hamburger, *The Logic of Literature*, 96–7.

Without wishing to resituate Hamburger's work altogether in that poststructural universe in which an Althusser can evoke science as a writing without a subject, the association must be made with Stanley Cavell's view of film as a world without me, that is, a world viewed as though in the absence of the viewer:[10] for it is with this conception of the aesthetic object that Hamburger's notion of narrative ("fiction") has its kinship. This is also the moment to place it in relationship with phenomenology, and in particular with Sartre's notion of an impersonal consciousness for which "I" or the ego is not a subject but rather an object, and indeed an object among others, although of a very special kind.[11] The reading of narrative is thus impersonal, and if we could find some equivalent for this formula in the realm of temporality we would also have solved the seemingly intractable dilemma of a temporal present with which the narrative conception of presentification (as we have seen) confronts us; in other words, we might find it possible to avoid terms like "eternal" which, tainted as they are, seem alone to offer an alternative to every purely temporal vocabulary.

Still, these are not the only dilemmas with which Hamburger's radical position leaves her. The problem of lyric is easily resolved by hiving lyric language off into a separate genre, one which accommodates the first-person pronoun and its subject position without any great difficulties. But there is also first-person narrative, and this is a more difficult nut to crack. I quickly resume Hamburger's unexpectedly satisfying solution: first-person narrative is distinctively fictive, not in its unreality but rather in that other root sense of the fictive which is the *feigned*. First-person narrative is therefore a form of acting, of posing, feigning, taking up positions, before that spectator who is the reader. The I-narrative thereby imperceptibly finds itself ranged in another category altogether from that of narrative prose: namely, the theatrical, whose relationship to rhetoric and melodrama we have already touched on in the previous chapter (as it was theorized by Michael Fried).[12] Despite the eminent examples of first-person literary narratives in German, from the eighteenth-century letter novel all the way to Thomas Mann, it is difficult to escape the impression that for Hamburger this essentially histrionic

---

[10] Stanley Cavell, *The World Viewed*, Cambridge: Harvard University Press, 1979.

[11] Jean-Paul Sartre, *The Transcendence of the Ego*, trans. Forrest Williams and Robert Kirkpatrick, New York: Hill and Wang, 1960, [1934].

[12] Michael Fried, *Absorption and Theatricality*, Chicago: University of Chicago Press, 1988.

and self-posing, self-dramatizing kind of narrative is somehow aes-
thetically inferior to the third-person classics: this is not an opinion
which need be binding on us, but it does obligate us to argue the case
for such narratives in a different way, which may require the theorization and opposition of two distinct systems rather than simply
judgements of value on individual writers and individual texts.

We must however forestall a simplification which would inevitably
put a premature end to the current discussion. We have had occasion
in the course of the preceding chapters to denounce from time to time
the false symmetries inevitably proposed by the inescapable opposition of subject and object. Garden-variety film criticism demonstrates
that we face this temptation again at this point, since our two kinds of
narratives—third and first—seem immediately to lend themselves to
the Hollywood classification of objective and subjective shots, camera
work that proposes itself as the scanning of an objective world (substituting its own apparatus for the position of the human spectator)
and views arranged so as to approximate what a given character in the
film sees (an impression carefully constructed and codified by editing
practices such as the matching shot and shot-reverse-shot, which now
pass themselves off as natural). This is the point at which we approach
problems like point of view and even (following Pasolini) *style indirect
libre*. We will postpone them for the moment.

It is enough at this point to repudiate this facile distinction and to
suggest that both "objective" or third person narrative and subjective
or first-person performances are far more complicated—the he or she
of the third person being based on a reifying system of names and
external personifications we can no longer accept today, while the
first-person narrative position itself, on closer inspection, proliferates
into a host of distinct subject-positions that cannot readily be subsumed and contained back into a single category. Thus, in the case of
Mark Twain, perhaps the most eminent of modern practitioners and
the one from whom, according to Hemingway (as Dostoyevsky said of
Gogol for the Russian), modern American literature emerged, a wild
succession of first-person dramatizations echoes restless self-transfor-
mations, and self-dramatizations challenge traditional boundaries
between public and private life. Indeed, it is as though "Mark Twain"
were himself a laboratory in which these structural confusions were
richly and experimentally exhibited.

I must here open a philosophical parenthesis on the relevance of this
seemingly generic discussion to contemporary psychoanalytic views

of consciousness and personality. I have already observed that Sartre's first publication[13] lays the groundwork for a theory of impersonal consciousness for which ego or self are as it were "objects" in Husserl's sense. *Being and Nothingness* (1943) was then elaborated out of this first conception of impersonality, to which is added the revolutionary theory of the Other and our alienation by the Other (neither impersonality nor the Other are present in Heideggerian existentialism in this form). Lacanian psychoanalysis, with its structural account of the "big Other" and the latter's formative relationship to the "subject of desire," then transforms the Sartrean picture of our traumatic alienation by the other into a whole permutation scheme, as it were a system of subject positions, which modify and vary unduly the sense of self or identity. Without wishing to overburden a discussion whose topic is the effect and function of pronouns in the narrative system of the novel, we may quickly detour Lacan's confusing distinction between the ideal ego and the ego ideal by suggesting that the sense of self depends on the mutilation and humiliation (I also evade the charged term "castration") of one or the other of these key positions of subject and Other. This presumably gives us four logical possibilities: the relationship of the mutilated self to the full Other (s/O) is one of dependency and subalternity, when not abjection; that of the ideal ego to the mutilated Other (S/Ø) is one of jubilation and euphoria; that of mutilated self to mutilated other (s/Ø) one of absolute melancholy and devastation; while that of full self or ego to unmutilated Other (S/O) can probably only be an imaginary relationship, but one which, imagined, might range from aggressivity and competition to some joyous and active celebration of collectivity (but discussion of such collective selves, which anticipate Sartre's *Critique of Dialectical Reason*, cannot be pursued any further here).

At any rate, we may hopefully now return to the question of first-person narrative with a suitably enlightened, if not chastened, sense of its possible complexities. Significantly, Hamburger identifies humor or the comic as a primordial form of first-person storytelling, while from another quite different perspective we may recall Sartre's own description of the way we act out our alleged identities in relationship to other people (the waiter "playing at being" a waiter)[14] as evidence that there is always something secretly comical in all public affirmations of

---

[13] See note 11 above.

[14] Jean-Paul Sartre, *Being and Nothingness*, trans. Hazel Barnes, New York: Washington Square Press, 1956 [1943], 101–3, 131.

identity (including the gender ones). And since we have mentioned Mark Twain, one cannot but be struck by the traumatic way in which his unexpected emergence as a public person made of him, his whole life long, a kind of privileged spectacle of the combined necessity and impossibility of "being" someone. For the "I" is at first a shame-faced kind of revelation, as though a character reluctantly stepped forward into the glare of the footlights to receive an unknown, unpredictable yet unavoidable judgement from those unseen others who constitute the public, hidden in darkness. Humor is then a fundamental weapon in this struggle with other people, and few anecdotes are more revealing of its aggressive powers than the story of Mark Twain's jubilation at making his quintessentially laconic friend General Ulysses S. Grant laugh out loud in public: "I fetched him! I broke him up utterly!... The audience *saw* that for once in his life he had been knocked out of his iron serenity...I knew I could lick him...I shook him up like dynamite."[15]

Such are the rhetorical and theatrical powers of the first person; yet even a cursory reading of *Huckleberry Finn* reminds us how distant and mysterious the first-person narrator is from even the most mysterious third-person subjective of narrative. In the former we do not confront the world side by side with the protagonist, looking along with him at the prospect, but are rather ourselves confronted by a mask that looks back at us and invites a trust that can never be verified. Yet this is a dialectic that is itself played out within many first person narratives such as this one, and the episode of the Duke and the Dauphin rehearse virtually all the subject-positions outlined above. At first, of course, they constitute the big Other for Huck and Jim alike (and Jim is there to articulate Huck's own subject-position, otherwise easily lost behind the first person). Royalty always thus demands the status of the big Other; and Twain's Americanism, in *Innocents Abroad* and even the first-person *Connecticut Yankee*, easily becomes an adversarial one, as does Huck's own: "It didn't take me long to make up my mind that these liars weren't no kings nor dukes, but just low-down humbugs and frauds."[16] The demotion of the Other by symbolic castration is thereby at once assured, and Jim and Huck freed from their position as subservient listeners and servants.

[15] Justin Kaplan, *Mr. Clemens and Mr. Twain*, New York: Simon and Schuster, 1991, 227.

[16] Mark Twain, *Huckleberry Finn*, in *Mississippi Writings*, New American Library, 1982, 747.

Theatricality enters the picture insofar as the Duke and the Dauphin are theatrical twice over: in their fraudulent public performances and in their private role-playing with Huck and Jim. Nor is Twain's anti-theatricality the only period expression of an exposure of the absurdity of contemporary European opera and stage-play: realists from Flaubert to Tolstoy inserted tell-tale scenes of the defamiliarization and a comic "making strange" of such spectacles, which leave their traces in the melodramatic "theater" of silent film as well (giving the would-be film realist of the next generation—Griffith straddled both—material to defamiliarize in its turn).

But what now needs to be laid in place is a fundamental complication of this first-person scheme: for this episodic narrative will seemingly turn on a series of two-step episodes—gullibility/disenchantment—which replicate the rhythm and structure of jokes themselves:

> Miss Watson told me to pray every day, and whatever I asked for I would get it. But it warn't so, I tried it. Once I got a fish-line but no hooks...I set down one time, back in the woods, and had a long think about it...No, I says to myself, there weren't nothing in it.[17]

Later, when "spiritual gifts" are on the agenda, Huck thinks about it again: "but I couldn't see no advantage about it, except for other people—so at last I reckoned I wouldn't worry about it any more, but just let it go."[18]

"Advantage" might be money or it might be making General Grant laugh. Either way, seeing through the joke no longer puts the subject at an advantage, but reduces him to the same mutilated condition as the now unmasked big Others themselves, so that the lot end up fleeing the townspeople's wrath all together, in the universal rout of the theatrical first person.

It is a paradoxical and contradictory situation which can be clarified by the realization that "lies" and "lying" are Mark Twain's technical terms for storytelling and narrative, at which point it will become obvious that storytelling in this situation is not only an autoreferential meditation on storytelling but a will to unmask it as such, as "lying." First-person theatricality is then an Enlightenment impulse to unmask everything spurious, from individual egotism and pretension

---

[17] Ibid., 635.
[18] Ibid., 635.

or mythomania to religion and collective delusions and derangements of all kinds: an impulse that preeminently characterizes Mark Twain's progressive politics. But it also raises the question of what to salvage out of the universal bonfire of all those innumerable stories and narratives which inevitably turn out to be little more than lies in the first place. Here the very meaning of the word "fiction" turns against itself and would seem on the point of destroying its own rationale in the process, and with it art in general. How to get back out of theatricality while saving everything that made it art in the first place? This is, of course, Michael Fried's question, and his answer—the painted figure who seemed to address you rhetorically from the painting and to solicit your response, your tears or your sentiment, must now turn away from the audience and become "absorbed" in his or her own being or "self"—this answer must now guide us in our search for what follows the first-person narrative in the novel.

Yet the unexamined third logical possibility in Fried's scheme—the Brechtian "first-person" turn of the character back to the public, which the actor addresses directly (as in the speech of the Fourth Knight in Eliot's *Murder in the Cathedral*)—does not seem endowed with the force and the shock it still has in a painting such as Picasso's *Demoiselles d'Avignon*. The latter's successive versions gradually divest themselves of their "third-person" and male fictional elements—the medical student carrying a skull, and the sailor ensconced at the heart of the brothel—and thereby determine a dramatic movement of the women towards the viewer, in the form of five enormous alien gendered beings whose gaze at us, not necessarily hostile or aggressive, is intense and yet unidentifiable: not so much that blast of raw sexuality as Leo Steinberg would have it, so much as the neutral presence of the Other, the impersonality of alien consciousness registered yet still aloof and denying us all recognition.

The fictional answer can thus only be a return to the third person, but with a difference; and it is a difference which will ultimately unravel the realist conjuncture we have been describing here and bring that uniquely realistic moment to an end. I am of course alluding to the difference between what we may now call the objective third person and the subjective third person, the swollen or blank unidentified third person with which we began this chapter. For it will now seem as though this new form (in some Borgesian sense absolutely identical to its predecessor at the same time that it is incommensurable with it) consists in the incorporation of everything we have attributed to the first-person narrator in order to reach some richer representation of subjectivity and thereby a more multidimensional representation of reality itself. The restructuration of this pronoun, the emergence of this new narrative entity, is related to that of several other literary phenomena—most notably *style indirect libre* and Irony—with which we will then subsequently deal, in order to form a more complete picture of what happens to realism as the initial realist synthesis begins to dissolve.

The most promising approach to this new (swollen or impersonal) third person will continue to be its effect in the beginnings of a given narrative, where its essential mystery can be felt most strongly. But this mystery has already been identified in our discussion of the first person, for it is that same blank wall of the mask or the face-to-face confrontation which has now been transferred to the third person and substituted for our sense of sharing the privileged point of view of the protagonist familiar from classical novelistic or realistic storytelling. I offer a few further illustrations:

> The telephone waked him. He waked already hurrying, fumbling in the dark for robe and slippers, because he knew before waking that the bed beside his own was still empty, and the instrument was downstairs just opposite the door beyond which his mother had propped upright in bed for five years.

> If he had been thirty, he would not have needed the two aspirin tablets and the half glass of raw gin before he could bear the shower's needling on his body and steady his hands to shave.

> The hard round ear of the stethoscope was cold and unpleasant upon his naked chest; the room, big and square, furnished with clumsy walnut—the bed where he had first slept alone, which had been his marriage bed.[19]

---

[19] All beginnings are taken from Faulkner's *Collected Stories* (New York: Random House, 1950). The first is "The Brooch" (647), where the main character (Boyd) is not named until well into the second paragraph. The second is "Golden Land" (701), where the name (Ira Ewing) only emerges many pages later. In the third, "Beyond" (781), the hero, Mothershed, is only named three pages later. I sense some deeper relationship between this pronominal development and the evolution described in G.R. Hamilton's curious essay *The Tell-Tale Article* (New York: Oxford University Press, 1950), which traces the evolution in poetry from the indefinite article to the definite, grasping it as a sign of modernity and its abstractions (his references are principally to Eliot and Auden): "the superior wink of the shared secret" he calls it (40), in other words the attempt of the isolated subjectivity to summon an elect collectivity around itself.

In effect, this kind of beginning incorporates our own confusion and perplexity, our own narrative curiosity, into the plot to come; and as such it supplements the growing plotlessness of the new narrative with a superimposed plot of its own. We have indeed seen how Zola's narrative conquest of the everyday needed to be supplemented (in the strongest philosophical sense) by a melodramatic and explosive dimension that reintroduced the Event back into the repetitions of the everyday. The new structural and pronominal mystery is a different, yet no less influential, solution to this same intensifying problem; and much of the power of the new Faulknerian narrative comes from the force of this cataphora, which is operative, not only on the micro-level of style, but on that of plot itself, as in the opening of *Sanctuary*, where we begin in the middle of an unexplained situation, where the secret to be revealed is not "profilmic" (that is to say, buried in the complexities of the narrative reality itself), but rather the result of the decision of the author.

This is the deeper structure of Faulknerian cataphora, to construct a secret and a mystery which is the result only of the author's withholding of information, rather than latent in the plot itself. The author of a detective story withholds the identity of the criminal no doubt, but this mystery is part and parcel of the plot itself, as all the characters experience it. In Faulkner, only the reader is inflicted with this mystery, inasmuch as the author has not seen fit to provide information which would at once make it clear what the situation is: and nameless third person or not, this peculiar beginning "*in medias res*" is characteristic of most of Faulkner's novels. They thereby bear witness to a modern necessity of constructing a narrative out of what were not initially narrative materials: in other words, they testify to the weakening of the pole of the récit, of the past-present-future system itself, by the dominance of an eternal present which seeks then to disguise itself as récit and narrative to be told and story or destiny to be revealed.

In Michael Fried's sense, then, we have here to do with an attempt to make absorption theatrical, to reannex the modernist moment of absorption—which Fried sees as the very logic of modernism itself as it more and more turns away from its spectators—to that "rhetoric of fiction" inherent in classical narrative.

The relationship of this modification of our distance from the characters then accounts for the kinship with detective stories, thrillers and commercial literature of all kinds, where the dual narrative—

formerly *syuzhet* and fable—now rearticulated as past criminal narrative and present narrative reconstruction by the detective, is simply an extrapolation of this structure.

So-called free indirect discourse then comes as a new solution to the problem of the unidentified consciousness of this "fourth person," as we may call the new narrative pronoun. For it is an unusual synthesis of third and first person which allows the latter's first-person thoughts to be represented in a way which avoids mimicry, dialectic, dramatic monologue and the like—in other words, which seems to evade precisely that theatricality from which the modernizing novel would like to turn away. What is unique about free indirect discourse can then be captured by the linguists' analysis and in particular by the incompatibility of present or deictic time words with sentences narrating the past.[20] The Faulknerian "now" is the most frequent and obvious signal of the lifting of this taboo in the new system ("now he was lifting the bale, now he was beginning to sweat," etc.).

And it should be clear from our earlier discussion that such a synthesis of the past (récit) and the present (scene) would seem to offer an ideal solution to the realist problem par excellence—except for the fact that realism was constitutively founded on an ineradicable tension between these two temporal realities, a tension that begins to dissolve into a facile practice of narrative mind-reading when free indirect discourse becomes the dominant sentence structure of the novel.

For Pasolini, in his idiosyncratic development of a theory of free indirect discourse (one which he ingeniously applied to film as well), the fundamental characteristic of this new stylistic device was the incorporation of an altogether different class discourse into the unavoidably bourgeois discourse of the novel as a form. Yet in order for its use to approach something like a Bakhtinian polyphony (not his reference), or something like a faithfulness of the form to the class structure (and struggle) of society itself, the radical otherness of the incorporated discourse must be retained— something not easy for bourgeois writers with a training in their class-specific style to achieve. The problem can be conveyed by a return to the simple-minded film-theory distinction between the objective and the subjective shots, whose images are sometimes

---

[20] Ann Banfield, *Unspeakable Sentences*, London: Routledge & Kegan Paul, 1982, 154; and see E. Benveniste, *Problèmes de linguistique générale*, Paris: Gallimard, 1966, 262 et passim.

"objectively" ambiguous, so that we cannot decide whose viewpoint we are adopting—that of the character or that of the camera apparatus. (Meanwhile, the exploitation of this uncertainty in horror films underscores the usefulness of the new procedure for commercial culture and its sub-genres). Pasolini's rage at the weakening of this constitutive tension and the loss of the class possibilities of the new stylistic device may not be misplaced here:

> The most odious and intolerable thing, even in the most innocent bourgeois, is that of not knowing how to recognize life experiences other than his own: and of bringing all other life experiences back to a substantial analogy with his own. It is a real offense that he gives to other men in different social and historical conditions. Even a noble, elevated bourgeois writer, who doesn't know how to recognize the extreme characteristics of psychological diversity of a man whose life experiences differ from his, and who, on the contrary, believes that he can make them his by seeking substantial analogies—almost as if experiences other than his own weren't conceivable—performs an act that is the first step toward certain manifestations of the defense of his privileges and even toward racism. In this sense, he is no longer free but belongs to his class deterministically; there is no discontinuity between him and a police chief or an executioner in a concentration camp.[21]

On the other hand, any evocation of *style indirect libre* in a discussion of realism surely has an obligation to come to terms with Flaubert himself, to whom traditional accounts (rightly) assign the merit of having invented both. But we cannot even pronounce the name of Flaubert without noting the multiple evaluations his writing objectively contains within itself. Read at different speeds, Flaubert successively becomes a realist (the content), a modernist (Joyce's master by way of his paragraphs) or a postmodernist (in the gaps and silences between his sentences described by Sartre and Nathalie Sarraute alike).[22] From the standpoint of production, I retain Barthes' account of Flaubert as essentially a handicraftsman, working in precious metals and jewels, and intent on making each sentence into an aesthetic object in its own right.[23] Flaubert's practice of free indirect discourse can in that case be seen as an attempt to withdraw thought (wordless or not) from the vague formlessness of subjectivity and endow it with all the materiality of an object of value (just as

---

21 Pasolini, *Heretical Empiricism*, 87.
22 See in particular Nathalie Sarraute, *The Age of Suspicion*, New York: Braziller, 1990.
23 Roland Barthes, *Writing Degree Zero*, New York: Farrar, Straus and Giroux, 1977, Part Two, chapter two.

Baudelaire did for the effusions of romantic poetry). That one of the consequences of this willful aesthetic reification was the transformation of Balzacian allegory into the bodily contingency of affect we have already claimed. But it is difficult to argue for any durable innovation of Flaubert in the area of novelistic forms. Zola learned the uses of the chapter as a form from *L'Éducation sentimentale*, no doubt, but we must also register Henry James's intense dissatisfaction with the ever-sameness and empty flow of that novel's pages.[24]

Instead, I offer the following parenthetical sketch of the novel's history as a form that can be reproduced and successfully exported, an apparatus which, like film later on, or the automobile, can open up new lines of manufacture in a variety of traditional internal and external cottage industries. Scott's historical novel, combining adventure, the past, the romantic costume drama and the great national heroes all together, may be said to be the first form of the successful and influential novelistic apparatus of the nineteenth century. But its progeny know a number of distinct outcomes: alongside Balzac, there is opera; alongside the feuilleton there is also Victor Hugo and Dickens. It is within this popular efflorescence that Flaubert marks a break and a decisive restructuration (remember how Proust compared his deployment of tenses with Kant's invention of the categories: it is a historical paradigm whose suggestiveness might well be further extended).[25] Flaubert's legacy was the new status of the novelist as artist, and not some new form, a task whose Edison or Ford was Émile Zola.

For naturalism quickly became the fundamental new form of the novel all over the world, and, as we have argued here, the fundamental form of novelistic realism. Beyond Europe, all the "first novels" in the various national traditions are indebted either to Scott's model or to Zola's, depending on their stage of industrialization. It is not until after World War II that a third export model of the novel becomes available (modernism having offered more than the Flaubertian example of the single "book of the world" and the ideal status of the great writer).

This model was the one Faulkner offered, and the Chinese reception

---

[24] Henry James, *Literary Criticism, Volume II: European Writers; Prefaces to the New York Edition*, New York: Library of America, 1984: "elaborately and massively dreary" (176), "an epic without air" (328).

[25] Marcel Proust, "À propos du 'style' de Flaubert," in *Contre Sainte-Beuve*, Paris: Gallimard/Pléiade, 1971, 586.

of Faulkner may be considered paradigmatic: before the Cultural Revolution, indeed, Chinese novels were specialized according to what may be termed professional genres—novels of the peasantry, novels of the military, novels of the party, and so forth. After the intellectuals returned from the countryside they could no longer sustain this segregation of the novel into class and social categories, which in any case themselves no longer existed. But of the many varieties of democratic or urban mass interaction available, Faulkner offered the additional advantage of a regionalism in which the life of the province subsumed land, town and city alike, and in which, most important of all, deep history existed and the memory of traumatic defeat subsisted into the present. The Faulknerian "now" at this point becomes something more than a feature of free indirect discourse and is transformed into a whole vision of the interpenetration of temporalities in a non-chronological experience of what is still place.

Faulkner's model thus breaks open a variety of traditions and enables the Latin American boom, with its magic realism, fully as much as all kinds of American "writing program" novels[26] all over the world, the Faulknerian sentence now becoming the excuse for a rebirth of rhetoric and its excesses (which take the place of any rebirth of melodrama or theatricality as such). These possibilities, for good or ill, allow for a flood of novelistic production—artistic and commercial alike—well beyond the bounds of the realistic structure described here.

Yet the weakening and dissolution of the latter must be documented in at least one additional way, by some account of the relationship of Irony to the transformation of the third person and the emergence of free indirect style we have been discussing here; and it is appropriate that this additional feature also be associated with the name of Flaubert. For it is noteworthy that in his account of the two stages of irony described by Wayne Booth in his *Rhetoric of Fiction*, the author of *Madame Bovary* is expressly singled out as the very fountainhead and source of that second "unstable" type[27] which Booth came to

---

[26] See Mark McGurl, *The Program Era*, Cambridge: Harvard University Press, 2009, along with my review of it in the *London Review of Books* 34:22 (November 22, 2012).

[27] Along with Céline. See *The Rhetoric of Fiction*. He reacted with anger to my characterization of him as "conservative" (I never saw the denunciation in the book's second edition), but I meant it in a purely literary and formal sense, in just such anti-modernist judgements as these.

abhor in his quest for those more stable moralistic judgements he found (paradoxically enough, as we shall see) in the fiction of Henry James. On his interesting narrative of the destinies of this literary phenomenon, what began life as a linguistic trope—stable irony as an effect—is with Flaubert transformed into something like an ideology and a nihilistic worldview; nor do I really wish to tell this story very differently, except for historicizing the change and for replacing the moral judgement with a structural description, in the process assigning Henry James a rather different historical role.

For if Flaubert is to be considered the inventor of unstable irony, as much on the strength of his "invention" of free indirect discourse as of anything else, then Henry James must be considered its ideologist, and its spokesperson throughout the literary landscape. This involves, no doubt, the substitution of the reproach of relativism for that of nihilism in the judgement that has been referred to; but such judgements are, in my opinion, like all political moralizing, simply category mistakes. We have here to do, not only with history, but with the history of forms; and it is better to begin with that kind of historical investigation rather than with taste and ideology.

Irony is to be sure intimately related to the emergence of point of view and its theorization; and the latter in turn to free indirect discourse and the feeling that the individual subject of perception and experience is an intelligible entity in its own right whose boundaries need to be respected. There thus arises a new kind of multiplicity, not that of objects and sensations, but of individual subjects. Free indirect discourse will mark the thoughts and perceptions of the subject in question on the level of the sentence; point of view will identify their mutual interrelationship on that of narrative as such. Both of these techniques, therefore, reflect that more general emergence of the subject of consciousness which we call individualism on the social level, as well as on the ideological one; and their codification as literary norms is then equally ideological.

If Flaubert is historically identified with the practice of *style indirect libre*, it is certainly Henry James whose name remains indissolubly related to the concept of point of view. But I think this association has less to do with his own narrative practice than with his critical and theoretical reflections on the art of the novel, which have been as fundamental for narrative analysis in modern times as Aristotle's for the classical world. James, indeed, wanted to be a professional writer, rather than an artist in Flaubert's sense, and I think it might clarify our view of his work—revived and virtually inescapable in the post-war period, with its elaboration of an ideology of modernism—if we step back to recognize that he was essentially a writer of short stories or of their longer cousin, the art-novella—both quite different in their requirements than the novel itself, where James's few great achievements are perhaps better considered to be accidents of the content rather than the triumphant demonstration of his talent as a born novelist. The aesthetic of the short stories then turned on the discovery of that unique anecdotal material he called a "subject," but which for clarity's sake in the present context it might be better to identify more vaguely as "inspiration," starting point, narrative kernel, *Einfall*, or suggestive anecdote. At any rate, few are as reflexive and revealing, as autoreferential as the "Beast in the Jungle" (whose opening sentence I quoted at the beginning of this chapter): yet its premise, a man whose destiny is to have no destiny, underscores the continuing significance, for Jamesian storytelling, of that older fundamental category of the *récit*, which is destiny itself and its (more stable) ironies. It is therefore immensely revealing that when James brings his own practice to bear on the theorization of the novel itself, this category of the uniqueness of the individual destiny (or at least of that of the "subject" of the individual story or tale) should mutate into the requirement of point of view as the form in which the individuality of each character should be framed. (I leave aside the question of voyeurism, central to James's own life, and obviously one component of the insistence on seeing, on presence, on scene as such.)

The mutation of irony into Irony is, however, a development closely related to this one (if it is not, in fact, simply the same phenomenon seen from a different formal perspective): for here too a stable irony in the content has been transformed into the irony of form as such. For this new unstable Irony is a matter of moral judgement, rather than one of the appreciation of the "ironic" contingencies and coincidences of life; and it depends on being able to compare as it were the inside and the outside of a character, which is to say, on being able to step back out of the text itself.

I want to argue that this particular narrative operation is not possible in classical realism, that is, in Hamburger's third-person narrative. It is certainly unavailable and unperformable in the classical tale, where characters are almost exclusively seen from the outside, so that if any divergence in judgement takes place it involves a distance from the text itself and the author, and not merely from within the text and from the character. In the older tale, such judgements generally fall into range of a melodramatic typology, in which there are, as we have shown, heroes and villains, secondary characters, helpers, lovers jealous, deceitful or devoted, comic caricatures and so forth.

This is a typology organized along the lines of traditional ethics and ruled by the ethical binary of good and evil; and it can of course undergo discovery—as when a villain is unmasked as a true friend, or a true friend unmasked as a villain; or in texts of increasing complexity, it could posit the slow development or transformation of a positive character into a negative one, as when a promising youngster goes bad, or a wastrel develops wisdom in his old age. But these are all functions of an external perspective, and they persist on into the nascent "true" realisms of the eighteenth and nineteenth centuries, where at best they are neutralized (by the attempt to eliminate melodrama and its standard plots and characters) and replaced by stretches of a greater introspection and a psychological notation which reduces our distance from the protagonists' thoughts and feelings without substituting new kinds of moral judgement for the older melodramatic ones.

The new developments to this early realism, then, are movements towards the impersonality of consciousness rather than towards irony. Lucien's weakness is still an external fact and judgement; and in that sense Balzac is always remorseless towards his own characters, however much from time to time he may sympathize with them: he has enough of them for the sympathies to go around, and if one falls short or goes to pieces, there will always be another one available. Stendhal would seem to be the exception here, yet his "ironies" are similarly based on side-taking, and on his identification with the protagonist, whom he constantly urges on, encouraging him even when he disappoints the author.

The point here is that judgements in the classical novel are made by the characters on one another, whether the author approves or not. Here in Jamesian point of view, we are so fully sealed into the protagonist's consciousness that we can scarcely see them from the outside: at best the outside judgement is an event within the story, a revelation and a shock, as when the father shows the protagonist of Kafka's "Judgment" what he really is. But in the Jamesian system, we have to step outside the text altogether in order to appreciate the fact that Densher is a gigolo and Kate a designing woman and a bird of prey. But is this judgement really the one *The Wings of the Dove* wants us to make? Is it extra-literary? And if you like moral judgements, does this form strengthen the practice and the habit, or on the contrary gradually do away with it? I will hazard the guess that it is only by association with the last traces of the traditional narrative category of destiny or the irrevocable (Milly dies, after all, the "crime" has been committed) that such moral reactions and evaluations remain possible, and that thereafter, in the floodtide of the everyday, they are quickly swamped by the sheer multiplicity of points of view, which clearly do render them relative, in the sense of irrelevant.

At this point, then, a parting of the ways becomes unavoidable. The "serious" writer—that is, the one who aspires to the distinction of literature—will keep faith with what alone authentically survives the weakening of all the joints and joists, the bulkheads and loadbearing supports, of narrative as such, of the récit on its point of submersion: namely affect as such, whose triumph over its structural adversary is that bodiliness that alone marks any singularity in the everyday, and which now turns to engage its new literary adversary in lyric and language. Its fate is henceforth the fate of modernism, and no longer has any place in this particular story.

As for narrative, however, we have seen how a new kind of third person, along with point of view and all its newly available techniques, allows a rough substitute for the older vehicle to be maintained. This is no longer the realism I have been describing here, as the preponderance of dialogue over description in the interest of easy reading may testify. I am tempted to call this new and omnipresent narrative form the "existential" novel, insofar as it stands as a grim caricature of Sartre's diagnosis of an inauthentic narrative temporality and his prescription for an open work, in which the future remains in suspension—a work that turned out unexpectedly to harmonize with a late-capitalist and consumerist present eager to persuade us that nothing is irrevocable and that everything is possible. This is indeed the context in which, in the illimitable standardization and repetition of the everyday, categories of the Event began to emerge, as if to testify to their own absence, their own structural impossibility.

What secures the inexpensive mass production of such novels and their efficient functioning is a conjuncture of point of view, *style indirect libre* and the loosely named stream of consciousness. One does not evade the subject-object gap by way of philosophical neologism and invention or by ingenious syntheses or the peremptory declaration that one side or the other does not exist: but one is also hesitant to endorse and reinforce it by using its terminology with abandon. Subjectivism is not the most useful reproach here, but rather the facile free association and the ease and speed with which a character can be shown to think when the truly ontological obstacles of objects and otherness have been evaded: a stream of perceptions, thoughts, desires, which are neither telling nor showing, but a performance that purports to offer both, at the same time that the novelist's narrative gets itself continued and then finished off. Such is the omnipresent production of realism after realism, as it lends its motor power to "serious" literature and the commercial kind alike.

It is not by adding a few metaphors, or interrupting these self-indulgent streams of consciousness with fragments of an alleged objectivity, that this historical situation and dilemma, which is that of contemporary literature, can be productively addressed. One does look back with a certain wistfulness at those mixtures of subject and object in which narrative carefully threads its way through the objective, its subject-centers brushing against this or that, luminously and momentarily transforming each passing thing into a flare of perception. So Galdós's multitude, with their varying mentalities, make their way cautiously and respectively through the new house, bestowing the admiration characteristic of the point of view of each, and pausing as is only fit to gape as follows at the bridal suite:

> They viewed the bridal chamber; the dressing-table, which in Doña Cándida's opinion was a *sweet little museum*; they rested in the rose-coloured boudoir, which seemed like one great open flower; they inspected the dining-room with its walnut chairs and sideboards in imitation of the old style; they admired the glass cabinets, in the dark depths of which there gleamed with a strange iridescence the silver and silver-plate. But what most interested the ladies was the kitchen range, one great cumbersome mass of iron, entirely of English manufacture, with a variety of plates, doors and divisions. It was an imposing contraption. "It only wants wheels to be a railway engine," said the knowledgeable Bringas, opening one door after the other to look inside this prodigy.[28]

It's too late to do this again, although it would be better than nothing: it has henceforth become the generic "novelesque," and

---

[28] *Torment*, trans. J. M. Cohen, New York: Farrar, Straus and Young, 1953, 215.

little is gained by redoing it in some *neue Sachlichkeit* or writing it up as a poem. Yet, historical destinies still exist somewhere and it is to be wondered what their literary fate may be now that affect has deserted them.

Chapter IX

Coda: Kluge, or, Realism after Affect

We have suggested that the breakdown of realism in the sense in which we have described it had essentially three historical outcomes: the first was clearly enough modernism, about which Roland Barthes' strategy of "tactical-style operations"[1] and local interventions seems the most prudent one. (In *A Singularity Modernity* I chose the option of describing a common situation from which the innumerable and varied modernisms all sprang, rather than seeking to invent some general theory under which they were all somehow subsumed.)

But who says modernism in the arts also says mass culture, since the two are dialectically and historically interdependent and arise at much the same moment. In the last and final chapter of this essay I showed how the breakdown of the realist tension between narrative and affect released uncontrolled linguistic production calculated to blacken endless pages of pseudo-realistic narratives classifiable by way of a return of the old genres and sub-genres that realism itself had attempted to dislodge (and had succeeded, but at the cost of its own destruction). At its best, the result, for which I could only find the term the "existential novel," now peoples the chain bookshops and the bestseller lists.

Yet beyond this symbiotic emergence of high modernism and mass culture, there now of course lies the postmodern and its narrative production (which in my opinion it is misleading to reduce to those playful autoreferential forms for which the intellectual media generally reserves that term). I want in conclusion to offer one remarkable example of a realism without affect: an utterly unpredictable one,

[1] Quoted in Alain Robbe-Grillet, *Why I Love Barthes*, trans. Andrew Brown, London: Polity, 2011, 39.

which has no parallels elsewhere in the world and is scarcely a paradigm for some generalized theory of the return of narrative or storytelling, but which may suggestively round out this particular literary-historical narrative.

In our mass cultural times the philosophical loftiness of Goethe's formula the *"unerhörte Begebenheit"* might better be rendered by Ripley's "Believe It or Not," which certainly offers an apt characterization of many of Alexander Kluge's tales. Let's illustrate it with his "Mass Fatality in Venice,"[2] of which I quote the opening lines:

> In the summer of 1969 the sun beat down for weeks without end on the urban and watery landscape of Venice. Steamers and motorboats plowed through green lagoons that surrounded the houses like thick soup. Some hundred elderly people were sheltered in the old people's home of San Lorenzo, a stone palace. They got no air. Twenty-four elderly residents died within a few hours on one of the last days of July. The survivors, taken unawares by these sudden events which they had no time to digest, refused to permit the removal of the bodies. They killed the director of the institute, Dr. Muratti, a respected gerontologist, equipped themselves with knives and lead pipes, as well as two revolvers which they found in the director's office. They drove the inmates of the home as well as its nurses and kitchen personnel into a capacious groundfloor room which seemed the coolest room in the building. Here several of the elderly, physically the strongest, established a dictatorship, promoting themselves to popes and cardinals.

As might be expected, the city brings in troops, the building is retaken and its leaders killed, and in a final twist, the few elderly survivors of the massacre are shipped off into the Tyrol, where they die of the cold.

This nasty little story will serve to illustrate, not postmodernism in general, which takes many forms and shapes, but at least what happens to both narrativity and affect after the end of their brief union. We will make two observations about narrativity as such in connection with the present illustration.

The first is a generic one: this is not a short story or *Novelle*, nor does it correspond to any of the official literary categories of the tradition. It has no author, for example, not even an implied one; and might well have merely been a clipping from a newspaper. This indeed puts us on the track of its structural identity: it is what the journalists call a *fait divers*, and what conversationalists might identify

---

2   Alexander Kluge, "Massensterben in Venedig," in *Chronik der Gefühle*, Frankfurt: Suhrkamp, 2004, Volume II, 461, translation mine.

as an anecdote. Most of Kluge's narrative work (at least in writing) falls into that no man's land between the two.

At best, from narrative analysis, we may retain a paradoxical intersection of two story lines: what the city government tries to do in this emergency of the heat wave; what the inmates do in the closed world which is their social home, presumably their last one. If there is any paradigmatic metaphor here it calls up the image of the prison revolt (and whatever meaning the fait divers has—or that we are tempted to assign it—comes from that analogy).

But the fait divers—and in gossip in general the anecdote as well—is also defined by its historical reality: it did really take place ("elderly woman robbed and killed for two dollars!"). The signed anecdote called *Massensterben in Venedig* raises the question I think we do not ask ourselves during the reading of it—namely whether such a thing really happened at all, or whether Kluge, in the seemingly infinite fertility of his imagination, made it all up in the first place. Is the generic frame of the fait divers a guarantee of its actuality? Does the absence of authorial presence make the attribution to a real individual named Alexander Kluge irrelevant? The evident futility of such questions confronts us with a unique development, namely the utter effacement of any separation between the fictive and the non-fictive. If this text is characteristic of the survival of an older récit impulse after the end of affect, then it also testifies to the disappearance of "fiction" as such, as a meaningful (narrative) category.

Indeed, the impending crisis of the fictional, and its consequences for art in general, was anticipated by Thomas Mann, in *Doktor Faustus*, where the devil warns the protagonist (a composer) about the public's increasing discomfort with *Schau* ("aesthetic appearance," here weakly translated as "pretence"):

"The historical movement of the musical material has turned against the self-contained work. It shrinks in time, it scorns extension in time, which is the dimensions of a musical work, and lets it stand empty. Not out of impotence, not out of incapacity to give form. Rather from a ruthless demand for compression, which taboos the superfluous, negates the phrase, shatters the ornament, stands opposed to any extension of time, which is the life-form of the work. Work, time, and pretence [*Schau*], they are one, and together they fall victim to critique. It no longer tolerates pretence and play, the fiction, the self-glorification of form, which censors the passions and human suffering, divides out the parts, translates into pictures. Only the non-fictional is still permissible, the unplayed, the undisguised and untransfigured expression of suffering in its actual moment.

Its impotence and extremity are so ingrained that no seeming play with them is any longer allowed."[3]

We could easily make connections with Freud's identification of our resistance to other people's fantasies and daydreams,[4] or on the other hand to the exhaustion of narrative itself, as well as the increasing attention to minute segments of the everyday, however narcissistic this may be. The intellectual's perpetual guilt about his preoccupation with art in the midst of universal suffering and starvation is also relevant here: Bourdieu's analyses, following the Sartrean notion of ontological self-justification, insist on the way in which all professional activities today (including intellectual labor) demand a kind of institutional vindication for their importance, and indeed their very existence. Meanwhile, after the short-lived bubble of the "nonfiction" novel, new defenses of reality and the factual have begun to reappear;[5] and we may well wonder whether "fictionality" or *Schein* plays any great part in the contemporary visual arts, which insist so strongly on our attention to their materials as such.

But the most interesting theoretical counterposition with which to place this one of Thomas Mann (which can be imagined to derive as much from Adorno) is the defense by Gilles Deleuze of the "*faux*":[6] the pleasures of the false and the counterfeit, of sheer appearance ranging all the way to delirium, a kind of ultimate apologia, in the face of that grim duty of realism to which Lukács seemed to summon us, of what we now call the postmodern in the more limited sense of the word: simulacrum, image, model or imitation without an original. Nor does it seem to me impossible that one form of contemporary narrative will consist in the absolute superposition of Deleuze's "*faux*" upon the strictest empirical fact.

I myself think, however, that the weakening of the fictional also tends to undermine its opposite number, the category of the factual;[7]

---

3 Thomas Mann, *Doctor Faustus*, trans. Helen Lowe-Porter, New York: Knopf, 1948 [1947], 240.

4 In Freud, "Creative Writers and Daydreaming," *The Standard Edition*, volume IX, London: Hogarth Press, 1959.

5 See, for example, David Shields, *Reality Hunger: A Manifesto*, New York: Vintage, 2011.

6 Gilles Deleuze, *Cinéma II*, Paris: Minuit, 1985, chapter 6, "Puissances du faux."

7 Catherine Gallagher's dramatic identification of fictionality—Barthes' "romanesque"—with the novel itself ("The Rise of Fictionality," in Franco Moretti, ed., *The Novel, Volume 1: History, Geography, and Culture*, Princeton: Princeton University

and that this is the point where we find ourselves on the threshold of a new world, which Kluge may be entering here.

But what about that disappearance of affect, what could possibly validate such a claim? Irony is not, to be sure, exactly an affective phenomenon in the ordinary sense of the word, but its utter absence from this blank text is revealing, and makes characterizations such as "terrible," "grotesque" or even the word "nasty" I myself used here with all due precaution—it makes all such characterizations absolutely irrelevant. Pity and terror? If so, then only in the form they might take in the mind of some glacial intelligence observing these events from over a great distance, as a researcher might examine a battle to the death of ant armies.

I want to stress the irrelevance as well of another category frequent (and quite appropriate) in much of contemporary criticism, and it is that of minimalism. How else is minimalism described in its essence than in the radical, even ostentatious omission of emotion and affect from the surface of the narrative, as in Hemingway or Raymond Carver? (Even though, as I should remark here, it is the absence of affect from their dialogue that is the most striking: while there is no dialogue at all in this narrative of Kluge, as indeed in many of his short narratives of this kind.)

But the withholding of emotion or affect (the dividing line between the two in both minimalist writers would also merit some discussion) is meant in them to make such feeling and inner turmoil emerge all the more powerfully for the reader. The absence is as profoundly expressive as its overt externalization in other writers, particularly those of a "maximalist" persuasion.

Here in Kluge there is nothing, not even a judgement on one of the players. We could imagine a denunciation of state bureaucracy, or an indictment of the irrepressible lust for power of human nature, or an arraignment of the social services which confine the elderly in this way, let alone a more metaphysical lament about man's vulnerability to natural catastrophe or to the elements; but none of those themes or interpretations takes with any plausibility on the icy surfaces of the text.

Nor is Kluge himself, the author (often with Oskar Negt) of numerous works of social theory, without ideas or philosophical theses to

---

Press, 2006) usefully refocuses this issue and helpfully complicates it—the purpose of theory being not to invent solutions but to produce problems in the first place.

defend. His political interests have tended to turn on pedagogy (as the title of the original collection from which our story is chosen— *Lernprozesse mit todlichem Ausgang*, or *Learning processes with deadly outcomes*—suggests): the proposition would seem to imply a capture of energies, their direction and investment in negative or positive activities. It is at best a quantitative rather than a qualitative concept, one of the measurement of intensities rather than any content-laden value. Indeed, in this sense this thought of Kluge seems closer to the affective intensities evoked earlier in these chapters; and perhaps indeed this is the last remnant of the affective dynamite persisting in a narrative in which the pure *récit* has somehow been reestablished.

I would also want to argue that the neutrality of the newspaper-style report also reflects a new and immensely heterogeneous global readership (not that Kluge himself enjoys this kind of reception): a massed population for which context and its explanations and interpretations is useless, their omission giving rise to the abstraction of the pure empirical facts themselves, the fait divers in all its shocking and contingent immediacy. No doubt such radically meaningless anecdotes are the result of the dissolution of both realism and modernism together, and an appropriate ending for the present speculative history; but they are unlikely to be the only kinds of narratives the future has in store for us.

PART II

THE LOGIC OF THE MATERIAL

Chapter I

The Experiments of Time: Providence and Realism

A happy denouement has at least as much justification as an unhappy one, and when it is a matter of considering this difference alone, I must admit that for my part a happy denouement is to be preferred.

Hegel, *Aesthetics*

I.

Happy endings are not as easy to bring off as you might think, at least in literature: but they are in any case a literary category and not an existential one. It is much easier to have your protagonist end badly; but perhaps here the perils of an arbitrary authorial decision are even more evident, and the outcome has to be more openly justified by some larger ideological concept—either the aesthetics of tragedy or that metaphysics of failure that dominated the naturalist novel and still very much govern our imagination of poverty and underdevelopment.

Nor is the happy ending quite the same as the "living happily ever after" with which youthful adventures so often terminate. Comedy, on Northrop Frye's account the phallic triumph of the younger generation over the older one,[1] is a theatrical sub-set of that plot-type; but its novelistic equivalents already tend in a different direction, the providential one, which is our topic here.

Not only does the *Aethiopica* add a reconciliation with the father to the reuniting of the lovers; it also (paradigmatically) separates them by way of a multitude of plots that must all be resolved in their individual stroke of good luck:

> "The child you regarded as your daughter, the child I committed to your keeping all those years ago, is safe," he exclaimed, "though in truth she is, and has been discovered to be, the child of parents whose identity you know!"
>
> Now Charikleia came running from the pavilion and, oblivious of the modesty incumbent on her sex and years, raced like a maenad in her madness towards

---

[1] Northrop Frye, *Anatomy of Criticism*, Princeton: Princeton University Press, 1957, 163ff.

Charikles and fell at his feet.

"Father," she said, "to you I owe as much reverence as to those who gave me birth. I am a wicked parricide; punish me as you please; ignore any attempts to excuse my misdeeds by ascribing them to the will of the gods, to their governance of human life!"

A few feet away, Persinna held Hydaspes in her arms. "It is all true, my husband," she said. "You need have no doubts. Understand now that this young Greek is truly to be our daughter's husband. She has just confessed as much to me, though it cost her much pain."

The populace cheered and danced for joy where they stood, and there was no discordant voice as young and old, rich and poor, united in jubilation.[2]

The greatest modern version of this narrative cunningly marshals its two immense trajectories (the plights of each lover) to map the geographical and the class levels of a whole historical society: at the same time, *I promessi sposi* now, at the end of the Christian era, includes the reflexive and philosophical questions about the providential and the salvational as its very content. At that price, the reunion of the young lovers turns out to include a temporal perspective far vaster than the triumph of youth over age.[3]

The point to be made is that the salvational is not a religious but a philosophical category. We must not grasp the tradition I want to propose as the mere secularization of a theological drama. Indeed, Blumenberg has famously taught us that this concept is a paralogism, designed either to discredit the alleged religious presuppositions of secularizations (such as Marxism), or to assert the unconscious persistence of religion throughout the seemingly modern and modernized world.[4] In reality, we have here to do with forms, which, inherited, are reappropriated for wholly new meanings and uses that have nothing to do with the historical origins of their borrowed articulations. Thus the very theme of resurrection itself—theologically the most glorious of all salvational representations—is scarcely to be understood in any religious sense: from its figural deployment in Proust ("*l'adoration perpétuelle*") to its literal celebration in Stanley Spencer's paintings (let alone in *The Winter's Tale*), resurrection expresses the euphoria of

---

[2] B. P. Reardon, *Collected Ancient Greek Novels*, Berkeley: University of California Press, 1989, 586–7.

[3] See also Jameson, "Magical Narratives: On the Dialectical Use of Genre Criticism," in *The Political Unconscious: Narrative as a Socially Symbolic Act*, Ithaca: Cornell, 1981, 103–50.

[4] Hans Blumenberg, *The Legitimacy of the Modern Age*, Cambridge: MIT Press, 1966.

a secular salvation otherwise inexpressible in material or social terms, religious language here offering the means of rendering a material possibility rather than the other way round.

It is this possibility that the providential work embodies: and if I claim that it does so philosophically, I mean by that to imply that (unlike the long-existing theological concept) no philosophical concept for the matter exists independently, and that therefore it is only by way of aesthetic representation that this reality can be grasped. But I also mean the word "philosophical" to imply that the local representation—the story of individuals, the empirical reality—must always in this form be shadowed by a more transcendental philosophical idea—just as I would assert that the naturalist rendering of bad luck and inevitable degradation is presided over by a constellation of more abstract and totalizing class and scientific ideologies (from entropy to the bourgeois terror of proletarianization, as well as that of the "decline of the West").

It will be appropriate to illustrate the process in the very different register of Science Fiction: indeed, at the heart of one of Philip K. Dick's grimmest novels, *Martian Time-Slip*, we encounter a salvational episode of the most radiant beauty.

Like so much paraliterature (the relationship between modern detective stories and specific cities is well-known), SF is often a literature of place and landscape, albeit imaginary ones: Dick's Mars is the prototype of his characteristic desert of misery, in which the most dismal features of a provincial 1950s America are unremittingly reproduced and perpetuated against a backdrop of ecological sterility and the intensive use of low-yield machinery. Cultural reminiscences of Australia waft off this unpromising colony, which still has remnants of its aboriginal population (here called Bleekmen) and nourishes Tasmanian fantasies of extermination. Dick's multiple alternating plots (whose virtuoso practice recalls Dickens or Altman), which typically include political corruption and dysfunctional families, mental illness and professional failure, would not be complete without the opening onto nightmare and hallucination, here incarnated in the autistic child Manfred, whose speech consists in the single word "gubble." It expresses Manfred's view through the appearances of things to "the skull beneath the skin," the horrible amalgams of machinery and garbage that constitute the deeper reality of the outside world and its population. It is a glimpse theorized by Lacan in his notion of *das Ding*, the monstrous indeterminate and inexpressible Other that bides its time in that "outside world" inside each of us.[5]

But in fact Manfred's situation is a time-travelling one: the real life of the mentally paralyzed child is "in reality" the aged, infirm, hospitalized old man he will in many years become, imprisoned in an early version of that "Black Iron Prison" ("the Empire never ended") which haunted Dick's later life and work.[6] But here a redemptive solution is still possible, owing to the temporal simultaneity of the Bleekmen (patterned on the aboriginal cosmos), who, fleeing their own immanent genocide, are able to save another orphan by rescuing the aged Manfred from his terminal confinement and carrying him off into the eternal Dreamtime:

> She and Jack pushed past the child, and into the house. Silvia did not understand what she saw, but Jack seemed to; he took hold of her hand, stopped her from going any farther.
>
> The living room was filled with Bleekmen. And in their midst she saw part of a living creature, an old man only from the chest on up; the rest of him became a tangle of pumps and hoses and dials, machinery that clicked away, unceasingly active. It kept the old man alive; she realized that in an instant. The missing portion of him had been replaced by it. Oh, God, she thought. Who or what was it, sitting there with a smile on its withered face? Now it spoke to them.
>
> "Jack Bohlen," it rasped, and its voice issued from a mechanical speaker, out of the machinery: not from its mouth. "I am here to say goodbye to my mother." It paused, and she heard the machinery speed up, as if it were laboring. "Now I can thank you," the old man said.
>
> Jack, standing by her, holding her hand, said, "For what? I didn't do anything for you."
>
> "Yes, I think so." The thing seated there nodded to the Bleekmen, and they pushed it and its machinery closer to Jack and straightened it so that it faced him directly. "In my opinion . . . " It lapsed into silence and then it resumed, more loudly, now. "You tried to communicate with me, many years ago. I appreciate that."[7]

---

[5]   L'Ethique de la psychanalyse (Le Séminaire, livre VII), Paris: Seuil, 1986, chapters iv and v, 55–86.

[6]   Philip K. Dick, Valis, New York: Vintage, 1991, 48 (chapter 4). I am grateful to Kim Stanley Robinson for this reference; he adds that "The Building, in A Maze of Death (chapter 9), is certainly a nightmare of a building, in a nightmare of a book. Then in A Scanner Darkly the ending happens in a forbidding mental hospital, 'Samarkand House,' and in Galactic Pot-Healer, the final Jungian project is to bring up The Black Cathedral (à la Debussy)."

[7]   Philip K. Dick, Martian Time-Slip, New York: Ballantine, 1964, 218–19 (chapter 16). For more on the relationship of this episode to Dick's world generally, see my

It is a deliverance into which one can no doubt read Dick's later religious mysticism; yet the theme of modes of production (the modern and the archaic) also reminds us to reverse this direction and to sense a social and historical redemption at work behind the individual one.

2.

And this is in fact the other axis that complicates our philosophical framework, and which runs, not from success to failure and back, but from the individual to the collective.

Kant's empirical/transcendental "doublet," and in fact the providential conundrum itself, organized as it is around categories of the individual subject, does not seem to me thinkable (which is not to imply that the thinkable can ever satisfactorily be resolved) unless we reconnect it with that other theological motif which takes history rather than individuality as its field of problems and paradoxes.

For rather than providence and the providential, the notion of predestination can illustrate our point here: for even in the realm of theology itself, this notion has been a "hard saying" that often and traditionally "sticks in the craw." Yet predestination illustrates Kant's two levels of the empirical and the transcendental[8] almost better than any other attempt at a concept, for it claims to solve this dilemma (which it merely names)—namely that of the distinction between the realm of freedom and that of necessity, that of the noumenon and that of the phenomenon, that of the transcendental and that of the empirical—by paradoxically locating the latter in the power of the divine, and the former in that of human subjectivity. What the concept of predestination asserts, in other words, is that an iron necessity governs my empirical acts and my personal destiny—this iron necessity is that of God's providence and of his determination of that destiny from all eternity, and before time itself.[9] I am, in empiri-

---

essay "History and Salvation in Philip K. Dick," *Archaeologies of the Future: The Desire Called Utopia and Other Science Fictions*, New York: Verso, 2007.

[8]   See the Introduction to the *Critique of Pure Reason*, Cambridge: Cambridge University Press, 1997, 117–52. For the contemporary relevance of this distinction, see Michel Foucault, *The Order of Things*, New York: Vintage, 1994, 241–4.

[9]   For the modern revival of Augustine's doctrine, see Bernard M. G. Reardon, *Religious Thought in the Reformation*, London: Longman, 1981.

cal reality, one of the elect or one of the damned, and I can exercise no freedom in influencing these outcomes. No individual act of mine exerts any kind of causality in their predetermined course. However, on the level of my individual consciousness or soul (Kant's noumenal realm of freedom), things stand utterly differently, and I can have no subjective sense of my election or my damnation: here I am left alone with my existential freedom and must necessarily choose my acts and make my decisions as though I were completely free.

This version of the problem now involves a dialectic of the sign or even of the symptom which is very contemporary indeed. It is resumed in the famous phrase "the outward and visible signs of inward election"; and this rather casuistical cutting of the Gordian knot can be summarized as follows: Nothing we do can ensure our election (rather than our damnation), but if in fact we happen to be one of the elect (chosen from all eternity) our behavior on earth will reflect this condition. It will therefore constitute an empirical sign of our noumenal and unknowable salvation in the transcendental realm. Hypocrisy is the tribute vice pays to virtue, someone famously said: and thus, even though it can have no causal effect, no genuine effectivity, we would do well to behave virtuously on the off chance our fate will be harmonious with this conduct. Only the more logical negative conclusion here—that if election is from all eternity, then it does not matter how I behave—has offered truly remarkable novelistic possibilities, above all in James Hogg's *Personal Memoirs and Confessions of a Justified Sinner* (1824). But the dilemma gets more productively restaged on the political and historical level.

Here we move from the individual destiny to the collective one; and the salvation of the soul is replaced by that of the human race itself, or in other words by Utopia and socialist revolution. But the well-known alternative within the Marxist tradition between voluntarism and fatalism absolutely coincides with the theological antinomy, which can thus be said to anticipate and to "prefigure" its more secular problematic in a distorted, still figurative and theological, and essentially individual way. The Mensheviks and the Bolsheviks are themselves mere personifications of this primordial opposition, in which a conviction as to the objective movement of history is opposed by a militant sense of the power of human beings to make history. Clearly, nothing is more debilitating than an opposition of this kind, which tends to sort itself out into a passive/active one in which neither alternative is satisfactory. For to oppose a placid Second-International confidence in the "inevitable" movement of history towards a socialist state is not necessarily only to show faith in the shaping powers of human beings; it is also to encourage the most mindless forms of suicidal attempts to "force" history, to break through its logic prematurely, to encourage young people to die in what are causes lost in advance owing to the fact that "the situation is not yet ripe," not yet a revolutionary one. As with predestination, however, there is nothing to guide us in this choice and no empirical signs are available to allow us to have any certainty of "election," that is to say, of the possibility of revolution as the one supreme salvational or providential Event.

But in this secular and collective version, in fact there is a kind of solution, and one not unrelated to the unconvincing theological one in such a way as to demonstrate that the latter was only really a distorted anticipation of the former. For here, what is taken as voluntarism—that is, the collective will to force history—is itself seen, not as a subjective choice, but as an objective symptom, in that sense very precisely an objective component of that history itself. Thus, an infantile leftism or anarchist voluntarism now becomes that "external sign" that revolution is not yet on the agenda and that the situation has not yet politically "matured." What was not solvable on the level of Hogg's theological hero here becomes a piece of historical evidence, a historical sign fully as significant as all the others. It is in the old theological spirit that one may also say that the passive "inevitabilism" of the Second International was itself a sign of immaturity and of an insufficiently developed political situation. This new symptomal interpenetration of the subjective and the objective thus now suddenly signals a transcendence of the old antinomy, and a moment in which the providential has become empirical, and Kant's two realms of transcendence and empiricism overcome as specific historical ratios. It thus also designates a new kind of social content for the novel as form, and the possibility of new kinds of narration.

It is to these that we must now turn, with the help of such findings: these last in effect signal the fundamental difference in possibility between the individual and the collective and suggest that we reinterrogate the novelistic form for just such consequences. The debate between revolutionaries about voluntarism and fatalism becomes, to be sure, a limited kind of specialized content for some officially political novel—what I have elsewhere called a kind of Third International literary dialectic in which this specific dilemma, most fully exacerbated by the peculiar position of Stalinist revolution in one country, gets played out.[10] (Sartre's works are some of the most interesting versions of these tragic paradoxes, which tend to be invisible in an anti-communist focus). But as with the theological material, it is not this specific content, but rather the larger form in general which interests us here.

3.

I now therefore want to return to the mainstream realist novel in order to make a few further remarks about the form-generating and form-producing value of the providential within realism itself. For the moment what is crucial for us is the distinction between the individual perspective and the collective one, when it comes to providence or happy endings. This turns out to be an evolutionary matter, for as in the purely theological realm, there is a decided historical movement from the individual destiny to the collective one (or from issues of individual salvation to those of political and revolutionary transformations, as in our preceding discussion).

But there are intermediate steps, and as it were external operators, which move us from the individual narrative to the collective one. To be sure, the first theological transfers take place naturally enough in the framework of an individual destiny, and it has been universally recognized that the very prototype of a truly individualized and isolated individual destiny, *Robinson Crusoe*, is saturated with providential impulses of various kinds.[11] The novel uniquely enables the interiorization of the various external adventures and episodes which had hitherto formed the space in which the happy or the tragic ending was played out—the realm of accidents, the contingent, chance of a meaningful kind, etc. Later on, these will be simply omens and not causes, as when Julien Sorel finds a prophetic scrap of paper in a church early in *The Red and the Black*. The interiorization of chance now means that contingency can offer the opportunity for an inward experience or development. But I think that the debate as to whether Defoe himself was a Christian is misplaced: we have here rather the

---

[10] See my Introduction to Peter Weiss, *The Aesthetics of Resistance*, Volume 1, Durham: Duke University Press, 2005.

[11] The classic discussions are those of G. A. Starr, *Defoe and Spiritual Autobiography*, Princeton: Princeton University Press, 1965; and J. Paul Hunter, *The Reluctant Pilgrim*, Baltimore: Johns Hopkins University Press, 1966.

template for the organization of experiences in a new way, in which religious influence is itself a mere external and enabling condition. Such developments need to be seen synchronically, in obedience to Blumenberg's warning about the pseudo-concept of "secularization." To be sure, it is not wrong to say that the *Bildungsroman* is then a secularization of this earlier, already secular "spiritual autobiography" of Defoe; but neither stage retains the meaning of the preceding one, but only the form. Thus it would be wrong to say that the *Bildungsroman* is still religious in its (now secular) concern for the state of the individual soul: no, what is deployed now is a mere form which organizes its new social material in an analogous way.

For our topic, it may be said that *Wilhelm Meister* is the decisive turning point, and as it were the true beginning of the nineteenth-century novel, the end of something as well as the beginning of something else, which is however its mutation and its adaptation to the new post-revolutionary society (a society which did not, of course, yet exist in Germany and scarcely elsewhere yet at that). This is a peculiarly central evaluation for such an odd and garbled book, immensely influential and yet a kind of literary white elephant, boring and fascinating all at once, and a perpetual question mark for the French and British traditions in which, as a text, it has played so small a role, yet which are incomprehensible without it, as we shall see.

The novel of formation, the novel of education?[12] It would be better to translate *Bildungsroman* as the novel of a calling or vocation, a *Beruf*, to use that word which Max Weber charged with its most intense Lutheran accents in order to make his point about the new inner-worldliness of Protestant behavior and virtue. Not that Wilhelm is at all secure in his ultimate vocation: the critics are at least sure that the latter is no longer the artistic calling or the surrender to genius that had been projected in the first draft (the *Theatralische Sendung*). Yet the rhetoric of the ending—so glorious and so determinate for several generations of *Bildungsromane* if not of providential narrative itself—is strangely at odds with the actual situation (Wilhelm is about to set off on a trip just like Goethe himself):

---

[12] The perspective adopted here does not allow me to endorse Franco Moretti's ideological analysis of the form, in *The Way of the World* (London: Verso, 1987), which remains the most stimulating and comprehensive discussion of this novelistic sub-genre. It will be apparent below that mine is rather an ideological indictment of what I call "ontological realism" as such.

To my mind thou resemblest Saul the son of Kish, who went out to seek his father's asses, and found a kingdom.[13]

Indeed, the principal role of "providence" here would seem to be a negative one: "Flee, youth, flee!" (313). Above all, he is not to become a mere actor, and his one-time success in *Hamlet* is owing, as Boyle rightly insists, to the pre-established harmony between his own personality and that of the Prince.[14] But for the greater part of the play the Prince is also tormented by the question of what to do, and what the superego—the father's Ghost (which also plays a significant part in *Meister*)—commands. Wilhelm's real father, however, proposes a life of commerce and trade, which, along with theatricals, is the one vocation quite decisively repudiated.[15] I will suggest in passing that by the end of the novel the authority of the Father has been displaced by that of the brothers; but I do not want to overemphasize this theme of the Big Other, which does not seem particularly important for Goethe here or elsewhere.

That "providence" is a fundamental theme of the novel, however, can be judged from recurrent discussions, which seem to propose a philosophical alternative between destiny and chance: "I easily content myself, and honor destiny, which knows how to bring about what is best for me, and what is best for everyone" (says Wilhelm). To which the first of his mysterious acquaintances replies:

Leider höre ich schon wieder das Wort Schicksal von einem jungen Manne aussprechen. Wehe dem, der sich von Jugend auf gewöhnt, in dem Notwendigen etwas Willkürliches finden zu wollen, der dem Zufälligen eine Art von Vernunft zuschreiben möchte, welcher zu folgen sogar eine Religion sei. Heisst das etwas weiter, als seinem eignen Verstande entsagen und seinen Neigungen unbedingten Raum geben? Wir bilden uns ein, fromm zu sein, indem wir ohne Überlegung hinschlendern, uns durch angenehme Zufälle determinieren lassen und endlich dem Resultate eines solchen schwankenden Lebens den Namen einer göttlichen Führung geben. (71)

---

[13] References to *Wilhelm Meister* in the text are adapted from Thomas Carlyle's English translation of the novel (New York: Heritage, 1959), in this instance, book 8, chapter 10, p. 657; and in the German original, to *Wilhelm Meisters Lehrjahre* (Frankfurt: Insel, 1982), p. 626.

[14] Nicholas Boyle, *Goethe: The Poet and the Age*, Volume II, Oxford: Oxford University Press, 2000, 336.

[15] Ibid., 239–40; and see also Giuliano Baioni, "Gli anni di apprendistato," in *Il Romanzo*, Volume II, Einaudi, 2002, 127–33.

It gives me pain to hear this word destiny in the mouth of a young person …
Woe to him who, from his youth, has become accustomed to search for something like will within necessity; to ascribe to chance a sort of reason, which it is a
matter of religion to obey. Is conduct like this aught else than to renounce one's
understanding, and give unrestricted scope to one's inclinations? We think it is a
kind of piety to move along without consideration; to let accidents that please us
determine our conduct; and, finally, to bestow on the result of such a vacillating
life the name of providential guidance. (63–4)

That this is not merely the expression of a standard Enlightenment
denunciation of superstition and religion, and an appeal to secular
reason, may be externally deduced by the obedience to one's daimon,
so dear to this author, as is apparent from texts like "Urworte
Ophisch." Here, however, it is enough to point out that the warning
of this stranger inserts itself into the very web of chance and coinci-
dence that make up the novel's stream of events: which is therefore
itself drawn inside the theme, and interrogated for its own function
as that predestined chance we call providence.

We thus arrive at the work's well-known secret: innumerable characters (although mostly divided socially between the wandering
theater people, whose triviality estranged Goethe's first intellectual
readership, and the aristocracy of this Germany of the principalities
in which Goethe was to make himself so eminent a place); a veritable orgy of interpolated stories and Gothic destinies, full of rather
random recognition scenes and rediscovered kinships of various sorts;
love affairs meanwhile, of the tentative sort riddled with flights and
avoidances with which Goethe's biography and psychology have
familiarized us. These materials scarcely seem to add up to any very
consistent focus of representation or stylization, nor are any of them
particularly powerful or commanding in their own right. But now, at
the center of the text, a long dream, in which characters from a host
of different plot strands come together:

Sonderbare Traumbilder erschienen ihm gegen morgen. Er fand sich in einem
Garten, den er als Knabe öfters besucht hatte, und sah mit Vernügen die bekannten
Alleen, Hecken und Blumenbeete wieder; Marianne begegnete ihm, er sprach
liebevoll mit ihr und ohne Erinnerung irgendeines vergangen Mißverhältnisses.
Gleich darauf trat sein Vater zu ihnen, im Hauskleide; und mit vertraulicher
Miene, die ihm selten war, hieß er den Sohn zwei Stühle aus dem Gartenhause
holen, nahm Mariannen bei der Hand und führte sie nach einer Laube.

Wilhelm eilte nach dem Gartensaale, fand ihn aber ganz leer, nur sah er
Aurelien an dem entgegengesetzten Fenster stehen; er ging, sie anzureden, allein
sie blieb unverwandt, und ob er sich gleich neben sie stellte, konnte er doch ihr

Gesicht nicht sehen. Er blickte zum Fenster hinaus und sah, in einem fremden Garten, viele Menschen beisammen, von denen er einige sogleich erkannte. Frau Melina saß unter einem Baum und spielte mit einer Rose, die sie in der Hand hielt; Laertes stand neben ihr und zählte Gold aus seiner Hand in die andere. Mignon und Felix lagen im Grase, jene ausgestreckt auf dem Rücken, dieser auf dem Gesichte. Philine trat hervor and klatschte über den Kindern in die Hände, Mignon blieb unbeweglich, Felix sprang auf und floh vor Philinen. Erst lachte er im Laufen, als Philine ihn verfolgte, dann schrie er ängstlich, als der Harfenspieler mit großen, langsamen Schritten ihm nachging. Das Kind lief grade auf einen Teich los; Wilhelm eilte ihm nach, aber zu spät, das Kind lag im Wasser! Wilhelm stand wie eingewurzelt. Nun sah er die schöne Amazone an der andern Seite des Teichs, sie streckte ihre rechte Hand gegen das Kind aus und ging am Ufer hin, das Kind durchstrich das Wasser in gerader Richtung auf den Finger zu und folgte ihr nach, wie sie ging, endlich reichte sie ihm ihre Hand und zog es aus dem Teiche. Wilhelm war indessen näher gekommen, das Kind brannte über und über, und es fielen feurige Tropfen von ihm herab. Wilhelm war noch besorg- ter, doch die Amazone nahm schnell einen weißen Schleier vom Haupte und bedeckte das Kind damit. Das Feuer war sogleich gelöscht. Als sie den Schleier aufhob, sprangen zwei Knaben hervor, die zusammen mutwillig hin und her spielten, als Wilhelm mit der Amazone Hand in Hand durch den Garten ging und in der Entfernung seinen Vater und Mariannen in einer Allee spazieren sah, die mit hohen Bäumen den ganzen Garten zu umgeben schien. Er richtete seinen Weg auf beide zu, und machte mit seiner schönen Begleiterin den Durchschnitt des Gartens, als auf einmal der blonde Friedrich ihnen in den Weg trat und sie mit großem Gelächter und allerlei Possen aufhielt. Sie wollten demungeachtet ihren Weg weiter fortsetzen; da eilte er weg und lief auf jenes entfernte Paar zu; der Vater und Marianne schienen vor ihm zu fliehen, er lief nur desto schnel- ler, und Wilhelm sah jene fast im Fluge durch die Allee hinschweben. Natur und Neigung forderten ihn auf, jenen zu Hilfe zu kommen, aber die Hand der Amazone hielt ihn zurück. Wie gern ließ er sich halten! Mit dieser gemischten Empfindung wachte er auf und fand sein Zimmer schon von der hellen Sonne erleuchtet. (458–9)

Strange dreams arose upon him towards morning. He was in a garden, which in boyhood he had often visited: he looked with pleasure at the well-known alleys, hedges, flower-beds. Mariana met him: he spoke to her with love and tenderness, recollecting nothing of any by-gone grievance. Erelong his father joined them, in his weekday dress; with a look of frankness that was rare in him, he bade his son fetch two seats from the garden-house; then took Mariana by the hand, and led her into a grove.

    Wilhelm hastened to the garden-house, but found it altogether empty: only at a window in the farther side he saw Aurelia standing. He went forward, and addressed her, but she turned not round; and, though he placed himself beside her, he could never see her face. He looked out from the window: in an unknown garden, there were several people, some of whom he recognized. Frau Melina, seated under a tree, was playing with a rose which she had in her hand: Laertes stood beside her, counting money from the one hand to the other. Mignon and Felix were lying on the grass, the former on her back, the latter on his face. Philina came, and clapped her hands above the children: Mignon lay unmoved; Felix started up and fled. At first he laughed while running, as Philina followed; but he screamed in terror when he saw the harper coming after him with large, slow steps. Felix ran directly to a pond. Wilhelm hastened after him: too late; the child was lying in the water! Wilhelm stood as if rooted to the spot. The fair Amazon appeared on the other side of the pond: she stretched her right hand towards the child, and walked along the shore. The child came through the water, by the course her finger pointed to; he followed her as she went round; at last she reached her hand to him, and pulled him out. Wilhelm had come nearer: the child was all in flames; fiery drops were falling from his body. Wilhelm's agony was greater than ever; but instantly the Amazon took a white veil from her head, and covered up the child with it. The fire was at once quenched. But, when she lifted up the veil, two boys sprang out from under it, and frolicsomely sported to and fro; while Wilhelm and the Amazon proceeded hand in hand across the garden, and noticed in the distance Mariana and his father walking in an alley, which was formed of lofty trees, and seemed to go quite round the garden. He turned his steps to them, and, with his beautiful attendant, was moving through the garden, when suddenly the fair-haired Friedrich came across their path, and kept them back with loud laughter and a thousand tricks. Still, however, they insisted on proceeding; and Friedrich hastened off, running towards Mariana and the father. These seemed to flee before him; he pursued the faster, till Wilhelm saw them hovering down the alley almost as on wings. Nature and inclination called on him to go and help them, but the hand of the Amazon detained him. How gladly did he let himself be held! With this mingled feeling he awoke, and found his chamber shining with the morning beams. (402–3)

Here suddenly we glimpse a principle of a wholly different formal nature at work: all these various characters are to be united in a central phantasmagoria just as musical themes are intertwined, in the contemporaneous emergence of the sonata form. The demonstration of a deeper unity now no longer has to be made in any logical or enlightenment or even causal way, but by the very logic of the dream as a formal moment, the moment of the reprise. Here is a form of closure utterly distinct from plot, allegorical of oppositions, yet demanding its own verisimilitude: do we not now finally believe that all this holds together in some new principle of coherence? It is enough to think of Joyce's prodigious reassemblage of all his daytime motifs in the Nighttown scene in *Ulysses* (beyond which everything is anticlimax), or in cinema, that remarkable final hour of Fassbinder's *Berlin Alexanderplatz* in which everything that has happened in thought or deed returns oneirically in a new unity, to grasp what is formally original in this extraordinary moment of *Wilhelm Meister*.

But in Goethe, the oneiric superstructure is doubled by a very different infrastructural unity as well, and it is this which sets *Wilhelm Meister* apart from all the generic norms and justifies its unique position as a synthesis of "world" and "soul" in Lukács' *Theory of the Novel*.[16] Nor would I want to characterize this alternate unification—although certainly redolent of the eighteenth century, of Freemasonry and of the *The Magic Flute* of 1790—as narrowly Enlightenment: its basis is not Reason as a faculty but the collective as such.

For it famously transpires that the various chance events and contingencies that have marked Wilhelm's youthful career so far are all planned out in advance, as necessary errors (shades of the Hegelian dialectic!), and are the doing of a shadowy group of conspirators known as the Society of the Tower, whose principal figures he will come to know at the end of the book, and whose existence—with a certain Masonic hocus-pocus ("all you saw in the tower was but the relics of a youthful undertaking" [512/564])—will be revealed to him. The plot is thus turned inside out: from a series of chance happenings it is suddenly revealed as a plan and as a deliberately providential design. And the Enlightenment emphasis on reasoned persuasion and pedagogy here reaches a kind of bizarre climax in which life itself becomes the "*leçon d'objets*," the theoretically calculated pattern of test and error which the old theological concept ("justify the ways of God to man") only dimly foreshadowed in distorted fashion. The Society of the Tower is a better pedagogue than God, and far more self-conscious and theoretical about its teaching method.

But it is important not to let all this slip (in the content) into a vapid kind of humanism and celebration of eighteenth-century virtue (there is very little of Plutarch and Rousseau here), although there is another kind of slippage, a purely formal one, which we will want to take more seriously. Yet it is significant that the Lukács of *Theory of the Novel*, only a year or so before his commitment to politics and to communism, should not have glimpsed the political significance of this "white conspiracy," which very obviously anticipates the structure of the Party itself, and the dialectic of a collective leadership which both reflects the social order and works back upon its already present tendencies to develop them. Lothario and his friends have just returned

---

[16] Georg Lukács, *Theorie des Romans*, Neuwied: Luchterhand, 1963, Part II, chapter 3.

from the New World, and the revolution of the colonists against the tyranny of the ancien régime. Their political party is not only out to transform the old social world by the modernization of agriculture— "Here or nowhere is America!" (407/446); it therefore carries within itself the explosive spark of that element of the American Revolution which was to expand into the French one, and to become an international movement for the transition from feudalism to the Republic—a movement then further elaborated in *Wilhelm Meisters Wanderjahre*, with Goethe's customary restraint (as befits that member of the late feudal bureaucracy he also was). This is the collective task into which Wilhelm is to be initiated, exchanging that microcosm of the social which is the theater—Faust's *"kleine Welt"*—for the "great world" of the socio-political. It is a unique solution to the formal problem of the political novel, which, a kind of *hapax legomenon*, can never be repeated, nor can it serve as a model, flawed in its very exemplarity, as though designating itself not as the concrete solution but rather merely the intent to find one. But this calls for a larger theoretical speculation about novelistic form, one which no doubt is deeply indebted to Lukács, but seeks to replace the notion of the unified subject or soul in his text with a less "humanistic" thematics.

Even before that, however, we need to bid farewell to that whole novelistic development of providential interiority which led from Defoe to *Wilhelm Meister* in the first place. The future of this formal path will no longer be subjective but objective, nor longer individualistic but rather collective. But it is important to see that Goethe himself liquidates this earlier tradition within his novel, in what has always struck readers of whatever period and generation as the most peculiar of his extrapolations, namely Book Six, or the *Confessions of a Beautiful Soul,* which from Hegel's famous discussion in the *Phenomenology* onwards has often been taken as a pathology of introspection. The form itself imitates, precisely by way of this self-sufficient extrapolation, the solipsism of interiority and of the subjectivity that seeks to enact its own virtue, even when issuing from a collective (the *Herrnhuter*), which still includes the ancient, almost extinguished vibrations of the great religious revivals and revolutions. Goethe has as it were sealed this noxious individualism away in a kind of cyst or crypt,[17] in which the subjectivity can be separated

---

[17] Jacques Derrida, "Fors," in Nicholas Abraham and Maria Torok, *Le Verbier de l'homme aux loups*, Paris: Flammarion, 1999.

out from the plot of his novel and as it were formally excised (even though the episode's author is as tightly knit by kinship into his cast of characters as all the other chance storytellers of the novel). Thus sealed off, the "confessions" then mark the grave of the "spiritual autobiography" and any reading of providence as an inward or psychologico-theological phenomenon.

4.

But, as Lukács so usefully warns us, the "novel" as a form is never a successful solution to any of its problems, and they merely change their terms when an older problematic individualism has been removed. The new terms in which I wish to codify the possibilities in a kind of structural permutation scheme will be the more Kantian ones (contemporaneous with Goethe himself) of transcendence and immanence.

But perhaps it is better to start with the more familiar older Hegelian terminology which passed into New Criticism without taking any of its dialectical baggage with it: namely the so-called concrete universal, or alternately the thoroughgoing fusion of form and content such that you cannot tell one from the other any longer.[18] This aesthetic was probably a neo-classical inspiration, produced by the return to antiquity popular in Goethe's circles, which Hegel frequented when he worked in Jena and with which he sympathized ever after. (Not many novels ever find mention in Hegel, who died just as the first great wave of modern fiction, with Balzac in the forefront, was about to hit land; Goethe of course famously reads Stendhal.[19]) Anyway, the unity of form and content thus far simply means that nothing stands out, there are no excesses either way, wherever you inspect the artifact: no extra stylistic frills, no "extrinsic" or extraneous content poking out of the pillowcase: all this very much in the spirit of epic; and of course the ambiguity of the German word *episch*, also used for the novel and for narrative in general, means that the novel gets no special treatment.

So this aesthetic of fusion can very conveniently be adapted to the language of immanence. *Episch* is immanent, in the sense that

---

[18] W. K. Wimsatt, "The Structure of the Concrete Universal in Literature," *PMLA* 62 (1947).

[19] *Conversations with Eckermann*, January 17, 1831.

meaning is inherent in all its objects and details, all its facts, all its events. They are meaningful in and of themselves, and require no outside commentary or explanation, as might be the case when you introduce modern technology of some sort, or events like financial crises, which are not self-explanatory and whose very nature as "events" in the first place is not secured in advance: which have to be explained in order to come into visible existence as temporal phenomena. Yet when this miraculously happens—not in older modes of production, but in our own—we call it realism, and have an interest in accounting for such texts, which we understand as being unusual and few in number. They are better explained, however, if we add the word transcendence to our repertoire in order to identify what is no longer present in them.

Or trying another alternative, that of Barthes' in a famous offhand sentence, that there is an incompatibility between meaning and existence in modern literature.[20] Transcendence is meaning, the immanent is existence itself, and so it is also best to enrich this layer of terms with an ontological significance. What is, whether in the text or in the life world, is not always meaningful (it is often therefore what we call contingent); what is meaningful is not always there as an existent, in the world, as is the case with Utopia or nonalienated relationships. What we may now perhaps call ontological realism is found where these two coincide to the point at which we cannot tell them apart any longer or worry about the distinction.

What would be the opposite of all this? What would be a truly transcendent kind of text? Myths, religious texts of all sorts? But after all, we are here working within the framework of the already secular novel, and have ruled those texts out in advance; we have thus presupposed a certain immanence to begin with by way of novelistic form.

Within this frame then, we can assume that what we call ontological realism is to be characterized as a truly immanent kind of immanence. In that case, and for purposes of differentiation, what would be a transcendental immanence? I think we can make a beginning by imagining this to be a kind of ethical literature, or a narrative in which the categories of ethics—vice, virtue, evil, kindness and

---

[20] Roland Barthes, "L'Effet de réel," *Oeuvres complètes*, Volume II, Seuil, 1994, 485: "La 'représentation' pure et simple du 'réel', la relation nue de 'ce qui est' (ou a été) apparaît ainsi comme une résistance au sens; cette résistance confirme la grande opposition mythique du vécu (du vivant) et de l'intelligible."

sympathy, and on into anger, melancholy and the like—are just at a slight distance from the narrated emotions and feelings of the characters or from their characterological properties. In this situation of a barely perceptible gap between the characters' existence and what they seem to mean, the old dualism of the immanent and the transcendent reinscribes itself, however faintly. The "ethical" characters are not yet mere examples or illustrations, nor have they gone all the way towards those allegories in which nameless figures bear their ethical designations on their backs in the form of signs: I am Envy, I am Complacency; but we are close; and the mere glimpse of such a possibility is enough to cast an unsettling doubt over the assurances of a hitherto ontological realism. No sensible secular and historical person can any longer believe that the ethical categories are "in nature," are in any way inscribed in being or in human reality; and for the most part an ethical literature has come to reflect the closure of class—whether it is that of Jamesian aristocrats or of Bunyan's tinkers. Ethical maxims and categories only work within a situation of homogeneous class belonging; when operative from one class to another, they absorb the signals of class struggle and tension itself and begin to function in a very different, socio-political way. At any rate, for the corpus of novels we are here considering, the novel which deploys ethical categories will be characterizable as betraying something like a transcendental immanence, that is to say, the promotion into a quasi-transcendental status of social elements—the ethical categories and judgements—which looked like intrinsic and even banal elements of the social situation itself, until closer inspection revealed their operation to be somehow and barely perceptibly trans-social, meta-social.

In that case, would it make any sense to propose a parallel category of transcendental transcendence? I think so, provided we understand once again that we are operating within a secular corpus from which all genuine transcendence has been eliminated. We no longer have to do with religious or sacred texts, with texts bearing within them anything having to do with the divine or the angelic or even the supernatural (although at some point very early in our historical segment—the history of the novel—the ghost story reappears, with Defoe's Mrs. Veal, or Schiller's *Geisterseher*). So the transcendence we are evoking will be a transcendence bound and limited by secular immanence, a transcendence within our own "realistic" and empirical world: what form can it possibly take, and what would possibly be above this realistic world and yet still of a piece with it and flesh of its flesh?

I think that such transcendence could only be detected in one possible place, namely in the space of an otherness from what is, a dimension freed from the weight of being and the inertia of the present social order. It seems possible to me that this transcendence could conceivably operate in the past, by way of the historical reconstruction of societies that no longer exist. Yet insofar as, no longer existing, they nonetheless have been, the law of an ontological realism would presumably still be binding on them, and there is a way in which *Salammbô*, or Walter Scott, or *Romola*, or *The Tale of Two Cities*, are no less realistic than their contemporary counterparts. At any rate, there here opens up the very interesting problem of the historical novel as such, which we can no longer pursue here.

But when we have to do with the future, with what does not yet and may never exist, it is a different story, and we are confronted with politics itself. Here we confront the knotty problem of the political novel and political literature in general, and their very possibility of existence. Is it conceivable, within the world of immanence, for this or that existent, this or that already existing element, to breathe "the air of other planets," to give off even the slightest hint of a radically different future? That the realistic novel absolutely resists and repudiates this possibility can be judged from its conventional treatment of political characters, of figures whose passion is political, who live for the possibilities of change and entertain only the flimsiest relationship with the solid ontology of what exists right now. We need only pass in review a few of the most famous representations of such figures to be convinced, and I will adduce three exhibits here.

There is Dickens's treatment of the "missions": all the crazed philanthropists who crowd the pages of *Bleak House* around the central character of Mrs. Jellabee with her African mission, and who wreak damage on all the people close to them. (Her husband literally pounds his head against the wall, her children are filthy and neglected, her oldest daughter escapes into a marriage of whose drawbacks she is scarcely cognizant, her own daily life is a shambles, ill-dressed, living only for the African correspondence and the African cause). When it is remembered that politics for Dickens, in any case in his supremely "liberalist" and free-market society, can only be embodied in philanthropy (but at best the personal, "ethical" type represented by Mr. Jarndyce, rather than this wholesale collective type), then it will be understood not only that these are figures of the political, but also that they represent the intellectual as well: the political intellectual, to whom these twin bugbears of abstraction and non-living, of the loss of ontological life and human reality to pure thought and idle speculation on the not-yet existent, must be conjoined.[21]

Once we learn to read these figures of the political, and to detect them throughout realism and in other places than the officially political—the parliamentary novels of Trollope, for example, where the political as such is a perfectly proper and respectable specialized dimension of life and being as such—we find that the satire of the anti-ontological is everywhere in ontological realism and indeed goes hand in hand with the very structure of the form and is inseparable from it.

Thus Henry James's feminists (in *The Bostonians*) are supremely emblematic of the political intellectual, and a far nastier and more malicious repudiation of politics than anything in the experiment of *The Princess Casamassima*, or indeed the contemporary treatment of anarchism generally (although Conrad's *Secret Agent* certainly comes close behind).

Finally, the whole animus spills over in Flaubert and is very far from being a mere personal ideology or idiosyncrasy. Whoever has read the extensive representations of the great political meetings in *L'Éducation sentimentale*—imitations in 1848 of the Jacobin clubs of the great revolution and far too long to quote here in the savorous detail they merit—knows of how much bile the political intellectuals are the recipients in Flaubert, who sees them as obsessives and maniacs necessarily plural in their nature, repetitions of each other and groups rather than individuals. Whatever the psychoanalytic interpretations of this unique passion and loathing of Flaubert, such scenes must also be taken as empty forms, structures of empty heterogeneity, which are reproduced throughout his work, most notably in *St. Anthony* but also in the *comices agricoles* in *Madame Bovary*, in court scenes in *Hérodias*, and at various key points in *Bouvard and Pécuchet*. As such, Flaubert has solved the formal problem of how to represent the unrepresentable posed here: in other words, how to

---

[21] Miss Wisk offers the generalized philosophy of the "mission" itself, being intent on showing "the world that woman's mission was man's mission; and that the only genuine mission, of both man and woman, was to be always moving declaratory resolutions about things in general at public meetings." (*Bleak House*, London: Penguin, 1996, 482 [chapter 30]).

lend ontological weight to the representation of figures and elements defined virtually in advance as lacking being, as having little ontological weight in their own right, either as characters or as meanings. The empty form of the obsessive exchange and multiplication of maniacs and their words (rather than thoughts) thus allows a representation to be set in the place of the ontologically thin and unreal (and indeed, in this respect, Flaubert's solution folds back over Dickens's, which equally relies on the multiplication and proliferation of such maniacs to fill in his canvas and give it the requisite density).

All of this, not merely to document the fragility of the new category of transcendental transcendence in the history of the novel, but also to make the usual point about the structural and inherent conservatism and anti-politicality of the realist novel as such. An ontological realism, absolutely committed to the density and solidity of what is—whether in the realm of psychology and feelings, institutions, objects or space—cannot but be threatened in the very nature of the form by any suggestion that these things are changeable and not ontologically immutable: the very choice of the form itself is a professional endorsement of the status quo, a loyalty oath in the very apprenticeship to this aesthetic. But since politics does exist in the real world, it must be dealt with, and satiric hostility is the time-honored mode of dealing novelistically with political trouble-makers. Only Stendhal and Galdós offer mild exceptions to this rule, the one on the basis of the youthful inexperience of his characters (and also Stendhal's internationalism and relative abhorrence of narrower French "realities"), and the other no doubt in part as a result of the extraordinary political changeability of Spain. But neither one loosens the lines that hold his work firmly to the ground of being, however much the narrative balloon surges and eddies in the winds of history. Were such lines cut, however, we would no doubt be confronted with truly Utopian forms, such as Chernyshevsky's *What's to be Done*, which would slowly drift out of the province of realism altogether.

Perhaps these two transcendental categories—the transcendental immanence of ethics and allegory, the transcendental transcendence of the political temptation—also open up a new space in which that formal and discursive phenomenon untheorizable in terms of realism might be grasped: I mean modernism, whose novels are, as I've insisted elsewhere, not at all to be understood as some opposite number of realism but in a very different and incommensurable aesthetic and formal fashion. Thus there are modernisms which can also be perfectly well interrogated with the categories and within the limits of realism as such—one thinks of *Ulysses* for example, certainly a prime example of a stubborn and hard fought attempt to hold onto the absolute being of the place and day, the untranscendable reality of a specifically limited secular experience. But such categories may no longer be the best ones to convey everything which is unique about such modernist works.

Yet there remains a fourth category in our scheme that has not so far been specified. We have positioned "great realism" in the space of immanent immanence, a kind of miraculous unity of form and content, a unique ontological possibility, on which we will waste no more effusions. We have then identified two slight yet menacing and perilous deviations from this formal plenitude, the first one in a kind of transcendental immanence in which certain of the categories of being—the ethical ones primarily—separate themselves out from reality and hover above it as a kind of organizing device which threatens to turn the events and narrative actions into so many examples and illustrations. And we have glimpsed a further possible deviation, the political one—transcendent transcendence—according to which the whole existing fabric of being is threatened by revolutionary and systemic overhaul and transformation.

But we have not yet taken into consideration the possibility that there could be something we might call immanent transcendence, in which a transformation of being would be somehow implicit in being itself, like a strange kind of wave running through matter, or a kind of pulsation of energy throbbing in the things themselves, without necessarily altering them or depriving them of their ontological status. The reader will have guessed that it is towards this final category that we have been working and that the immanent transcendence we have in mind is nothing less than the providential as such, its production what we have sporadically been calling the providential novel. Here truly we find what Lukács imagined himself to be describing when he evoked a realism of tendencies, which he understood as a representation of ontological change.[22] The examples were very precisely the passage of history throughout the regime changes of the early nineteenth century, as in

---

[22] See especially *Writer and Critic* and the *Studies in European Realism*. I believe that the theory of realism promoted in these essays is best grasped in terms of the way plot is able to represent historical tendencies, rather than as any static notion of "typical" social individuals.

La Cousine Bette, which ranges from Napoleon to the first Algerian expeditions in the late 1820s; yet no one ever suggested that onto-logical realism could not handle history or the passage of time. It is systemic change that we have tended to rule out; yet Lukács' description of the "tendency" seems far better to describe the prov-idential drifts at work in the novels we have been describing than anything else.

We may now return to those, and, in the light of this "ontologi-cal typology" and also mindful of the unique structural properties of the *Wilhelm Meister* experiment, will now need to offer some conjectures as to the historical development of these possibilities, that is to say, their concrete evolutionary realizations in those his-torically determined "evolutionary niches" (Moretti)[23] that the secular societies uniquely offered, in their various contingent ways.

The replacement of Providence by uniquely human energies was always a temptation for Balzac: the very character of Vautrin himself, as he desperately races to release Lucien (at the end of *Splendeurs et misères des courtisans*), just as he has magisterially pulled strings to secure the latter's good fortune in the early moments of this novelistic series—this image of supreme know-how and savoir-faire mesmer-ized the author of *La Comédie humaine* throughout his life, offering an image of action to be narrated as well as a subject-position for the novelist himself. In this sense, we must accustom ourselves to rethink-ing the pallid category of the "omniscient narrator" in terms of sheer passion, as an obsession to know everything and all the social levels from the secret conversations of the great all the way to the "*mystères de Paris*" and the "*bas fonds.*" Balzac was supremely what the Germans call a "*Besserwisser,*" a know-it-all at every moment anxious to show off his inside expertise (which he was unfortunately less able to put into practice). But surely Dickens had the virus as well, who was so proud of knowing all the streets in London; and we may safely attrib-ute an analogous concupiscence of knowledge to all the other great encyclopedic fabulators, from Trollope to Joyce.

What interests us more for the moment is the way this concep-tion of absolute knowledge spills over into the intrigue itself. Vautrin's status as the superman is sealed by his ultimate failure (with its human reward in his eventual promotion to chief of police—like the real-life Vidocq): but this failure simply marks the sterility of the dialectic of

23 See his *Atlas of the European Novel 1800–1900*, London: Verso, 1998.

the One and the Many. What if the task of knowing the Many were rather assigned to the Many themselves, in the form of a Meister-like Society of the Tower?

This is precisely what happens in Balzac, beginning with the *Histoire des Treize* (1833):

> Il s'est rencontré, sous l'Empire et dans Paris, treize hommes également frappés du même sentiment, tous doués d'une assez grande énergie pour être fidèles à la même pensée, assez probes entre eux pour ne point se trahir, alors même que leurs intérêts se trouvaient opposés, assez profondément politiques pour dissimuler les liens sacrés qui les unissaient, assez forts pour se mettre au-dessus de toutes les lois, assez hardis pour tout entreprendre, et assez heureux pour avoir presque toujours réussi dans leurs desseins; ayant couru les plus grands dangers, mais taisant leurs défaites; inaccessibles à la peur, et n'ayant tremblé ni devant le prince, ni devant le bourreau, ni devant l'innocence; s'étant acceptés tous, tels qu'ils étaient, sans tenir compte des préjugés sociaux; criminels sans doute, mais certainement remarquables par quelques-unes des qualités qui font les grands hommes, et ne se recrutant que parmi les hommes d'élite. Enfin, pour que rien ne manquât à la sombre et mystérieuse poésie de cette histoire, ces treize hommes restés inconnus, quoique tous aient réalisé les plus bizarres idées que suggère à l'imagination la fantastique puissance faussement attribuée aux Manfred, aux Faust, aux Melmoth; et tous aujourd'hui sont brisés, dispersés du moins. Ils sont paisiblement rentrés sous le joug des lois civiles, de même que Morgan, l'Achille des pirates, se fit, de ravageur, colon tranquille, et disposa sans remords, à la lueur du foyer domestique, de millions ramassés dans le sang, à la rouge clarté des intendies.

In Paris under the Empire, thirteen men came together. They were all struck with the same idea and all endowed with sufficient energy to remain faithful to a single purpose. They were all honest enough to be loyal to one another even when their interests were opposed, and sufficiently versed in guile to conceal the inviolable bonds which united them. They were strong enough to put themselves above all law, bold enough to flinch at no undertaking; lucky enough to have almost always succeeded in their designs, having run the greatest hazards, but remaining silent about their defeats; impervious to fear; and never having trembled before public authority, the public hangman or even innocence itself. They had all accepted one another, such as they were, without regard to social prejudice: they were undoubtedly criminals, but undeniably remarkable for certain qualities which go to the making of great men, and they recruited their members only from among men of outstanding quality. Lastly—we must leave out no element of the sombre and mysterious poetry of this story—the names of these thirteen men were never divulged, although they were the very incarnations of ideas suggested to the imagination by the fantastic powers attributed in fiction to the Manfreds, Fausts and Melmoths of literature. Today this association is broken up, or at least dispersed. Its members have peacably submitted to the yoke of civil law, just as Morgan, that

Achilles among pirates, gave up buccaneering, became a colonist and, basking in the warmth of his domestic fireside, made profitable use, without any qualms of conscience, of the millions he had amassed in bloody conflict under the ruddy glare of burning ships and townships.[24]

Here, this promising conspiracy results in little more than episodes (although they are among the most remarkable episodes in all of Balzac). Elsewhere, however, a rather different dialectic sets in motion, which suggests that the providential conspiracy is trans-ethical. It is beyond good and evil, to the degree to which it can serve feudal or individualistic passions (as in the *Histoire des Treize*) or philanthropic ones indifferently. So it is that Balzac will fantasize a white conspiracy with equal enthusiasm, this one however nourished by the more conservative traces of the religious orders, rather than the sulphurous fumes of the Carbonari and the other great political confraternities of Balzac's youth. Charity also needs its Machiavellis; as the organizational figure in *L'Envers de l'histoire contemporaine* (1842–1847) serves:

> N'avons-nous pas à déjouer la conspiration permanente du mal? à la saisir dans ses formes changeantes qu'on les croirait infinies? La Charité, dans Paris, doit être aussi savante que le vice, de même que l'agent de police doit être aussi rusé que le voleur. Chacun de nous doit être candide et défiant; avoir le jugement sûr et rapide autant que le coup d'œil.

> Is it not our task to undermine the permanent conspiracy of evil? to apprehend it beneath forms so mutable as to seem infinite? Charity, in Paris, must be as cunning as the thief. Each of us must be at one and the same time innocent and mistrustful; we must have powers of judgement that are as reliable and as swift as a glance.[25]

But if these "*frères de la Consolation*" are less exciting than the Thirteen, this has less to do with the moralism of the former than it does of the increasing "transcendence" of the providential conspiracy, which little by little comes externally to intervene in a situation to which it has a merely contemplative relationship of pity and moral judgement. Here, then, we can observe the slippage of more purely immanent plots into

---

[24] Honoré de Balzac, *La Comédie humaine*, Volume V, Paris: Pléiade, 1977, 787 (first paragraph of *Ferragus*). Balzac, *History of the Thirteen*, trans. Herbert J. Hunt, Middlesex: Penguin, 1974, 21.

[25] Ibid., Volume VIII, 323 (*L'Envers de l'histoire contemporaine*, premier épisode), trans. mine.

their transcendental opposite numbers. Whether this movement can be reversed, and develop into some more original novelistic structure, is a question better addressed to Dickens.

Our Mutual Friend—for many readers the darkest and most excit- ing, Willkie Collins–like of Dickens's completed novels, and also the one in which the salvational note is most satisfyingly sounded, and the lifting of sentimentalism into a truly providential realm of being—this late novel testifies to the temptation of conspiracy in Dickens as well, and to the "master-strokes of secret arrangement"[26] whereby the great feuilletonist attempts to hold together plot strands so numerous as to defy memory itself. But here conspiracy reveals its structure by promoting itself to a heightened power: for that system- atic promotion of illusion fostered by the symbolically eponymous protagonist ("mutual" also means a participation in several plots at once)[27] when he decides to take on a second existence after his alleged and public death—something that cannot yet be called a conspir- acy exactly—now promotes a deception on the part of Mr. Boffin, the Golden Dustman (or junk collector) and ostensible heir of the miser's fortune. Here, then, we enter the realm of genuine conspiracy, not diminished by its moral uses as test and lesson. It will no doubt promote the fortunes of the good and the discomfiture of the wicked, who do indeed recognize this human agency for Providence as such: such is for example the last glimpse of meaning of the obsessed Bradley Headstone, one of the darkest characters in Dickens, as he comes to understand his failure to dislodge his rival for Lizzie (the "separation" referred to in the following):

> For then he saw that through his desperate attempt to separate those two for ever, he had been made the means of uniting them. That he had dipped his hands in blood, to mark himself a miserable fool and tool. That Eugene Wrayburn, for his wife's sake, set him aside and left him to crawl along his blasted course. He thought of Fate, or Providence, or be the directing Power what it might, as having put a fraud upon him—overreached him—and in his impotent mad rage bit, and tore, and had his fit.[28]

Yet however glorious the apotheosis of the Golden Dustman in this salvational dénouement (which Dickens, evidently uncertain

26 Charles Dickens, *Our Mutual Friend*, New York: Modern Library, 1960, 794 (Book IV, chapter 13).

27 See p. 116: "'I may call him Our Mutual Friend,' said Mr. Boffin" (Book I, chapter 9).

28 Ibid., 816 (Book IV, chapter 15).

of himself, then redoubles in his postscript, in which Mr. and Mrs. Boffin miraculously survive a destructive railway accident), it cannot for most readers match the outcome of *Bleak House* itself, which will therefore have some lessons as to the providential slippages of the later work.

Dustbins, to be sure, they have in common, and old Krook—he of the spontaneous combustion, as in Zola—is no doubt a match for Mr. Boffin.[29] But we will understand nothing of the providential if we imagine it has only to do with the conventional happy ending and the marriage of Esther to her true beloved. On the contrary, the supremely providential moment, the truly sublime note of salvation-ality, lies elsewhere: it is an Event, in the most august sense of the term, and one that people feel approaching in the street:

> an unusual crowd…something droll…something interesting…everyone pushing and striving to get nearer…and presently great bundles of paper began to be carried out—bundles in bags, bundles too large to be got into any bags, immense masses of papers of all shapes and no shapes, which the bearers staggered under, and threw down for the time being, anyhow, on the Hall pavement, while they went back to bring out more.[30]

Laughter, universal glee, is the sign of this event, in which a whole old world is swallowed up and a new one born: and no reader who has worked through the thousand pages and nineteen installments of this extraordinary novel will fail to be electrified by the outcome:

> Even these clerks were laughing. We glanced at the papers, and seeing Jarndyce and Jarndyce everywhere, asked an official-looking person who was standing in the midst of them, whether the cause was over. "Yes," he said; "it was all up with it at last!" and burst out laughing too.[31]

And this in an ante-penultimate chapter entitled "Beginning the World"!

These passages return us to the euphoria of our initial quotations, with a few additional findings. For one thing, it has become clear that the jubilation will necessarily be a collective one, it will tell the

---

[29] Edgar Johnson compiles an impressive list of the items collected in such "dust bins," among them "soot, cinders, broken glass, bottles, crockery, worn-out pots and pans, old paper and rags, bones, garbage, human feces and dead cats," etc. Ibid, xi, note 6.

[30] Charles Dickens, *Bleak House*, 973–4 (chapter 65).

[31] Ibid., 974 (chapter 65).

climax of the story of the Many rather than the One. In that sense, it bears a strong relationship to Kant's idea of enthusiasm, which he associated with the French Revolution, and whose jubilation at least partly underscores its kinship with the Sublime, a parallel we cannot further explore here, save to recall the profound ambivalence of the Sublime, for Kant as for Burke, which must awaken monstrous feelings of terror and revulsion fully as much as those of the expansion of joy.[32]

5.

But we must also recall the fundamental shift, in the evolution of this kind of novel, from the question of individual salvation to the interweaving of many plots and many destinies. George Eliot is subversively outspoken on the matter of point of view, democratically insisting on everyone's right to this narrative centrality, and reminding us, in the middle of a chapter gravitating to Dorothea as naturally as water finding its own level, that her unattractive spouse, Mr. Casaubon, also "had an intense consciousness, within him, and was spiritually a-hungered like the rest of us."[33] Such reminders are virtually a social Bill of Rights (or *Droits de l'homme*) for the novel as a form, and will be programmatically enacted by later novelists like Joyce or Dos Passos.

What this implies most immediately, however, is the shift from the diachronic to the synchronic: now not the fateful destiny of this or that privileged or at least narratively favored protagonist, but rather the immense interweaving of a host of such lots or fates will involve a prodigious shifting of the axes of the novel, and usher in the serials of Dickens we have been examining no less than the late work of George Eliot herself, virtually our central exhibit in this discussion.

For not only the fact that the very word "providence" is dropped fatefully in the course of virtually every chapter of *Middlemarch*, sometimes by the characters, sometimes by the author herself; but the deeper sense of this recurrence—the drawing into the light of this

---

[32] See Immanuel Kant, "General Comment on the Exposition of Aesthetic Reflective Judgements" (it follows paragraph 29), in *Critique of Judgement*, Indianapolis: Hackett, 1987, 126–40; and also J.-F. Lyotard's interesting commentary in *Le Différend*, Paris: Minuit, 1983, 238–40 (Kant 4).

[33] George Eliot, *Middlemarch*, London: Penguin, 1994, 278 (chapter 29).

omnipresent ideology of providence and destiny, of the providential character of good or bad fortune—makes of this great work a reflexive practice of providential realism as such. This is to say, using a term that is more meaningful when sparingly appealed to, that *Middlemarch* can be seen as an immense *deconstruction* of the ideology of providence as such, a tracking down of its religious overtones and undertones, and an almost surgical exploration of its results and effectivities. I insist on the term "ideology," for other ideas of interrelationship and inextricability would have been possible in this period of the Paris Commune and the unification of Germany: Darwinian visions, nationalist programs, the bitter experience of class antagonisms—all of these, along with later ethnic or gender forms, might well have presided over the narrative of collective necessity, and in fact sometimes did. But Eliot's peculiar identification of this essentially social experience uniquely reflects the survival and ideological function of religion in the English class compromise, and allowed her to double a remarkable narrative synchronicity with a secondary investigation of the concepts through which the participants thought their experiences. (The term "deconstruction" was chosen to underscore the non-partisan nature of the investigation, which does not overtly denounce these religious survivals, as outright ideological analysis would surely have wanted to do).

But her word "spiritual" is also misleading, to the degree to which it suggests otherworldliness. To be sure, there is here a remarkable emphasis on intellectual labor. Earlier novelists were willing to tolerate glorified images of various artists, reunited under the general Romantic rubric of "genius": Balzac even indulged in alchemical inventors of genius (*La Recherche de l'absolu*), and thinkers of genius (*Louis Lambert*), but can scarcely be said to have had the sympathy for what would later in the century develop into scientific research (as Eliot follows it, with technical curiosity, in the story of Lydgate). "Idealistic" in Hegel's usage, we may recall, simply means "theoretical"; and Eliot brings a passionate curiosity to her depiction of all kinds of productive activity (including Garth's engineering).[34]

But what is certainly central in *Middlemarch*, and non-theoretical fully as much as non-spiritual, is the "cash nexus" and the synchronic role of money in the play of these individual destinies (which bear the name of a collectivity). The novel is a historical one, no doubt (set in 1830), and the intensifying grip of a money economy over the

---

[34] Ibid., 250–1 (chapter 24).

provinces is one ostensible theme the book shares with Balzac (in the France of an earlier period). But the financial essence of "providence" is the key to this particular unmasking or deconstruction, and it is worth comparing it with Dickens's version, only a generation earlier.

For *Bleak House* shares a character with *Middlemarch*, and Fred Vincy's "great expectations" is a virtual replay, in a wholly different register, of the fate of poor Richard Carstone, that equally amiable young man famous for being able to spend the numerical sum he has economized in previous purchases without ever having had it in the first place.

But Dickens has concentrated this thematics of money in one site, the famous trial, thereby allowing him to denounce the psychological corruption of expectation as such ("there's a dreadful attraction in the place," says Miss Flyte; "there's a cruel attraction in the place. You *can't* leave it. And you *must* expect")[35] rather than in the money economy as such. But in *Middlemarch* there is no destiny which is not in one way or another touched by money. Dickens's "web" is thus occasional:

> There, too, [at Jo's sickbed] is Mr. Jarndyce many a time, and Allan Woodcourt almost always; both thinking, much, how strangely Fate has entangled this rough outcast in the web of different lives.[36]

But George Eliot's web is constitutive, as the multiplicity of her figures suggest—besides webs, threads, lines, scratches (on a burning glass), interweavings, etc. I leave it to the Mr. Casaubons of the English Departments to take the inventory of these recurrent figures (it being understood that no one with any interest in allegory and interpretation can afford utterly to despise Mr. Casaubon's labors, however ill-fated).

We need to dispel two persistent errors about this narrative "fabric" and the meaning to be assigned to it. The first, despite what we have said about money and the material basis of this alleged attention to "spirituality," is the religious connotation of a novel which begins with St. Teresa and ends with a memorable celebration of Dorothea's goodness:

---

[35] *Bleak House*, 566 (chapter 35).
[36] Ibid., 732 (chapter 47).

for the growing good of the world is partly dependent on unhistoric acts; and that things are not so ill with you and me as they might have been, is half owing to the number who live faithfully a hidden life, and rest in unvisited tombs.[37]

Surely, despite the strength of all arguments against the concept of secularization which have been referred to above, such words, and the portrait of Dorothea that precedes and justifies them, testify to an unmistakable intent to secularize on George Eliot's part: the will to invent a figure of saintliness for a worldly and commercial society, and to reinvent a demonstration of the well-nigh material power of the kindness that radiates from Dorothea, gripping those around her with an almost physical force. It it clear enough that Eliot wishes to celebrate modernity (Lydgate's scientific passion, Garth's satisfaction in sheer productivity) without sacrificing the components of an older communal and religious culture virtually extinguished by it. But the ideological intent of the author never constitutes the "meaning" of the book, but rather, as Adorno pointed out, functions as a component of its raw materials. It will be possible to reinterpret Dorothea's centrality in another, non-ethical way, as we shall see in a moment.

The other fundamental misconception about the novels of this period (and of the later nineteenth century in general) is that, on the strength of their keen sensitivity to the movements of feeling and inner perception, they are somehow "introspective." But to range George Eliot (or Dostoyevsky, for that matter) among the novelists of introspection from Benjamin Constant's *Adolphe* to Proust is to obscure everything that is truly and formally original about her work. What we have here—as compared to Dickens, for example—is a significantly enhanced proximity to the relationships between individuals, a kind of intensified and well-nigh photographic enlargement of those barely perceptible adjustments to the Other, which Nathalie Sarraute, long after the fact, called "tropismes." What was wrongly identified as a self-consciousness or reflexivity of the individual self (now increasingly endowed with that private or personal reservoir entitled the Unconscious) can on closer inspection be seen to be a minute and microscopic negotiation with the shock and scandal of the Other, a reverberation of muffled reactions back and forth, as with the dance of insects confronting one another and attempting to gauge degrees of danger or attraction, if not neutrality. If a new theory

---

[37] *Middlemarch*, 838.

of modernity be wanted, then it might just as well be this one, the discovery, in philosophy and in artistic representation as well, of the existence of the Other as what Sartre called a fundamental alienation of my Being. Philosophy, except for Hegel's Master/Slave dialectic, altogether ignored the existence of other people as a philosophical problem that changed the very nature of philosophizing; as for literature, as long as the "other person" or character is imagined to be a kind of self-sufficient substance in itself, which occasionally comes into momentary or violent contact with other objects like it, but whose being is not fundamentally modified by the being of others, then it matters very little what kinds of psychological experiences are attributed to these independent tokens of narration. But when, as here, the other is seen to call me into question in my very being; when relationships take precedence over the beings in relationship, and a registering apparatus is developed which can detect such perpetual changes; when relationships are focused close-up in their intolerable proximity ("marriage is so unlike everything else," Dorothea reflects, "there is something even awful in the nearness it brings"),[38] then a new dimension, a new social continent has been discovered, which is the microcosm corresponding to the new macrocosms of collectivity on the level of cities and social classes.

After this, the intricate molecular patterns of a Henry James; or the violent spasms of cruelty and self-abasement of a Dostoyevsky; and on into the multiple sub-atomic languages of what we are pleased to call modernism itself. We have already observed that the alternative of modernism and realism does not correspond to a classification system, but rather to a methodological focus, in such a way that it can scarcely be paradoxical for a "great realist" like George Eliot also, and from another angle, to be identified as a nascent modernist.

What needs to be taken into account for this to become more plausible is the ostentatiously omniscient and relatively archaic character of the style itself. But the latter imitates proverbs and traditional collective wisdom rather than anything redolent of Proustian self-expression, and thus disguises the innovative nature of its intersubjective raw material at the same time that it seeks to incorporate the latter into a quintessentially social knowledge, rather than to document the discoveries of some "new science" such as psychology or psychoanalysis.

---

[38] Ibid., 797 (chapter 81).

This "web" of interrelationships is now, on the one hand, to be grasped as an immense and mobile concatenation of events—encounters, looks, demands, self-defenses—rather than a static table of equivalences; and on the other hand—as synchronic nature also necessarily becomes visible—it is to be grasped in the form of interconnections that fan out well beyond the field of vision of the reader of any individual notation, and are yet modified by the most minute adjustments in the "lives" thereby brushing against each other.[39] What we must observe about Dorothea's saintliness is that it not only prolongs and perpetuates its effects across a multiplicity of neighboring connections, but that pain and suffering do so as well, and the various Dickensian wills—Mr. Casaubon's, Mr. Featherstone's, along with the deployment of money in his various projects by Bulstrode—are here transmuted into the vehicles of the transmission of bad vibrations across the same immense capillary system. But what has been lost in the shift from a diachronic providentiality—an attention to the salvation of the individual—to this synchronic vision is simply the ethical itself, or better still, any sense of evil as such. There is, in George Eliot, goodness, but its opposite is simply unhappiness; and we are forbidden to judge either Casaubon or Bulstrode as evil, even though their contemporaries may well do so.

The point is that, reinscribed in the web of interrelationships, what is painful or unhappy for one subjectivity in this immense network can, as it is transmitted over the links of a whole series, be transformed into something positive for others; just as the reverse can happen too.[40] But this possibility of the transformation of negative into positive, of suffering into happiness and back, clearly lifts these categories up into another supra-personal dimension and tends to efface older ethical or eudaimonic meanings. (It also forfeits the great game of the omniscient narrator, which is to know secrets which none of the characters involved will ever learn, ironically taking their unhappy

---

[39] Ibid., 795 (chapter 81). And see also David Ferris's exploration of the figure of the web in *The Romantic Evasion of Theory*, Baltimore: Johns Hopkins University Press, 1994, 222–223.

[40] Mr. Skimpole's Panglossianism (in *Bleak House*) may be said to anticipate this transcendence of good and evil in a comic register: "'Enteprise and effort,' he would say to us (on his back), 'are delightful to me … Mercenary creatures ask, "What is the use of a man's going to the North Pole? What good does it do?" I can't say; but for anything I *can* say, he may go for the purpose—though he don't know it—of employing my thoughts as I lie here.'" (*Bleak House*, 294–5 [chapter 18]).

ignorance to their graves. Here, "essence must appear," as Hegel says, and the secrets, already appearing under the guise of their effects, must necessarily be revealed.)

But is not their misery—so vividly registered here in ways unequalled in the other novels of the time—a proof of George Eliot's supreme insight into psychology? In fact, in both Casaubon and Bulstrode, what we confront are masterful diagnoses of what Sartre will later on call *mauvaise foi*, the bad faith of self-deception and agonizing and impossible attempts at self-justification.[41] But these moments already contain otherness within them, in the form of judgement, in which the suffering subject interiorizes the gaze of the other and seeks to master and reorient it in his own favor. Indeed, as these tropismes become magnified by way of the novelistic or narrative medium, we glimpse a parallel magnification in the social itself, which is none other than the dimension of gossip, which enlarges the facts of interrelationship and transmits them onward to a circulation through the collectivity. It is the other face of my alienation by the other, and extends on into George Eliot's vision of history as "a huge whispering-gallery" in which we are ultimately privy to "the secret of usurpations and other scandals gossiped about long empires ago."[42]

Yet now providentiality returns, in an extraordinary and unexpected guise, at the moment when its actions and effectivities seemed all but undecideable. Casaubon and Bulstrode end unhappily; Lydgate's scientific ambitions are dashed and his marriage loses all its enchantment; yet contrary to all expectations, Dorothea's story ends well, and the renunciation (*Entsagung*) for which the German tradition, from Goethe to Fontane, had prepared us—let alone the terrible and emblematic solitude of spinster and widow from Balzac to Maupassant—is here dispelled by an utterly unexpected happy ending, for which we did not even dare to have "hope against hope" (and which, in hindsight, renders somewhat exaggerated the elegiac last lines about her which we have quoted above).

But the truly providential in *Middlemarch* lies elsewhere; and to appreciate it, we must note another significant feature of the providential-synchronic which we have hitherto omitted. We have learned, to be sure, that the synchronic and the diachronic are not to each other as space to time, nor even as the ahistorical to the historical, let

---

[41] See above, Part One, chapters VII and VIII.
[42] *Middlemarch*, 412 (chapter 41).

alone the non-narrative to the narrative; yet we would be justified in expecting time, history and narrativity to undergo some fundamental modifications as they pass under a synchronic regime. When, as here, we have to do with the synchronic as a simultaneity of destinies and a coexistence of a host of different narratives, what happens to temporality is this: the simultaneous time-lines become, as in Einsteinian relativity, difficult to reckon off against each other. It is simultaneity itself which becomes spatial, and in this new spatiality the various distinct temporalities can be adjusted against each other only with some difficulty, as in the voluminous historical concordances we might expect to find in Mr. Casaubon's papers.

Indeed the two series of events run side by side like Einstein's trains: who can tell what time it is outside, let alone inside? There are many train tracks, parallel and infinite, they keep overtaking each other in some ideal present; their own times overlap, cancel, outleap each other, overtake, fall behind. But every so often they overtake, not the other's, but their own past; they speed ahead of themselves and run through the line a second time.

Here, then, occasionally, something miraculous happens; and it is just such a miraculous happening that we are able to witness in the destiny of Fred Vincy, whose hopes of an inheritance and the estate called Stone Court are properly dashed at an early crisis in the novel, in which "realism" demands that the unrealistic hope and expectation be brought to its realistically anticipated unhappy end. This play with expectation constitutes a kind of novelistic "reality principle," which we find historically realized twice over in the classic Balzacian "hope against hope," and then in the gloomy fatalities of naturalism.

Here, on the contrary, it is the reality principle which must be joyously discredited; yet it is the test and the obligation of the form of providential realism to outwit sheer wish-fulfillment and daydream, to overtrump both fairy-tale endings and naturalist certainties with a new form of necessity. Fred Vincy will administer the estate after all (even if he does not technically inherit it), and this loop in time, in which the lost chance comes again against all odds, and the old hope is fulfilled after its definitive disappointment, is the concrete narrative embodiment of that religious iconography of resurrection with which we began, and the recuperation, by Eliot's voluminous realism, of the coming alive of the statue in *The Winter's Tale*: it is the salvational temporality of Ernst Bloch's privileged fable of the *Unverhofftes Wiedersehen* (a story by Hebel later rewritten and recapitulated by

Hoffmann), in which in extreme old age the widow of a dead miner is able to glimpse her long-lost husband once last time again as youthful as on the day he disappeared. What interests us here, however, is the way in which these stirring images find their own unexpected resurrection in the most seemingly unpropitious of forms, the nineteenth-century novel itself. It is an ecstatic ending which previous novels could only achieve by the glimpse of the ghosts of Heathcliff and Catherine wandering together over the moor.

6.

Now we must rapidly conclude, with only the briefest of glances at the descendency of this form in contemporary culture, and in particular in contemporary film. For both Quentin Tarantino's *Pulp Fiction* (1994) and Goran Paskaljević's *Cabaret Balkan* (1998, also known as *The Powder Keg*), if not indeed Milčo Mančevski's 1994 *Before the Rain*, seem to testify to a revival of effects structurally dependent on the apparent simultaneity of narrative time lines. Despite the bloodiness and violence of all these films, each conceals a salvational note underscored by the conversion of a professional killer, in the first-named of these works, to the old-time religion.

But it is to their prototype, in Robert Altman's *Short Cuts* (1993), that we must turn for some more fundamental structural insight into this new and old form, which seems to reflect an intensifying feeling for the interrelatedness of the social totality. In much of Altman's work, indeed (*Nashville*, 1975; *A Wedding*, 1978; *Pret-à-porter*, 1994; *Cookie's Fortune*, 1999; *Dr. T and the Women*, 2000), the multiplicity of plot lines and characters frequently leads to providential sparks and fires; and these are also, as we have seen with George Eliot, beyond good and evil, which is to say that the providential outcome can absorb either a happy or an unhappy ending indifferently, from what is a kind of Spinozan elevation.

But *Short Cuts* is the most revealing of these works, insofar as it reveals the very gesture of totalization itself. The film is based, indeed, on a compilation of stories by Raymond Carver, which for the most part offer unrelieved glimpses of failure and private misery. The one exception, "A Small, Good Thing," in which a fatal accident is unexpectedly transfigured by a symbolic wake, is then itself amplified, in its providential content, by Altman's combination of all these separate stories into a web of episodes or multiple plots. Speaking of one of Balzac's shorter stories, Lukács once observed: "To treat this theme in a novel instead of a short story would require entirely different subject matter and an entirely different plot. In a novel the writer would have to expose and develop in breadth the entire process arising out of the social conditions of modern life and leading to these ... problems."[43] Altman's unification, however, achieves this miraculous transformation without any modification of the subject matter or plots of the stories, simply by a prodigious enlargement of their frame and context and a virtual creation, ex nihilo, of the totality they now come to express and represent. It is a passage from the private to the collective, from the static-ontological to the dynamic and the historically actual—the whole concatenation of episodes ominously overflown by the notorious med-fly fumigations of 1988 and shaken climactically by the major earthquake to come—which reinvents the providential narrative anew for late capitalism.[44]

---

[43] Georg Lukács, "Art and Objective Truth," in *Writer and Critic*, New York: Grosset and Dunlap, 1971, 54.

[44] See, for further elaboration of this thesis, my "Altman and the National-Popular" in *The Ancients and the Postmoderns* (Verso, forthcoming).

Chapter II

War and Representation

A vast entity, a planet, in a space of a hundred million dimensions; three-dimensional beings could not so much as imagine it. And yet each dimension was an autonomous consciousness. Try to look directly at that planet, it would disintegrate into tiny fragments, and nothing but consciousnesses would be left. A hundred million free consciousnesses, each aware of walls, the glowing stump of a cigar, familiar faces, and each constructing its destiny on its own responsibility. And yet each of those consciousnesses, by imperceptible contacts and insensible changes, realizes its existence as a cell in a gigantic and invisible coral [*polyp*]. War: everyone is free, and yet the die is cast. It is there, it is everywhere, it is the totality of all my thoughts, of all Hitler's words, of all Gomez's acts; but no one is there to add it up. It exists solely for God. But God does not exist. And yet war exists.

          –Sartre, *The Reprieve*

Stalingrad is like a painting that cannot be observed from close up, but from which one must step back in order to do it full justice.

          –Joseph Goebbels

I.

War offers the paradigm of the nominalistic dilemma: the abstraction from totality or the here-and-now of sensory immediacy and confusion. For Tolstoy, as for almost everybody else, the representational consequence was most memorably drawn by Stendhal in *The Charterhouse of Parma*: its naive young hero setting forth to join the Emperor's army and blundering into the middle of the battle of Waterloo without even recognizing his hero as the latter gallops off what he does not even understand to be the battlefield. The protagonist thereby gives expression, avant la letter, to what the Formalists called "*ostranenie*" or "estrangement" (defamiliarization), in which a preexisting stereotype is dismantled and brought before us in all its nameless freshness and horror. Whether this is to be grasped as an essentially modernist operation, or on the contrary is something all the realisms are by definition called upon to do, is a question we will for the moment leave open.

Still, it suggests that there exists some preexisting stereotype of war for such passages to defamiliarize, and that there must then also be representations of war that are content to reconfirm the stereotype. Indeed, one often has the feeling that all war novels (and war films) are pretty much the same and have few enough surprises for us, even though their situations may vary. Indeed, we can enumerate some seven or eight of those situations which more or less exhaust the genre. If so, and despite experience which confirms this opinion, this would be in itself an astonishing fact, given the radical changes in warfare the historians document since the hand-to-hand combat in the plains before Troy (Hegel's prototype of that human and unalienated form, the epic, as opposed to the modern "prose of the world," denatured by money, commerce and industry): there is then, marked by technological advances (gunpowder, machine guns and tanks, aircraft, unmanned cybernetic weaponry), a whole periodization of structural changes in warfare and its accompanying strategies which needs to be combined with the narrative typologies we are about to enumerate and to examine in more detail. Add to this complication a periodization of properly aesthetic modes and transformations (allegory, realism, modernism, postmodernism), and we confront a combination scheme of no little complexity which may strike us ultimately as serving less to explain these representations than simply to classify them. But perhaps such possibilities, which account for the organization of the notes that follow into a sampling of exhibits rather than a unified and systematic theory, may also be reduced and simplified by the rather different consideration which cuts across all of them— namely the suspicion that war is ultimately unrepresentable—and by the attention to the various forms that the impossible attempt to represent it may have taken.

As for the narrative variants, which seem to me to hold for film as much as for the novel, I enumerate eight of them: 1) the existential experience of war; 2) the collective experience of war; 3) leaders, officers, and the institution of the army itself; 4) technology; 5) the enemy landscape; 6) atrocities; 7) attack on the homeland; 8) foreign occupation. The final category does not include the related subject-matter of spies and espionage (now largely settled into a generic category of its own); nor does it exhaust the phenomenon of guerrilla warfare, from the current US occupation of Iraq and Afghanistan all the way back to the Vendée and indeed to the earliest institutionalization of armies as such; for guerrilla warfare—the result of uneven development and of the incursion of an "advanced" mode of production into an "underdeveloped" one—can also offer the very prototype of war itself and not its savage exception. Yet these very exclusions suggest a different way of cutting across these plot-types, for the typical events of foreign occupation (and of espionage for that matter) take us back to institutions and to the state as actor and agency; while the horror of guerilla warfare (whether urban or rural) would seem rather to lie in the unidentifiability of its actors, who emerge from their surroundings without warning and just as unexpectedly disappear again.

What may prove most helpful here, then, is Kenneth Burke's "dramatistic pentad," which differentiates between act, agent, agency, purpose and scene as so many distinct perspectives through which the narrative material can be focused.[1] To use a different, more structural terminology, we may say that each of these categories constitutes a different kind of dominant and thereby produces a somewhat different projection of the material, it being understood that there is no correct or "true," photographically accurate rendering of such multidimensional realities. Still, narrative semiotics, by reidentifying Burke's first three categories with each other—an act always somehow implying an agent and the agent in turn implying an agency— suggests a different ordering of these perspectives, in which purpose somehow withdraws (as a feature of interpretation rather than of representation), while scene begins to emerge as a whole new element in its own right, in which the anthropomorphic gets eclipsed and some new and as yet unrecognizable narrative reality comes into view. For the act and its accompanying actantial categories always presuppose a name, and thereby a preexisting concept of the event thus identified (as already with the word "war" itself), while action and agency themselves seem to be determined and simplified in advance by this or that institutionalized and organized agent. Scene, however, remains at an unmodified level of narrative complexity, only becoming concrete in the course of the representation. Spatiality is only one possible

---

[1] See Kenneth Burke, *A Grammar of Motives*, Berkeley: University of California Press, 1953.

dimension of scene, to which anthropomorphic elements are subordinated in unaccustomed and estranged ways.

Technology, meanwhile, as alienated and reified human labor and energy, is always a slippery category, moving back and forth between allegory and external (or proto-natural) doom, yet sometimes also celebrated as the triumph of human inventiveness and the expression of human action (or its prosthetic extension). It wanders back and forth across all our tale-types, sometimes organizing their very periodization (as we have suggested above), sometimes generating a uniquely nightmarish experience in its own right, as in the sheer terror and panic aroused by the appearance of the first tanks at the Battle of the Somme in World War I; or that of the V-2 rockets in its sequel. Yet technology is truly the apotheosis of a properly modernist teleology, describing, as Adorno put it, a direct line from the sling-shot to the megaton bomb. Each innovation is somehow also the same in its embodiment of radical difference: as witness Ermanno Olmi's wonderful film *Il mestiere delle armi* (2001) on the development of artillery in the sixteenth century.

The first category, of the existential experience of war—which has its classical literary realization in Stephen Crane's *Red Badge of Courage* (1895)—most often expresses the fear of death and that somewhat different thing, the death anxiety: as such, although this category is surely the quintessential form the representation of war will take in most people's minds, its content (personal danger, decisions and hesitations, contingency, apprenticeship) can be transferred to other generic frameworks. War then becomes that laboratory in which, as with the bullring for Hemingway, such experiences are most unfailingly aroused and observed. Yet it tends towards the category of the *Bildungsroman* to the degree to which it is generally a question of a very young and inexperienced soldier, whom the event does not leave untouched.

With the collective focus, however, everything changes; yet here also we find ourselves in the presence of a content fully interchangeable with several other familiar and well-defined genres which call the generic specificity of the war film back into question. For the collective war story turns on the interaction of various character types apparently gathered at random. The experience is the national one, of universal conscription as the first occasion in which men from different social classes are thrown together, at least until the public high school dramas of more recent memory. In the Europe of emergent nationalism, the experience was called upon to level the old regional cultures (Sicily, Brittany) and to standardize language and the claims of authority and the state—discipline as well as obedience, and acknowledgement of national unity. The American films, taking class difference for granted and only gradually absorbing racial difference, found their originality psychologically, in the typology of personalities thrown together in the group (or war machine). The intelligent upper class figure, the sociopath, the weakling, the bully, the fixer, the jokester, the trickster, the Don Juan, the ethnic type (generally southern European, but a black man, a Chicano, an Indian, comes later on), the religious fundamentalist, the "nice guy," the nerd. The list is endless but the combinations—that is to say, the fundamental dramatic conflicts and clashes—are probably statistically limited and certainly generically predictable.

The crucial thing about this collective system is that it is itself the abstraction of something else. We may focus the action in terms of male bonding or the psychology of hierarchical institutions, with the problem of authority figures (either incompetent or psychotic, etc.) added in later on. The first versions of the form emerge in what we may call a pre-feminist world; and certainly the absence of women is a significant structural part of the form—later on, women will be admitted as yet another variation on the male character types—but it is above all the absence of the family and of peacetime, indeed of wage labor itself, that is the crucial feature here. This is why a juxtaposition with the heist or caper film is so interesting: for in this last we find the same abstract structure, the same variety of character types and their clashes, the same as it were sealed social world in which now even the legitimacy of the institution of the army and the "declaration" of war has been stripped away, giving us all this in a different kind of defamiliarization, where the overall aim of the collective action is not even "war aims," defeating the enemy, defending freedom, or some such socially plausible motive, but rather simply money itself—the ultimate abstraction, the ultimate "axiomatic" emptied of all concrete content. Yet the absence of wage labor or commodified labor is here retained; and as with many other kinds of crime films, there is a Utopian overtone in which the characters are allowed to live in a disalienated world, and in which activity is akin to play. (I have elsewhere tried to show that these Utopias can be invested with very different valences: thus the mafia film quintessentially appeals to nostalgia for the family by way of unconscious collective envy for the southern European clan system).[2]

Thus, what both war films (of the collective buddy type) and caper films abstract from and yet dramatize in their own specific generic ways is the division of labor itself: each of these character types stands for a certain type of competence, something brought out much more strongly in the caper films, where each is precisely selected on the basis of that competence. The overall small or micro-group is the Deleuzian nomadic war machine, literally or figuratively, that is to say, the image of the collective without the state and beyond reified institutions. Still, such "groups-in-fusion" as Jean-Paul Sartre calls them in the *Critique of Dialectical Reason*, are also, as they themselves harden and ossify, forerunners of the institutional as such. Indeed, when the peacetime army comes into its own mode of representation (or indeed the police force itself, in current procedurals), it is rather bureaucracy whose epic is here sung before us (without being named as such, except in socialist realism), and the collective structure of the nomads is reappropriated for the celebration of the state. Both are indeed themselves afterimages of the social, and we make a more productive use of Deleuze when we grasp his dualism as an alternating possibility and realize that libidinal investment in the nomads can be no less reprehensible (but also no more so) than libidinal investment in the state itself.

As for the third category, of leaders and institutions, it initiates a shift of gravity towards the exterior of the experience of war, whether individual or collective, for the officers are ordinarily as much a part of the external environment of the soldier as the enemy itself, and are indeed equally often objectified into what gets identified as the bureaucracy or the state. Initially, however, such characters furnished the staple of the older chronicle history, with its great men and world-historical figures—what Lukács assigns to the potentialities of the stage, as in Schiller's *Wallenstein* or Strindberg's *Gustavus Adolfus*, or even Shakespeare's war-ridden history plays (and the short-hand German imitations that come out of them, like Goethe's *Goetz von Berlichingen* or even Kleist and Büchner). This is, on one traditional yet rather narrow acceptation of the term, the place of politics as such; and it cannot be doubted that the various populist representations of

---

2 See "Reification and Utopia in Mass Culture," in *Signatures of the Visible,* NY: Routledge, 1990.

the simple soldier and the common man in uniform are dialectically later than these less and less glorious figures striding about the stage and vocalizing their decisions, with or without a note of human, all-too-human pathos.

Yet Tolstoy's notorious loathing for Napoleon is in that sense merely the other face of his hero-worshipping portrayal of the uniquely Russian bluffness and acumen of Kutuzov, a historical figure Tolstoy himself had not many years before this characterized as "sensual, cunning and unfaithful"—just as he had called such patriotism "a fairy tale which aroused national feeling"[3] in earlier times. Perhaps the classic defamiliarization of the "great general" comes closer to Tolstoy's representation of "world-historical" decision-making and his inveterate resistance to it (a stance to which we owe the concluding "theory of history" in *War and Peace*):

> But at that moment an adjutant galloped up with a message from the commander of the regiment in the hollow and news that immense masses of the French were coming down upon them and that his regiment was in disorder and was retreating upon the Kiev grenadiers. Prince Bagration bowed his head in sign of assent and approval. He rode off at a walk to the right and sent an adjutant to the dragoons with orders to attack the French. But this adjutant returned half an hour later with the news that the commander of the dragoons had already retreated beyond the dip in the ground, as a heavy fire had been opened on him and he was losing men uselessly, and so had hastened to throw some sharpshooters into the wood.
>
> Prince Andrew listened attentively to Bagration's colloquies with the commanding officers and the orders he gave them and, to his surprise, found that no orders were really given, but that Prince Bagration tried to make it appear that everything done by necessity, by accident, or by the will of subordinate commanders was done, if not by his direct command, at least in accord with his intentions. Prince Andrew noticed, however, that though what happened was due to chance and was independent of the commander's will, owing to the tact Bagration showed, his presence was very valuable. Officers who approached him with disturbed countenances became calm; soldiers and officers greeted him gaily, grew more cheerful in his presence, and were evidently anxious to display their courage before him.[4]

This pretense of freedom in the face of necessity, however, pales in comparison with the criminality of the officers' decisions in World War I, as so memorably exemplified in Kubrick's *Paths of Glory*

---

[3] Boris Eikhenbaum, *Tolstoi in the Sixties*, trans. Duffield White, Ann Arbor: Ardis, 1982, 149 and 144.

[4] Leo Tolstoy, *War and Peace*, New York: Norton, 1966, 163.

(1968); and it is to be remarked at this point that many mass cultural genres—the police procedural, the spy novel—end up turning less on the pursuit of the enemy or the official other, than they do on their own institutional framework itself, with its ineffective and ill-informed command system and the internal subversion of moles and double or triple agents.

Perhaps the abstract theoretical debates on strategy and tactics are relevant here in a new and more formal way. The debate on the influence of Clausewitz, for example—whose notion of war as a duel is as anthropomorphic as Hegel or Homer; his notion of the decisive final battle a thoroughly narrative one (which has wrongly been criticized for omitting the very different dynamic of guerrilla warfare); and even the famous maxim of war as the continuation of politics by other means—suggests a way of translating warfare and its specialized personnel back into more familiar peacetime and civilian realities amenable to the techniques of the more conventional realist novel.

Yet behind all such discussions lies a narratological problem, a challenge to anthropomorphic representation and the mimesis of human actions and characters: the question of whether such possibilities are not altogether obsolete in the age of nuclear weapons, drones and suicide bombers. These are the debates waged back and forth across history by the generals and commanders, the dictators (in both ancient and modern senses) and the war leaders. They reenter the narrative representations of war in the form of unwarranted hero-worship and blind allegiance, or the sense of betrayal, or the contempt of foot soldiers for stupid officers, or the cowardice of the general staff. These are all what semiotics terms "actantial" questions, issues about action and human agency; and even our fourth category of technology seems to move uneasily in and out of the whole area of personification and anthropomorphism.

When it comes to the next set of categories, however, my sense is that the focus of the war narrative subtly changes, and that in Kenneth Burke's dramatistic pentad, we have begun to move from the first four Burkean categories to the fifth, which he called scene and to which he attributed a different and perhaps more diffuse kind of rhetorical and representational power.

2.

For even atrocities might seem to us today to belong rather to the malignant properties of evil or cursed landscapes than to the savagery of an individual actor; and it is as though with this and our other later plot-types we pass from a world of acts and characters to that of space itself—scene, landscape, geography, the folds of the earth that determine military campaigns in the sense of contingency or the main chance, a heterogeneous element which is that of *Stimmung* or affect fully as much as of some mere stage or "context" for human gestures. The bombs falling out of the sky are part of it, along with the lunar landscape of trench warfare; the silence of deserted villages is a narrative player in such tales, along with the menace of empty windows and the complicity of nature in ambush or pursuit, in concealment as well—camouflage being the way that humans acknowledge the primacy of Scene, just as maps are another.

Meanwhile this category then abolishes or suspends the distinction between the enemy's landscape and our own, the latter no less fraught with peril than some unknown, hostile terrain. For here the great hand-to-hand duels of the armies—Napoleon versus Kutuzov, Wallenstein versus Gustavus Adolfus—give way to the imagery of penetration—the first glimpse of a sea of tanks at the battle of Kursk, the smell of sweating armies miles away in World War I, the screaming of the dive bombers, the first exposed steps in an abandoned hamlet—the space of modern warfare is vulnerable by definition, and no longer belongs to anyone.

But that was also the case in the Thirty Years' War, whose most extraordinary literary document begins in full incursion and horror, as the mercenaries (of whatever affiliation) loot the villages and torture the peasants for food and gold:

> Da fing man erst an, die Stein von den Pistolen und hingegen an deren Staff der Bauern Daumen aufzuschrauben, und die armen Schelmen so zu foltem, als wenn man halt Hexen brennen wollen, massen sie sich einen von den bereits in Backoven Steckten, und mit Feuer hinter ihm her waren, ohngesehen er noch nichts bekannt hatte; einem anderen machten sie ein Seil um den Kopf und rettelten es mit einem Bengel zusammen, das ihm das Blut zu Mund, Nas und Ohren heraus sprang.

> Then they used thumbscrews, which they cleverly made out of their pistols, to torture the peasants, as if they wanted to burn witches. Though he had confessed

to nothing as yet, they put one of the captured hayseeds in the bake-oven and lighted a fire in it. They put a rope around someone else's head and tightened it like a tourniquet until blood came out of his mouth, nose, and ears. In short, every soldier had his favorite method of making life miserable for peasants, and every peasant had his own misery.[5]

The period has indeed virtually become defined by such atrocities, which I am tempted to count into the Scene and space itself as one of its properties during this long war in which most of central Europe is consumed, at all scales from macroscopic to microscopic: armies pursuing each other from one end of Europe to another, enemy battalions unwittingly colliding in marshes during the night, bands of marauders burning villages, a deserter ransacking an empty house:

> "Noses and ears cut off to make hatbands"… "the robbers and murderers took a piece of wood and stuck it down the poor wretches' throats, stirred it and poured in water, adding sand or even human feces…" "'they tied our honest burgher Hans Betke to a wooden pole and roasted him at the fire from seven in the morning until four in the afternoon, so that he gave up the spirit amidst much shrieking and pains.'"[6]

With such nightmares, indeed, one has the sense that the two categories—of internal invasion and intervention and of war carried to foreign, unfamiliar territory—somehow coincide and dialectically reinforce each other. This is not so much the pseudo-synthesis of a "civil war" (an oxymoron if there ever was one) as rather an utter transmogrification of the familiar into the alien, the "*heimlich*" into the "*unheimlich*," in which the home village—the very limit of the world itself and the boundary of the real and the everyday—is transformed into a place of unimaginable horror, while the neighbors of the home country—the eternal peasants, the stock characters of village life—become sly faces of evil and of menace, ambushing the soldier who strays from his company and lynching the few they can safely overpower, concealing the food and hiding in the woods like savages (anachronistically to redeploy that Fenimore Cooper imagery

---

[5] Hans Jakob Christoffel von Grimmelshausen, *Der abenteuerliche Simplicissimus,* Munich: Artemis & Winkler, 1956, 17. English translation: *The Adventures of Simplicius Simplicissimus,* trans. and abridged by G. Schulz-Behrend, Columbia, SC: Camden House, 1993, 7.

[6] Christopher Clark, *Iron Kingdom: The Rise and Downfall of Prussia, 1600–1947,* Cambridge: Harvard University Press, 2006, 32–4.

that Balzac so relished). But this is something that happens, not so much to people or individuals—characters as such—as to the landscape itself, which fades in and out of nightmare, its mingled dialects now intelligible, now the gibberish of aliens.

Some such Gestalt-like metamorphosis from familiar to unfamiliar, from the anthropomorphic to the micro- or macroscopic play of the material elements themselves, can be observed in what the Thirty Years' War itself imposes on our attempts to conceptualize it as a whole. On the one hand, the great strategic trajectory of the armies of a Wallenstein or a Gustavus Adolphus, of ferocious condottiere like Mansfield or the Bavarian general Tilly, of the Spanish armies of intervention in search of the enemy and of some final and decisive bone-jarring clash; on the other, a well-nigh optical enlargement, an eyelash-brushing approach in which the seemingly intelligible units of the official armies disintegrate into minute bands of individual marauders spreading across an everywhere identical landscape of fields and woods, huts and paths, and offering the same scenes of carnage and flight over and over again, beyond history, beyond narrative.

Nor is this only caused by the complexity of this block of historical time, with its innumerable agents and actors (who constantly change position and swap their functions with one another), a multiplicity only momentarily simplified by the conventional stereotype of religious war and the climactic struggle between the Counter-Reformation and Protestantism as such. For the Counter-Reformation is already divided and multiplied by the triple centers of the papacy, Madrid and the Habsburg Emperor Ferdinand II (more Catholic and fanatical than the pope, or than his own Spanish relatives); while what is loosely called Protestantism—already locked in internecine warfare between its two, Lutheran and Calvinist, branches both of them anathematized by innumerable millenarian sects—is itself susceptible to infinite fission and the propagation of innumerable subsidiary local and foreign conflicts.

To assign the guilt of striking the first blow is a philosophical quandary of the first magnitude; while even the most warlike of the participants—Wallenstein for example—can also be read as embodying a humane will to peace, to the ending of the indefinite proliferation of the war and an establishment of central European unity on a new basis. (Even Schiller's Hamlet-like version of the great generalissimo's assassination leaves us with multiple interpretations of his motives:

Does he want to found a dynasty and make himself Emperor? Does he want to unite Germany in some prefiguration of nineteenth-century nationalism? Is he indeed, against all appearances, a moderate and a peacemaker? Or even a Protestant sympathizer? Etc., etc.)

In fact, although Ferdinand would like to repeal many of the confessional compromises of the preceding century, it is the Protestant side which provides the provocative and incendiary pretext: the Protestant elites of Prague, dissatisfied by Habsburg sovereignty, persuade Friedrich, the Elector of the Palatinate, a son-in-law of James I of England, to assume the throne of Bohemia, normally a prerogative of the Emperor's dynastic lineage. But the Elector only wins the mock title of Winter King, owing to his brief tenure, cut short by the decisive battle of White Mountain (1620), and leaving the unhappy Friedrich to wander from ally to ally in search of a renewal of fortune, in a hapless quest which turns him into the very allegory of weakness and indecision. Here is a modern version of this uninspiring and vacillating figure, perking up somewhat at the prospect of meeting his mercenary generals, themselves revived by the intermittent and sluggish streams of cash flowing reluctantly into the Hague, "refreshed by the sums like flowers in the dew," as they ride out to greet their sometime employer:

> Die beiden, von den Summen erquickt wie Blumen vom Tau, ritten ihrem Kurfürsten auf der Landstraße zum Haag entgegen; sein Herz schlug kräftiger, als er die starken Pferde und die gepanzerten unbändigen Männer antraben sah. Erzählten ihm vom König Christian und den prächtigen Niedersachsen, wie gern der Kaiser auch Magdeburg schlucken wolle und von dem neuesten Ankerseil des löblichen Hauses Habsburg, dem gewissen Wallenstein. Und sie freuten sich zu dritt über den gewissen. Der schlaffe Friedrich fühlte sich wieder erwachen, hineingerissen in das alte Leben zwischen den davontosenden schweren Kürissern.[7]

> His heart beat strongly in his breast as he saw powerful hooves drive these armored and undisciplined men towards him. They told of the Danish king, Christian, and of Lower Saxony, magnificent in its prosperity; told also how the Emperor lusted to swallow up Magdeburg, and gave news of the latest effort of the distinguished house of Habsburg to acquire a reliable mooring, namely a certain Wallenstein, the three making merry over this unknown name. And the slack Friedrich felt himself awakening to life again, swept back into the old excitement by the proximity of these two stormily galloping, heavily ironclad warriors.

---

[7] Alfred Döblin, *Wallenstein*, Munich: DTV, 1983, 248, trans. mine.

The stereotypical vacillation (shared by the Emperor) does not equip this personage to be a protagonist, any more than the grim but indistinct determination of the true instigator of this war, the Bavarian Elector Maximilian, entitles him to be the villain of the piece.[8] But we must also pause here a moment to register the existence of that extraordinary literary document, the novel entitled *Wallenstein*, an untranslated and visionary nightmare dreamed out and written up by the young surgeon Alfred Döblin in the evenings of the bloody trench warfare of World War I and published in 1920, nine years before the *Berlin Alexanderplatz* that made him world-famous. No background in Döblin, no preparation, no perspective, it comes before us as a perpetual present which is at every moment, on every page, in every sentence, filled space, not a pause or backward or forward glimpse— the armies in movement even when they are at rest in their temporary quarters—the army's pauses are themselves movement, they hint at some sly signal of Wallenstein, rebuking the Kaiser by not following his directions, feinting the enemy, pretending to obey the commands to stop (says one of the imperial counselors, "es ist mir nicht klar, gegen wen der Herzog Krieg führt").[9] Yet filled at every moment with names, with all the characters of history, some known, some only mentioned in passing; and with place names as well, not even the map is enough to accommodate them all. It is a pulsing interminable uninterrupted flow, true textuality (not mere form without content) in which everything is in perpetual change back and forth across Central Europe yet driving forward temporally so that time itself, the passing instants, become invisible, only the events are generated and they never stop, the writer never stops (he thereby disappears also), and the sources are so thoroughly used up that nothing is any more allusion, Schiller has long since vanished, there can be no longer any competition with this unending flow of text but only the affect that pulses through it and changes color from pallor to flush, purple to yellowish-sallow, all the tonalities of the affective spectrum stream through the interminable moments, none of them truly fulfilled or effectuating any lasting pause or destiny.

Not the least interest of this novel is indeed the recurrence in the form of an allegorical habit profoundly consanguineous with the baroque content of its setting in the Counter-Reformation. Thus here

---

8   Golo Mann, *Wallenstein*, Frankfurt: Fischer, 1971, 299–300.

9   "I'm unclear as to whom the Duke is waging war against," ibid., 254.

it is money itself that ultimately revives the unhappy Winter King: the lifeblood of the money that runs through the immense continental expanse of the conflict, feeding it locally and reorganizing its forces into impermanent groups, from the foraging deserters and guerillas all the way up to the official and unofficial warlords and officials of the official royal and imperial adversaries. The great and bloody rhizome of the war then becomes a representation of money, riches, wealth, taxes levied, the very sustenance of potatoes impounded from villages in flames and peasants dead or in flight. Everything here— from the penniless imperial court, who count on Wallenstein to raise forces for them at the same time that they try to give him orders, all the way down to the brutal *soldateska* who live off the countryside—has to do with money, and with an immense coral polyp that refuses to starve or die away but keeps itself in life for unforeseeable years by the very strength with which it draws money out of its hiding places, like magnets drawing, or blood from a stone, soaking it up interminably, reproducing itself, using its population of generals, peasants, priests, burghers, kings, lepers and landless, heiresses, as so many divining rods, so many instruments for draining the last drops of wealth or riches from the devastated land. Wealth then becomes the very conduit of energy itself, whether blood, sexuality and libido, activity, irritability, sensation, impulse, drive, propulsion, it is what makes the sentences pound forward like horses' hooves as well as the human individuals themselves to their otherwise incomprehensible yet irrepressible heat-seeking clashes. The libidinal apparatus of the war—of this extraordinary, unique war—thus ensures the most fully realized representation of finance and its networks and capillary extremities, it makes wealth in its "early modern" sense appear before us as a phenomenon in its own right, in the strong Heideggerian sense of the *phainesthai*, the appearance of Being, in ways frontal narratives of trading companies and usurers were unlikely to convey, or the abstractions of religious moralizing or economic philosophy.

Yet all this eventuates in blood and landscapes of dead bodies, the world of Callot anachronistically revived within that of World War I, which reproduces it only for reasons of historical underdevelopment, because its generals failed to grasp the proper use of machine guns or of tanks. Still, we may wonder what forms the representation of agents and agency takes under the regime of the Scene, in this interminable narrative of events and sequence of grotesque or nightmarish figures, more human in their caricaturality than any of the genuine human beings of realism or of our acquaintance. No causes, to be sure, and yet immense allegorical figures, like the famous frontispiece of Hobbes's *Leviathan*, or better still, Arcimboldo's vegetable portraits, in which the sovereign is called upon to incarnate his own multiplicity and his own multitudinous subjects. But here the "world-historical figure" allegorizes not subjects or a people, not even the collectivity of the men under his command, but rather his own victims and the corpses he has in effect become. Here is Tilly, one of the more fearsome of these legendary imperial warlords, as he entertains an audience with the equally fearsome Wallenstein himself:

> Der Brabanter, steif, gespenstig, mit einer weissen Schürze, zwei Pistolen und einem Dolch im Gurt, kurze weisse Haare; an den Haarspitzen schwankten ihm wie Ähren die Tausende erschlagenen Menschen. Sein bleiches spitzes Gesicht, buschige Brauen, starrer borstiger Schnurrbart, überrieselt von den verstümmelten Regimentern eines Menschenalters; sie hielten sich rutschend an den Knöpfen seines grünen Wamses, an seinem Gurt. Seine knotigen Finger bezeichneten ein jeder die Vernichtung von Städten; mit jedem Gelenk war ein Dutzend ausgerotteter Dörfer bezeichnet. Über seine Schultern schoben sich her, zappelten die Körper der gemetzelten Türken, der Franzosen, der Pfälze, und doch sollte er damit erscheinen vor Gericht einmal, samt ihren Pferden und Hunden, die uber dem andern, eine ungeheur Last, so daß sein Kopf samt dem Hütlein darunter verschwand. Die aufgerissenen roten und borkigen Hälse, Bäuche mit weißen regsamen Farben, geädert, triefend über die geschlitzten zurückdrängenden Arme und die einknickenden Beine. Darmschlingen am langen Gekröse, in die er sich verwickelte, wampend und schwabbelnd über die sich stemmenden leder verwahrten Knie, eine riesenlange weiche wurmartige rieselnde Schleppe, an der er ruckte riß keuchte, wenn er ging. Ein Mammut belastete er den Boden; aber eisig hielt er sich, hörte nicht das Gebrüll der Menschen, das markerschütternde der Schweine, schrillen Pfeifen der Pferde, die sich alle an ihn hielten, ihr Leben aus ihm saugen wollten, aus den feinsten Röhrchen seiner Haare; herumlangende Pferdehälse, nüsternzitternd, scheckig, schwarz; zerknallte Hunde, die nach seinem Mund, seiner Nase schnupperten, gierig seinen Atem schlürften. Er mußte längst ausgeleert sein, sie sogen an einem dürren Holz, er klapperte drin und sie brachten ihn nicht zum Sinken.
>
> Hinter ihm vierzehn Regimenter zu Fuß und sechs zu Pferd.
>
> Der Friedländer ihm gegenüber ein gelber Drache aus dem böhmischen blasenwerfenden Morast aufgestiegen, bis an die Hüften mit schwarzem Schlamm bedeckt, sich zurückbiegend auf den kleinen knolligen Hinterpfoten, den Schweif geringelt auf den Boden gepreßt, mit dem prallen, breiten Rumpf in der Luft sich wiegend, die langen Kinnladen aufgesperrt und wonnig schlangenwütig den heißen Atem stoßweise entlassend, mit Schnauben und Grunzen, das zum Erzittern brachte.

Hinter ihm vierundzwanzigtausend Männer.[10]

The Brabanter [Tilly], stiff and ghostly, with a white scarf and two pistols and a dagger in his belt, and short white hair; at the hairs' tips like ears of corn there waved the corpses of a thousand men cut down. His pale sharp features, bushy brows, stiff brush-like moustache rippled with the mutilated regiments of a whole generation; they clung in slippage to the buttons of his jerkin, to his belt. His gnarled fingers each one testified to the annihilation of whole cities; with every knuckle a dozen exterminated villages. Over his shoulders there crowded forward, writhing, the bodies of slaughtered Turks, Frenchmen, Palatiners, and yet someday he would meet his judgement with them on himself along with their horses and dogs, hanging every which way in front of each other and one on top of the other, a burden so immense his very head and little hat vanished beneath it. Necks ripped open and scabby, stomachs with white and livid colors, veined and dripping on the slit and restrained arms and the spastic legs. Guts in loops of intestines in which he was wrapped, sloshing and flabby over the braced knees encased in leather, an interminable limp wormlike rippling train which as he dragged it creaked with every step. He weighed the earth down like a mammoth; but bore himself icily, deaf to the screams of the men and those, bone-shattering, of the swine, the shrill cries and piping of the horses, all of them holding to him, seeking to suck their life out of him, out of the most minute hairs on his head; horses' necks straining, their nostrils trembling, piebald, black; dogs shot to pieces and yet snuffling at his mouth and nose, greedily sucking up his breath. He should have long since been drained; they were sucking dry wood; he clicked and clattered around inside and yet could not be brought down. Behind him fourteen regiments of infantry and six of cavalry.

In front of him Friedland [Wallenstein], a yellow dragon emerging from the bubbling bogs of Bohemia, plastered with black slime to the hips, drawn back onto his knobby hind legs, sulphur pressed into the earth ringing him, waving his broad elastic rump the air behind him with his big jaws wide open, blissfully and with the fury of a serpent exhaling hot breath in intermittent blasts, with a panting and grunting that struck fear.

Behind him, twenty-four thousand men.

These portraits, which we may characterize as rehearsing the modes of allegory and symbol respectively, are drawn into an uninterrupted stream of filled time and space, of a visual writing only occasionally punctuated by dramatic scenes, by a "showing" which mainly takes second place to the "telling" of the visionary nightmare which feeds on the interminable war as on indefinitely renewable fodder.

Wallenstein's biographer gives us a more articulated picture of the perpetuum mobile of this infernal machine, which seems unable to

---

[10] Ibid., 243–4

run down and stop (and indeed Wallenstein's function, for good and ill alike, is to have been able to supply the gradually less and less enthusiastic Kaiser with ever renewed reserves of troops):

> After not much more than a year [after White Mountain], people began to fear that the rapid exhaustion both sides felt was premature. A definitive victory would have to be a universal one and could never have existed. Partial victories, however, each of which related to the whole in a different way, called new enemies into the field, who then gave new energies to the old adversaries, humiliated and pillaged. Bohemia, although isolated in its captivity, remained a part of Europe and Germany even more so, owing to its size. This is not merely an individual opposition, a struggle between two power centers or the aggression of a single one of them. It is a tidal succession of wills in conflict, some of which claim to be able to form them into a single unified will and campaign against another one, and yet never do completely subsume the wills of their individual allies. A fencing court. Individual pairs joust. Suddenly they form two fronts which begin to move in opposition to each other. Yet as they do so, the ballet of betrayal sets in within each. One party withdraws into a corner, exchanges meaningful looks with its former adversary, manoeuvers between the two fronts, seeking to mediate. Another tries to entice this or that participant out of both fronts and to form a third. All this laden with illusion, mistakes, deception. No one knows enough about the other, and some don't even know their own minds.[11]

This fencing ballet of the war as a whole, as in an aerial shot, stands in sharp contrast to the horrors on the ground, as recorded by Grimmelshausen and others—a kind of no man's land in which all spaces are identical and all the atrocities as well, a kind of nightmarish repetition moving from Bohemia to the Baltic and back, as it were a triumph of space and identity over time and its differentiations, a virtually non-narrative flow for which the only appropriate registering apparatus or point of view would seem to be the eyes of an idiot or of a child, as in Ambrose Bierce's terrifying story "Chickamauga."

3.

And this is indeed how *Der abenteuerliche Simplicissimus* begins—the supreme literary monument produced by this war by one of its participants, its six books published in 1668 and 1669, some hundred and fifty years after *Don Quijote* and *Lazarillo de Tormes* and another fifty before *Robinson Crusoe* (1719). Yet it is clearly incorrect to characterize

---

[11] Golo Mann, op. cit., 287–8, trans. mine.

Simplicissimus as a picaresque novel or even as a *Bildungsroman* (the hero is certainly a naif, who seems to maintain his innocence even during those episodes in which he has technically become a trickster figure). Not only is this enormous text episodic in the extreme, it is also rhizomatic, a kind of hyper-text throwing off all kinds of ancillary episodes, at least one of which, *Courasche* (1670), has known a prodigious afterlife in Brecht's theatrical version.

But we will argue that *Simplicissimus* is more than episodic, it is an extraordinary machine for generic production, for the narrative space tirelessly generates one new genre after the other, from the "war novel" and the "lives of saints" all the way to the final Utopia and desert island narrative. How to account for this unparalleled literary autopoesis, this non-teleological proliferation of generic exercises, which goes well beyond what has been identified under the term "generic discontinuities"? Is it possible that it is precisely out of that undifferentiated space of local yet universal conflict, whose fever chart runs from the plundering of villages to the sacking of whole cities and back, that in the absence of ready-made narrative micro-forms the various genres are themselves summoned into existence?

At any rate, we begin virtually in the state of nature, in which the youthful protagonist scarcely has language, and in particular either does not know his own name or has none, being ordered around the field by his brutal father (whose very status is registered in dialect— "*knan*"—equally bereft of a family name). He flees into the woods during the mercenaries' sacking of the village from which we have quoted above, and there meets a pious hermit who instructs him both in religion and, even more remarkably, in the classical languages and their rhetorical traditions. (The causes of this saintly hermit's withdrawal from the world, a premonition of Simplicius' own eventual destiny—it is indeed the hermit who thus baptizes him—will be related in a later discovery, which recapitulates the different genre of unhappy love). Upon the death of the hermit, the boy returns to the world of social beings, first becoming page to the governor. He is then abducted by Croatian mercenaries and incorporated into the imperial troops, where, after a number of humiliations, he reemerges generically as the trickster figure we have mentioned above, a *Jäger* supremely gifted in warfare and plunder or theft of all kinds, after which he marries, and then in a more magical episode discovers treasure.

Yet these potential destinies are all abruptly broken off, whether out of impatience or boredom, or owing to the serial production of the various books, if not the fermentation of new genres at work in Grimmelshausen's feverish imagination. There follows a salacious episode in Paris, a spell as a travelling salesman, and a fall into the truly bad company of a real thief who tries to teach him the way of the real world ("du bis noch Simplicius, der den Machiavellum noch nit studiert hat"[12]). The boy then undergoes a religious conversion, founds a new landed estate and family, undertakes a Vernian journey to the center of the earth, and finally sets forth on travels that ultimately lead to his shipwreck and a hermit-like existence on a desert island, where autobiographical notes are found by a Dutch sea captain, who brings them back to Europe and to publication.

Finally, it is not so much the narrative quality of the various episodes that strikes the reader, as rather the restlessness of the character's exploration of his various possible destinies, and that of the author's experimentation with the various narrative genres they carry within themselves. We are here, in the German principalities of the empire, still very far even from the sophistication of the Spanish monarchy, in which the first realisms flourished so many generations earlier, and in which the urban worldliness of commercial life and colonial and military power generate the picaresque, along with an extraordinary theatrical culture. Germany is here still profoundly pre-novelistic, and indeed the first crystallizations of form in Grimmelshausen's seemingly interminable text take the form of immense allegorical dream frescoes—most strikingly that of the class divisions and struggles of the feudal world, with its prelates and nobles at the top of the allegorical tree and the nameless peasantry at its very base,[13] along with the dream transformation into an animal, reminiscent of *The Golden Ass* of Apuleius. But it would be equally incorrect to read such allegorical episodes as the mere self-indulgence of an autodidact reveling in his classical education. For in this great laboratory of forms, Baroque allegory is closely affiliated with Utopia as such, which one may perhaps thereby in hindsight identify (in More) as itself an allegorical form.

The devastated landscape, indeed, calls out for the relief of Utopian transfiguration: such is the first crossing of the border into Switzerland:

> The landscape struck me compared with other German lands, as strange as Brazil or China. I saw people trading and strolling about in peace, barns full of cattle, courtyards full of chickens, geese and ducks, the streets were used by travelers in

---

[12] *Der abenteuerliche Simplicissimus*, 353.
[13] Ibid., 45.

safety, taverns full of people making merry, no fear of the enemy, no worry about plundering and sacking, no anxiety about losing land or life and limb, everyone lived safely under his grape arbor or fig tree, and in comparison with other German lands in pleasure and content, so that I took this country for an earthly paradise, although it seemed primitive enough.[14]

Later on, among the hallucinations of the desert island, this earthly paradise will be transformed into a vision of primeval bliss—"so we lived like the first men in the golden age, where a bountiful heaven lets all the fruits of the earth flourish without work"[15]—until the devil in the form of a woman shatters the vision and sends the text itself, in the generic reversion, back into the anchoritic withdrawal of its own beginnings.

I want to draw the conclusion that war, perceived at this existential proximity of Scene, is virtually non-narrative, and that this raw material seeks to appropriate its missing protagonist from any number of narrative paradigms, ranging from the conventions of generic war novels or films enumerated at the outset, to the multiplicity of generic experiments of Grimmelshausen's peculiar text.

4.

It is a hypothesis we may now test on the aerial warfare of World War II, about which it will be recalled that the most famous representation of its most famous (European) atrocity—*Slaughterhouse-Five*—sets the firebombing of Dresden offstage, behind the sealed door of the protagonist's eponymous cellar. About this kind of warfare, W. G. Sebald, who grew up in a part of Germany untouched by the air war and exiled himself to England at an early age, has oddly maintained that the Germans have repressed its experience, and indeed that of the defeat in general.[16] He excepts from this accusation one of the most remarkable writers (and filmmakers) of modern Germany, Alexander Kluge, whose portrayal of the battle of Stalingrad (*Schlachtbeschreibung*) already presents many of the features to be noted in the account of the bombing of his native city of Halberstadt on April 8, 1945.

---

[14] Ibid., 391, trans. mine
[15] Ibid., 582, trans. mine
[16] See W. G. Sebald, *On the Natural History of Destruction*, New York: Random House, 2003. And see also Sven Lindqvist, *A History of Bombing*, New York: New Press, 2003.

It was indeed Kluge from whom we selected the remark of Goebbels that figures as a motto to the present essay; and it is in precisely this sense that Stalingrad seems to disintegrate into a host of unrelated colors and brush-strokes as we gradually approach our eyes and faces to the canvas itself.[17] It would be facile to characterize this text as a deconstruction, either of the traditional narrative account of the battle, or of the battle itself. Yet in some literal sense the word is apt, provided that we take it backwards, as the account of the various elements and raw materials which went into the building of the phenomenon hereby unbuilt: indeed, the subtitle of this work is very precisely "the organizational construction of a catastrophe." Kluge here redistributes the building blocks of the defeat in what may be called non-existential segments; which is to say non-narrative units set side by side in a kind of collage. We here find extracts from an army manual on winter warfare side by side with historical accounts, pictures of the landscape, interviews with survivors, medical descriptions of the most characteristic wounds and mutilations, a chronology, the propaganda rhetoric of pastors and preachers on the subject, the language habits of the officers and staged press clippings and conferences, dispatches from the front, the whole interlarded with anecdotes and other stray observations and testimonies, among which Hitler's own vacillations and tactical inattention are duly registered in passing—in what could, I suppose, be called a "non-linear" narrative if one still likes that kind of terminology. It should be understood that Kluge's interest lies in the enumeration of destinies and the deployment of anecdotes, and not in any sustained or "novelistic" storytelling or longer sustained narrative breath; it may be said that he practices a unique type of didactic abstraction, in which a given outcome is x-rayed for the components it incorporates of life-promoting or lethal energies respectively.

"The Bombing of Halberstadt" (*Chronik* II, 27–82) is another such collage, in which individual experiences, in the form of anecdotes, are set side by side not so much for their structures as the acts of traditional characters (Burke's agents), so much as names and destinies, the latter being reduced in many cases to peculiar facts and accidents, of the type of Ripley's Believe It or Not. The juxtaposition of these anecdotes with quotations from academic studies of the history of

---

[17] Alexander Kluge, *Chronik der Gefühle*, 2 vols., Frankfurt: Suhrkamp, 2004, Volume I, 509–791. All page numbers in text refer to this edition, and translations are mine.

bombing and of the RAF techniques, scholarly conferences on the relationship between aerial strategy and ethics ("moral bombing" is for example specified as a matter, not of morals, but of morale), or indeed interviews with the allied pilots who participated in this particular raid—all these materials, which we take to be nonfictional (although they may not be, the interviews in particular bearing the distinctive marks of Kluge's own provocative interview methods) raise the question of the fictionality/non-fictionality of the personal stories of the survivors as well. Halberstadt is to be sure Kluge's hometown, and he is perfectly capable of having assembled a file of testimonies and eyewitness documentation, and of using the names of real people. On the other hand, these stories with their rich detail afford the pleasures of fictional narrative and fictional reading.

Is this text (written in the 1970s) a nonfiction novel? I believe that we must think our way back into a situation in which this question makes no sense and in which—as with the storytelling that precedes the emergence of the so-called Western novel—the distinction between fiction and nonfiction (or history) does not yet obtain, any more than that (so closely related to it) between figurative and literal language. This is not to say that Kluge marks a regression to pre-capitalist storytelling, but rather on the contrary that postmodernity as such has now rendered those distinctions obsolete in the other direction: now, it is not so much a question of all narrative being fictional as it is of a reading process which is always literal, even when we are reading what is technically a fiction.

At any rate, it can be argued that the opening section of "The Bombing of Halberstadt" is less a matter of assembling the personal experiences of the survivors, the moments of the first bombs—in what amount to six successive waves of bombers—than it is of a use of named individuals to map the small city itself (64,000 inhabitants) as they try to make their way across streets increasingly blocked by fires and rubble. (Indeed, we will learn shortly that such attacks follow a specific and intentional pattern: first, strikes calculated to identify targets by columns of smoke identifiable from the aircraft; then the systematic blocking off of streets so the fleeing population is trapped; then an initial destruction of roofs and top storeys, with a calculated time lapse in order to allow a later wave of bombers to drop new explosives through the holes and set fire to the buildings as a whole: procedures carefully designed in order to produce the so-called fire storm characteristic of such raids.) A certain amount of curious detail is amassed here, such as the effort of the civilians to get rid of flammable materials such as the stocks of paper in the newspaper offices, or hosing down groups to survive the heat. Mainly, however, these opening chapters document the regression of the civilians into their private obsessions and neuroses and their decidedly meaningful and intentional, yet aberrant, activities, as with the random scattering of an ant-hill. Thus, in the opening section, which, so characteristically for this writer-filmmaker, deals with the local movie theater, the Capitol, and its manager, Frau Schrader (the owners are on vacation in the country), this particular character is at first worried about the next matinees at three and six o'clock (the first bombs begin to fall at 11:20 a.m.), and only later about the bodies of the initial spectators. Her emotional low-point is reached, however, when she finds nothing to do and "feels herself 'useless'": not danger and death, but the blockage of activity is the phenomenon that interests Kluge here.

The agitated movements of these named and presumably real-life characters, however, serve to map out the streets they attempt to negotiate, the routes in and out of town, and the position of key buildings—the institute for deaf-and-dumb children, for example, or the church tower on which civilian volunteers are stationed, in order to observe and report the attacks, which of course exceed anything they had expected and at the same time destroy any number of telephone lines and other channels of communication. Both these situations will be given a turn of the anecdotal screw in the second part, in which the postwar interviewer inquires into the possibility that a white flag of surrender had been shown on the tower ("surrender to whom?" the American pilot asks; "how do you surrender to a squadron of bombers?"); while a colonel attempts to get information by telephone about the state of things around his sisters' home outside of town (from Magdeburg, owing to the destruction of the lines, he has to "make connections via Kroppenstedt, Gröningen, Emersleben, Schwanebeck, and then back through Genthin, Oschersleben and further south via Quedlinburg"; he never gets through, although the operators realize that this is not official but rather private business). From the two parts we may retain (and compare) the initial attempt of Hen Grämert to rescue his twelve thousand tin soldiers, which represent Napoleon's winter campaign in Russia, along with the episode of the "unknown photographer" (characteristically, the surviving photographs are here reproduced, along with much visual material in Part II); and the episode in Part II in which a teenager succeeds in mastering his piano lesson but not in persuading his piano teacher to reschedule his lesson for the next day, upon which, escaping the burning city, he takes refuge in a village where he practices non-stop so energetically that the owners have to tell him to give it a rest.

Part II, indeed, lets us into the formal secret of this work (I will not say its message or its meaning exactly) with its differentiation of a strategy from below and a strategy from above (the latter, to be sure, outlines the bombing techniques and conveys what it would be improper, as we shall see, to call the "point of view" of the American pilots). Thus Gerda Baethe has learned that the pressure from the bomb blasts will damage the lungs; she tries to make her small children hold their breath during the explosions. Meanwhile, Karl Wilhelm von Schroers, a convalescent veteran in charge of the prisoner-of-war camps in Halberstadt, eagerly visits key points in and out of the city, giving and taking orders, but above all satisfying his keen scientific curiosity. This characteristic, like Gerda's "strategies," is not to be understood in any subjective way, even though the two are vivid personalities succinctly conveyed in a page or two. In keeping with the neutrality of this text and with the generic focus of the anecdote as a form, these are external or objective traits, of the type one registers for other people, as when we note that someone (a proper name) is "quick to anger," or that some other proper name is "indecisive."

But Schroers is more significant than that, insofar as his "scientific curiosity" constitutes something like an "aspiration to totality" which his position on the ground can scarcely satisfy. He is indeed a "collector of strong sense impressions" (66).

> His capacity to feel increasingly curiosity rather than anxiety is not based on any lack of imagination. To be sure, with his physical eyes he only sees this particular tavern, a partial view of Wherstedter Bridge (and nothing of the torn up rails) and perhaps a few houses, but he can imagine the whole city. What he doesn't know [we are still in the night before the bombardment] is that this will be the last conscious glimpse of the cityscape intact. (68)

Like Frau Schrader, he has his later moments of depression (owing to the absences of goals and intentions to be fulfilled, activities to be carried out), but at length recovers his original energy and "curiosity."

Another cameo appearance is made by the head of the fire brigade, who deplores the ignorance of the city officials and their haste to extinguish fires that will be controllable only at the later stage of their chemical life and development, and who takes a reasoned decision to allow the city archives and its museum contents to go up in flames: "I was virtually the last person in this city to see its valuable memorabilia, to say farewell, to estimate the value of the collection" (78).

Here the micro-perspective, the view from beneath, dwindles to its vanishing point. Yet it should not be imagined that the view from above, that of the pilots and crew, is any more comprehensive or reliable. Indeed, as has already been hinted, there is in fact no view from above insofar as the pilots are not expected to see but rather to determine their movements by map and by mathematical calculation, by radar rather than by "sight" (an expression that here in any case signifies strategy rather than the personal organs of the participants [54n12]). All of the studies of aerial warfare and its techniques foreground the depersonalization of the individuals involved and their assimilation into the larger machinery, first of their own aircraft, and then of the squadron as a whole. "Here there do not fly individual airplanes as in the Battle of Britain, but rather a whole conceptual system, an intellectual construction in metal" (51, to quote from one of the discussants at the aerial warfare symposium also represented here).

Abstraction versus sense-datum: these are the two poles of a dialectic of war, incomprehensible in their mutual isolation and which dictate dilemmas of representation only navigable by formal innovation, as we have seen, and not by any stable narrative convention. It is not to be imagined, however, that we can return to some earlier state of wholeness, in which, as in Homer, the individual hand-to-hand combat would at one and the same time somehow epitomize the totality.

On the other hand, the contradiction can be exacerbated even further, as it continues to be in contemporary warfare. Michael Hardt and Antonio Negri have evoked a kind of dialectic of the body in the most recent American wars, in which the solitary body of the suicide bomber, on the one hand, finds itself opposed, on the other, to the smart bombs and pilotless drones of an aerial warfare visible only on monitors at thousands of miles of distance—a contradiction itself reproduced in the distance between the conventional duel of armies ("mission accomplished") and the house-to-house urban resistance of guerilla warfare.[18] Does this opposition then not correspond to what we have previously identified as a distinction between the named (or

---

[18] Michael Hardt and Antonio Negri, *Multitude*, New York: Penguin, 2005, 45.

institutionalized) action and the blooming, buzzing confusion of scene, from which as yet no formalizable actantial categories have emerged? This category may also stand in constitutive opposition to what we have called the existential experience of war, through which an equally undefined subject or consciousness finds representation. But Scene is in its fullest reality necessarily collective, and it is the multiplicity of the collective which marks the difference between the representational problems we have rehearsed here. The language of the existential individual already possesses an elaborate history with all kinds of stereotypes that it can be the task of representation to correct, disrupt, undermine or metaphysically challenge. That of the collective does not yet exist. Group, nation, clan, class, general will, multitude—all these remain so many linguistic experiments for designating an impossible collective totality, a manifold of consciousnesses as unimaginable as it is real. War is one among such collective realities which exceed representation fully as much as they do conceptualization, and yet which ceaselessly tempts and exasperates narrative ambitions, conventional and experimental alike.

As for the thing itself, to minimize its horrors is to pass for callous or historically privileged, and in any case naive; yet to insist on its elimination as the central task of politics is willfully to ignore or to condone the immemorial record of peacetime oppression which is the burden of class history. To paraphrase Horkheimer on fascism, he who would not mention capitalism and class struggle has nothing to say about war. The concept of violence is an ideology, however real its existence. Nor should we underestimate its ambiguity, and in particular its potential excitement. I think it was John Aldridge who pointed out that the powerful anti-war novels written in the wake of World War I to warn their readers occasionally had the opposite effect, fascinating young people bored and frustrated by peacetime. Meanwhile, the beginning of a war has often been a source of collective elation, as with World War I in particular.[19]

---

[19]   Here is Robert Musil on what he called "the August experience":

Those for whom the nation simply does not exist make it too easy for themselves. This mentality, which declares itself extraterritorial and supranational in the name of the spirit, pursues ostrich politics in response to the contempt and slavery that weigh on all of us. This way of thinking sticks its head in the sand, but cannot prevent the blows meant for us all from striking it where its ostrich feathers are. This individualistic, separatist spirit overlooks something else: that well-known summer experience of 1914, the so-called upbeat to a Great Age, and I do not at all mean this entirely ironically. On the contrary, what was

And what of Hegel's infamous remark that war is the health of nations? I would like to think he meant something else and something more than this fleeting experience of the transformation of the nation into an all-too-ephemeral Utopian collectivity. I believe he had in mind the destruction of immense quantities of capital which war brings with it. In our system, the accumulation of undestroyed capital, unproductive, and in the hands of wealthy fanatics and obsessives who are free to use it in the perpetuation of their own privileges, is a burden it is very difficult indeed for a people, even a democratic one, to overcome. I would like to think that Hegel meant the demolition of all that and the possibility for a poor and laborious society of survivors to begin again. André Gide thought that convalescence from illness was one of the most precious human experiences. In that case, not the exhilaration of the beginning of a war, but the collective convalescence that sets in with its conclusion is the better meaning of Hegel's sentence.

---

stammered at the outset and later allowed to degenerate into a cliché—that the war was a strange, somehow religious experience—undoubtedly corresponds to a fact; that it degenerated says nothing against the character of the original insight. It became a cliché in the customary way precisely because we called it a religious experience, and in doing so gave it an archaizing mask, instead of asking what it actually *was* that was pounding so strangely and violently on a realm of ideas and feelings that had been asleep for the longest time. Still, it cannot be denied that mankind (and of course people in all countries in the same way) was touched at that time by something irrational and foolish, but awesome, that was alien, not from the familiar earth, and which therefore, even before the actual disillusionments of war arrived, had already been declared a hallucination or a ghost simply because its atmospherically undefined nature prevented it from being held or grasped.

Contained in this perception too was the intoxicating feeling of having, for the first time, something in common with every German. One suddenly became a tiny particle humbly dissolved in a suprapersonal event and, enclosed by the nation, sensed the nation in an absolutely physical way. It was as if mystical primal qualities that had slept through the centuries imprisoned in a word had suddenly awakened to become as real as factories and offices in the morning. One would have to have a short memory, or an elastic conscience, to bury this insight under later reflection.

Robert Musil, "'Nation' as Ideal and as Reality," in *Precision and Soul: Essays and Addresses,* Chicago: University of Chicago Press, 1990, 102–3.

Chapter III

The Historical Novel Today, or, Is It Still Possible?

> Greifst in ein fremdestes Bereich,
> Machst frevelhaft am Ende neue Schulden,
> Denkst Helenen so leicht hervorzurufen
> Wie das Papiergespenst der Gulden.
>
> Goethe, *Faust*, Part II

Even in the throne room scene, Mephistopheles reminded the future treasure-hunters of the proximity of the underworld. For the treasures abandoned and forgotten by History ... await their rediscoverers like the historical figures in Hades. What the past buried and hid away, the present seeks to resurrect, if only as the deceptive image of what they imagine the past to have been. There is thus an archaeological dimension to all these seemingly so different appearances: conjuration or treasure hunt replace excavation, reality hesitates uncertainly between the offerings of magic and the value of paper money.

Heinz Schlaffer

Perry Anderson, in his landmark survey of the genre,[1] reminds us that the historical novel has never been so popular nor so abundantly produced as at the present time: an assertion that seems counterintuitive in the light of present-day enfeeblement of historical consciousness and a sense of the past only until you grasp that production as symptom and as symbolic compensation.

But what kind of historical novel is being reproduced here? Harlequin "histories," in which a romantic tale is played out against this or that costume setting? *Annales*-school reconstruction of the peculiar mores and customs of a selected segment of the past? The attempt faithfully to reconstruct the historical situation in which this or that "real" historical figure made his fateful decision? The "feel" of

---

[1] Perry Anderson, "From Progress to Catastrophe," *London Review of Books* 33:15 (July 2011).

a great event (Pompei, the conquistadors arriving on the shore of the New World) through the eyes of an imaginary character (one probably doomed to reproduce the movements of this or that sub-generic plot paradigm at least as stereotypical as the "romance" with which we began this enumeration)? The historical novel seems doomed to make arbitrary selections from the great menu of the past, so many differing and colorful segments or periods catering to the historicist taste, and all now, in full globalization, more or less equal in value (or a Ranke liked to say, "immediate to God"). Meanwhile, as for the protagonists, they are also by now more or less equivalent: Julius Caesar, Huang Di, Genghis Khan, Stalin, Shaka—take your choice depending on your mood of the day, in that reflecting the now ambiguous and imperiled status of the individual subject or identity, no longer centered or unified, and capable of breaking down into so many distinct subject-positions (let alone confronting its own extinction, as in the famous poststructuralist "death of the subject"). How to have confidence in the presence and stability of any of the allegedly world-historical figures of the past when we have lost our own? In short, we have to do here, as with realism, with an impossible form or genre that, as Anderson suggests, is still assiduously practiced.

But this may well be an excellent reason for arousing further suspicions about this genre, which has so often been marshaled to serve political ends, of which nationalism is only the most obvious. Yet the inventor of the modern form itself, often thought to be at one with his narrative persona—the Scottish antiquarian and collector of anecdotal folk materials (as other contemporaries collected fairy tales and folksongs)—had in fact a more complex, if no less ideological agenda—namely the production of Britishness and of the new identity-concept of "Britain." As for the greatest American novelist of the last century, his testimony to the experience of defeat is placed in a more ambiguous light by the pioneering demonstration by Peter Novick that having lost the Civil War, the South then successfully conquered the academic profession of history in the US,[2] opening the floodgates of a nostalgia no less toxic than that of a postwar British celebration of the good old class system or of the Raj. Is it possible, then, that a socially levelled and plebeianized population finds fantasy gratification in images of hierarchical social relations and by-gone systems of privilege? Meanwhile, Harlequin romances and the like

---

[2] Peter Novick, *That Noble Dream*, Cambridge: Cambridge University Press, 1988.

suggest that such settings are also propitious to libidinal fantasies and wish-fulfillments as well, so that the historical novel proves formally adequate to gender as well as to class needs (let alone racist ones). A genre of this kind demands an ideological testing system a good deal more complex than what the everyday reader would instinctively bring to the celebration of other people's heroes and historical moments of heroic resistance, defeat or even triumph. Today, when the rhetoric of the nation has largely been supplanted by that of small groups (of whatever variety), we may be excused for wondering what such a tainted form can legitimately do for us.

Meanwhile, victory and its triumphalistic celebrations have everywhere fallen under a cloud, as it is assumed that winners, always instantly corrupted, turn into the "state" in no time. The conviction that revolutions are always confiscated, when not already defeated, then inspires, not an effort to rethink and revitalize the concept of revolution as such, but rather the glamorization of testimony and memory and the fetishization of so-called "*lieux de mémoire.*" The Holocaust industry ought then to offer renewed legitimation for the historical novel as a form,[3] except that oral histories and local documentation, massively in place, would preempt the fictional were it not already paralyzed by the formal problem of narrating the collective.

In the previous essay, we simplified Kenneth Burke's "dramatistic pentad" into an opposition between act and agency on the one hand and scene on the other, thereby finding that we had ended up merely reproducing a time-honored and philosophically stigmatized opposition between subject and object that no one has any great interest in perpetuating. But this reluctance has less to do with the form of the binary opposition as such, than with its omission of a fundamental element in the scheme, a missing third in all these definitions and conflicts, which is simply the collectivity as such. We may let Brecht's great poem on dynastic change in traditional societies evoke its unseen omnipresence:

> When the houses of the great collapse
> many little ones are slain.
> Those who had no share in the fortunes of the mighty
> often share in their misfortunes.
> The plunging wagon drags

---

[3] See footnote 39 below for a brief discussion of just such a historical novel.

the sweating oxen with it
into the abyss.[4]

Individual and collectivity are here opposed in the persons of lord and subject, but each are opposed in different ways to Scene, in the sense of the mode of production in which this class struggle takes form (here the so-called Asiatic mode, today that of capitalism). It is tempting to characterize the historical novel as the intersection between individual existence and History, the lightning bolt of wars and revolutions that suddenly strikes a peaceful village or an urban daily life. I have myself elsewhere borrowed the Heideggerian formula that expresses the simultaneous emergence and withdrawal of Being, in order to characterize texts which, in one way or another, and exceptionally, "make History appear," no matter how fitfully.[5] Unfortunately for literary theory, such texts do not always have to be historical novels. Indeed, as we will see later on, the most eminent theorist of the historical novel (Georg Lukács) is led by his commitment to the representational glimpse of deeper underlying historical trends and tendencies (the future of society secretly at work within its present) to the implicit conclusion that our true historical novel, today, is not the historical novel at all but rather realism as such.

So if we want to keep the novel "historical," it looks as though we will be forced back upon our subject/object alternative and obliged in spite of ourselves to make a choice between some dated and named Event in history (Savonarola's downfall, the Sicilian Expedition, Napoleon's invasion of Russia) and that more general scenic thing which is a historical period, a setting or a culture (Tenochtitlan, the era of the whaling ships, some far future dystopia, or New York in the 1950s), all of which we tend to visualize spatially rather than temporally.

But inasmuch as History also has a history, the ratio between these poles will vary considerably ever since its quasi-invention around the time of the French Revolution. Before that, the chronicle of the reigns of kings and queens (which passed for historiography) left little room for difference and social or cultural change, for historicity or historicism, a form of consciousness that

---

[4] Bertolt Brecht, "Der Kaukasische Kreidekreis," *Grosse Kommentierte Berliner und Frankfurter Ausgabe*, Berlin: Suhrkamp, 1992, Vol. 8, 107 (Scene 1), trans. mine.

[5] In the last chapter of my *Valences of the Dialectic*, London: Verso, 2010.

may be said to date from the "Querelle des anciens et des modernes" (1687–1714).[6]

But the kings and queens, dynastic history, certainly outlived the chronicles, and in the form of those protagonists nobler than our-selves (as Northrop Frye, following Aristotle, might put it), and under the guise of what Hegel infamously called "world-historical individu-als," they dominated the historical novel at least until more modern forms of nationalism—the allegorical protagonists of the nation and the people—took their place, and the lower classes of peasantry and proletariat began to make sporadic appearances.

The great modern ideological leaders (or dictators) then appeared at the very moment in which historiography began to doubt its own anthropomorphic methods, and to project *Annales*-style accounts of the past that did away with narrative actors altogether. The calling into question of the category of the Event, however, scarcely leaves the historical novel without any reason for being, since it can then energetically assume the task of dismantling all the inherited illu-sions, beginning with those having to do with the historical heroes themselves and their "victories." So we have protagonists in whom we no longer believe, and masses who are at best imaginary, and to this unpromising material we bring our incredulity about the grand narra-tives of decisive events and genuine historical change or development. What seems to survive at best are a host of names and an endless warehouse of images. What kind of History can the contemporary historical novel then be expected to "make appear"?

I.

What is most frequently retained from the essays of *The Historical Novel* is the distinction between the world-historical individual and the average hero, a formal and structural opposition derived from Scott's *Waverley* (1811), on most accounts the first modern histori-cal novel, and certainly the model of most of what was done in this vein in the first half of the nineteenth century as well as the paradigm of the most fertile operatic tradition. Paradoxically, the two greatest

---

6   Hans-Robert Jauss, *Studien zum Epochenwandel der ästhetischen Moderne*, Frankfurt: Suhrkamp, 1990.

7   Georg Lukács, *The Historical Novel*, trans. Hannah and Stanley Mitchell, Lincoln: University of Nebraska Press, 1983; page numbers in text refer to this edition.

historical novels of the period seem neither of them to obey this formula, as we shall see; we will return to them later.

What is less often noticed about Lukács' discussion is first, that what underpins his proposed opposition is the generic distinction between the theater and the novel; and second, that in the course of it, Scott's own paradigm vanishes, giving way to Balzac, who writes, not historical novels, but contemporary novels which are profoundly historical. A Hegelian *Aufhebung* is then at work here, and the historical novel of Scott becomes the vehicle for a historicization of the novel in general, which leaves the specialized sub-genre called the "historical novel" as a kind of evolutionary dead end for the rest of the (bourgeois) century after 1848, only to revive, but far more weakly, in the era of the popular front. It turns out, then, that despite appearances, Lukács is not really interested in the historical novel at all, but rather in the novel as such, in realism and the realistic novel, which when it comes into its own will be profoundly historical and will let History appear more effectively than its earlier, more specialized vehicle.

This can all be said in a different way by attention to the ways in which the content of a given historical moment enables or limits its representational form, or better still, its narrative possibilities. The tension, in Marxism and elsewhere in social thought generally, between sociology and history, or better still, between structure and the event, between everyday life and its cultural continuities and the cataclysm of a genuinely historical turning point or paradigm shift— this tension, which we will confront as a genuine opposition or formal alternative in the next section, also makes possible moments in which the two kinds of realities overlap, and in which therefore complex or dual possibilities are momentarily available.

This overlap explains the privileged situation of Scott in Lukács' system, for his focus on a specific kind of historical catastrophe allows him to write a kind of social description of the past as well as to single out a historical event. This involves his relationship to what is translated as "gentile" society and social relations. The reader today will probably first find religious-sectarian associations flashing up at the use of this word, which however has nothing to do with non-Jews and everything to do with the *gens*, that precapitalist society explored by Morgan in *Ancient Society* (still a fundamental work in the Marxian canon), and there represented by the Iroquois. The society of the gens (or "gentile society") is a clan-based society which is neither feudal nor organized according to the contentious category of "oriental despotism" or the so-called Asiatic mode of production. It is closer to Tacitus's Germans and is thereby relatively more democratic and perhaps closer to the simpler groups ranged under primitive communism, which, coming out of pre-agricultural hunters-and-gatherers, are organized by gender and by age (the elders having priority in decisions and distribution of goods). These classificatory uncertainties account for the springing up of further categories of modes of production within the standard ones (four or five from primitive communism to socialism) and very much include the nomadic societies dear to Deleuze and Guattari[8] and perhaps most extensively theorized by Owen Lattimore.[9] Clan society is another one of these developmental routes, and obviously in the world of Sir Walter Scott it is embodied in the Gaelic highlanders, whose social order is extinguished by the genocide which followed the end of the 1745 uprising and the battle of Culloden. Scott is, as we shall see, and whatever his other political sympathies, the epic poet of the end of this mode of production.

But its pre-bourgeois or pre-capitalist social relations are then those of the epic as such, and they thus entitle Scott to a characterological and literary identification which, far from being a deficiency and a defect, turns out to be one of his strengths. At this point, therefore, the investigation will seek less to differentiate epic from novel but momentarily to draw them closer together. "Scott's historical subject-matter ... is linked not with his interest in history as such, but with the specific nature of his historical themes, with his selection of those periods and those strata of society which embody the old epic self-activity of man, the old epic directness of social life, its public spontaneity. This it is that makes Scott a great epic portrayer of the 'age of heroes,' the age from which the true epic grows, in the sense of Vico and Hegel" (35). In fact, the analysis here is taken directly from Hegel (Lukács has already discussed his analysis of epic); and this residuality and survival (in both content and form) will be a crucial indication for a rereading of Scott according to different categories and standards than those of the novel as a successor and replacement of epic.

---

8 Gilles Deleuze and Felix Guattari, *The Anti-Oedipus* (see chapter 3: "Savages, Barbarians, Civilized"), Oxford: Oxford University Press, 1989.

9 Owen Lattimore, *The Inner Asian Frontiers of China*, Oxford: Oxford University Press, 1989 [1940].

In one sense, then, Scott confirms our obscure suspicion that all genuinely historical novels must have a revolutionary moment as their occasion: a moment of radical change, which lifts their content out of the placid continuities of mere custom and of the picturesque daily life of this or that exotic moment of the past. The implication is then that all great historical novelists must in one way or another harbor conservative sympathies, and have a deep ontological investment in the old ways of life in the process of being destroyed by the new order, whether that be the new English hegemony over the Scots or that of the Normans over the Anglo-Saxons, the emergent post-revolutionary capitalism of Balzac's Restoration (in name only), the encroaching Europeans of Fenimore Cooper, or indeed all those later capitalist industrialisms which destroy village life and tradition, or even the seemingly eternal American small town. The protagonists of these later revolutions—Zola's Saccard or even Faulkner's Snopses—are from this perspective rarely seen as world-historical individuals in Hegel's sense, for in Hegel this kind of figure consciously or unconsciously prepared the future and epitomized a kind of historical progress that the conservative historical novelists reject. For them, the world-historical figures are the heroes who fail, who succumb fighting against history, like the Pretender in *Waverley*; and it may be suggested that wherever a vision of history embodies this struggle between past and future in a way that approaches the radical dichotomy of class struggle and genuine revolution, the text and its characters are likely to take on an allegorical function.

Still, the prototypical content of historical novels has always been war, about which we will affirm that to the degree to which its representation is authentically historical in Lukács' sense, it will always be in one way or another a figure for class struggle as such. The greatest historical novels of this first period, however—Scott's *Heart of Midlothian* and Manzoni's *Betrothed*—do not have warfare as their central object of representation; and they also offer more specific hints as to the uses and formal function of the world-historical figures we have been discussing here. In *The Heart of Midlothian*, for example, the world-historical individual appears only in the final meeting with the Duke of Argyle (one of the great historical mediators between England and Scotland in the period of the Union and the 1715 invasion); in Manzoni, it takes the form of the archbishop, whose ministrations are in many ways the climax of the narrative, which almost literally moves towards him with much the same momentum as Jeannie's voyage south to seek the King's pardon for her sister. This confers on the narrative the great spatial and geographical form of the adventure as such, which unites the episodic and the linear, looping the melodramatic elements back into epic movement. Lukács specifies the limits of Manzoni's novel wrongly, in my opinion, by identifying Italy's historic dilemma as that of unification. (Machiavelli is often interpreted as turning on this issue, which is rather the production of the nation as such.) One might say the same about *Midlothian*, insofar as the unification of England and Scotland is at its center, overlaid by the twin contradictions of a tripartite class system (highlanders, lowland Scots and English) and a tripartite religious and ideological struggle (between the Anglican Church, the Presbyterians and the Cameronians—these last the remnants of the radical Calvinists). But to give contradiction a physical and spatial form, and to enlarge the province of the novel to include geography, are obviously both essential components in the invention of this genre, in which time becomes space and the past is transformed into the sensory and the visible.

Meanwhile, in both works, the collective, and that even rarer and more unique event which is Revolution, replaces the relatively specialized background of war itself by way of the social content shared by each, namely masses of people in aggressive protest and demonstration. These "mob uprisings"—the Porteus riots in Scott, a protest against a brutal police officer, and the bread riots in Manzoni—then stand as figures of the collective and of revolution against the state and against the old order: transparent figures, which the Queen is not slow to interpret as resistance to the Union itself, even though her Scottish subjects (and no doubt Scott himself) go to some lengths to minimize the political meaning of this disturbance organized by mere agitators. The historical novel as a genre cannot exist without this dimension of collectivity, which marks the drama of the incorporation of individual characters into a greater totality, and can alone certify the presence of History as such. Without this collective dimension, history, one is tempted to say, is again reduced to mere conspiracy, the form it takes in novels which have aimed for historical content without historical consciousness and which remain therefore merely political in some more specialized sense.

What must also be emphasized is that the named historical figure, the so-called world-historical individual, already exists: "we do not follow his life step by step; we see him only at moments when he is significant" (Otto Ludwig, quoted by Lukács, 45). The events with which he is associated have already happened, they are fixed, however one wishes to reinterpret them. In that sense, the world-historical figure is the result of prior knowledge: a name familiar from the school books, as they pass the various official versions of national and international history on down to successive generations. Our approach to them must therefore include a kind of voyeuristic curiosity: so this is how they looked and acted! This is how they spoke to their subordinates (or their superiors)! These were their reactions on hearing the news or on confronting a crisis! And so forth: such prior knowledge is absolutely required (for we approach the unknown heroes of other people's history only by analogy), and it is also what determines Lukács' positioning of them in drama. For as opposed to the "totality of objects" central to the epic, drama stages the moments of decision of these already familiar historical actors themselves, which it must necessarily stage from the outside, if necessary by way of the great monologues and soliloquies. The agonies of their decisions remain alive before us on stage, but the outcomes cannot be changed, we know the facts in advance from our history books. Whence the problematic transfer of such figures to the novel, where stream of consciousness and interior monologue ought to provide an even closer approach to subjectivities which must however forever remain closed and mysterious. When Tolstoy provides us with an account of Napoleon's thoughts, the results must always be derisory (we note that he is careful not to show us Kutuzov's stream of consciousness). Clearly, then, the famous "average hero" whose presence Lukács posits as a necessary mediation between everyday life and the great historical events is precisely the theatrical spectator, who observes the great episodically and from afar.

Yet we must also understand that this "rule" of historical fiction is part and parcel of a whole Lukácsian attack on biography as a form (André Maurois is singled out as a particularly egregious specimen of this new twentieth century bourgeois decadence)[10] and testifies to his

---

[10] Oddly enough, Lukács does not here include the most ancient warning of this kind, in Aristotle's *Poetics*, paragraph 8: "The unity of plot does not consist, as some suppose, in its having one man as its subject. An infinity of things befall that one man, some of which it is impossible to reduce to unity; and in like manner there are many actions of one man which cannot be made to form one action." (*Aristotle's Rhetoric and Poetics*, trans. W. Rhys Roberts and Ingram Bywater, New York: Random House, 1954, 234.)

conviction that subjective analysis and interpretation of characters—fictive or historical—inevitably leads to the pathological, just as the modern (bourgeois) taste in events tends towards violence and the atrocity. (We may of course in turn psychologize Lukács himself on the basis of his hostility to psychoanalysis.) I will in a moment suggest that this aversion to psychologism risks overlooking one important political function of the historical novel; but it might also be interpreted as a reaction to the more general subjectivization which leads in the modern period to a problematization of narrative itself.

Meanwhile, we need to return for another moment to Scott, whose defense by Lukács ("the classical form of narrative must be shielded against modern prejudices" [40]) is reinforced by just such attacks on the interest in complex psychological states and on the taste for the violent and the exotic. Lukács does not provide anything like a political analysis of Scott's own historical situation; indeed at some point he calls him an "English" writer, by which one assumes that this Hungarian intellectual writing in German means only to designate the language of the texts (but one might have some difficulty in sustaining even this in a discussion of *The Heart of Midlothian*, for example). At any rate, it is important to stress the room for manoeuver afforded Scott by the three-sided situation of an opposition between highland and lowland Scots confronted by the English overlord: of these, it is only the highlanders who constitute that "gentile society" in the course of extermination, nor do the recent theorists of Scottish devolution ever claim Scott for any cultural resistance to English assimilation.[11] What they do point out is that his literary operation—whatever else it may be as a vision of history—is also an ideological one, namely the construction of a Britishness in which the lowland Scot can henceforth coexist with the English as a single entity: and to that degree the royal pardon at the end of *The Heart of Midlothian* is as ideological a gesture as the handshake between labor and capital that concludes Fritz Lang's *Metropolis*.

To be sure, Lukács is not a practitioner of ideological critique, despite the theoretical innovations of *History and Class Consciousness*;[12] indeed, one misunderstands the whole thrust of his "Marxist literary criticism" if one does not understand that he is there attempting to

---

[11] See Robert Crawford, *Devolving English Literature*, Oxford: Oxford University Press, 1992.

[12] See my discussion in *Valences of the Dialectic*.

substitute a Marxist formalism for Soviet class-affiliated literary judgements of the current 1930s. Still, it seems to me that we do not fully grasp Scott's narrative possibilities (or Balzac's either) if we remain content with Engels's famous formulations on the way in which the conservative Balzac is nonetheless forced by history to write against himself.[13]

Perhaps the problem of class affiliation may be approached in another way by observing that the moment of revolution—the absolute Event, so to speak[14]—is always a matter of absolute dichotomization: whatever happens later on, the "lyric illusion" is always the moment in which everyone has to take sides, for or against, and that this stark simplification then poses unique dilemmas for

---

[13] Friedrich Engels, letter to Margaret Harkness, April 1888: "The more opinions of the author remain hidden, the better for the work of art. The realism I allude to may crop out even in spite of the author's opinions. Let me refer to an example. Balzac whom I consider a far greater master of realism than all the Zolas *passés, présents et à venir*, in *La Comédie humaine* gives us a most wonderfully realistic history of French "society," describing, chronicle-fashion, almost year by year from 1816 to 1848 the progressive inroads of the rising bourgeoisie upon the society of nobles that reconstituted itself after 1815 and that set up again, as far as it could, the standard of *la vieille politesse francaise*. He describes how the last remnants of this, to him, model society gradually succumbed before the intrusion of the vulgar moneyed upstart, or were corrupted by him; how the *grande dame* whose conjugal infidelities were but a mode of asserting herself in perfect accordance with the way she had been disposed of in marriage, gave way to the bourgeoisie, who cornered her husband for cash or cashmere; and around this central picture he groups a complete history of French society from which, even in economic details (for instance the re-arrangement of real and personal property after the Revolution) I have learned more than from all the professed historians, economists and statisticians of the period together. Well, Balzac was politically a Legitimist; his great work is a constant elegy on the irretrievable decay of good society, his sympathies are all with the class doomed to extinction. But for all that his satire is never keener, his irony never bitterer, than when he sets in motion the very men and women with whom he sympathises most deeply—the nobles. And the only men of whom he always speaks with undisguised admiration, are his bitterest political antagonists, the republican heroes of the Cloître Saint-Méry, the men, who at that time (1830–36) were indeed the representatives of the popular masses. That Balzac thus was compelled to go against his own class sympathies and political prejudices, that he *saw* the necessity of the downfall of his favourite nobles, and described them as people deserving no better fate; and that he *saw* the real men of the future where, for the time being, they alone were to be found—that I consider one of the greatest triumphs of realism and one of the grandest features in old Balzac."

[14] I take Alain Badiou's philosophical and political work as turning centrally around the analysis of revolution as absolute Event.

narrative representation. An analogy may be made (and is often made in practice if not in theory) with the representational problems of war, about which Lukács quotes Balzac with approval: "It is impossible for literature to go beyond a certain limit in painting the facts of war" (he recommends that writers confine themselves to "small encounters, revealing through them the spirit of the two contending masses") (43).

Leaving aside the question of whether there have ever been successful revolutions in the first place, we may suggest that an absolute dichotomization, which leaves only two adversaries face to face, leads at once to a kind of allegorical treatment unsuitable to the novel as a form and presenting impossible obstacles for any genuinely novelistic narration. (For one thing, it then becomes impossible for either one of the opposing sides to avoid taking the role of the villain—a category of melodrama rather than of realism, let alone historical realism; and it will be remembered that the greatest historical works—Malraux's *l'Espoir*, where the principle is articulated explicitly, or Peter Weiss's *Äesthetik des Widerstandes*—deliberately avoid any account of the other side, in this case Spanish fascism or Nazism respectively.)

Is it still possible that the word revolution is historically and even dialectically ambiguous? That what we call a revolution in the passage from the old order or feudalism to capitalism is not at all the same structurally or substantively as the passage from capitalism to a post-capitalist or revolutionary order? And this, despite the continuing existence of capitalist urban elements (in Czarist Russia and pre-revolutionary China) alongside feudal ones—peasantries, landlords and the like? In other words, to use the same word, revolution, for historically different transitions from one mode of production to another is to suggest an identity between them which is misleading, despite the absence of different words for these different transitions (as in the various Inuit words for snow or the various Arabic words for sand).[15] This ambiguity suggests some doubt as to whether the historical novel—historically a narrative form generated by the passage from the old order to a bourgeois society, as well as the representation of that historical passage—can function as a useful generic category for novels which issue from and represent wholly different kinds of historical convulsions. This does not mean that revolutions

---

[15] But now see, for the most exhaustive discussion of this problem, Neil Davidson, *How Revolutionary were the Bourgeois Revolutions?*, Chicago: Haymarket, 2012.

are henceforth impossible, or that history is at an end, or that capitalism is eternal; only that our use of the generic term is metaphorical or even analogical, and demands the most vigilant suspicion as we go along.

At any rate, the historical novel, condemned to such unique raw material, will demand a multiplicity and differentiation of standpoints, in such a way that the Event itself is grasped on either side of its absolute moment, either in the multiplicity of class positions that precede the revolutionary moment, or in the dispersal that follows its repression.

This clarifies the advantages of Scott's three-sided situation, which is replicated in the novel in the "average hero's" distance from both the English and the Jacobite positions. But perhaps it may also be well to open a parenthesis here on the question of parties or factions in such situations: for it is clear that later anti-political novelists such as Flaubert will use the multiplicity of parties and factions as a demonstration of the vacuity of revolution itself, as in the great assemblies of the political clubs in *L'Éducation sentimentale*,[16] as artfully grotesque as anything in Daumier. When we reach this stage of a babel of political opinions, what has happened is that the "political," hitherto a convulsive stirring of the Event as such and an eruption of History, has become specialized as subject matter, and points ahead to those institutionalized genres which deal with parliamentary or representational dramas and characters (as in Trollope). The debates on the Communist Party in modern literature (from Malraux to Weiss) are debates within socialism (generally written by party sympathizers or former adherents rather than current members), and thus are not to be classified as novels about the flora and fauna of a specific institution, and not representations of revolution as such.

But now we need to assess the promotion of Balzac to Scott's legatee as the archetypal representative of the historical novelist, when in fact he wrote so few such works (and there is little reason to rate *Les Chouans* any higher than Hugo's *Quatre-vingt-treize*, for example). The dialectical argument will consist in positing a transformation of the historical novel into the novel in general and as such (and the confluence of an English eighteenth-century social novel without historical focus into a form social and historical all at once). In Balzac, all novels are historical novels, or, to put it another way,

---

16 See "The Experiments of Time" above in this volume.

when a standpoint has been reached in which the present can itself be apprehended as history, a novel set in any of the periods through which the author himself lived, from the Restoration to 1848, can be said to qualify as a "historical novel" in the generic sense. Scott's tripartite situation is then here reproduced in an oddly asymmetrical way. For besides the two sides in conflict during the Revolution (and setting the romantically ambiguous figure of Napoleon aside), the ostensible winners of the revolutionary struggle, the aristocrats who return to power during the Restoration, are in fact in Balzac's eyes the true losers, since they are politically incompetent and—mostly provincial—are destitute, while the beneficiaries of the revolution (those who bought church properties for example) remain in place. This is, indeed, as Lukács liked to point out (following Engels), why the one true revolutionary hero in Balzac—the martyr of the 1832 uprising, Michel Chrestien—is on the left, and an opponent of the "bourgeois monarchy" fully as much as the Bourbons.[17]

It may be worth devoting a little more thought to this unique position of Balzac in literary history and in the history of the historical novel. Why should we consider Balzac's novels more profoundly historical than Stendhal's *Charterhouse of Parma*, for example, the very epitome of the historical novel, with its popular uprisings, its court intrigues, its despots, and its Napoleonic and post-Napoleonic background? Indeed, was not Stendhal himself the very theorist of the political novel, with his slogan—a pistol shot in the middle of a concert?

The comparison incites us to two questions, the first of which has to do with the obvious absence of mob scenes in Balzac's most characteristic works, that is, the absence of that collective dimension we have affirmed to be essential to the form. The second is the absence of the Event, even though, to be sure, all of Balzac's novels document the consequences of that Event which is the Revolution (and its Napoleonic world sequel). I think that collectivity is in Balzac figured by Paris itself (or its force of gravity on the rest of France in the provincial novels). Paris, the indispensable center of revolution in French history, and the unique space around which all of French social life turns (unlike other European capital cities or great metropolises, such as London), figures the collective totality in ways not available to

---

[17] This fictional "world-historical protagonist" appears off stage in the novella "Les Secrets de la Princess de Cadignan," for Lukács (as well as for Engels) one of the most revealing moments in *La Comédie humaine.*

274 ANTINOMIES OF REALISM

other novelists. Meanwhile, the fact that the action of Balzac's novels is always dated—we always have to do with the 1830s or '40s, with the Restoration period, and that not in general but in the annual specifications of their changes, their fashions, their power systems—is what links them to the great "axial events" as it were (Ricoeur's expression) which constitute History itself in its more specific sense. This is what Dickens's novels lack, inasmuch as there is in modern English history no such axial event from which to date the fictional action (in George Eliot, to be sure, it is the moment of the Reform Bill which is selected as a historical center and which lends her work its greater historicity); and as for Galdós, there is always the Revolution of 1867 which we approach and from which we recede in significantly more historicist fashion. Tolstoy is of course, as we shall see later, diverted from his "axial event" by the failure of the Decembrist rebellion (which was to have been the official subject of *War and Peace*). But French history is unique in its punctuation by crucial revolutionary moments (which could be prolonged into the twentieth century by the Popular Front, the Liberation of Paris, May '68), which confer a profound historicity even onto the most inconspicuous of peacetime years. (Sartre's little fable is instructive: when the Second World War broke out, he says, our entire youth was reified into a period called "*l'entre-deux-guerres*").

With Balzac's formal transformation, then, the historical novel in its earlier authenticity disappears; its place taken by "realism"; but what particularly interests us here is that by the same token, the world-historical individual also disappears: Michel Chrestien, a fictive character, takes his place; later on, but off-stage, Rastignac becomes prime minister, however much his death in the plague resembles that of Casimir Perier; various figures represent Fouchet or Talleyrand, but Napoleon is absent from *Une ténébreuse affaire*, save for his fatal decision, etc. Political intrigue and the dialectical complexity of revolutionary and post-revolutionary French political history have not disappeared, but the great historical actors have been effaced to the benefit of the period itself, which comes to the forefront as social reality rather than historical event.

But to be sure, the genre itself survives, now emptied of its genuine historical content; and we may follow it on through its next stages as Lukács sees them (the true historical novel living on briefly outside of France in Cooper and Manzoni and Pushkin, as well as in the special case of Tolstoy to whom we will come later on). What happens as historiography itself becomes theorized in terms of class struggle, first on the right by its ideologues, and then on the liberal left by Thierry and novelists like Merimée, Vigny, and Hugo, is that the world-historical individual again occupies center stage and the form is undermined by a dialectical opposition between "picturesquely fashioned anecdotes" (the empirical facts) and "moral reflections," the political and ideological judgements of the authors (77). "Merimée wishes to draw general lessons from history which hold good for all time (including the present) but he draws them *directly* from a keen and detailed observation of the empirical facts of history" (79), which is to say that he does not grasp either "history" or its "lessons" historically, and as a result these well-meaning and moralizing or idealizing efforts lead on into the decadence of post-1848 literature, of which Flaubert's *Salammbô* is the terrible object lesson, and in which the philosophical and ideological triumph of empiricism leads to decorative exoticism, if not the excesses of violence and atrocities for their own sake. Meanwhile, what was once the authorial judgements of these novels becomes the place of a subjectivity which either surrenders to the pathological and the exceptional or to the reified form of the biographical (if not indeed to both at once).

In effect, this turn spells the extinction of the historical novel as a form until we come to the progressive literature of the twentieth century, whose specimens, from Romain Rolland and de Coster to Feuchtwanger or Heinrich Mann, do not arouse much excitement, even in Lukács. But it will be remembered that the modernism debate casts its shadow over such debates in the contemporary period, just as Stalinist nationalism casts another. Lukács is therefore scarcely in

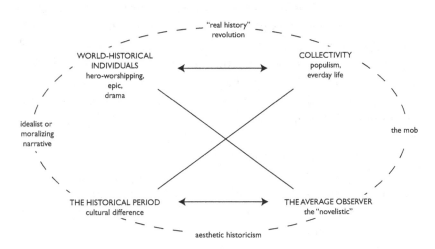

a position to assess the possibilities of anything like a modernist historical novel, while its possible evolution into a historical novel of the future (just as with Balzac we saw it evolve into a historical novel of the present) is not yet for him conceivable in the state at which socialist construction found itself at the end of his lifetime.

He also failed to note the way in which the historical novel could function as an intervention into the political situation and not merely a representation of the past. This is something we may observe at work in one of the rare successful novelizations of a genuine revolution, namely Hilary Mantel's *Place of Greater Safety*, which, transgressing all the Lukácsian warnings and injunctions, offers a remarkable picture of the lives and psychologies and personal and social relations of the three major actors of the French Revolution itself—namely Camille Desmoulins, Danton and Robespierre. She thereby transfers what is minimally permissible on stage (Büchner's *Dantons Tod*) and psychologizes and presumably modernizes real historical figures, whose thoughts she makes available to us, and this in the form of personal relationships, solidarities, jealousies, envies, and private judgements, which might well have been depoliticized and modernized in the form of this or that intimate novel or play staging purely fictional individuals. The great "events" of the French Revolution here indeed come before us in the form of echoes, rumors, reports from the outside, sounds in the street, documents to be signed or decisions to be made or evaded: as rich as the texture is, there is something of the closet drama about all this and a reduction of the collective dimensions of this unique revolutionary situation, an Event which included many events and truly contained multitudes.

One can indeed prefer to this fictionalization the truly novelistic proportions of Michelet's great history, or indeed the varieties of its contemporary tellings and reinterpretations; indeed, the prior knowledge required here is not only that of the elaborate chronology of the Revolution itself, portrayed as I suggested only in its effects and scarcely in itself and according to its own extraordinary and well-nigh autonomous inner momentum, but also that of the various interpretations themselves, which can mainly be reduced to a taking of sides, now for the monarchists (the Mirabeau of the beginning), now for the Girondins, now (and far more frequently) for the genuinely humanistic populist Danton, and scarcely anyone at all for the prim monster Robespierre—each of whom represent a specific political solution and program.

The taking of sides, the partisanship, generally stops there, as it is assumed that Thermidor effectively answers the question all revolutions ask themselves, namely when the revolution is considered to be at an end. Not only do we have Michelet's extraordinary picture of the emptiness of the assembly on all sides as Robespierre confronts it towards the end of his work of ideological purification. We also have Michelet's coda, one of the most remarkable envois to be found in any histogriographic narratives (the other, quite different, which I do not quote, is to be found on the last page of Vargas Llosa's *War of the End of the World*; and we will have to return to this matter of the "end," if not of history, then of the historical novel, later on):

> Peu de jours après Thermidor, un homme, qui vit encore et qui avait alors dix ans, fut mené par ses parents au théâtre, et à la sortie admira la longue file de voiture brillantes qui, pour une première fois, frappaient ses yeux. Des gens en veste, chapeau bas, disaient aux spectateurs sortants: «Faut-il une voiture, *mon maitre?*» L'enfant ne comprit pas trop ces termes nouveaux. Il se les fit expliquer, et on lui dit seulement qu'il y avait eu un grand changement par la mort de Robespierre.

> A few days after Thermidor, a man still living who was ten years old at the time was taken to the theater by his parents, and coming out after the spectacle gazed with amazement on the long row of splendid vehicles waiting for their customers, he had never seen such a thing before. People with coats on, holding their hats respectfully, were asking the emergent theater-goers, "Does *monsieur* require a carriage?" The child could not quite understand this new language, but on inquiring what it meant, he was told that only with the death of Robespierre a great change had come over the world.[18]

What Hilary Mantel's novel achieves is a political intervention of a quite unexpected type: she manages to turn Robespierre into a believable character. It is an achievement that transforms our received opinions on *le vraisemblable*, on political intervention, and indeed on Robespierre himself. She has also in passing given us her philosophical opinions on history and revolution, in a properly unbelievable dialogue between Danton and Sade, but that is of little moment here.

What counts is that, in keeping with that dramatic and externalizing stage distance we observe in the representation of the world-historical individuals in our history books, the picture we have of Robespierre himself has never been believable (quite unlike the figures of other "tyrants" like Hitler or Stalin, whom we understand only too well,

---

[18] Jules Michelet, *Histoire de la revolution francaise*, Paris: Gallimard, 2 volumes, 1952, Vol. II, p. 990. English translation, mine.

mainly on account of their fearsomeness). Robespierre is alternately indifferent, aloof, rigid, puritanical, coldly fanatical, or preposterous, comical, a Malvolio without even passion to excuse him, awkward, mocked behind his back, etc., etc. Michelet himself indulges in this mockery, which only Daniel Guérin has managed to endow with any genuine historical irony, when, taking for the end point of the Revolution not Thermidor but Babeuf, he stages Robespierre as an unwitting tool of the new bourgeois order, tossed aside contemptuously when his historic task has been completed and he is no longer required as an agent.[19]

Now it would not seem to be an extraordinary literary feat to rescue such a peculiar personage from the satiric weight of political vilification and the caricature of his personality and private habits; but surely much in the politics of the past as well as the present turns on just such anthropomorphic assessments: the political is the personal, and the identification of violence with the Law becomes even more intolerable when incarnated in so grotesque a figure. To humanize Robespierre, then, to show the moments when he is a friend and even a lover, to turn the susceptibility to flattery into an excusable failing, to show his anguished hesitation at shipping his childhood comrade Desmoulins off to the gallows (indeed, it is by way of a strange new caricature of Camille that much of this neighboring characterization is achieved)—all this makes it possible once more to reconsider Robespierre's more general political strategy with other standards than the traditional humanist ones whereby his "fanatical" ideals are contrasted unfavorably with the all-too-human weaknesses of Danton (whose personal political hesitations are also foregrounded in what allows a reinterpretation of his own role as well.)[20]

All of this implies a different distance from human relationships and personalities than the older humanist sympathies; yet the shift in psychology and evaluation would be inconsequential—or would be more interesting in the context of Mantel's own literary work rather than in the historiography of the Revolution—were it not for the signal fact that with this intervention in the portrayal of Robespierre, his political program can now again be taken seriously. Its watchwords had little to do with economics in a pre-industrial capitalism, but the social and political diagnosis of corruption is surely not without its

---

[19] Daniel Guérin, *La lutte de classes sous la première république*, Paris: Gallimard, 1946.

[20] On Mantel's presentation, Danton, after the mobilization of the Parisian masses, decides to withdraw from politics into private life, abandoning power to others.

significance today, where the center and the margins of late capitalism alike are predicated on its omnipresent facilitation of business great and small, and where the universal tolerance of corruption tells us more about what is apolitical in our societies than any number of party-oriented opinion polls. In the current absence of any genuinely socialist politics, Robespierre's politics of Virtue may well have something active and constructive to offer us; it is in any case a genuine political intervention to have made it narratively conceivable again, and Mantel has given us a possibility of rethinking the uses of the historical novel in a mode distinct from that of hagiography or the legend of martyrs.

2.

But we have not yet mentioned the work which for most readers constitutes the very summit of what the historical novel can achieve; nor have we examined the unique way in which Tolstoy inherits and confronts the formal problem of the "world-historical individual" in his historical constructions. For Tolstoy not only includes such figures in a good deal more forthright manner than the distance recommended by Lukács (although there are here and there mediatory characters such as Prince Andrew, whose personal life and psychology is however far more vivid and pronounced than Waverley's, or those of any other characters in Scott). Here the opposition between Napoleon and Kutuzov bears a symbolic weight which dispenses Tolstoy from any more rigorous settling of accounts with Westernizers or Slavophiles in his own immediate intellectual environment (and indeed is complicated by the fact that he identifies fully with neither of these positions: we may well wish to remember Lenin's judgement that he made himself into a kind of ideologue of the peasantry and its worldview,[21] even though that is something perhaps more tangible in *Anna Karenina* and in some of the stories than here). Meanwhile, his opinions on these figures, however aberrant, is not without interest either: Perry Anderson has objected strenuously to the transformation of the old reactionary Kutuzov into a culture hero,[22] while any number of admirers of Napoleon will surely have their word to say

---

[21] V. I. Lenin, "Leo Tolstoy as the Mirror of the Russian Revolution," in *Collected Works*, Vol. XV, Moscow: Progress, 1973.

[22] See note 1 above.

about that particular caricature. Neither of these reinterpretations, in any case, carries the political weight and value of the intervention we have attributed to Mantel's novel.

Tolstoy's most perceptive critic already casts doubt on the standard view of *War and Peace* as the greatest of all historical novels, not only by insisting on the anachronicity of most of the social materials in the novel (which reproduce Tolstoy's own experiences in the 1840s and '50s), but also by insisting on the generic discontinuities within the work, as a combination of the domestic or family novel with the war narrative.[23] Boris Eikhenbaum then adds, significantly, that in the final version a third "genre"—"the philosophy of history"—is added into the mix. This last, introduced here and there but worked up as an independent treatise in the Second Epilogue, is the least popular part of the book for most readers and for the specialists a testimony to the unphilosophical nature of Tolstoy's mind, as it grapples with abstract problems such as determinism and free will, or historical necessity.

I propose, however, to grasp these ruminations as the attempt to solve a properly narratological issue, and as a logical complement to the unique form-problems posed by the historical novel as such. We have indeed from the outset chosen to couple the two unique characteristics of the historical novel: the presence of "world-historical," which is to say "real" historical, individuals, and the concomitant presence, however shadowy, of the collectivity itself—nation, people or multitude—whose "history" is here in question. But we have linked these two features (which can be omitted from definitions of the novel as such and its other sub-genres) as opposites, whose tension makes up the specificity of this form and on whose resolution depends the literary value and distinctiveness of the work in question. It will therefore be to this second feature of the historical novel—the problem of the representation of collectivity—that we turn in this second section; and it is in this context that Tolstoy's Second Epilogue takes on its narratological significance. Contrary to received opinion, then, we will argue that the relationship of the two great leaders—Napoleon and Kutuzov—to their respective collectivities is not at all an allegorical one, nor is either identified with his "people" or "culture" (what to call this collective background is very much a part of the problem we want to raise here, and we will return to it): indeed, read closely it becomes clear that Tolstoy works hard to exclude this identification on both sides.

---

[23] Boris Eikhenbaum, *Tolstoi in the Sixties*, Ann Arbor: Ardis, 1982, 242–3.

The way this exclusion is achieved on the French side is obvious enough from episodes such as this one, in which Napoleon receives a Russian emissary:

> It was plain that Balashov's personality did not interest him at all. Evidently only what took place within his own mind interested him. Nothing outside himself had any significance for him, because everything in the world, it seemed to him, depended entirely on his will.[24]

That this is something more than mere caricature (which of course it also is) will become clearer if we recall that contradiction between spontaneity and will power that Tolstoy shared with Stendhal and which became the ideological and moral foundation for his critique of an artificial *mondanité* as well as for a well-nigh ontological attraction to the peasantry. That the episode might also be understood as a more general commentary on the French or Western character (and thereby on the nature of their—revolutionary—collectivity) is not to be excluded either, and will ultimately constitute the philosophical stumbling block of the Second Epilogue: yet the Emperor's egotism and self-centeredness would seem to preclude any easy identification between Napoleon as an individual and whatever collectivity he may be thought to "represent."

It would seem more difficult to argue such a disjunction in the case of Kutuzov, so often taken as the very epitome of the slyness of the Russian peasant and the latter's quintessential stubbornness and suspicion ("it was evident that Kutuzov despised knowledge and cleverness, and knew of something else that would decide the matter— something independent of cleverness and knowledge" [828]). But in order to determine what this "something else" is, we must abandon Kutuzov for the moment and turn to the Second Epilogue.

The language of the Second Epilogue—and the philosophical code into which Tolstoy's thinking is locked—is that of freedom and determinism (or necessity). The problem he poses, however—the dilemma he seeks to resolve—is the political problem of representation as it is raised most dramatically in Rousseau's *Social Contract*; and it will have been clear, I hope, that I take this term "representation" in all its senses and grasp this problem fully as much a narratological problem as a political one. For Rousseau, in other words, the problem of the

---

[24] Page references to *War and Peace* throughout are to the translation by Louise and Aylmer Maude, New York: Simon and Schuster, 1942, here 685.

One and the Many is that of the possibility of the emergence of a single General Will from the multitude of opinions and factions, ideologies and positions, which constitutes a people or a nation. In our literary context, however, the issue is that of the representation of a collectivity by individual characters; and the discomfort with the obvious recourse to allegorical representation is not unrelated to Rousseau's reluctance to solve his problem by way of mathematical majorities and pluralities: not that he fears for the minority and its fate in an electoral system, but he senses the absence of any available concept for a multiplicity of individuals; there is for Rousseau no available genus of which the individual could possibly be a species, and therefore the very "General Will" itself is the name for an absence, for an impossible concept.

In Tolstoy's version, there clearly exists a bias against the notion of individual freedom, as an illusion that must somehow be eradicated: "consciousness gives expression to the essence of freedom" (1347), and individual freedom can never be disproven… at least in the conscious present of the individual. But here too it is a question of knowledge and of an infinite limit, for "the farther I go back in memory, or what is the same thing the farther I go forward in my judgement, the more doubtful becomes my belief in the freedom of my action" (1342).

The eradication of this illusion will of course at once dispose of the "world-historical individual," whose will no longer has any authority over the course of the world; but it also tends to dissolve the individual character as well, whose decisions (Lukács thought they were best acted out in drama) come to seem less credible and more and more symptomal, in the spirit of modernism or of Freudian psychoanalysis. Meanwhile, in historiography, the waning of the grand historical figures gives rise to the anonymity of cultural collectives of the kind promoted by the *Annales* school, and historical events themselves begin to wane and to disappear. Under such circumstances it would seem difficult to project a historical novel at all, except in the form of sheer anthropological description.

But Tolstoy still holds to his Event, and stubbornly confronts it with his insistence on causes and causality. It may well be so that individual freedom need no longer concern us: "In history what is known to us we call laws of inevitability, what is unknown we call free will. Free will is for history only an expression for the unknown remainder of what we know about the laws of human life" (1348).

But "what is power? What force produces the movement of the

nations?" (1335). It is not an abstract question, but has to do with Kutuzov's strategy in 1812, when he is ordered by the Czar and his general staff (mostly Germans, I might add) to stand and to defend Moscow against the approaching French army. Instead, Kutuzov retreats, abandons the city, and lets it burn, leaving the French nothing but an empty shell for all their victory. This hollow victory is thus Napoleon's defeat, who would have won any official frontal engagement. But does this seemingly suicidal strategy confirm the greatness of Kutuzov as a world-historical individual? Let us return to Prince Andrew's impressions:

> Prince Andrew could not have explained how or why it was, but after that interview with Kutuzov he went back to his regiment reassured as to the general course of affairs and as to the man to whom it had been entrusted. The more he realized the absence of all personal motive in that old man—in whom there seemed to remain only the habit of passions, and in place of an intellect (grouping events and drawing conclusions) only the capacity calmly to contemplate the course of events—the more reassured he was that everything would be as it should. "He will not bring in any plan of his own. He will not devise or undertake anything," thought Prince Andrew, "but he will hear everything, remember everything, and put everything in its place. He will not hinder anything useful nor allow anything harmful. He understands that there is something stronger and more important than his own will—the inevitable course of events, and he can see them and grasp their significance, and seeing that significance can refrain from meddling and renounce his personal wish directed to something else." (831)

It is time to resolve this conundrum: "the something stronger and more important than his own will," the "something else that would decide the matter—something independent of cleverness and knowledge"—that something else is simply the "will" of the people. The Russian people know that Moscow is doomed and that they cannot resist Napoleon; and they also know that they do not want to leave the city to him. The conclusion, then—drawn by the General Will—is to destroy it in the moment of abandoning it. This unconscious collective will is the cause of History. Tolstoy calls the "cause" of an event such as 1812 "a force commensurate with the movement observed" (1321): unsurprisingly, this force will be here identified as the people ("power is the collective will of the people transferred, by expressed or tacit consent, to their chosen rulers" [1313]).

But this philosophical conclusion does not solve our literary one: what is the transfer in question, and how is it to be represented? The "greatness" of Kutuzov is in fact implicit in Prince Andrew's reflections: it consists in letting history happen, in abandoning his own will, his own self, his own personal assessments, and entrusting his decisions to history itself. This is, to be sure, on one level a well-nigh religious abnegation of self, which can eventually be related to Tolstoy's mysticism on the level of personal ethics and "belief." On the level that interests us here, this position leaves history intact, with all its cataclysmic events, merely stripping it of its actors and decision-makers. As I read it, this is a narratological position, and its seeming "determinism," which does underscore necessity at the heart of its conception of history, is in fact a kind of actantial law: "we see a law by which men, to take associated action, combine in such relations that the more directly they participate in performing the action the less they can command and the more numerous they are, while the less their direct participation in the action itself, the more they command and the fewer of them there are; rising in this way from the lowest ranks to the man at the top, who takes the least direct share in the action and directs his activity chiefly to commanding" (1333).

This is in fact a position which leaves a good deal of play as far as the characters are concerned. Kutuzov's "wisdom" consists in knowing his powerlessness. But there are also comic versions of this knowledge, as witness Bagration's leadership during the battle of Ulm, of which we have already quoted a portion in the previous essay:

> Bagration called to him, and Tushin, raising three fingers to his cap with a bashful and awkward gesture not at all like a military salute but like a priest's benediction, approached the general. Though Tushin's guns had been intended to cannonade the valley, he was firing incendiary balls at the village of Schöngrabern visible just opposite, in front of which large masses of French were advancing.
>
> No one had given Tushin orders where and at what to fire, but after consulting his sergeant major, Zakharchenko, for whom he had great respect, he had decided that it would be a good thing to set fire to the village. "Very good!" said Bagration in reply to the officer's report, and began deliberately to examine the whole battlefield extended before him. The French had advanced nearest on our right. Below the height on which the Kiev regiment was stationed, in the hollow where the rivulet flowed, the soul-stirring rolling and crackling of musketry was heard, and much farther to the right beyond the dragoons, the officer of the suite pointed out to Bagration a French column that was outflanking us. To the left the horizon was bounded by the adjacent wood. Prince Bagration ordered two battalions from the center to be sent to reinforce the right flank. The officer of the suite ventured to remark to the prince that if these battalions went away, the guns would remain without support. Prince Bagration turned to the officer and with his dull eyes looked at him in silence. It seemed to Prince Andrew that the officer's remark

was just and that really no answer could be made to it. But at that moment an adjutant galloped up with a message from the commander of the regiment in the hollow and news that immense masses of the French were coming down upon them and that his regiment was in disorder and was retreating upon the Kiev grenadiers. Prince Bagration bowed his head in sign of assent and approval. He rode off at a walk to the right and sent an adjutant to the dragoons with orders to attack the French. But this adjutant returned half an hour later with the news that the commander of the dragoons had already retreated beyond the dip in the ground, as a heavy fire had been opened on him and he was losing men uselessly, and so had hastened to throw some sharpshooters into the wood.

"Very good!" said Bagration.

As he was leaving the battery, firing was heard on the left also, and as it was too far to the left flank for him to have time to go there himself, Prince Bagration sent Zherkov to tell the general in command (the one who had paraded his regiment before Kutuzov at Braunau) that he must retreat as quickly as possible behind the hollow in the rear, as the right flank would probably not be able to withstand the enemy's attack very long. About Tushin and the battalion that had been in support of his battery all was forgotten. Prince Andrew listened attentively to Bagration's colloquies with the commanding officers and the orders he gave them and, to his surprise, found that no orders were really given, but that Prince Bagration tried to make it appear that everything done by necessity, by accident, or by the will of subordinate commanders was done, if not by his direct command, at least in accord with his intentions. Prince Andrew noticed, however, that though what happened was due to chance and was independent of the commander's will, owing to the tact Bagration showed, his presence was very valuable. Officers who approached him with disturbed countenances became calm; soldiers and officers greeted him gaily, grew more cheerful in his presence, and were evidently anxious to display their courage before him. (192–3)

I have dwelt on Tolstoy's theories of history at some length in order to demonstrate that the unique position of *War and Peace* in the history of the historical novel is formally dependent on this idiosyncratic "solution" in which named characters are able to stand for the masses behind them in a non-allegorical way, and in which the narrative can "include" history without utterly abandoning those protagonists without whom it risks sinking back into either a chronicle of the facts or an ethnological account of customs and mentalities. It should be added that Tolstoy's personal relationship to that peasantry of which Lenin saw him as a kind of spokesperson falls into exactly this pattern of passive acceptance and reliance on a force greater than the individual: his story "Metel" paradigmatically shows us a Westernized landlord attempting to reform his peasants and to teach them new and efficient agricultural methods (a drama central to the eighteenth-century Enlightenment in the West), until, frustrated and exhausted, he gives in and adapts himself to their immemorial ignorant behavior and relationship to the earth (and to Being).

We must now, in conclusion to this section, ask ourselves what kind of historical novel can be possible if Tolstoy's view of reality prevails and if the individual historical protagonists disappear altogether. The answer is, paradoxically, that a narrative possibility still subsists, and retains ideological as well as literary power. It is the tale of the mob, as literature first glimpses it in the counter-revolutionary rhetoric of an Edmund Burke:[25] the revolution seen as a lynching— a vision retained by bourgeois literature, whether in the scientific mode of Freud's appropriation of LeBon in *Group Psychology and the Ego*, or in the far more progressive vision of Zola's *Germinal*. This synecdoche, in which the skirmish stands in for the battle, as Balzac recommended, is a far more forthright and energetic assault on the impossible problem of collective representation than anything on the Left, which is reduced to demonstrations and marches, and whose dilemmas are vividly dramatized by the fact that more actors and extras took part in Eisenstein's filming of *October* than the number of actual participants in the Bolshevik revolution itself.

There is, to be sure, a price to be paid for any narrative solution to the issues grappled with in the *Social Contract*; and it is the oneiric spirit in which collective History and action here for one brief moment make their appearance. I believe that the concept of the uncanny is appropriate for this phantasmagoric state, in which the individual being is briefly raised to another ontological level: that *Aufhebung* which bourgeois and reactionary thinkers saw as a dissolution of individuality and a loss of self in the crowd. For Americans, the story is told most effectively in one of Hawthorne's most successful historical visions, "My Kinsman Major Molineux," in which a youth from the countryside wanders into the midst of a revolutionary event, searching for his Tory kinsman in what it is difficult to distinguish from a carnival.[26] But we may remain with Lukács' classics by citing an

---

[25] Edmund Burke, *Reflections on the Revolution in France* (1790).

[26] The referent peeps through the festivities in the form of a man tarred and feathered and run out of town on a rail, whereby the hero's acquaintance concludes the tale with a flourish magnificent in its irony: "Some few days hence, if you continue to wish it, I will speed you on your journey. Or, if you prefer to remain with us, perhaps, as you are a shrewd youth, you may rise in the world, without the help of your kinsman, Major Molineux." (Hawthorne, *Tales and Sketches*, New York: Library of American, 1982, 87.)

early climax in Walter Scott's finest novel, in which the Edinburgh mob seizes the city and metes justice on a tyrannical lawman, in the process pressing into service the young clergyman who for the moment figures Lukács' average hero and observer:

> "I would it were a dream I could awaken from," said Butler to himself; but, having no means to oppose the violence with which he was threatened, he was compelled to turn round and march in front of the rioters, two men partly supporting and partly holding him.
>
> While this was going on, Butler could not, even if he had been willing, avoid making remarks on the individuals who seemed to lead this singular mob. The torch-light, while it fell on their forms and left him in the shade, gave him an opportunity to do so without their observing him. Several of those who appeared most active were dressed in sailors' jackets, trowsers, and sea-caps; others in large loose-bodied great-coats, and slouched hats; and there were several, who, judging from their dress, should have been called women, whose rough deep voices, uncommon size, and masculine deportment and mode of walking, forbade their being so interpreted. They moved as if by some well-concerted plan of arrangement. They had signals by which they knew, and nick-names by which they distinguished each other. Butler remarked, that the name of Wildfire was used among them, to which one stout Amazon seemed to reply.[27]

Transvestism is to be sure itself one of the prime characteristics of carnival, on the Bakhtinian or any other point of view, expressing the "world turned upside down" of this moment, which is here and in Bakhtin himself the figure for the revolutionary Event as such. (Le Roy Ladurie's *Carnival in Romans* offers a striking narrative of the same moment in an anthropological mode). At any rate, the authorities in London are under no illusions as to the hermeneutic significance of this moment of disorder in Scotland; and as for Bakhtin, I have suggested that his theory is weakened by its insertion into a cyclical temporality which domesticates and "anthropologizes" it. He himself clearly intended his account of a moment of Renaissance licentiousness and liberation to stand for the revolutionary culture of the Soviet 1920s, compressed between the Czarist old regime (in his narrative, the middle ages) and the repressive new order of Stalinism (here figured as the Counter-Reformation). Bakhtin's is then in effect yet another historical novel;[28] and the oneiric carnival it celebrates is

---

27 Walter Scott, *The Heart of Midlothian*, London: Penguin, 1994, 59–60.

28 Mikhail Bakhtin, *Rabelais and his World*, Bloomington: Indiana University Press, 1984, 72: "The disintegration of the feudal and theocratic order of the Middle Ages

the last possible representation of the Event of a multitude without named actors.

3.

The next logical and formal possibility will then be that of names without events, and indeed I believe this reduction of the world-historical individuals to little more than their names is what characterizes one of the two distinctive forms of the historical novel today. Names are indeed the remnants of historical "prior knowledge," the detritus of the schoolbooks, nouns from the General Intellect stagnating in the collective unconscious and attempting organically to reconnect amoeba-like in the Internet. As we shall see, such historical names, bloated with biography, tend towards an autonomy of their own as the history of which they were once a part becomes spongy. But it is the mode of this autonomization which is curious and even paradoxical.

For it may be said to begin precisely in that process of critical reexamination, of historical intervention into the stereotypes of the past, of fresh historiographic revision, which we have seen at work in an inconspicuous way in Mantel's Robespierre. Nowadays, it is not so much an ideological belief in the past as multiple narratives—in all its versions as so many different ways "the story is told"—as it is the sheer accumulation of all those versions in what has complacently come to be called the Archive ("after Foucault"). It is sheer multiplicity itself which guarantees that none of these narratives can or should be taken at face value—a serious blow to the serious historian. But even in a less saturated period there were several ways in which the name could survive the fact and even the story.

The most traditional was of course the hero-worshipping or hagiographic mode stoutly and anachronistically championed by Carlyle and continuing to draw its strength from the inherited stereotypes, with "interesting" minor variations, so that John Ford's *Young Mr.*

---

also contributed to the fusion of the official and nonofficial. The culture of folk humor that had been shaped during many centuries and that had defended the people's creativity in nonofficial forms, in verbal expression or spectacle, could now rise to the high level of literature and ideology and fertilize it. Later, in times of absolute monarchy and the formation of a new official order, folk humor descended to the lower level of the genre hierarchy. There it settled and broke away from its popular roots, becoming petty, narrow, and degenerate."

Lincoln becomes a detective, Gore Vidal's a racist, and a contemporary version, modishly enough, becomes a vampire-killer. But there is more often the mode of caricature, such as Melville's version of Benjamin Franklin in *Redburn*, in which the existence of the historical personage is reconfirmed by his all-too-human feet of clay. In both modes, interrogation, a hermeneutic curiosity about the past, is steadily maintained and pursued; and perhaps it is a matter of autoreferentiality when, as in his unexpected appearance at the end of *Lotte in Weimar*, Thomas Mann's Goethe proves to be an enigma, glacially persisting in his undecideability, which turns out to be the undecideability of the past as such.

Finally, it is precisely this undecideability which ends up detaching the name from its "referent." The most conspicuous modernist view of the past has posited a longing to recapture or recreate it. Proust generally serves as the canonical demonstration of this will to make the past live again, but Joyce's elaborate literary reconstruction of 1904 Dublin, Thomas Mann's endless musings on time, moments in Pound and Eliot, political nostalgia in Yeats, all among much else document this strange vocation of the modernists, which does not seem to have any real equivalent, either among the so-called realists of the nineteenth century novel, or among ourselves. But if you had a great deal of money, and no particular literary gifts as such, you might imagine going about it in a different way. Here, for example, is Dos Passos's evocation of the old age of Henry Ford in *The Big Money* (the last volume of the *USA* trilogy):

Henry Ford as an old man
is a passionate antiquarian
(lives besieged on his father's farm embedded in an estate of thousands of
millionaire acres, protected by an army of servicemen, secretaries, secret agents,
dicks under orders of an English exprizefighter,
always afraid of the feet in broken shoes on the roads, afraid the gangs will
kidnap his grandchildren,
that a crank will shoot him,
that Change and the idle hands out of work will break through the gates and the
high fences;
protected by a private army against
the new America of starved children and hollow bellies and cracked shoes
stamping on souplines,
that has swallowed up the old thrifty farmlands
of Wayne County, Michigan,
as if they had never been).

Henry Ford as an old man
is a passionate antiquarian.
He rebuilt his father's farmhouse and put it back exactly in the state he
remembered it in as a boy. He built a village of museums for buggies, sleighs,
coaches, old plows, waterwheels, obsolete models of motorcars. He scoured the
country for fiddlers to play oldfashioned squaredances.
Even old taverns he bought and put back into their original shape, as well as
Thomas Edison's early laboratories.
When he bought the Wayside Inn near Sudbury, Massachusetts, he had the new
highway where the newmodel cars roared and slithered and hissed oilily past (*the
new noise of the automobile*)
moved away from the door,
put back the old bad road,
so that everything might be
the way it used to be,
in the days of horses and buggies.[29]

This is less an interpretation of Ford (about whom a modern biographer—the director of the Henry Ford museum itself—has implausibly asserted that he "built this place [Greenfield Village] out of guilt")[30] than it is an imputation to him of Dos Passos's own aesthetic, as it wavers uneasily between modernism and a postmodernism to come. But the emphasis on accuracy, authenticity and "complete restoration" in Ford's project may turn out to be less a Proustian recovery of the past than a whole new construction, as in this account by a contemporary witness, of Ford's transfer of Edison's laboratory in Menlo Park to the new site in Michigan:

> Before he moved the laboratory here, he went out to New Jersey—the land where
> the building was originally—and dug up tons of dirt, just tons of it. Then he had
> it all earthed out here and dumped it all over this site before they stuck the build-
> ing down on top of it. That was his idea of complete restoration. This place had
> been built on New Jersey soil, so it should be restored on New Jersey soil. Stuff
> like that drove the experts crazy.[31]

The element of hero-worshipping, so central to Ford's later personality, is here allied to something closer to time-travel, the not necessarily so materialist urge to recreate a physical site in which one could oneself

---

[29] John Dos Passos, *The Big Money*, New York: New American Library, 1960, 76–77.
[30] David Lowenthal, *The Past is a Foreign Country*, Cambridge: Cambridge University Press, 1999, 328.
[31] Ibid., 288.

stroll about. It is this urge which was so memorably recaptured in Philip K. Dick's *Now Wait for Last Year*, where we confront a three-hundred-year-old industrialist and millionaire—his body regenerated through countless organ transplants over the years while his mind is arguably somewhat more senescent—who shows many of the features of Henry Ford's strange passion.

Virgil Ackermann is, for example, a passionate collector of authentic memorabilia, items increasingly rare in this bleak future world. When his staff feel the need to underscore their devotion, for example, they find nothing quite so suitable as to acquire, at great expense, from the businesses who specialize in such rarities, a green Lucky Strike cigarette package wrapper certified as having been produced in the pre-World-War-II period. He receives these metonymic objects with real delight, but it should not be thought that he simply accumulates them in a random way. Rather, he owns a complete lunar estate or encampment, significantly named Wash-35, which is to say a reconstruction of Washington, D.C. in the year 1935, or at the time of the millionaire's boyhood. Here, as with Ford's boyhood farmhouse, the whole neighborhood has been lovingly rebuilt just as it was, including robot or android simulacra of familiar childhood figures:

> The emphases of Wash-35, a five-story brick apartment building where Virgil had lived as a boy, contained a truly modern apartment of their year 2055 with every detail of convenience which Virgil could obtain during these war years. Several blocks away lay Connecticut Avenue, and, along it, stores which Virgil remembered. Here was Gammage's a shop at which Virgil had bought Tip Top comics and penny candy. Next to it Eric made out the familiar shape of People's Drugstore; the old man during his childhood had bought a cigarette lighter here once and chemicals for his Gilbert Number Five glass blowing and chemistry set.
>
> "What's the Uptown Theatre showing this week?" Harv Ackerman murmured as their ship coasted along Connecticut Avenue so that Virgil could review these treasured sights. He peered.
>
> It was Jean Harlow in *Hell's Angels*, which all of them had seem at least twice. Harv groaned.[32]

But it is worth revisiting this historical figure (or name) one last time, in a fully postmodern guise where Ford—no longer a mere insert as in Dos Passos—reappears as a minor character, whose typically American slyness and practicality (we have just been treated to a presentation of the innovation of the assembly line) finds itself

32 Philip K. Dick, *Now Wait for Last Year*, New York: DAW, 1966, 27.

unexpectedly conjoined to an (equally typical?) weakness for the occult and for mysticism. The scene takes place during a visit of the inventor to J. P. Morgan:

> When he had satisfied himself that he understood, he nodded his head solemnly and replied as follows: If I understand you right, Mr. Morgan, you are talking about reincarnation. Well, let me tell you about that. As a youth I was faced with an awful crisis in my mental life when it came over me that I had no call to know what I knew. I had grit, all right, but I was an ordinary country boy who had suffered his McGuffey like the rest of them. Yet I knew how everything worked. I could look at something and tell you how it worked and probably show you how to make it work better. But I was no intellectual, you see, and I had no patience with the two-dollar words.
>
> Morgan listened. He felt that he mustn't move.
>
> Well then, Ford continued, I happened to pick up a little book. It was called *An Eastern Fakir's Eternal Wisdom*, published by the Franklin Novelty Company of Philadelphia, Pennsylvania. And in this book, which cost me just twenty-five cents, I found everything I needed to set my mind at rest. Reincarnation is the only belief I hold, Mr. Morgan. I explain my genius this way—some of us have just lived more times than others. So you see, what you have spent on scholars and traveled around the world to find, I already knew. And I'll tell you something, in thanks for the eats, I'm going to lend that book to you. Why, you don't have to fuss with all these Latiny things, he said waving his arm, you don't have to pick the garbage pails of Europe and build steamboats to sail the Nile just to find out something that you can get in the mail order for two bits![33]

Reincarnation does seem to be a better technical characterization for the postmodern relationship to historical names than any modernist "*recherche du temps perdu*," and this not only for the obvious constructivist reasons and the commitment to a present which forecloses the indirections of memory, remembrance or mere commemoration. We must also here reinscribe the fortunes and the aftereffects of contemporary semiotic philosophies, which displace that dualism of words and things, signs and referents, that continue to motivate the aesthetics of the modern. But the latter's commitment to mimesis must not be misunderstood as a belief that the representation can somehow fully reproduce its original. Rather, the point is to demonstrate its failure, its structural incapacity to represent reality, to designate its grandiose project of doing so as "mere" art and artifice, in an autoreferentiality of the aesthetic as such and its overweening autonomy.

---

[33] E.R. Doctorow, *Ragtime*, New York: Random House, 1975, pp. 173–4.

In the postmodern, where the original no longer exists and everything is an image, there can no longer be any question either of the accuracy or truth of representation, or of any aesthetic of mimesis either. Deleuze's "*puissance du faux*"[34] is a misnomer to the degree that, where the true is ontologically absent, there can be nothing false or fictive either: such concepts no longer apply to a world of simulacra, where only the names—Lacan's "*points de capiton*," Kripke's "rigid designators"—remain, like time capsules deposited by aliens who have no history or chronology in our sense in the first place.

Significantly, Doctorow's "portrait" of Ford is accompanied by a far more elaborate "fictional" character to whom he attributes the invention of the movie camera and indeed of motion pictures as such. Ford's contribution—the model-T whose theft sparks the main plot, the stirring pastiche of Kleist's *Michael Kohlhaas*—is thus subtly displaced by this non-narrative of the inventor and his daughter, who take the trolley to the end of the line and then walk to the beginning of the trolley of the adjacent township, thereby tracing a network of the imaginary that is ultimately more durable than Ford's highways, which are after all not replicated in his own museum, remaining imaginary, very much in Malraux's sense.

This is also a move from the narrative to the non-narrative. Dos Passos's original and fundamental isolation of the great historical name and its insertion by fiat into a world of imaginary characters is to that degree unable to generate a new narrative mode for the historical novel, but at best a kind of lateral return of the repressed, as an interesting contemporary German practice of the form suggests. *Die Vermessung der Welt* (*Measuring the World*) offers a lively cartoon version of the travels of Alexander von Humboldt intercalated with episodes from the life of the great mathematician (and astronomer) Christian Gauss.

The passage I want to quote evokes a perilous ascension of mount Chimborazo, a volcano now situated in Ecuador:

> With groping steps they made their way alongside the cliff. Bonpland [Humboldt's travelling companion] remarked that he actually consisted of three people: one who moved, one who observed the Bonpland in motion, and one who tirelessly accompanied them with a commentary in a language unknown to anyone. As a test he hit himself on the ear. That helped for a moment or two, and for those moments he thought more clearly. But that did not change the fact that earth

---

[34]   Gilles Deleuze, *Cinéma II*, Paris: Minuit, 1985, chapter 6.

now lay where the sky ought to be and vice versa, or in other words that they were actually descending upside down.[35]

Humboldt himself is accompanied, incidentally, not by doubles or triples, but by the vision of a homeless dog he has abandoned. Kehlmann's own intent is not without interest for us: "to tell the past anew," as he puts it, "and to deviate from the official version into the realm of invented truth." In fact, part of Kehlmann's invention has consisted in leaving something out: for the original expedition actually included a third person, a guide, whom the novelist has omitted, supplying instead the physical sickness, distress, hallucinations, which are amply recorded in the literature of mountain climbing but which Humboldt's own account itself omits. "In the sovereign cool tone of Humboldt's report there thus lies no less fiction than in the confused and staggering episode I have made it into," concludes Kehlmann, in his interesting essay "Wo ist Carlos Montúfar?" (the name of the real life guide he has omitted from his own narrative).[36] The hallucinated third person is also, however, one of the characters in virtually the most canonical classic of modernism itself:

> Who is the third who walks always beside you?
> When I count, there are only you and I together
> But when I look ahead up the white road
> There is always another one walking beside you
> Gliding wrapt in a brown mantle, hooded
> I do not know whether a man or a woman
> – But who is that on the other side of you?

These verses, from the climax of *The Waste Land*, have often been taken to have a religious meaning (nor are they without any connection with Philip K. Dick's "religion" of Mercerism in *Do Androids Dream of Electric Sheep?*); but I mean to think of them now in another way. Here is Eliot's footnote to this passage: "The following lines were stimulated by the account of one of the Antarctic expeditions (I forget which but I think one of Shackleton's); it was related that the party of explorers, at the extremity of their strength, had the constant delusion that there was one more member than could actually be counted."[37] And here is the actual account by one of the three

---

[35] Daniel Kehlmann, *Die Vermessung der Welt*, Hamburg: Rowohlt 2005, 175.

[36] Daniel Kehlmann, *Wo ist Carlos Montúfar?*, Hamburg: Rowohlt, 2005, 12.

[37] T. S. Eliot, *The Waste Land*, note 360.

survivors of the Endurance crew, the navigator Frank Worsley: "Sir Ernest and I, comparing notes, found that we each had a strange feeling there had been a fourth in our party and Crean [the third survivor] afterwards confessed the same thing."[38] To be sure, from the religious standpoint the change in number is significant. From ours, however, it is the multiplication of characters or participants which is the point of interest.[39]

---

[38]   Frank Worsley, *Endurance*, New York: Norton, 2000 [1931].

[39]   It is worth comparing this experience with the narrative of another historical novel, *Götz and Meyer* (trans. Ellen Elias-Bursac, New York: Harcourt, 2004), a kind of pre-Holocaust and magic-realist or "postmodern" novel about two SS truck-drivers who are instrumental in the experiments in gassing people in busses before the actual construction of the gas chambers as such. The narrator (a teacher) is very much a character in this novel, or rather the novel explicitly represents his attempt to imagine these two drivers of the lethal truck in which his own family was murdered. The question is then, not whether the facts of the narrative are true or false, but whether the imagining itself really happened; that is to say, is the experience of this imagining to be attributed to the biographical novelist called David Albahari (leaving out of it the question of whether his own family was thus involved), or is one not to assume that the whole thing is a novelist's idea for a new and interesting kind of Holocaust novel no one had quite written in this way before? (We thereby also omit the final suicide of the narrator himself.) It is at any rate one of the most successful works in that genre of the novel about the wilting of the novel as it has evolved since *Tristram Shandy*, with the qualification that the Holocaust material (itself a genre) serves to mask or cancel the frivolity of the postmodern play of genres as such. At any rate, the passage that will now concern us tells the story of the appearance of yet a third (or fourth) unwanted and fictional character within his narrative: "I would rather tilt at windmills, even the old and decrepit kind, the way they are now, Götz and Meyer, if they are alive. I never met them, I can only imagine them. I'm back where I began. This is what my life has turned into: stumbling, looking back, starting anew. One of those three lives I was living in parallel, maybe even a fourth. The rest continued to follow me, unchanged, and I'd wake up like Götz, or Meyer, eager to work, and go to sleep like a thirteen-year-old boy preparing for his bar mitzvah and repeating words in a language that made his throat ache. None of my relatives in the camp could be described as a thirteen-year-old boy, nor do I know where he came from, nor which life he belongs to. Götz and Meyer are also unable to help me. If we had remembered all those faces, they say, we'd remember nothing else. The boy kept popping up, and on one occasion, instead of my own hands, I saw his, clear as day. He was clutching a mug of milk and he was thirsty. He was in me that day, when, in a voice squeaky with excitement, I proposed to my students that we spend our next class in a hands-on demonstration. Although beside themselves at the thought that they wouldn't have to be in school, they wanted to know what was going to happen. The boy had, in the meanwhile, faded, leaving me to respond. It was going to be about the difference between the tangible world and art, I explained, but also about the similarity between an instant of reality and a figment of the imagination.

We might have added that, according to another character (the impresario-photographer Daguerre, yet another historical name included here), Humboldt's "long-awaited travel report disappointed the public: hundreds of pages of measurements and statistics, scarcely anything personal, practically no adventures."[40] But Kehlmann's historical novel can scarcely be said to constitute an attempt to substitute the narrative of those missing adventures (which one can imagine a traditional historical novel doing in abundance). Rather, setting forth from the surviving names, it ends up generating another anthropomorphic phantom of an unnamed third, in an account hallucinogenic rather than hallucinatory. This is not the delirium of collectivity we witnessed in the previous section, but rather simply the production of an additional character alongside the names he began with. The path of the historical names is anthropomorphic, it leads to multiplication rather than multiplicity. It remains to be seen whether a different path to the renewal of the historical novel in our time is still available.

4.

We have followed the vicissitudes of the great as they shrink from their elaborate costume settings and adventures into the empty shell of mere names and their most unlikely combinations. It remains to complete this diagnosis of the contemporary transformations of our historicity, pathological or not, with a brief look at their opposite number, namely the collectivity and its imaginary metamorphoses.

I was pretty busy for a few days. I had to find a school bus, collect money from the students, work out the route, get my thoughts together" (126–7). This shadowy third figure might well be theorized as the return in exteriority of the new "subjective" third person identified in Chapter VIII of Part One, above.

40 Kehlmann, *Vermessung*, 239. The generic term "postmodern novel" already seems to be current for "textual" or severely "reflexive" books of the type of *House of Leaves*, with more traditional historical-novelistic precursors in *The French Lieutenant's Woman* or *Possession*. Related texts, such as Cesar Aira's *An Episode in the Life of a Landscape Painter*, New York: New Directions, 2000 (a reference I owe to Emilio Sauri), or Doctorow, or those of writers like Ken Kalfuss, suggest the need for a new generic category for narratives organized, not around the feel of a period, but rather around historical proper names which circulate through what is often sheer fictional play, of a type quite distinct from the period simulacra of nostalgia film.

In that tug of war between chronology and structure, diachrony and synchrony, history and sociology or anthropology, to which we have already referred, it is clearly the latter that wins out on this side of the tension. A history without names, whether it is the description of a mode of production or an ethnological report, whether it follows the various codes and inscriptions of Deleuze and Guattari in "*sauvages, barbares, civilisés*" (Morgan's classification) or the detailed graphs of Lévi-Strauss's villages (or Bourdieu's in "La maison Kabyle"), will inevitably tend towards a tableau without events; nor is it terribly different for our purposes of classification from those historicisms of the late nineteenth century which found their delectation in the exoticisms of this or that period of the cultural past (always different, alien, and thereby virtually by definition exotic in the first place). And to be sure, narration and the event can always be pressed into service as a pretext for the panorama of otherness, the time travel of historical tourism.

Oddly enough, insofar as the temporal thinkers seem to agree that no historicity can function properly without a dimension of futurity, however imaginary, it is we ourselves who normally stand in for the place of the future, as we peer into the various pasts offered by novels claiming to be historical. And we remember our peculiar position occasionally by way of our irritation with too conspicuous modernization in the feelings or sayings of these allegedly long-dead figures, and the anachronism of their unwanted contemporaneity.

Still, the problem of what to do with the future in the historical novel is scarcely an unrewarding one, as witness the question of endings, and their relationship to the reader's prior knowledge. As for the history of the future itself, unless it is understood to be a literary genre (Science Fiction), we often tend to abandon it to prophets and Cassandras, if not to the writers of best-sellers on the subject, without remembering that every present of time in which we move includes its own dimension of futurity, of fears and expectations, which (realized or not) at once accompany that present into the past along with it, as what Sartre called "dead futures." Of those, no doubt, one could write a history, or at least a historical novel. (Francis Spufford's *Red Plenty*, for example, is one such registration of a future history we do not find in the history books.)[41]

---

[41] Francis Spufford, *Red Plenty*, London: Greywolf, 2012. See also my review in *New Left Review* 75 (May–June 2012).

I suspect that in these areas it is the notion of the fictional that creates the greatest mental confusion: for the historical novel was traditionally a contract whereby we agreed to tolerate a certain number of fictional characters and actions within a framework equally agreed to be factual. And no doubt we are willing to tolerate fictional characters in an imaginary future as well, since it is itself a fiction which will eventually be factual, no matter what we do about it.

But who would the world-historical individuals of such a future be, and are not the great names of such a future inevitable projections of our own present and past, as with the Caesar who will in a few years from now found the hegemony of the apes over our own species? Yet the invention of Science Fiction was assuredly a modification of our historicity to which a genuine historical cause can be assigned with some precision: the emergence of imperialism on a world scale in the Berlin Conference of 1885. (Wells' *War of the Worlds* specifically evokes the extermination of the Tasmanians as his inspiration.) The only other genre which can be thus clinically interrogated as an analogous symptom of a structural modification of history and our consciousness of it is, of course, the historical novel, whose relations with the French Revolution are complex and demonstrable. (Those who, on the contrary, take Mary Shelley's 1811 *Frankenstein* as the true emergence of modern Science Fiction can then adopt this argument as well.)

In what follows I will want to claim, however outrageously, that the historical novel of the future (which is to say of our own present) will necessarily be Science-Fictional inasmuch as it will have to include questions about the fate of our social system, which has become a second nature. To read the present as history, as so many have urged us to do, will mean adopting a Science-Fictional perspective of some kind, and we are fortunate to have at least one recent novel which, against all expectations, gives us an idea of what that might look like.

Before examining it, however, I will take the liberty of introducing a filmic exhibit, less as a text than as a model and a kind of thought experiment. To be sure, film has always been an avid accomplice of the historical novel, from costume dramas to special effects, from local color to the unexpected resurrection of the Titanic. In particular, what I have called "nostalgia films" very much belong in our current category of the milieu without the character, of a historicist reconstruction in which not only the world-historical figures but even the everyday street life have vanished, transformed into a caricatural realization and simulacrum of that "world of objects" Hegel and Lukács associated with epic, a world dated by costume and fashion, haircuts and coiffures, hit songs, popular music, the yearly make of the automobile and the occasional distinctive building style, which (all of them twentieth century) mark our visual experience as the neo-epic of a named period, whether the '20s or the '50s: for finally it is periodization and its styles which, as we shall see, are central to this new version of the form. The present as history nowadays requires us to turn it into just such a named period, and to endow it with a period style, on which we look back.

The film I wish to take as a point of departure here is however not a nostalgia film in the technical or generic sense, and I only need it to help me make a few points which will be useful later on. As so often in SF (in *Necromancer*, for example) the plot is borrowed from another genre, in this case the heist or caper film, even though it is here less a question of stealing a priceless object than of breaking and entering the mind of another character, in order to modify a crucial decision. But what is crucial here, and original in Christopher Nolan's film *Inception* (2010), is that its working premise is neither magical nor subjective. Indeed, as with much of modern philosophy, it evades the subject/object division altogether, by way of a new distribution of elements: the team is able, collectively, to enter the "mind" of the target by modifying it objectively in order to secure another outcome and a different decision. But the "real" cast of characters of the targeted individual's mind and environment persist in being and remain in place; and the plot is animated by their sense of an intrusion and a violation by the team of thieves and by the collective hostility they are able to marshall in opposition—a device which advances the action but is of no further interest to us here. What is significant is that this new system advances cinema itself to the degree to which it absolutely repudiates the latter's older conventions of subjectivity. These are neither dream-sequences of the traditional kind, nor hallucinations, nor even flash-backs. (It is ironic that the film DiCaprio made immediately before this one, Scorsese's *Shutter Island*, was a pastiche of all these old subjective illusions, thereby risking a fatal misunderstanding on the part of the public of *Inception* and leading it to misconstrue its true originality.) At best, today, the flashback is underscored by a shift from color (the present) to black-and-white or sepia (the past); but most often by a radical shift in style, so that a memory of the '30s, for example, is staged in the manner of '30s films. (I believe it was Ingmar Bergman who pioneered this device in the magnificent silent-movie sequence of *Sawdust and Tinsel* [1953].) The use of style itself as an index or a connotation (in Barthes' early sense) is important, and we will come back to it later.

But the contemporaneity of *Inception* (its postmodernity rather than its postmodernism) is to be found in this aesthetic of an absolute present, where, as Adorno warned about late capitalism, all negativity has been tendentially reduced and extirpated—and this not only in his sense of the distances still maintained by critique and "critical theory," but even in the temporal sense of the gaps left by the past and the mirages fitfully generated by the future: an absolute reduction to the present (what Adorno called "nominalism") and a mesmerization by the empirically and sensorially existent. Film always moved towards this absolute plenitude of a present of sight and sound: *Inception* has "motivated the device" (to use Shklovsky's expression for the rationalization of an aesthetic necessity) and has turned what was a historic tendency into a one-time structural premise. To which we may also add two more features: the modification of architecture around stable characters is very consistent with the structural alternatives just outlined for the temporary historical novel itself; and the fact that the newly invented environment or constructed world is a Potemkin-like projection which only exists in the general and not in the detail strongly confirms its relationship to stereotypes (and images) rather than to an older mimetic realism.

Now we can draw the lessons we need from *Inception*: the various situations it needs to construct around its targeted characters are also so many worlds which need to be coordinated in some way. The Golden Age of SF did this by means of that narrative part of speech I will call the doorway: the portal whereby a bemused character of van Vogt stepped from her darkened rundown North American bedroom into an exotic landscape (bright with sun, tropical in its vegetation).[42]

To be sure, all narrative requires such syntactical conjunction: "the art of transitions," as Wagner called it, and as Flaubert practiced it. The historians conventionally called upon that fictional category named Causality to do this work for them and to suture their disparate moments, the heterogeneity of their times and places. But causality has fallen into a neglect justified by philosophical skepticism and just that nominalism diagnosed by Adorno; and one cannot say that its

---

[42] See my *Archaeologies of the Future*, London: Verso, 2005, chapter 6.

much-maligned "linear history" has been any better served by loops and cyclical time, simultaneities and alternate worlds, repetitions and eternal returns, the demon of analogy, and the various other conceits remaining at the bottom of the tool-kit of Western grand narratives.

What is not wrong about these attempts, however, is that they confirm the implication—in Deleuze's formulations of "the image of thought," for example[43]—that what is needed is not so much a new theory or system, as precisely a new image of time, a one-time ad-hoc invention which can be discarded after productive use: "shapes of time," to use George Kubler's useful formula,[44] against which Lyotardian incredulity is quite unnecessary, since no one really believes in them in the first place. Still, here are a few:

> It is difficult to tabulate dates from different calendars, for example, speculative Biblical dates against confirmed Roman dates. This leads drafters of time-lines to experiment with almost every imaginable graphic design. A survey of the history of time-lines reveals time-"lines" pictured as time-trees, time-rivers, concentric time-wheels, kaballistic time-bodies, frenzied gothic lines, time-mazes, time-atlases, time-hydraulics, time-cartoons, time-palaces, Doomsday docks and astrological convergence-charts, palm-lines readied for chronological palm-reading, immense fold-out "synchronologies," and time-line graphics that look more like piles of hair or over-wired computer chips.[45]

The shape *Inception* provides us with is that of its massive central elevator, which rises and falls to the levels of its various worlds, its portals opening on past or future indifferently, and on the weathers of the globe's named spaces and the interiors—modern or antique, glass or dark wood—of its innumerable yet distinct and disjoined situations.

The historical novel today must be seen as an immense elevator that moves us up and down in time, its sickening lifts and dips corresponding to the euphoric or dystopian mood in which we wait for the doors to open. For historicity today—an acute consciousness of what Heidegger would call the historicality of our historical situations—demands a temporal span far exceeding the biological limits of the individual human organism: so that the life of a single character—world-historical or not—can scarcely accommodate it;

---

43 Gilles Deleuze and Felix Guattari, *Qu'est-ce que la philosophie?*, Paris: Éditions de Minuit, 1991, 39.

44 George Kubler, *The Shape of Time*, New Haven: Yale, 1962.

45 Jay Lampert, *Simultaneity and Delay*, London: Continuum, 2012, 3.

nor even the meager variety of our own chronological experiences of a limited national time and place.

The traditional historians placidly enumerated their chronicles with little enough existential anxiety, when they did not mark their materials as legendary hearsay or myths swimming up from the distant past. (Indeed, they rarely possessed a conception of such "distance" in the past, all their stories told "as if" of yesterday.) Novelists have not had it much easier: Kim Stanley Robinson's immense counterfactual epic of an alternate world[46] has recourse to reincarnation in order to control his temporal open spaces and to preserve the identity of his ambassadors to History.

Inception's problem in this respect is somewhat different: it must ward off those illusions and categories of a bad subjectivity we have already denounced, and prevent characters and audience alike from falling into the trance of "virtual dream" or a P. K. Dick-inspired schizophrenic hallucination. The trick will be turned by way of a small and insignificant object, about which much might be said philosophically: it is the small and quite undistinguished "jack" (as in the game of jacks) which DiCaprio carries in his pocket and which assures the passage of identity from one world to another. Neither fetish nor token, with neither use nor exchange value, by definition a "lost object" (as beneath a sofa cushion) which must not be lost at all costs, the skeleton of an object, its abstraction, a cube reduced to a few transversal bars so denuded you can scarcely tell their color—the little jack is the Lacanian "quilting point" or "upholstery nail" that holds all this together; and History also needs just such a material leitmotif, which might be a birthmark, a tell-tale word, or any other inconspicuous material sign whose presence is enough to reassure us that history has a meaning after all. Or such is the constructional conceit of *Cloud Atlas*, that unique contemporary "historical novel" with which we will conclude this essay.

---

[46] Kim Stanley Robinson, *The Years of Rice and Salt*, New York: Bantam, 2002. The lifetime allotted to the historical observer is obviously a crucial problem for the representation of long-term change, inasmuch as our biological existence does not correspond to the temporal rhythms of socio-economic history. Woolf's *Orlando* solves it one way, Luther Blissett's *Q* another (mainly by distracting you from calculating the protagonist's real age; its authors are the Italian collective now known as Wu Ming, Chinese for "anonymous.") Meanwhile there are still the continuities of the family novel available in those parts of the world where remnants of the clan system still persist, but no longer in the "West."

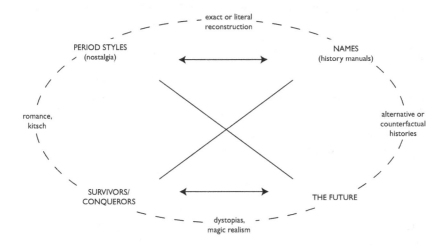

This is an elevator of a novel that stops briefly at a number of disparate floors on its way to the far future; and their relation to each other in space and time is preponderantly centered on the Pacific Rim—with some Scottish and Belgian exceptions—and connected in the unmistakable zigzags by which a hacker conceals the source of his transmission, or the random order on a bookshelf of a set of travel guides and memoirs jumbled in their dates and places in time. This unsystematic stacking of unfinished manuscripts which might have remained buried in various drawers stimulates that unconscious part of the dream work Freud called *Überdeterminierung* (a word since hijacked for other theoretical, but paradoxically not unhistoriographic, purposes) in which, in its function as "secondary elaboration" (an earlier translation I prefer), it impels us to invent as many connections and cross-references as we can think of in an ongoing process. Probably all of modernism arouses this not necessarily admirable drive we often assimilate to Interpretation as such; but here, at least, we can wonder whether the interest lies in the content of such symbolic themes and interconnections or in the ontological foregrounding of the process itself.

At any rate, a composition planned by the young composer-protagonist of one of the earlier segments lays out the plan of his Cloud Atlas Sextet in a fairly inescapable hint:

> overlapping soloists: piano, clarinet, cello, flute, oboe and violin, each in its own language of key, scale and color. In the first set, each solo is interrupted by its successor: in the second, each interruption is reconstituted, in order.

> Revolutionary or gimmicky? Shan't know until it's finished, and by then it'll be too late.[47]

The sextet, and thus by extension and magnification the novel itself, both practice what may be called an aesthetic of singularity, in which what is constructed is not meant to be the elaboration of a style or the practice of a genre (even a newly hinted one), but rather the experimental projection of a single one-time conceit, unimitable and without a legacy or any intention of founding a tradition formal or otherwise: not a new style, but the assemblage of various styles, as we shall see.

So we begin with 1) a narrative of the sea and of Pacific colonization, whose hero is a lawyer traveling halfway around the world to execute a contract—shades of Jonathan Harker!—in a Melvillian world which follows the footsteps of Captain Cook, reminiscent of *Mason and Dixon*, until we realize that the confusion it generates between an eighteenth-century journal or daybook and the nineteenth-century reality of its squalid colonies is simply the continuity of a whole world to which the steamship will in a year or two put an end; 2) a fin-de-siècle or *symboliste* drama in which the fictionalized life of the young composer who helped the semi-paralyzed Delius write his final works is expressed in cynical letters which combine the autonomy of art and a semi-incestuous eroticism à la Thomas Mann; 3) a corporate thriller about a young investigative reporter exposing the ecological predations concealed behind government contracts in a California setting; 4) a first-person and very British gossip-columnist memoir of an impecunious and aging upper-class publisher whose family has confined him ito an old-person's home; 5) a Science-Fictional far-future dystopia about the repression of androids in one of those North-Korean dictatorial fantasies which have suddenly become so popular (see also *The Orphan Father's Son*) as though in an informational universe this last hermetically sealed non-nation-state were the final place in which our bleaker imaginations of the future could still run riot, although furnished with rudimentary SF technology and pajamas à la Star Trek; 6) a post-Holocaust reversion to simple village life on a Hawaii menaced by more advanced and bloodthirsty neighboring tribes and told in the manner of *Huckleberry Finn*, intersecting with a small surviving minority of

---

[47] David Mitchell, *Cloud Atlas*, New York: Random House, 2004, 445. Page numbers in text refer to this edition.

scientifically trained and knowledgeable experts from a future now past, much as the inhabitants of Camelot confront the Connecticut Yankee.

A variety of genres surely, about which it is hard to say whether any one of them brought to true novelistic completion would be finally worth reading in its own right. The combination certainly incites us to wonder whether it is a random sample, or whether taken together these episodes somehow form a coherent picture of the stereotypes which govern our current view of history, past, present and future, or even project some ideal caricature of that Pacific Rim culture to which David Mitchell (himself an Englishman) seems personally attached. If so, then the selection, whose arbitrariness somehow does not seem arbitrary in the reading of it, has that legitimacy of authentic dead pasts and dead futures, the legitimacy of our own collective Imaginary, as I have suggested, however spurious its details might be. But it is not clear to me that the combination—Bruges, the South Seas, nuclear power plants on the San Andreas Fault, British gangsters and skinheads, let alone North Korean dystopias and neolithic Hawaian villages—exhaust our cultural and historical stereotypes, even the mass-cultural ones. That they offer some kind of grand narrative, however, does seem to me to be the case, or at least they make the search for one somehow inevitable and unavoidable. But is this inclusion of two Science-Fictional futures enough to justify the characterization of *Cloud Atlas* as a new form of the historical novel defined by its relation to future fully as much as to past?

The great television interviewer Larry King was once asked the kind of question with which he liked to probe his own celebrities, namely what his own attitude—now retired himself and "getting on in years" as people say—was towards death. His memorable answer ran as follows: the worst thing about dying is that I will never find out what comes next. You may feel that this forthright answer blurts out a doubly unacceptable submission to the plot of linear history. Still, it has the merit of reminding us of a historicity we rarely take into account in this age of extraordinarily intricate and paradoxical theories of time and history, and it certainly characterizes the most striking feature of the experience of reading *Cloud Atlas*.[48]

---

[48] It might be well at this point to take into account Jean-François Lyotard's novel interpretation of the Kantian sublime in temporal terms, as the terror "kindled by the threat of nothing further happening." J-F Lyotard, "The Sublime and The Avant-Garde," in *The Inhuman*, Stanford: Stanford University Press, 1991, 99.

For we do want to find out what can possibly come next, in this series of stories broken off as surely as Sheherezade's; and while the rather disreputable notion of mere garden-variety suspense lies ready to hand, it scarcely suffices to cover the suspense we are also made to feel about history itself in the peculiar structure of this novel. I want to say, with Victor Hugo, that this masks that; and that the philosophical question about future history and indeed about the future history of the planet itself is one which all true historical novels must raise today. That "*grand récit*" is then subtly displaced and substituted by the "language game" of the unfinished narratives and their succession. We do not stop asking the illicit question about the former, modestly resigning ourselves to the latter in its absence; we use the latter to pose the former, which we ask through its material disguise. We do not, after all, ask the question, What happens next? at the end of *Waverley* or *War and Peace*, nor even after *Gone with the Wind* or *Shogun*.[49]

The trick is of course the substitution of one form of curiosity with another: for the anxiety about what happens next in history is substituted our immediate concern about what happens next in the cliffhanger we are reading right now. It is a stepped structure, in which we read the beginnings of the various stories in chronological order, reversing our direction at the apex where we descend the other slope, closing each narrative parenthesis until we reach our beginning again (which is not, of course, our own present.) So a smaller "language-game" answer is provided for each "grand-narrative" question, and instead of the satisfaction of learning our ultimate destiny, we are given that of solving riddles that move further and further into the past, concluding with the sequel and happy ending to Adam Ewing's *Pacific Journal* of 1849 which opened the text. Has *Cloud Atlas* then succeeded in making the whale-like bulk of History heave into view even briefly like the marine life Adam Ewing views from his railing? The historicity of Mitchell's novel derives from a good deal more than its unique form which we have associated with the most famous and illustrious collection of tales in existence (offering yet another "image of the thought of time" not noted in our previous enumerations), but

---

[49] But in SF the ending is sometimes achieved by positing a future of this future, as in London's *The Iron Heel* (or the withdrawal of the camera into a far future at the end of *Road Warrior*):

And they are gone–ay, ages long ago
These lovers fled away into the storm.

which also takes the linguistic form of embedding, or the intercalation within a simple-sentence syntax of all manner of dependent clauses. The anthropological linguists, indeed, believe that this form is at the origin of properly human thought itself; while its most outlandish embodiment is to be found in that most peculiar of all modernist artifacts, the *Nouvelles Impressions d'Afrique* of Raymond Roussel, a poem in the form of one gigantic sentence within which parentheses begin to open within parentheses until, at the other side of the watershed, they start to close again, much to the reader's relief, whose human mind, it should be added, is structurally incapable of recalling their beginnings after a very limited opening number. (How high can the Unconscious count? was indeed a favorite problem on which Lacan liked to ruminate.)

The truly historical nature of *Cloud Atlas*'s materials lies elsewhere, however, and takes two possibly related forms. The first can be identified as the postmodern practice of pastiche, which offers one answer to our positioning of this work in opposition to those founded on a postmodern play with historical names. The latter was indeed posited as the formal descendent of a high Lukácsian historical realism in which world-historical named individuals constituted a horizon of event and a mid-range of summits in the middle distance. The position we are trying to block out here would then be the alternate one of the novel of the anonymous masses, the movements of the peoples, the historical period itself (whose events are little more than its symptoms). It is a dimension of history we have associated in passing with nostalgia film, and it is time to reveal the deeper kinship of this contemporary version with pastiche, or in other words with historical periods grasped as styles. If the aesthetic of the modern consisted in the effort to invent new styles as so many approaches to the Absolute, the postmodern, ratifying the exhaustion of that project and of the possibilities available to it, now indexes the styles it left behind as so many modes in which periodization is reified and available in a kind of postmodern forgery in the loftiest sense (forgers of great talent working their reincarnations effectively as holograms or androids). To be sure, there remains a necessary and causal relationship between form and content here, where the latter provides the raw material demanded by the style in question in order to be reproduced. Yet style, besides being a historical category in the spirit of the modernist aesthetic (as a historical moment in its own right), is also anthropologically historical in the deeper sense of what constitutes the superstructure of a mode of production as such, or at least what can be recovered and described of that superstructure.

It is therefore of no little significance that *Cloud Atlas* proceeds by a series of distinct genres and pastiches. Unlike a modernist equivalent, such as the "Oxen of the Sun" chapter of Joyce's *Ulysses*, which purports to follow the evolution of English style from its earliest beginnings, as an analogue of the formation of the embryo in the womb (it takes place in a maternity hospital), the generic sequences of *Cloud Atlas* mime style as the evolution of taste, experience and the social constraints that determine "adventure" in history, beginning with English seamen's limited thoughts on what constitutes civilized, or on the contrary "uncivilized," behavior. This is the sense in which the final Hawaiian episode can perhaps be considered a picture of regression and the collapse of "civilization" as such, the reversion to barbarism. Once again, however, the form plays tricks on us, as it substitutes a different kind of cyclical reversion—the gradual working our way back down through the episodes to the initial Pacific journal—for the larger cyclical "philosophy of history" or grand narrative implied by this particular far future.

But this is only one of the language games, or experiments of time, that *Cloud Atlas* has in store for us. A beginning, a middle, and an ending, but not necessarily in that order, a great filmmaker once said, neglecting to add that they could not only be shuffled and rearranged at will but also superimposed within a single framework. For in *Cloud Atlas*, and from a different perspective, we may say that the endings come in the middle, at the moment of reaching the farthest point "that thought can reach"; and these points are very familiar to us, since they are the farthest points our own thought can reach, namely dystopia and regression, world dictatorship and the reversion to savagery, civilization and barbarism, *1984* and *Road Warrior*, states and nomads, with their respective lines of flight in religion and science, the transmission of salvational legend and the safeguarding of the last great scientific discoveries. *Cloud Atlas* thereby fulfills one of the great indispensable functions of ideological analysis: namely to show the contradictions in which we are ourselves imprisoned, the opposition beyond which we cannot think. These alternatives are today and for the moment the only ways in which we can imagine our future, the future of late capitalism; and it is only by shattering their twin dominion that we might conceivably be able again to think politically and productively, to envisage a condition of genuine revolutionary difference, to begin once again to think Utopia. Meanwhile, we are here abandoned with our twin absolute limits, take your choice, no other futures conceivable, so that relief has to come in the gradual stepping back down from those twin inevitabilities onto the respective happy endings in reverse order, ending up in the past of our own present, in a nineteenth century that looks more like our eighteenth century, Captain Cook instead of Melville, a past present already resolved and reassuringly over for us and simpler than our own unfinished problems: not the present as history but the future as over and done with.

There is, however, yet another history hidden in these sequences, one perhaps more materialistic than the stylistic variations, even though intimately associated with them; and that is what must be called the medium as such. Each segment, each story, is indeed registered by a different material apparatus of transmission, so that to that extent *Cloud Atlas* offers a kind of experimental history, not so much of styles and events, as rather of communicational technology: indeed the deeper continuity of the work, itself a kind of narrative one, if you like, but an inconspicuously narrative thread at that, lies in the ingenious linkage of each of these segments to the next one, which at one point or another explicitly thematizes it. Thus Adam Ewing's handwritten seaboard journal partially survives into the second segment, where it is read by the composer with some interest (the missing part is then found in the concluding sequence). As for the composer (whose Sextet is actually played in a number of contexts later on), he writes letters, some of which are read by the reporter in the third segment (and the rest of the packet appropriately rediscovered in its concluding sequel). As for the reporter herself, whose adventures we imagine we are reading as a straightforward narrative, the latter is in fact a manuscript submitted to the publisher-protagonist of the fourth segment, whose story we also imagine "*en direct*," until we find that it has been made into a fiction film, viewed in the far future of the next segment. That one is in fact Suonmi's interrogation by her executioners and has been registered on a kind of hologram device, which has been preserved somehow into the still farther future, inasmuch as she has by then been transformed into the central figure of a new religion, to whom the final narrator prays. So the heterogeneity of narratives has been revealed to be a multiplicity of informational and communicational technologies, à la Kittler; and thereby a materialist infrastructure of narrative and historiography restored, much as in *Krapp's Last Tape* it is the tape player itself who becomes the central figure and interlocutor on an empty stage.[50]

The term "postmodern novel" seems indeed to have become a generic category in recent years; but it is important to distinguish this kind of materiality of the communicational systems from the complacent writing about writing that the term generally designates. The effects here are on the contrary reminiscent of those of the *nouveau roman* rather than of Gide's *Counterfeiters*. In Robbe-Grillet, for example, we find descriptions of a suitably sadistic kind in which a naked young woman is described, bound and gagged by some unknown assailant. As in certain moments of cinema, however, the uncertainty as to whether the shot is "objective" or "subjective," whether in other words we are witnessing the scene through the eyes of another character or merely from the neutral vantage point of the camera, comes into play in a more specifically literary or linguistic mode: the next sentence draws back, as it were, away from what turns out to have been a keyhole, and the hitherto living and writhing victim turns out to be a semi-pornographic photograph on the cover of a magazine. It is a shock effect which on the one hand turns

---

50 I have been interested in the adaptation of novels into films for too long to be able to avoid commenting on the ambitious new film version of *Cloud Atlas* (directed by the Wachowskis and Tom Tykwer, 2012). My conclusion (see my Afterword to Colin MacCabe, et al., eds., *True to the Spirit*, Oxford: Oxford University Press, 2011) was that unless both are bad, either the original or the film adaptation must necessarily be superior to its opposite number. If both are equal in value and impact (as for example in the Lem/Tarkovsky *Solaris* texts), then each will necessarily be radically different in spirit from the other. The film version of *Cloud Atlas* would seem to refute these conclusions and in particular to offer an instance in which some equivalence is achieved. Yet here, I think, one has only to recall the great Dickens adaptations of the immediate postwar period, and it will begin to dawn on us that these films (and the excellent *Cloud Atlas* film along with them) are not filmic as much as dramatic adaptations, as it were for the stage, with prodigious feats of character acting, of which one can agree that, yes, the Beadle must have been something like that, the young composer must have been something like this. These performances, then, do not cancel out other versions, as a genuine filmic adaptation always seems to do (Laurence Olivier will always be Heathcliff, no matter what new versions are presented, and without any thought as to what this permanent identification might do to the book). So the film version of Mitchell's novel may not be a great film, even though one cannot say that it is inferior to the book, but it is a magnificent collection of performances. I would also want to add, and this is a more serious critique, that the medium has the unfortunate effect of reifying all the thematic references (the birthmark, for example), thereby unifying its time scheme illicitly into this or that religious or supernatural interpretation, which the novel so subtly evades.

(fictional) reality into an image, and on the other foregrounds the medium itself in what I have called a materialistic fashion.

In *Cloud Atlas* this is something that happens *après coup*, as it were, and retroactively, after we have moved into the next-story segment which reveals the nature of what we have been reading in the last. I am tempted to see this as a serious defamiliarization of the whole ideological thematics of information and communication which has become omnipresent today and a virtually official philosophy of the postmodern. This intrusion of technological consciousness into the reading process at once demotes that official philosophy to a conceptual reflex of the mode of production and in its own way rewrites the history of the alleged "break" of the newer technologies with the older modern ones. It is in any case significant that *Cloud Atlas* overleaps the moment of computers and the Internet in its temporally ambitious chronology, and stages our own present as historical by diminishing it to a passing stage between nostalgia-pasts and a Science-Fictional far future.

I have been promoting the idea that the most valuable works are those that make their points by way of form rather than content, that relativize their themes and ideas, their "meanings," to the benefit of formal demonstrations that do not require interpretation to "produce" their problems (or their problematic, to revive a useful word from yesteryear). Indeed, Lyotard's very notion of the "*grand récit*" aimed in a parallel direction, it seems to me, insofar as the "philosophies of history" he denounced (liberalism and Marxism) all in one way or another involved the transformation of history into ideas and meanings: the one "freedom," the other "emancipation." So it was not so much narrative that he was calling into question as rather the illicit interpretation of narrative by the organization of equally illicit continuities: Hegel is here the fundamental paradigm, even though his notion of the movement of human history towards an ever greater realization of freedom was argued in subtle and complex fashion by way of his conception of the "ruses" of History or Reason—something like an unconscious of history in a quasi-pre-Freudian sense.

But *Cloud Atlas*, alas, does also seem to have a meaning and an interpretation of that kind (and ironically one in which freedom and emancipation are conjoined, as it turns out). For it is a history of imprisonments: the enslavement of the Moriori, the confinement of Ewing to his exiguous cabin, the penniless destitution of the young composer, the surveillance of the atomic energy site, the confinement of the elderly publisher, the arrest and condemnation of the android, and finally the island itself, on which the more peaceful inhabitants are threatened by a seemingly invincible warlike tribe next door. But in the second part—the descending curve of the stacked narratives—these desperate situations are all somehow resolved, and happy endings provided to what looked like any number of nightmares of History. Do we then have to accept this authorial intention, which has been reinforced by any number of demonstrations of the inherent evil of mankind: "the weak are meat, the strong do eat" (503)? Or is this particular "philosophy of history" simply thrown out, like the repetitive patterns, as a sop to the reader who still needs "meanings"?

Yet this immense glissando through all the styles and affects of history, whose unremitting greed it handles with comic precision, leaves behind it the taste of that immemorial cruelty which is human history itself and which Hegel could only think of as one endless slaughterhouse. The joyousness of this art, captured page by page by the thematics of transmission and the technological media, is scarcely contradicted by our other sense of prolonged horror, itself not cancelled either by the salvational assurance that we have come through! We have escaped the inevitable, inescapable peril, and the doom of history's desperate and repeated emprisonments, and are still alive! The far-future of the scientific survivors, reminding us of Kim Stanley Robinson's insistence on science as the true non-alienated labor as which art was once seen, is radically distinct from this closing quasi-religious devotion of Adam Ewing to his new mission; and yet the two strands, sheerly ideological in the isolation of each, are comparable to distinct orchestral voices heard together, as at one and the same time are the notes of cannibalistic violence and unremitting greed scarcely effaced from this articulate mass of sound by its other dimensions. The aestheticians return again and again to the problem of the extra-artistic and referential dimensions of art, in its shabby ideological messages and its altogether insufficient and rather pitiful calls to this or that action, this or that indignation or "call to arms" (as Lu Xun put it), this or that coming to consciousness. But the moment of the aesthetic is not that call but rather its reminder that all those impulses exist: the revolutionary Utopian one fully as much as the immense disgust with human evil, Brecht's "temptation of the good," the will to escape and to be free, the delight in craftsmanship and production, the implacably satiric, unremittingly skeptical gaze. Art has no function but to reawaken all these differences at once in an ephemeral instant; and the historical novel no function save to resurrect for one more brief moment their multitudinous coexistence in History itself. After that, the reader sinks back into the current situation, which may or may not have some similarity to what has just been glimpsed.

So it is that Lukács' warning about "modernization" in the historical novel, recreating the past in the image of ourselves and omitting its radical difference and the originalities of its cultures and miseries, its class oppressions, turns into something like the injunction of the Red Queen: getting so far ahead of ourselves that only our imaginary futures are adequate to do justice to our present, whose once buried pasts have all vanished into our presentism. "Our philosophies" want to absorb all these foreign totalities as identical with us and flesh of our flesh; Science Fiction wants desperately to affirm them as different and as alien, in its quest for imaginary futures. In an ideal world, perhaps, they would be different and identical all at once at one and the same time: at any rate, for better or for worse, our history, our historical past and our historical novels, must now also include our historical futures as well.

Index

Ackermann, Virgil, 291
Adam Bede (Eliot), 122, 155, 159
Adorno, Theodor, 35, 190, 225, 235, 300
The Aesthetics of Resistance (Weiss),
    202n10
Aethiopica, 195
affect, 10, 27–44, 46–93, 139;
    autonomization of, 35–6, 38,
    50, 55, 65; and body, 28, 32, 42,
    98; denarrativizes action, 83; and
    destiny, 50, 186; disappearance of,
    191; and emotion, 29, 32, 40, 44,
    73; and everyday, 143, 153, 184;
    and language, 37; and literature,
    184; and material support, 65,
    69–70; and melancholia, 71–2,
    148; and modernity, 34; and
    music, 38–40; and naming, 30–1,
    34–5, 166; and narrative, 76, 83,
    85; and perception, 43, 49; and
    psychology, 78, 154; and realism,
    10, 76, 140; realism after, 187–9;
    and revolution in form, 40; and
    scene, 240; and subject, 92; and
    tales, 35; unequaled in Tolstoy, 93
Affective Mapping (Flatley), 29n4
Afghanistan, 234
Agamben, Giorgio, 91
Aldridge, John, 257
Althusser, Louis, 169
Altman, Robert, 197, 231; *Short Cuts*,
    230
Ancient Society (Morgan), 264

Anderson, Perry, 147n16, 259–60, 279
Angenot, Marc, 128, 149
Anna Karenina (Tolstoy), 279
Annales school, 111, 259, 263, 282
antinomies, 2, 6, 11, 26, 69, 76, 83, 88,
    96, 108–9, 177, 201
Anti-Oedipus (Deleuze and Guattari), 28
Apuleius, *The Golden Ass*, 250
Archaeologies of the Future (Jameson),
    199n7, 300n42
L'Argent (Zola), 55, 70
Arikha, Noga, *Passions and the Tempers*,
    29n5
Aristotle, 1, 25, 29, 38n22, 78, 120, 168,
    182, 263, 268n10
The Art of the Novel (James), 22n13
article, (in)definite, 175n19
L'Assommoir (Zola), 56, 76
attention deficit disorder, 87
Auerbach, Erich, 1, 27, 141–3, 153,
    163, 167; on everyday, 142–3; on
    mimesis, 3–4
Augustine, 199n9
Austen, Jane, 164
autonomization, 35–6, 38, 50–5, 65,
    153, 288. *See also* Zola, Émile,
    sensory automatization in

Bachelard, Gaston, 38
bad faith, 129–37, 228; and narrative,
    135–7
Bakhtin, Mikhail, 138, 287; "Epic and
    Novel," 3

Balzac, Honoré de, 8, 22, 32, 37,
50–1, 66, 71, 99, 110, 112, 146,
147n15, 153–4, 156, 161, 179,
210, 217–18, 223–4, 229, 231,
264, 266, 271–2, 275, 286;
characters in, 183; Engels on,
270; *Eugénie Grandet*, 96; *Histoire
des Treize*, 218–19; and historical
novel, 272–3; as know-it-all, 217;
retour des personnages, 96, 108;
and senses, 32–4
Banfield, Ann, 164
Barthes, Roland, 9, 23, 64, 86, 178, 187,
211, 300; and modernity, 33; on
novel, 161–2; reality effect, 34,
36–7; *Writing Degree Zero*, 36
Baudelaire, Charles, 20, 32, 34–5, 42,
55, 69, 72, 146, 153, 179
Beethoven, Ludwig van, 39
Being and Nothingness (Sartre), 171
Benjamin, Walter, 20, 23, 72n24; "The
Storyteller," 19
Bennett, Arnold, 166n5
Bergman, Ingmar, 300
La bête humaine (Zola), 25
Betrothed (Manzoni), 266–7
Bierce, Ambrose, 248
Bildungsroman, 145–6, 150, 152, 203,
235
binary opposition, 2, 7, 29, 73, 115. *See
also* antinomies; ethical binary
biography, 268, 288
Blissett, Luther, 302n46
Bloch, Ernst, 229
Blumenberg, Hans, 196
Boccaccio, Giovanni, 23–5; *The
Decameron*, 23
body, 28, 256; and affect, 28, 32,
42; bourgeois, 32, 34, 42, 65;
character becomes, 76; and
language, 32; new dimensions of,
59
Au Bonheur des Dames (Zola), 57
Booth, Wayne, 99, 164, 180
boredom, 30. *See also* distraction
Borie, Jean, 95

Bourdieu, Pierre, 190, 297
bourgeois: and body, 32, 34, 42, 65;
decadence, 268; and déclassement,
149; literature, 286; novelists, 102,
113; order, 278; and realism, 5;
society, 107, 109, 146, 148, 271;
and temporality, 28; terror, 197;
writers, 177
Bouvard and Pécuchet (Flaubert), 45,
214
Boyle, Nicholas, 204
Brecht, Bertolt, 133, 160, 167, 174, 249,
261–2, 312
Brennan, Teresa, *The Transmission of
Affect*, 35, 92
Buñuel, Luis, 45, 148
Burke, Edmund, 286
Burke, Kenneth, 234, 239, 261
butterfly passion, 86

carnival, 286–7
Carver, Raymond, 191, 230
Casalduero, Joaquin, 108
cataphora, 165, 176
Cavell, Stanley, 169
Cervantes, Miguel de, 100; *Don Quijote*,
4, 113, 139, 248; literary impact,
139n1
Cézanne, Paul, 56
chance, 202, 205, 208; and destiny, 204.
See also contingency
chapter as form, 179
characters: dialogue, 98; in Eliot, 126–7;
existential states of, 97; in Galdós,
96–113; minor/secondary,
99–113, 126; supersession of, 183,
240, 242; in Tolstoy, 88–92, 285;
view of, 182–3; in Zola, 76. *See
also* hero; protagonist; villain
The Charterhouse of Parma (Stendhal),
232, 273
Chernyshevsky, Nikolay, 79, 215
China, 180
chromaticism, 41
cinema *See* film
civilization, 72n24, 80, 86. *See also* society

class: déclassement, 148–9; and
    ethics, 212; and literature, 149;
    lower classes appear, 263; and
    naturalism, 149–50
Clausewitz, Carl von, 239
Cloud Atlas (Mitchell), 302–12;
    ideological analysis of, 308
Coleridge, Samuel Taylor, 140
collective, 261, 273, 296; and historical
    novel, 267, 273, 280; and history,
    267; and individual, 200–2, 262;
    and representation, 280–2; and
    revolution, 276; and war, 235–7;
    will of people, 282–3
Conrad, Joseph, *Secret Agent*, 214
consciousness, 78, 129; impersonal, 169,
    171; impersonality of, 25, 183;
    self-, 130–1
conspiracy: and history, 267; and
    providence, 219–20
contingency, 37, 52, 202. *See also* chance
Cooper, Fenimore, 241, 266, 274
corruption, 50, 278–9
The Counterfeiters (Gide), 17
Craft of Fiction (Lubbock), 21
Crane, Stephen, *Red Badge of Courage*,
    235
Le crime de M. Lange (Renoir), 108
La Curée (Zola), 46–50

Dahlhaus, Carl, 70
Daniel Deronda (Eliot), 123–4, 130,
    155–6, 158–9, 161
Danton, Georges, 277–8
Davidson, Neil, 271n15
de Man, Paul, 164
Débâcle (Zola), 43, 66, 74, 93
The Decameron (Boccaccio), 23
déclassement, 148–9
deconstruction, 223–4, 252
defamiliarization *See* ostranenie
Defoe, Daniel, 203, 212; *Robinson
    Crusoe*, 202, 248
Deleuze, Gilles, 7, 28, 36, 45, 64, 70,
    121, 148, 190, 237, 265, 293,
    297, 301; *Anti-Oedipus*, 28

Derrida, Jacques, 6, 209n17
Descartes, René, 29
description, 33, 48, 163; and affect,
    51–2; transformation of, 50–1
Desmoulins, Camille, 278
destiny, 21, 46, 75–6, 121, 149; and
    affect, 50, 186; and chance,
    204; deconstruction of ideology
    of, 223; vs eternal present, 26;
    and everyday, 184; individual vs
    collective, 200–2; and money,
    224; predestination, 199–201;
    and reality, 143; and tale, 182; waning
    of, 109, 160. *See also* irrevocable
diachrony/synchrony, 227–9
dialogue, 98
DiCaprio, Leonardo, 299, 302
Dick, Philip K., 197–9, 302; *Do Androids
    Dream of Electric Sheep?*, 294;
    Martian Time-Slip, 197; *Now Wait
    for Last Year*, 291
Dickens, Charles, 148, 153, 156, 179,
    197, 215, 222, 225, 274; *Bleak
    House*, 213, 221, 224; as know-it-
    all, 217; *Our Mutual Friend*, 220;
    Pickwick Papers, 96; *The Tale of
    Two Cities*, 213
distraction: in Galdós, 102; in Tolstoy,
    86–8. *See also* boredom
Do Androids Dream of Electric Sheep?
    (Dick), 294
Döblin, Alfred, *Wallenstein*, 242–7
Le docteur Pascal (Zola), 74
Don Quijote (Cervantes), 4, 113, 139,
    248
Dos Passos, John, 222, 289, 291, 293
Dostoyevsky, Fyodor, 4, 22, 166n5, 170,
    226; on Tolstoy, 79

eccentric, 97
L'Education sentimentale (Flaubert), 179,
    214, 272
Eikhenbaum, Boris, 79, 81–3, 88–90,
    238n3, 280
Einstein, Albert, 229
Eisenstein, Sergei, 20; *October*, 286

Eisler, Hanns, 62
ekphrasis, 8, 51, 163
Eliot, George, 8, 98, 109–10, 113,
    120–35, 139, 156, 226–30, 274,
    289; *Adam Bede*, 122, 155, 159;
    and bad faith, 130–7; characters
    in, 126–7; *Daniel Deronda*, 123–4,
    130, 155–6, 158–9, 161; evil in,
    122, 128, 133; *Felix Holt*, 155,
    158; history as whispering gallery,
    228; and melodrama, 156–7,
    161; *Middlemarch*, 112, 123, 130,
    133, 155–7, 222–5, 228; *The Mill
    on the Floss*, 155, 161; multiple
    centers in, 121; Nietzsche on, 120;
    plot in, 124–5, 128; on point of
    view, 222; and politics, 157–60;
    psychological complexity in, 125;
    Romola, 123–4, 130, 133, 155,
    161, 213; *Silas Marner*, 155
Eliot, T. S., 72; *Murder in the Cathedral*,
    174; *The Waste Land*, 294
emotion, and affect, 29, 32, 40, 44, 73
Engels, Friedrich, 273; on Balzac, 270
epic, 167, 210; and novel, 265
equality, 109
eternal present, 24, 26, 28, 36, 39–41,
    99, 160, 176
ethical binary, 115–16, 120, 137,
    183. *See also* antinomies; binary
    opposition
ethics, 227; and class, 212
Eugénie Grandet (Balzac), 96
everyday, 142–3, 146–7, 153, 264; and
    affect, 143, 153, 184; and destiny,
    184; and narrative, 153; triumph
    of, 109
evil, 117–18, 121–3, 128–9, 137, 140,
    157, 227; and good, 115–16,
    120, 183; non-existence of, 122,
    133
existential novel, 184, 187

Fassbinder, Rainer Werner,
    Alexanderplatz, 207
fate *See* destiny

Faulkner, William, 96, 166n5, 175–7,
    180, 266; "now" in, 177, 180;
    Sanctuary, 176
Faust (Goethe), 122, 155, 159, 259
Fernandez, Ramon, 16–17
Ferris, David, 121, 156
Fichte, Johann Gottlieb, 61
fiction, 167, 174, 189; and nonfiction,
    253; science fiction, 197, 297–
    300. *See also* characters; literature;
    narrative; novel; plot
fictionality, 168, 190
film, 48, 51, 170, 178, 207, 236, 293,
    299, 310; crime, 236–7, 299;
    nostalgia, 298; theory, 136–7,
    140, 170, 178. *See also* individual
    filmmakers
finance *See* money
first-person narrative, 169–75, 177
Flatley, Jonathan, *Affective Mapping*,
    29n4
Flaubert, Gustave, 32–4, 37, 40, 42, 45,
    61, 72, 142, 156, 164, 178–9,
    215, 272, 300; *Bouvard and
    Pécuchet*, 45, 214; *L'Education
    sentimentale*, 179, 214, 272; and
    free indirect discourse, 164, 181;
    and irony, 181; *Madame Bovary*,
    45, 101, 124, 141, 148, 150–1,
    153, 180, 214; *Salammbô*, 72,
    213, 275; and *Ulysses*, 150–1, 153
Ford, Henry, 289–91
Ford, John, *Young Mr. Lincoln*, 289
Fortunata y Jacinta (Galdós), 100,
    102–5
La Fortune des Rougon (Zola), 50
Foucault, Michel, 32, 115–16, 199n8,
    288
Fourier, Charles, 86
Frankenstein (Shelley), 298
Frankfurt School, 1
free indirect discourse, 130, 135–6, 164,
    170, 175, 177–8, 180–1, 185
French Revolution, 146, 222, 262, 276,
    298
French theory, 136

Freud, Sigmund, 28, 86, 125, 129, 160, 190, 282, 286, 303, 311
Fried, Michael, 139–41, 154, 169, 174, 176
Frye, Northrop, 142, 195, 263
future, 309
future history, 306

Galdós, Pérez, 95–113, 139n1, 146, 185, 215, 274; characters in, 96–113, 153; *Fortunata y Jacinta*, 100, 102–5; as mimic, 98; *That Bringas Woman*, 97; triumph of everyday, 109
Gaultier, Jules de, 142
genre, 141–2, 144, 152; and novel, 138
Germinal (Zola), 76
ghost, 15, 212, 230
Gide, André, 16–17, 122, 258; *The Counterfeiters*, 17; on tale vs novel, 17
Gilman, Stephen, 100
Girard, René, 143
Goebbels, Joseph, 252
Goethe, Johann Wolfgang von, 19–20, 51n7, 92n20, 122, 167, 188, 203–5, 208–10, 237, 259, 289; *Faust*, 122, 155, 159, 259; "unerhörte Begebenheit," 188; *Wilhelm Meister*, 203, 208–9, 217
Gogol, Nikolai, 72, 170
The Golden Ass (Apuleius), 250
good, and evil, 115–16, 120, 183
Goody, Jack, 16n1
Griffith, D. W., 9
Grimmelshausen, Hans Jakob Christoffel von, *Simplicius Simplicissimus*, 248–51
Gross, Daniel M., *The Secret History of Emotion*, 29n5
Guattari, Félix, 28, 265, 297; *Anti-Oedipus*, 28
Guérin, Daniel, 278
Gunning, Tom, 9
Gustavus Adolfus (Strindberg), 237

Hadji Mourad (Tolstoy), 93
Hamburger, Käthe, 182; *The Logic of Literature*, 166–71
happiness, 81–3
happy endings, 195, 202, 230. *See also* providence
Hardt, Michael, 256
Harrow, Susan, 45
Hauser, Arnold, 2
Haussman, Georges-Eugène, 50, 55, 146
Hawthorne, Nathaniel, "My Kinsman, Major Molineux," 286
The Heart of Midlothian (Scott), 266–7, 269
Hegel, G. W. F., 7, 30, 113, 130–1, 167, 209–10, 226, 228, 233, 263–6, 299, 311–12; and novel, 210; on war, 258
Heidegger, Martin, 21, 38, 82, 136, 301
Hemingway, Ernest, 170, 191, 235
here and now, 168, 177, 180
heredity, 46, 50, 73–4, 76
hero, 20; backgrounding of, 96, 109, 111; and villain, 115; worship of, 91, 111, 288, 290
Heyse, Paul, 23
historical novel, 146–7, 151, 179, 213, 259–313; and Balzac, 272–3; characteristics of, 280; and collective, 267, 273, 280; extinction of, 275; first, 263; future of, 297–8; and history, 263; and names, 288; in question, 271; and realism, 262, 274; and revolution, 266; and Tolstoy, 285–6; and war, 266
The Historical Novel (Lukács), 111, 263–4
history, 262; and collective, 267; future, 306; and historical novel, 263; and names, 297; passage of, 216–17; as whispering gallery, 228; and Zola, 73–4
History and Class Consciousness (Lukács), 269
Hobbes, Thomas, *Leviathan*, 246

Hogg, James, 200–1
Homer, 165; *Odyssey*, 152
Horace, 165
Horkheimer, Max, 257
Hugo, Victor, 148, 154, 179, 272, 306
Humboldt, Alexander von, 293–4, 296
Husserl, Edmund, 167, 171

Ibsen, Henrik, 51; *Peer Gynt*, 20
identity, 78; and self, 25
ideology: providence, 223; of realism, 5–6
immanence, and transcendence, 211–12, 216
impersonality, 25, 169, 171, 183
impressionism, 41
Inception (Nolan), 299–302
individual, and collective, 200–2, 262
individualism, 209–10
Ingarden, Roman, 167; *Literary Work of Art*, 166
intensity, 36, 69–70, 72, 75–6
introspection, 209, 225
Iraq, 234
irony, 99, 175, 180–1, 191; and point of view, 181–2
irrevocable, 19–21. *See also* destiny

Jakobson, Roman, 89
James, Henry, 4, 21–3, 26, 51, 66, 82, 99, 101, 124, 155–7, 164, 179, 181, 214, 226; *The Art of the Novel*, 22n13; and point of view, 181, 183; *Prefaces*, 21; as writer, 182
Jameson, Fredric, 202n10; *The Ancients and the Postmoderns*, 231; *Archaeologies of the Future*, 199n7, 300n42; "The End of Temporality," 28; *The Modernist Papers*, 152n22; *The Poetics of Social Forms*, 11; *The Political Unconscious*, 147, 196; *A Singular Modernity*, 9n15, 187; *Valences of the Dialectic*, 262

Joyce, James, 222, 289; *Ulysses*, 25, 98, 150–3, 207, 216, 308; and *Madame Bovary*, 150–1, 153
jubilation, 221–2

Kant, Immanuel, 70, 116, 179, 199, 201, 222
Kehlmann, Daniel, 294, 296
Kierkegaard, Soren, 42
King, Larry, 305
Kittler, Friedrich, 309
Kleist, Heinrich von, 237, 293
Kluge, Alexander, 10, 188–9, 191–2, 251–4
knowledge, absolute, 217
Kubler, George, 301
Kubrick, Stanley, *Paths of Glory*, 238

La Rochefoucauld, 93
Lacan, Jacques, 89, 171, 197, 293, 307
landscape *See* scene
Lang, Fritz, *Metropolis*, 269
language: and affect, 37; and body, 32; comparisons of, 72, 82; and experience, 34; and historical transformation, 32; and literature, 166; and perception, 54; of protagonist, 99; "unspeakable sentences," 164. *See also* name/ naming
Laocoon (Lessing), 8
Latin America, 180
Lattimore, Owen, 265
Leavis, F. R., 156–7
Lenin, Vladimir, 1, 279, 285; on Tolstoy, 79, 285
Lessing, Gotthold Ephraim, *Laocoon*, 8
Lévi-Strauss, Claude, 297
Leviathan (Hobbes), 246
Levin, Harry, 152n21
life, 32
Literary Works of Art (Ingarden), 166
literature: and affect, 184; bourgeois, 286; and class, 149; and language, 166; and war, 271. *See also* characters; fiction; narrative; novel; plot

The Logic of Literature (Hamburger), 166–71
Lubbock, Percy, *Craft of Fiction*, 21
Luhmann, Niklas, 153
Lukács, Georg, 1, 5, 45, 51n6, 83, 138, 146, 190, 209–10, 216–17, 231, 237, 262, 266–8, 271, 273–5, 279, 282, 287, 299, 313; on biography, 268; *The Historical Novel*, 111, 263–4; *History and Class Consciousness*, 269; and realism, 264; on Scott, 269; *Theory of the Novel*, 4, 208; the typical, 144
Lyotard, Jean-Francois, 36, 222n32, 305n48, 311

Madame Bovary (Flaubert), 45, 101, 124, 141, 148, 150–1, 153, 180, 214; and *Ulysses*, 150–1, 153
Maddox, Brenda, 150
magic realism, 180
Mahler, Gustav, 85–6
Malraux, André, 22, 271
Manchevski, Milcho, *Before the Rain*, 230
Manet, Édouard, 41, 45, 56, 67
Mann, Thomas, 67, 189–90, 289
Mantel, Hilary, 277–80, 288; *Place of Greater Safety*, 276
Manzoni, Alessandro, 274; *Betrothed*, 266–7
Marcuse, Herbert, 147
Marx, Karl, 6n12, 32n10, 42
Maupassant, Guy de, 17–18, 23, 147
Mauriac, Francois, 18
McKeon, Michael, *Origins of the Novel*, 1
McLuhan, Marshall, 27
meaning, 33, 50, 142; liberation from, 64
medical speculation, 74–5
melancholia, 35, 43, 71; and affect, 71–2, 148
melodrama, 139–40, 145, 154–5, 159–60, 183; and Eliot, 156–7, 161; supersession of, 183
Melville, Herman, *Redburn*, 289

Merleau-Ponty, Maurice, 38
Il mestiere delle armi (Olmi), 235
metaphor, 25–6
Metropolis (Lang), 269
Michelet, Jules, 276–8
Middlemarch (Eliot), 112, 123, 130, 133, 155–7, 222–5; money in, 223–4; providence in, 228
Milton, John, 72; *Paradise Lost*, 114
mimesis, 1, 3–5, 141
minimalism, 191
Mitchell, David, 304–5
modernism/modernity, 3, 9, 37, 73, 113, 138, 140, 144, 175n19, 176, 187, 225–6, 313; and affect, 34; and Barthes, 33; as breakdown of realism, 187; dissolution of, 192; liberation from tradition, 39; and realism, 215–16
The Modernist Papers (Jameson), 152n22
Molière, 51, 107
Monet, Claude, 41, 50
money, 106, 133, 223–5, 236, 245. *See also* wage labor; worker
Montaigne, Michel de, 92
morality, 120, 122, 133
Moretti, Franco, 5, 16n1, 145, 190n7, 203n12, 217
Morgan, Lewis H., 297; *Ancient Society*, 264
Mozart, *The Magic Flute*, 208
Munch, Edvard, 72
Murder in the Cathedral (Eliot), 174
music, 85; and affect, 38–40
Musil, Robert, 117, 257n19

name/naming, 289, 293, 296; and affect, 30–1, 34–5, 166; and discovery, 87; and historical novel, 288; and history, 297
narrative: affect appropriates, 76; and affect in Tolstoy, 83, 85; after affect, 188–9; and bad faith, 135–7; beginnings, 166; for elites, 111, 262; endings, 160–1; epic, 167; and everyday, 153; existential,

184, 187; first-person, 169–75, 177; impulse for, 8; and pronoun, 171; vs realism, 15; relations precede beings, 226; representation of villainy, 117, 122; showing and telling, 21–6; statement, 167; and tale, 15; third-person, 170, 172, 174–6, 180, 182, 184; in Tolstoy, 285–6; waning of, 109; and war, 233, 251–2. *See also* fiction; literature; novel; plot; space
nationalism, 158–9, 236, 260, 263
naturalism, 148–50, 152, 179, 229; and class, 149–50
Nausea (Sartre), 18, 37
Negri, Antonio, 256
Negt, Oskar, 191
New Criticism, 49, 73, 210
Ngai, Sianne, *Ugly Feeling*, 29n4
Nietzsche, Friedrich, 42–3, 87, 115, 117–19, 129, 156; on Eliot, 120
Nolan, Christopher, *Inception*, 299–302
novel: of adultery, 147–8, 150, 152; Barthes on, 161–2; Bill of Rights for, 222; closure of, 160–1; components of, 153, 155; and epic, 265; and evil, 116; evolution of, 108, 222; existential, 184, 187; existential states of characters in, 97; first novels, 179–80, 210; and genre, 138; history of, 3–4, 179, 215; idealist, 2n3; nineteenth century turning point for, 203; and other, 116–18; and politics, 213–16; postmodern, 296n40, 310; and pronoun, 171; and providence, 204; and psychology, 118; and realism, 161–2, 264; and status quo, 215; vs tale, 16–21; and theater, 264; types of, 7–8; word for, 16. *See also* characters; fiction; historical novel; literature; narrative; plot; realism
Novick, Peter, 260
now, 168, 177, 180

odor *See* sense/sensation
Olmi, Ermanno, *Il mestiere delle armi*, 235
The One vs. The Many (Woloch), 96
ontological realism, 211–17
Origins of the Novel (McKeon), 1
ostranenie, 51, 55–6, 232–3, 241, 311
other, 116–18, 225–6

Paradise Lost (Milton), 114
Pascal, Blaise, 75
Paskaljevic, Goran, *Cabaret Balkan*, 230
Pasolini, Pier Paolo, 164, 166, 170, 177–8
passions: psychology of, 118; sad passions, 117–18, 129, 133
Passions and the Tempers (Arikha), 29n5
past-present-future, 10, 25, 39, 73, 81, 88, 176
pathetic fallacy, 49–50, 73
Paths of Glory (Kubrick), 238
Peer Gynt (Ibsen), 20
perception, 46–7, 49, 56, 59, 64; and language, 54
periodization, 3
Picasso, Pablo, *Demoiselles d'Avignon*, 174
Pickwick Papers (Dickens), 96
Place of Greater Safety (Mantel), 276
plot, 65, 207, 216n22, 268n10; in Eliot, 124–5, 128; supersession of, 109, 153, 160, 183; and villain, 138
The Poetics of Social Forms (Jameson), 11
point of view, 170; and déclassement, 149; Eliot on, 222; floodtide of, 184; as ideology, 164; and irony, 181–2; and James, 181, 183; in Tolstoy, 82, 88; in Zola, 51, 56
The Political Unconscious (Jameson), 147
politics, 237; and Eliot, 157–60; and novel, 213–16; and Tolstoy, 78–9; war by other means, 239
postmodernism, 187–8, 190, 253, 293, 296n40, 310–11
predestination, 199–201
Prefaces (James), 21

present, eternal, 24, 26, 28, 36, 39–41, 99, 160, 176
presentification, 167
pronoun, and narrative, 171
Propp, Vladimir, 114
protagonist, 146; deterioration of, 96, 109, 111–12; in Eliot, 121; for elites, 111; language of, 99; and minor character, 106, 108, 126; in Tolstoy, 285–6. *See also* characters
Proust, Marcel, 25, 35, 83, 90n16, 119, 122, 179, 196, 289
providence, 204–5, 216–17, 219, 221–2, 228, 230; and conspiracy, 219–20; deconstruction of ideology of, 223–4; and novel, 204; replacement of, 217. *See also* happy endings
psychology, 118–19; and affect, 78, 154; in Eliot, 125; in Tolstoy, 80
public sphere, 109

rationality, 39
realism, 143–4; and affect, 10, 76, 140; without affect, 187–9; antinomies of, 2, 6, 11, 26, 69, 76, 83, 88, 96, 108–9, 177, 201; and archetypes, 160; and bourgeois society, 5; breakdown of, 187, 192; chronological endpoints of, 10–11; defined, 5–6; developments in, 183; genres of, 145–52; and historical novel, 262, 274; ideology of, 5–6; and Lukács, 264; and modernism, 215–16; vs narrative, 15; and novel, 161–2, 264; ontological, 211–17; and psychology, 118; and semiotics, 36; and temporality, 10; and withdrawal of protagonist, 111. *See also* mimesis; novel, the
reality effect, 34, 36
reality principle, 229
Reardon, B. P., 196
récit *See* tale
Red Badge of Courage (Crane), 235

relations, 226
Renoir, Jean, *Le crime de M. Lange*, 108
representation: and collective, 280–2; of villainy, 117, 122; and war, 233, 256–7, 271
revolution, 267, 270–1, 276; and collective, 276; French Revolution, 146, 222, 262, 276, 298; historical ambiguity of, 271–2; and historical novel, 266
rhetoric, 140
Ricoeur, Paul, 25, 274
Rise of the Novel (Watt), 1
Robbe-Grillet, Alain, 1, 9n15, 45, 310
Robespierre, Maximilien de, 276–9, 288
Robinson Crusoe (Defoe), 202, 248
Robinson, Kim Stanley, 198n6, 302, 312
Romola (Eliot), 123–4, 130, 133, 155, 161, 213
Ropars, Marie-Claire, 62
Rousseau, Jean-Jacques, 80, 282; *Social Contract*, 281, 286
Roussel, Raymond, 307

sad passions, 117–18, 129, 133
Said, Edward, 161n30
Salammbô (Flaubert), 72, 213, 275
Sarraute, Nathalie, 45, 178
Sartre, Jean-Paul, 5, 16, 20–1, 23, 38, 73, 115–16, 119, 121, 126, 167, 169, 171, 178, 184, 202, 226, 228, 237, 274, 297; bad faith, 129–32, 228; *Being and Nothingness*, 171; *Critique of Dialectical Reason*, 171, 237; impersonal consciousness, 169, 171; *Nausea*, 18, 37; on tale vs novel, 17–19
scene, 11, 153, 160, 234, 240, 242, 245, 251, 257; and affect, 240; and war, 251. *See also* space
Schiller, Friedrich, 167, 212, 237; *Wallenstein*, 237, 242
Schlaffer, Heinz, 259
science fiction, 197, 297–300
Scorsese, Martin, *Shutter Island*, 299

Scott, Walter, 109, 123–4, 147, 154, 179, 213, 263–7, 269–70, 272–3, 279, 287; *The Heart of Midlothian*, 266–7, 269; Lukács on, 269; *Waverley*, 147, 263, 266
Sebald, W. S., 251
The Secret History of Emotion (Gross), 29n5
self: consciousness, 130–1; and identity, 25
sense/sensation, 6n12, 28, 33–5, 54–6, 61, 64; autonomization of, 55; transformation of, 32. *See also* affect; autonomization; Zola, Émile, sensory autonomization in
Shelley, Mary, *Frankenstein*, 298
showing, and telling, 21–6, 247
Shutter Island (Scorsese), 299
Simplicius Simplicissimus (Grimmelshausen), 248–51
simultaneity, 229–30
A Singular Modernity (Jameson), 9n15, 187
singularity, 36
Sirk, Douglas, 140
Slaughterhouse-Five (Vonnegut), 251
smell *See* sense/sensation
Smith, Barbara Herrnstein, 161n30
Social Contract (Rousseau), 281, 286
society: bourgeois, 107, 109, 146, 148, 271; differentiation of, 110; Tolstoy on, 80, 91
Sorkin, Andrew Ross, 161n31
space, 70–1, 153, 240, 248–9, 267. *See also* scene
Spenser, Edmund, 118
Spenser, Stanley, 196
Spinoza, Baruch, sad passions, 117–18, 129, 133
Spitzer, Leo, 167
Spufford, Francis, *Red Plenty*, 297
state, 237, 261
Stein, Gertrude, 41, 62
Steinberg, Leo, 174
Stendhal, 30, 82, 88, 91, 93, 95, 183, 210, 215, 232, 273, 281; *The*

Charterhouse of Parma, 232, 273; *The Red and the Black*, 202
Stimmung, 38, 77, 143, 148, 240
storytelling, 8, 46, 173, 253; art of, 24; impulse for, 15; origin of, 20n7; and realism, 10
Strauss, David, *Life of Jesus*, 120
Strindberg, August, 42; *Gustavus Adolfus*, 237
Stroheim, Erich von, 45
style, 41, 307
style indirect libre, 130, 135–6, 164, 170, 175, 177–8, 180–1, 185
subject: and affect, 92; death of, 78
synchrony/diachrony, 227–9
synesthesia, 55

tale/récit: and affect, 35, 46; and destiny, 182; and irrevocability, 19–21; and narration, 15; vs novel, 16–21; reestablished, 192; survival of, 73; and temporality, 24–5, 27; typology of, 183; weakening of, 176; word for, 10, 16
Tarantino, Quentin, *Pulp Fiction*, 230
technology, 235
telling, and showing, 21–6, 247
temporality, 10; as agitation, 85; end of, 28; here and now, 168, 177, 180; past-present-future, 10, 25, 39, 73, 81, 88, 176; and tale, 24–5, 27; two systems of, 24–6. *See also* chance; contingency; destiny; everyday; present
Terada, Rei, 32
La Terre (Zola), 47
Thackeray, William Makepeace, 117
That Bringas Woman (Galdós), 97
theater, and novel, 264
theory, French, 136
Theory of the Novel (Lukács), 4
third-person narrative, 170, 172, 174–6, 180, 182, 184
Thirty Years' War, 240, 242
Todorov, Tzvetan, 21
Tolstoy, Leo, 77–94, 111, 164, 232, 238,

268, 284–5; affect and narrative in, 83–5; affect unequaled in, 93; *Anna Karenina*, 279; characters in, 88–92, 285; on civilized society, 80; distraction in, 86–8; on free will, 282–3; *Hadji Mourad*, 93; happiness in, 81–3; and historical novel, 285–6; and liberalism, 79; peasant pupils of, 89; and political, 78–9; psychology in, 80; on society, 80, 91; and war, 93; *War and Peace*, 78, 80, 83, 87, 91, 93, 238, 274, 280–1, 285

Tolstoy on Education, 89n14

torture, 241

transcendence, and immanence, 211–12, 216

The Transmission of Affect (Brennan), 35, 92

Tristan (Wagner), 39, 69–70, 72

Trollope, Anthony, 214

Twain, Mark, 170, 172–4; *Connecticut Yankee*, 172; *Huckleberry Finn*, 172; *Innocents Abroad*, 172

typical, 144

Ugly Feelings (Ngai), 29n4

Ulysses (Joyce), 25, 98, 150–3, 207, 216, 308; and *Madame Bovary*, 150–1, 153

uncanny, 286

Upfield, Arthur, 166n5

Upheavals of Thought (Nussbaum), 29n5

Utopia, 28, 55, 86, 110, 133, 158–9, 200, 211, 215, 236, 249–50, 258, 309, 312

Valences of the Dialectic (Jameson), 262

Vargas Llosa, Mario, *War of the End of the World*, 277

Le ventre de Paris (Zola), 46, 50

Verlaine, Paul, 154

Vidal, Gore, 98, 289

villain, 114–18, 121–2, 138–40; and hero, 115; narrative representation of, 117; non-existence of, 122, 133; and plot, 138

Vonnegut, Kurt, *Slaughterhouse-Five*, 251

wage labor, 236. *See also* money; worker

Wagner, Richard, 39, 41, 67, 87, 109, 300; and affect, 40; *Tristan*, 39, 69–70, 72

Wallenstein (Döblin), 242–7

Wallenstein (Schiller), 237, 242

war, 232–58; civil war, 241; collective experience of, 235–7; existential experience of, 235, 257; guerilla, 234; and historical novel, 266; leaders and institutions, 237–8; and narrative, 233, 251–2; politics by other means, 239; and representation, 233, 256–7, 271; and scene, 251; and Tolstoy, 93; torture, 241; transformation of, 233

War and Peace (Tolstoy), 78, 80, 83, 87, 91, 93, 238, 274, 280

War of the End of the World (Vargas Llosa), 277

War of the Worlds (Wells), 298

The Waste Land (Eliot), 294

Watt, Ian, *Rise of the Novel*, 1

Waverley (Scott), 147, 263, 266

wealth *See* money

Weber, Max, 4, 39, 203

Weimann, Robert, "Mimesis in Hamlet," 1

Weiss, Peter, 271; *The Aesthetics of Resistance*, 202n10

Wells, H. G., *War of the Worlds*, 298

Welsh, Alexander, 155

White, Hayden, 164

Whitman, Walt, 61

Wilhelm Meister (Goethe), 203, 208–9, 217

will, 282–3

Woloch, Alex, 97; *The One vs. The Many*, 96

women, 147–8, 158, 236

Woolf, Virginia, 37, 43, 151, 302n46

Wordsworth, William, 140
worker, 97, 148, 158. *See also* money;
   wage labor
world-historical-figures, 109, 111, 148,
   237–8, 246, 263, 266–8, 273n17,
   274–5, 277, 279–80, 282–3, 288,
   298, 301, 307
Worringer, Wilhelm, 2
Worsley, Frank, 295
writing: and affect, 184; as profession,
   156
Writing Degree Zero (Barthes), 36
Wu Ming, 302n46

Zola, Émile, 44–77, 110–13, 146–7,
   154, 156, 161, 164, 176, 179,
   266; *L'Argent*, 55, 70; *L'Assomoir*,
56, 76; *La bête humaine*, 25; *Au
Bonheur des Dames*, 57; *La Curée*,
46–50; *Débâcle*, 43, 66, 74, 93;
Le docteur Pascal, 74; doctrine
of intensity in, 76; enumeration
in, 52–4, 61; *La Fortune des
Rougons*, 50; *Germinal*, 76, 286;
and heredity, 46, 73, 76; history
in, 73–4; light in, 68–9; medical
speculation in, 74–5; rhetoric of
things, 66; sensory
autonomization in, 55–6, 59,
smelly cheese as, 55, 59–64,
white linen as, 44, 54, 56–8, 60,
65; *La Terre*, 47; transformation
of description, 50–1; *Le ventre de
Paris*, 46, 50–2, 59

Printed in the United States
by Baker & Taylor Publisher Services